Lecture Notes on Coastal and Estuarine Studies

Managing Editors:
Malcolm J. Bowman   Richard T. Barber
Christopher N.K. Mooers   John A. Raven

31

G. Lopez   G. Taghon
J. Levinton   (Eds.)

Ecology of Marine Deposit Feeders

Springer-Verlag
New York Berlin Heidelberg London Paris Tokyo

ISBN 3-540-97001-0 Springer-Verlag Berlin Heidelberg New York
ISBN 0-387-97001-0 Springer-Verlag New York Berlin Heidelberg

Printing and binding: Druckhaus Beltz, Hemsbach/Bergstr.
2837/3140-543210 – Printed on acid-free paper

Dedication

The editors would like to dedicate this volume to Donald Cave Rhoads, one of our contributors. Don is not only a pioneer in the study of the ecology of deposit feeders, he has been a great innovator in instrumentation, experimental design, and field studies. He first recognized the relationship of hydrodynamics, sedimentary processes, and deposit-feeders and published a remarkable series of papers which are truly interdisciplinary in nature. These studies developed from his unique education in geology and marine biology.

Rhoads was born in Rockford, Illinois in 1938 and earned his bachelors degree at Cornell College in Iowa. He received his masters degree at the University of Iowa and earned his Ph.D. in Paleozoology at the University of Chicago, working under Ralph Gordon Johnson. It was during this period that he and his wife Christy first came to New England and breathed a fragrance unfamiliar to those from the heartland of America: that of the sea. The intoxication of the ocean never wore off. After his degree, he joined the Geology faculty of Yale University in 1965, rose to the rank of Professor, and moved to Woods Hole in 1986 as a Senior Scientist for Science Applications International Corporation. He is also an adjunct Professor of Geology at Boston University, and a participant in the Boston University Marine Program.

Preface

Most of the seabed throughout the world's oceans is covered with sediment. Sediments are a complex mixture of organic and inorganic materials derived from marine and terrestrial sources. A diverse array of organisms live in sediments, and by far the majority of them derive their nutrition from the organic matter present in the sedimentary deposit. These "deposit feeders" have been studied from a variety of perspectives, ranging from their contribution to the decomposition and remineralization of organic matter reaching the sediments, to their importance as food items to commercially important fishery resources.

In this book, the basic goal of the contributing authors has been to identify the critical research problems pertaining to deposit feeders, and to suggest promising approaches for dealing with those problems. In many cases, the reader will find that the problems and possible solutions discussed in the study of marine deposit feeders have applications to other organisms which face the same general problem of obtaining sufficient nutritional resources from food-poor environments. It is also apparent that much future research on deposit feeders will depend on the integration of such disparate areas of research as nutritional physiology and sediment geochemistry.

In Chapter 1, Levinton provides an historical overview of the study of deposit feeders, primarily from the contextual setting of coastal environments where much of the research has been focused. He reviews the evolution of ideas about the food sources of deposit feeders, and points out that "clearly the most important unresolved issue is the role of POM [particulate organic matter] in the nutrition of deposit feeders and, conversely, the effect of deposit feeders on the decay of particulate material." This theme is reiterated throughout the volume.

Carney shifts attention to deposit feeding in the deep sea in Chapter 2. Deposit feeders in this environment must subsist on even more attenuated and potentially more refractory supplies of organic matter than those in coastal environments. Carney reviews recent data from organic geochemistry about the flux of carbon to the deep sea, its variation with depth of the water column, its distribution in the deep sea (i.e., in the nepheloid layer, at the sediment-water interface, and within the sediment), and variations in flux on ecological and evolutionary time scales. Again, a central conclusion of this chapter is the need for measures of labile organic carbon.

The next two chapters take an organic geochemical viewpoint. In Chapter 3, Rice and Rhoads develop a model for the vertical transport of sedimentary organic matter as driven by subsurface-feeding deposit feeders. They present a framework to examine the availability of particulate organic matter and how it changes during subduction. Their model serves as an important link between the biology of deposit feeders and early diagenesis of sedimentary organic matter, and is illustrated by a case study of a population of subsurface deposit-feeding polychaetes from a coastal site in Maine. An especially intriguing aspect of the model is the description of how the balance in competitive interactions among surface deposit feeders, subsurface deposit feeders, and bacteria for newly input organic matter might be shifted by changes in subduction rate.

Mayer, in Chapter 4, addresses directly the need for biologically relevant measures of the organic matter in sediments. Clearly, susceptibility to enzymatic digestion and decomposition rates vary with organic type. Mayer discusses the physical forms of organic matter in sediment (adsorbed to mineral phases, dissolved, particulate, polymeric versus monomeric) and reviews methods for quantifying the amount of biologically available material. He presents several outstanding problems that require resolution: the importance of discrete (particulate) versus adsorbed organic matter; the role of partially humified organic matter; and the role of microbial exudates.

The next nine chapters are concerned with various aspects of the acquisition and utilization of food items by deposit feeders. In Chapter 5, Jumars and Penry present a novel approach to the study of digestive dynamics. They adapt theory and models developed by chemical engineers to optimize the design and operating characteristics of chemical reactors to the case of a deposit feeder's gut. Thus, predictions emerge about how gut throughput time and extent of digestive conversion should vary with changes in food concentration in order to achieve digestive homeostasis, maximization of rate of digestive conversion, or maximization of conversion efficiency.

Kofoed, Forbes and Lopez (Chapter 6) continue the theme of the dynamics of the digestive process and construct a model focusing on time-dependent absorption. Their basic premise is that digestion and absorption are time-dependent processes, and the rapid feeding rates of many deposit feeders can result in short gut residence times. What are the consequences for absorption of nutrients under these conditions? Kofoed et al. develop a model and describe experiments to measure absorption as a function of gut residence time. Ingested bacteria can be absorbed at a rate of several percent per minute, so that even for very short gut residence times absorption efficiency is high. Bacteria were absorbed more rapidly than were sediment microalgae, which were in turn more digestible than seaweed detritus. The absorption rate constant may be an important measure of the quality of a given food type for an animal.

It has long been known that many deposit feeders are quite selective during feeding, but quantification of their selective abilities, especially when feeding on natural sediments, has been a knotty problem. Lopez, Tanti-chodok and Cheng (Chapter 7) discuss the use of radiotracer techniques both for measuring selection of organic matter from bulk sediments during ingestion and its subsequent absorption. They suggest that an ideal label would bind strongly (by chemisorption) to organic matter in sediment, be relatively nonspecific for different types of organic matter, and would not desorb easily. Experiments using ^{14}C formaldehyde to label sediments are described.

All organisms grow, and in Chapter 8 Forbes considers how size changes during ontogeny affect feeding rate and rate of metabolic carbon loss. Study-ing a deposit-feeding polychaete, Forbes shows that adults are not geomet-rically scaled-up versions of juveniles. In contrast to the usual practice of fitting a single power function to describe allometric data, Forbes uses mov-ing regression analysis to demonstrate an abrupt shift in the scaling exponent for egestion rate as a function of body volume. This suggests that constraints on energy intake and growth may change during different stages of growth. Forbes points out that these shifts may indicate "critical periods" in an animal's life.

Cammen addresses in Chapter 9 the continuing controversy of what or-ganic components of sediment are used by deposit feeders. It seems clear that bacteria alone cannot supply all the carbon required by deposit feed-ers. Both physiological and geochemical approaches lead to the conclusion that deposit feeders must obtain most of their energy from "detritus," the non-living organic matter that comprises most of the organic matter in sedi-ments. However, bacteria may supply most of the needed protein or organic nitrogen, a point also made by Rice and Rhoads. Cammen also addresses the topic of ingestion rate of sediment, and how it is affected by the nutritional quality of sediments. He presents data indicating a peak in feeding rate at intermediate levels of sediment food quality.

In Chapter 10, Taghon reviews models developed to predict particle se-lectivity and ingestion rate of deposit feeders as these processes are affected by the physical and geochemical nature of the sediment. A literature review reveals that the vast majority of species exhibit varying degrees of selectivity for smaller or organic-rich particles. Recent experimental studies have shown that truly non-selective deposit feeders are much rarer than thought earlier.

Continuing with the theme of variation in feeding rate begun in the chapter by Cammen, studies are reviewed that show both increased and decreased feeding rate as a function of sediment food quality. It is possible that these separate studies represent different subsets of a continuum, as suggested by Cammen. If so, then our challenge is to determine where natural systems fall along such a continuum.

Nowell, Jumars, Self and Southard inject a refreshing air of natural history in Chapter 11. The fact that deposit feeders dominate in depositional environments has undoubtedly contributed greatly to observations and experiments skewed towards still- water situations. Water motion is, however, pervasive in aquatic environments. Nowell et al. describe a laboratory flume designed to simulate accurately real-world boundary flows and present a series of observations on the behaviors of different species of deposit feeders under sediment transport conditions. The often abrupt and dramatic changes in behaviors they observe as flow conditions change serve as a sobering reminder of the necessity of incorporating biological realism in models and experiments.

Watling continues this theme of realism in Chapter 12, in this case in reference to the structure of the sedimentary environment inhabited by deposit feeders. Watling argues for the need to more realistically visualize the structure of marine sediments, if we are to understand how deposit feeders operate. He suggests applying the techniques used regularly in the study of terrestrial soils, especially thin sectioning in order to study sediments in a more natural state than is achieved by dispersing a sample on a microscope slide. He summarizes the morphological features that are revealed by thin sectioning, including fecal pellets, burrows, tubes, and pore spaces. The take-home message of this chapter is that deposit feeders most likely do not perceive individual particles while foraging. Particles are embedded in a continuous "matrix" whose nature is poorly known.

Whitlatch (Chapter 13) reemphasizes the idea that it is time to move beyond overly simplistic particle size-selection experiments. He presents models showing how selectivity patterns can reflect different foraging mechanisms ("line-trappers" versus "gulpers"). In the search for unifying principles, Whitlatch employs the concept of functional response, which has been applied to study the feeding behavior of a wide range of animals, to deposit feeders. Although appropriate data are scarce at present, evidence that functional response of feeding rate to changes in food quality is affected by particle size is discussed. This suggests another layer of complexity must be added to future experiments if they are to be more realistic.

In a valuable coda, Tenore presents an ecologically oriented review in Chapter 14. He focuses on the larger picture of those factors, in addition to food abundance and composition, that affect deposit feeders at the population level. This chapter serves to remind us that narrowly directed field or laboratory studies, while extremely valuable, are a means towards the final goal of understanding the distribution and abundance of deposit feeders in marine sediments.

It is our hope that the reader will find the book a useful forum for discussion of critical problems and promising approaches in the study of deposit feeders. In particular, we encourage that these and other approaches (e.g. geomicrobiology, physiology) be merged in future study of deposit feeders and their sedimentary environment.

This book is the product of a workshop, funded by the National Science Foundation, held at the Marine Sciences Research Center, SUNY at Stony Brook, May 20- 22, 1985. Contribution number 636 from the Marine Sciences Research Center, S.U.N.Y. at Stony Brook, and contribution number 707 from the Graduate Studies in Ecology and Evolution at Stony Brook.

We would like to thank the staff of the Marine Sciences Research Center at Stony Brook for help with organizing the workshop. Tom Forbes, Valery Forbes, I-Jiunn Cheng, Cynthia Decker, Pitiwong Tantichodok, and Matt Liebman were also very helpful at the workshop. Marie Eisel and Catherine Sexton helped with graphics. The book was typeset at the Biological Sciences Computing Facility at Stony Brook. The photograph of Don Rhoads was provided by Josie Aller.

Glenn Lopez, Gary Taghon, Jeffrey Levinton
Stony Brook and Corvallis, January 21, 1989

Table of Contents

Chapter 1

Deposit Feeding and Coastal Oceanography

Jeffrey S. Levinton
Department of Ecology and Evolution
State University of New York
Stony Brook, New York 11794-5245

Introduction

Deposit feeders satisfy their nutritional requirements from the organic fraction of ingested sediment. This noncommittal statement masks a number of problems and controversies that have occupied the efforts of nutritional biologists, biological oceanographers, and sedimentologists. The exact mode of nutrition of deposit feeders is of great interest to those working on nutrient recycling in the water column. Deposit feeders may ingest and assimilate phytodetritus and they may influence the rate of mineralization and return of dissolved nutrients to the water column. In some cases detritus is probably digested and assimilated directly, but some detritus is relatively indigestible and may have to be cycled through the microbiota before it becomes available to deposit feeders. The effects of deposit feeders on the physical and chemical properties of sediments can strongly influence sediment resuspension and transport. These interactions explain why deposit feeders are of central importance in coastal oceanography and why the resolution of certain specific problems may take oceanographic research in alternate directions. It is the purpose of this introductory chapter to outline the major issues and to place them in perspective.

The Particulate Organic Matter Controversy

The focal importance of deposit feeders derives from the classical hypothesis (Petersen and Boysen-Jensen 1911; Blegvad 1914; Petersen 1918) that particulate organic matter (POM) from seagrasses is the principal nutritional base for shallow-water benthos. POM in Danish waters was believed to be derived mainly from the decomposition of eelgrass (*Zostera marina*). POM entered as particles into nearshore sediments, which were ingested by deposit feeders. Petersen appreciated that it would be difficult to relate fresh seagrass to the amorphous organic matter found in sediments. Nevertheless, this hypothesis emphasized the importance of deposit feeders in the processing of organic matter, and conversion into fish food.

While the eel grass epidemic of the 1930s failed to cause a collapse of nearshore fisheries (see Rasmussen 1967), the POM subsidy hypothesis survived and was revived in the "outwelling" hypothesis (Odum 1980; Odum and De La Cruz 1967). POM derived from *Spartina* salt marshes was believed to subsidize shelf fisheries. This claim has also proved controversial; some have suggested that very little salt marsh POM reaches the open shelf (e.g. Haines 1977; Woodwell et al. 1977). Others have shown that *Spartina* and *Zostera* are relatively refractory (Harrison and Mann 1975) and therefore would not be of immediate importance to secondary consumers, even if large amounts of material did reach the shelf. Digestible microorganisms, however, could ride piggy back on the detrital particles and be consumed and digested by shelf benthos. Longer-term decomposition might also make this material available. The interested reader should consult the review by Nixon (1980).

While marine vascular plants consist primarily of complex and indigestible carbohydrates, the broad range of marine seaweeds include species that are digestible and easily decomposed by saprophytes (e.g., Tenore 1977; Tenore et al. 1979). Nitrogen content seems best correlated with deposit feeder growth, but carbon (or available energy) may be limiting at high nitrogen levels (Tenore and Rice 1980). In their nutritional budget, Rice et al. (1986) concluded that the intertidal polychaete *Scoloplos* was limited by microbial nitrogen, but must have obtained a significant fraction of their carbon from detrital sources. Thus in areas of high seaweed productivity, the supply of particulates to the benthos may be important, especially in habitats where herbivore grazing is not significant. High winter-spring production of ulvacean seaweeds may provide a source of digestible organic matter for shallow water benthos, or may decompose and subsidize growth of more accessible benthic diatoms and bacteria (Levinton 1985). Some shallow embayments may be alternately dominated by attached plants or by phytoplankton, depending upon the basin shape and exchange with open shelf waters (Mann 1975).

This controversy is further complicated by a consideration of the particulate organic matter falling to the bottom from surface waters. Petersen dismissed the importance of detritus derived from the rain of sinking dead phytoplankton, but a large fraction of shallow shelf phytoplankton reaches the bottom during the spring diatom increase (Riley 1956). D.C. Rhoads (pers. comm.) has documented this with *in situ* photographs of Long Island Sound USA muddy bottoms. The benthos respond to the spring rain of detritus with increased production; summer temperature may cause an increase of community respiration and a concomitant decline of secondary benthic production (Grassle et al. 1985). In very shallow systems, such as Narragansett Bay, Rhode Island, USA (Nixon et al. 1976) and in open beach bottoms where surf diatom blooms occur (Lewin et al. 1975), the release of dissolved nutrients from the bottom probably fuels phytoplankton growth, and large amounts of phytoplankton probably serve as the food base for both suspension feeders and deposit feeders. POM supply must therefore by considered a vertical water column problem, as well as a horizontal shoreline-lagoon to offshore process. While shelf phytoplankton may subsidize the adjacent deep-sea bottoms, current evidence suggests no pattern of export from the shelf-slope phytoplankton towards the open ocean (Rowe et al. 1986).

Nutrition

The question of deposit feeder nutrition is related directly to the more general issue of nutrient dynamics on the continental shelf and in coastal embayments and marsh systems. With the exception of some work on the importance of bacteria (Zobell 1938; Zobell and Feltham 1938), most early work presumed that deposit feeders digested organic matter from the sediment and that the known inverse correlation between deposit feeder abundance and grain size resulted from the correlation of increasing grain size with decreasing organic content (e.g., Sanders 1958).

Several studies helped focus the problem by demonstrating that certain types of POM were digested inefficiently, as opposed to the efficient digestion of sediment microbial organisms such as bacteria and diatoms (Newell 1965; Hargrave 1970; Fenchel 1970; Yingst 1976). These results were not specific to any given phylum, and led to the view that the organic matter in sediment must be converted to bacteria before it would be available to the consumer (Hargrave 1970). Deposit feeders were to be regarded as sediment microbial strippers, although their activities, such as tearing of particles, might increase the rate of decomposition by providing more surface area for the decomposers (Fenchel 1970).

A number of considerations have raised some doubts about the microbial conversion hypothesis. Although microbial organisms can be the bulk of the sedimentary organic carbon in some sandy sediments (e.g., Cammen 1982), they usually account for much less than 1-5 percent of the total organic carbon. Thus a very low assimilation rate on non-living organic matter may be undetectable in an assimilation assay, but of equal importance to the total assimilation of microbial carbon, even if the assimilation efficiency on the latter approaches 100 percent (Hargrave 1976)! In some cases, assimilation of non-living organic matter is sufficiently great to make this a concern (e.g., Hargrave 1970; Findlay and Tenore 1982; see Lopez et al.; Cammen; Rice and Rhoads, this volume).

Some calculations suggest that microbial organisms are an insufficient source of energy for typical macrobenthic populations, given the measured feeding rates and absorption efficiencies (Baker and Bradnam 1976; Cammen 1980a; Findlay and Meyer 1984; Cammen, this volume). This discrepancy could only be explained by selectivity for microbes during feeding, but in some cases enrichment of up to two orders of magnitude would be required, relative to the sediment. In one study, where the deficit was only a factor of two (Cammen 1980a), selective feeding could account for the difference. On sandy beaches of Oregon, bacteria cannot account for even ten percent of the respiratory requirements of the polychaete *Euzonus mucronata*. Benthic or deposited planktonic diatoms, however, might account for the discrepancy (Kemp 1987).

The microbial stripping hypothesis has been tested with POM mainly derived from plants composed of complex and relatively indigestible carbohydrates. Indeed, Bianchi and Levinton (1984) showed that the mudsnail *Hydrobia totteni* grew as well on sediment bleached of POM derived mainly from *Spartina* as it did on normal salt marsh sediment, as long as microalgae were abundant. Most deposit feeders have cellulase activity, but perhaps not sufficient to digest such material (Hylleberg 1976). Gut passage times are typically less than an hour, making efficient digestion of this material unlikely in any event. But it is not clear that the range of POM is sediments is sufficiently dominated by grassy material to preclude a significant degree of digestion and assimilation of organic matter derived from other source materials. We are only beginning to approach the problem of discerning among the mixture of sources. One promising technique is the use of stable isotopes, which are diagnostic of detritus source (e.g. Haines 1977). Single elements may not be definitive, but a multi-element approach may be more fruitful. A study of *Spartina* consumers demonstrated that their stable isotopic composition reflected a strong *Spartina* fingerprint (Peterson et al. 1986). Unfortunately, this study failed to include an analysis of benthic diatoms, which may have been intermediaries and the food that was directly assimilated, as opposed to *Spartina*. Differential labeling has also demonstrated a heterogeneity of ingestion selectivity from sediments (Lopez and Cheng 1982; Carman and Thistle 1985).

A recent experiment suggests that POM may be important in the nutrition of the subsurface marine oligochaete *Paranais litoralis* (Levinton and Stewart 1988). A comparative study was done of secondary production of the worms on sediment versus sediment spiked with detritus derived from *Ulva* and green *Spartina*. While the conversion of nitrogen from sediment to animal flesh was an order of magnitude lower that the conversion rate from detritus, the great abundance of particulate organic nitrogen in the sediment made it a significant nutritional source. The same conclusion applied for carbon. Thus the complex array of sources in sediments (fresh detritus, microbes, algae, humified organic matter, etc.) will have to be studied carefully to understand the nutrition of deposit feeders.

Functional Morphology and Feeding

The POM-microbe controversy outlined above can be resolved to a degree by partitioning modes of feeding and habitats. Deposit feeders used to be visualized as indiscriminate bulk ingestors of sediment, and this masked a considerable diversity of feeding mechanisms and degrees of specialization. As mentioned above, selection for organic matter in sediments may permit some deposit feeders to survive in a seemingly nutritionally deficient environment.

The diversity of deposit feeding can be partitioned among means of:

1. Particle Selection

   Particles are collected by a variety of structures, including mucus-laden tentacles (e.g., spionid polychaetes), tentacles with ciliated tracts (protobranch bivalve mollusks), siphons directing particles towards a ciliated tract (some tellinacean bivalves), and crustacean mouthparts, which can tear detrital particles apart or scrape microbes from particle surfaces. While some animals such as some sea cucumbers and arenicolid polychaetes are capable of ingesting larger particles, most deposit feeders collect particles greater than 100μm with difficulty. This must be related to the concentration of both fine-grained organic matter and microbes in sediments dominated by small particles. When presented with a mixture of particles, many species prefer small particles (e.g., Hylleberg and Gallucci 1975; Taghon 1982; Lopez and Kofoed 1980; Levinton 1987) but not all (Whitlatch 1974; see Taghon, this volume). The very smallest particles, i.e. clay size particles, may be a poor substrate for bacteria (Deflaun and Mayer 1983; Yamamoto and Lopez 1985), and the mud snail *Hydrobia totteni* apparently avoids this size fraction (Doris 1983). Selection of particles may also be on the basis of surface texture, specific gravity, and chemical composition (Whitlatch 1974; Hylleberg and Gallucci 1975; Self and Jumars 1978). In the tentaculate forms mucus adhesion plays a strong role in particle collection, and this may reduce the degree of particle size selectivity (Hammond 1982; Dauer 1983; Whitlatch, this volume).

2. Digestion and Gut Complexity. Deposit feeders may have intracellular or extracellular digestion. Intracellular digestion is often associated with the ability to partition particles in a caecum, so the gut retention time is greater than for less desirable food particles (see Kofoed et al., this volume). Extracellular digestion, on the other hand, may be the most efficient means of rapidly stripping microbes from particle surfaces. There are probably strong differences among species in digestion ability. The extracellularly digesting amphipod *Corophium volutator* is capable of digesting a considerable amount of the material that passes through the gut of the mudsnail *Hydrobia ventrosa* (Lopez and Levinton 1978). The nassarid gastropod *Ilyanassa obsoleta* seems capable of digesting algae that pass through the guts of *Hydrobia totteni* (Bianchi and Levinton 1981). Some species employ both extracellular and intracellular digestion (Kermack 1955; Reid and Rauchert 1972).

There is a considerable degree of diversity among groups in the digestive spectrum. While cellulases are present widely, they are usually not important, except perhaps in some suspension feeders (Crosby and Reid 1971). Some detritus-ingesting insects have strongly alkaline guts and this may permit solution or desorption of small molecules associated with humified material (see discussion in Lopez and Levinton 1987). At present, there is a need for more surveys that correlate digestion mechanisms with food supply.

3. Feeding responses to flow and other factors.

Because deposit feeders live in a diversity of hydrodynamic microenvironments, their feeding is probably affected by the many different flow regimes (see Nowell et al., this volume). The manufacture, for example, of a chimney can greatly increase flow through a U–shaped burrow (Vogel 1978). Even the size scale of an organism can greatly change the flow regime in the vicinity of a feeding organ (summary in Vogel 1981, chapter 5). Moving water creates microtopographic features such as ripples, which may cause organic matter to accumulate in troughs. In order to increase feeding efficiency, deposit feeders must be capable of locating microenvironments that are food rich, and sites that permit efficient deployment of feeding structures without damage from bottom turbulence.

Many deposit feeders have the ability to switch between deposit feeding and suspension feeding (Hughes 1969; Taghon et al. 1980). As many food particles saltate above the bottom, this switch may not involve a qualitative change in food supply, only an adjustment to differing hydrodynamic regimes. While some species can switch behavior quite rapidly, studies of the tellinacean bivalves demonstrate that alternate modes may be fixed by constraining morphological features. Species such as *Scrobicularia plana* can alternate feeding modes owing to the presence of a simple tubular siphon that can collect particles from the sediment surface or from suspension (Hughes 1969). Some tellinaceans, such as species of the genus *Donax*, have tubercles within the inhalant siphon that can reject large particles, but they also preclude deposit feeding (Pohlo 1969). Some species of *Donax* occur in wave swept beaches and have a migratory cycle that is finely tuned to the local hydrodynamic regime and to the moisture of the sediment (Trueman 1971). These would be interesting to study as they must deal with saltating particles, but are clearly suspension feeders.

Potential Limiting Resources for Deposit Feeders

The potential limiting resources of deposit feeders include space, food, and ingestible particles. Space appears to be an important limiting factor both for surface dwellers and infaunal groups. Woodin (1974) showed that tube-building polychaetes limit the available infaunal space sufficiently to inhibit the colonization of mobile forms. Rapid burrowing by some mobile bivalve mollusks can also inhibit other bivalves that maintain more permanent burrows (Levinton 1977). At the surface, spatial interference is sufficiently great to affect growth rates (Levinton 1985) and intertidal interspecific zonation (Race 1982) of gastropods. Spatial crowding may (Holme 1950) or may not (Gilbert 1977; Levinton 1972a) result in intraspecific territoriality.

Ingestible particles may also limit deposit-feeding populations. Many deposit feeders produce compact fecal pellets that effectively increase the grain size of the sediment (Rhoads 1967). But they may not reingest such pellets, which may provide insufficient reward if immediately reingested. When the sediment is completely pelletized, *Hydrobia ventrosa* will emigrate (Levinton and Lopez 1977). The ampharetid polychaete *Amphicteis scaphobranchiata* has a specialized branchium that flings fecal pellets out of possible reach of the feeding organ (Nowell et al. 1984). When this is not possible, the balance of pelletization and pellet breakdown can be used to predict the sustainable standing stock, with respect to pellets (Levinton and Lopez 1977). With advection and erosion, other parameters must be introduced into such a model (Miller et al. 1984).

If microbial food is important, then resource limitation depends upon the recovery rate of the microbes following grazing, and the limitation of microbial population growth (Levinton 1979). Some microbial resources, such as bacteria, probably recover from grazing too rapidly to ever be depressed by deposit feeders (Levinton and Bianchi 1981), while others, such as large diatoms, recover slowly and may limit deposit feeders (Fenchel and Kofoed 1976). Laboratory experiments on microbial exploitation demonstrate a food depression by deposit feeders that is correlated with diminished somatic growth. As microbial levels are close to those found in the field, this may suggest food limitation (Levinton and Bianchi 1981). Standing microbial biomass therefore would represent a steady state between grazing and microbial recovery. For the mudsnail *Hydrobia totteni*, diatoms seem to limit growth in the field, while bacteria are unimportant.

Although it is relatively easy to identify the potential contributing factors, relatively few studies have attempted to estimate the contributions of different renewable resources. Peterson (1982) examined the relative roles of infaunal space and sediment-water interface space in the regulation of infaunal bivalves. One presumes that sediment-water interface space is related to food supply. He found that both seemed to contribute significantly to growth of the clams. Levinton et al. (1984) reported an experiment with the oligochaete *Paranais litoralis*, where a two-factor balanced experiment compared sediment-surface area and sediment volume. A two-way analysis of variance demonstrated that surface area did not affect population growth, whereas volume was of great importance. This could be related to both infaunal space and particle availability. Levinton (1985) used a balanced experiment to contrast surface space with microbial food availability and found both factors to be of importance to the gastropod *Hydrobia totteni*, though spatial interactions dominated. It will be necessary to take this multifactorial approach in the future, since no model predicts the necessary precedence of any of the suggested component limiting resources.

Foraging Theory

Natural selection should favor increased efficiency in gathering food, which should increase somatic growth and reproduction, i.e. fitness (see Taghon, this volume). The simplest approach to this problem is to calculate an optimum strategy, given a series of boundary conditions of both the environment and the organism's biological limitations (e.g., tentaculate feeding structure, physical properties of mucus, etc.). As it is well known that both microbial organisms and amorphous organic matter are generally correlated inversely with grain size (Zobell 1938; Dale 1974; Yamamoto and Lopez 1985), it is to be expected that a model of optimal ingestion will predict selection for fine particles, assuming a minimal cost of rejection of the "wrong" particles (Taghon et al. 1978). The microbial feeding and pelletization activities of deposit feeders may actually stimulate microbial growth, suggesting an optimum sediment pelletization rate (e.g., Levinton 1979). Finally, increased feeding rate brings more food into the gut, but tends to decrease gut passage time and the concomitant rate of digestion of material (Kofoed et al., this volume). This balance sets an optimum feeding rate, which should increase with increasing food quality (Taghon 1981; 1982). Calow (1975a, b), however, has argued that, as food quality decreases, the appropriate strategy is to increase gut residence time, in order to increase digestion. With extremely poor foods, such as lignin, it would be beneficial to increase feeding rate and therefore decrease gut passage time in order to expel the nutritionally useless food item. The strategy of increasing gut residence time in order to increase absorption seems at odds with Taghon's model. One mechanism of increasing gut residence time, without changing ingestion rate, is to increase gut length. This occurs in some marine consumers that ingest large amounts of relatively indigestible organic matter, such as mullet (Marais 1980), deep-sea bivalves (Allen and Sanders 1966), and sea -grass feeding turtles (Fenchel et al. 1979).

It has been found that overall the feeding rate of a deposit feeder on organic matter is positively correlated with body size (Cammen 1980b). This relationship occurs over a broad range of feeding rates and body sizes, and was calculated using different species as data points. It may indicate that, on a gross level, a given deposit feeder requires a certain amount of carbon per unit time. Within small ranges of body size, however, significant alterations of behavior may be required to achieve an optimal intake of food.

Stability and Trophic Structure in the Deposit Feeding Realm

Levinton (1972b) argued that deposit-feeding populations were stable and food limited. This conclusion derived from the commonly observed correlation of deposit feeder abundance with food related parameters and the commonly low spatial variation in abundance. The microbial nutrition hypothesis could be an important part of this stability. If microbes themselves are resource limited, then deposit feeders have a limiting amount of food available from the sediment. Evidence for food depression at high densities, especially of intertidal benthic diatoms (Fenchel and Kofoed 1976, Pace et al. 1979; Connor et al. 1982; Levinton et al. 1985), further suggests the possibility of food limitation. As Levinton and Lopez (1977) note, the range of densities of populations of *Hydrobia* is quite small, suggesting some sort of population control. Levinton (1972) made a similar argument. At Flax Pond, New York, this population stability is maintained despite the fact that the population has an annual life cycle (Levinton and Bianchi 1981).

Olafsson (1986) tested the trophic stability hypothesis by using a bivalve species that suspension fed in sands, but deposit fed in muds. His density manipulations failed to elicit a slowdown in growth in sand, but dense populations in mud showed reduced growth. This suggested that food was limiting for deposit feeders, but not for suspension feeders, and the experiment was obviously controlled for taxonomic group. My recent work on the American west coast bivalves *Macoma nasuta* and *Macoma secta* shows that the distance that the siphon extends from the siphon hole decreases with increasing flow and surface sediment stability. This suggests that there may be hydromechanical factors that influence the deposit feeding–suspension feeding switch in different regimes.

While this argument seems reasonable for fairly long-lived species, it is apparent that there is also a great deal of instability in the deposit feeding realm; this instability seems related to strong seasonal cycles in POM supply, both in intertidal and in subtidal flats. In the intertidal of Flax Pond, New York, spring blooms of the benthic green alga *Ulva rotundata* initiate a considerable detritus supply to mudflats in the late spring. At this time a number of polychaetes recruit, but of special note are large-scale invasions of the oligochaete *Paranais litoralis* (Levinton and Stewart 1982, Stewart, in preparation). These invasions disappear in the summer. While some resident invertebrates inhibit the population growth of *P. litoralis* (Levinton and Stewart 1982), their experimental removal in summer only results in a modest population surge, suggesting that the absence of labile POM is the main cause of reduced population growth.

A similar cycle of seasonal POM supply occurs subtidally, especially in temperate and boreal shallow shelf and bay environments. The spring diatom increase may result in a large scale supply of POM to the bottom and invertebrates with short life cycles may respond appropriately. As noted above, the rapid supply can result in a layer several mm thick on the bottom. Two independent estimates suggest that this input may provide the bulk of the annual requirements for benthic productivity (Christensen and Kanneworff 1986, Peinert et al. 1982). Grassle et al. (1985) have documented the response to this supply in Narragansett Bay, Rhode Island, USA. The abundance of these species declines in summer, as temperature rises and POM supply declines. This indicates a shifting balance between community respiration and food availability to fuel the overall metabolic requirements. Rudnick et al. (1985) saw a similar cycle in Narragansett Bay of meiofaunal increase in spring and decrease in summer–fall. In colder environments, it is possible that cold-adapted species might rapidly take advantage of the spring diatom fall.

Deep conveyor belt feeders also live in both intertidal and shallow subtidal environments. These animals depend upon a continual cycling of POM between the sediment-water interface and the depth where feeding occurs. Because this process has a longer time scale, we might expect that such populations are more stable than those bound by supply to the surface. Indeed, it would be expected that juvenile conveyor belt feeders would have population dynamics that mimic shallow feeders. This has been found by D. Rice (personal communication) for a species of *Scoloplos* (Polychaeta) living in a tidal flat in Maine. Juveniles feed near the surface and fluctuate strongly in numbers from year to year and from place to place. In contrast, deeper feeding adults have remarkably stable populations.

These considerations suggest that Levinton's hypothesis of stability is incomplete. There seem to be at least three main modes of deposit feeding: (1) surface microbe feeding (principally microalgae in intertidal sediments), (2) surface POM dependent feeding (intertidal or subtidal, short life cycle), and (3) deep conveyor belt feeding. Each has its own trophic stability features. The surface POM dependent type is not particularly different from suspension feeding, which is subject to the vagaries of the water borne supply of phytoplankton. These modes, moreover, may coexist in the same habitat.

Deposit Feeding and the Stability of the Sediment-Water Interface

Sediments are strongly affected by the activities of most benthos, but actively burrowing and feeding deposit feeders are the most important component. The burrowing and feeding activities of deposit feeders greatly increases the water content of sediments with high silt-clay contents (Rhoads and Young 1970), and the production of fecal pellets may greatly increase the effective grain size of the sediment (Rhoads 1967). Vertical sorting of fine particles can produce biogenically graded beds, especially in intertidal poorly sorted sediments. When subjected to tidal or storm-derived currents, the roughness aspect introduced by pelletization into an otherwise very fine-grained sediment tends to increase the degree of erosion. As a result, the water column near the sediment-water interface is typically laden with bottom sediment (Rhoads and Young 1970; Levinton 1977). Thus the activities of deposit feeders strongly affect the sedimentary regime.

In shallow environments of high wave stress, bed forms are largely determined by the grain size spectrum of the sediment and the pattern of wave and current actions. In environments such as beaches of moderate exposure, deposit feeders are more the subjects, than the partial determinants, of the sedimentary regime. In such environments, advection and erosion of inorganic and organic particles both contribute considerably to the trophic regime (Miller et al. 1984). Microbes seem to occur in crevices of sand-size particles, and particle collisions may partially determine microbial abundance in wave swept environments. If transport of absorbable POM is considerable, higher feeding requirements may be sustained, relative to quieter bottoms.

Deposit feeders may respond to increased advection and erosion in a number of ways, but these have only been explored incompletely. Under high particle fluxes, a tentaculate spionid polychaete is known to change its feeding by orienting its tentacles in a spiral in order to efficiently capture particles saltating above the sediment- water interface (Taghon et al. 1980).

Conclusion

Deposit feeders have been extensively studied, and we now appreciate their central importance in coastal oceanography. Along with saprophytic microorganisms they mediate the processing of particulate organic matter. They also affect the grain size, chemical microenvironment, water content, and erodibility of fine-grained sediments. In order to understand these larger processes, basic aspects of feeding, digestion, and burrowing must be understood. This requirement justifies the necessity for a tightly integrated team of autecologists, nutritional biologists, sedimentary geochemists, and coastal sedimentologists. Only such a group can hope to solve the unsolved problems in deposit feeding research.

Clearly the most important unresolved issue is the role of POM in the nutrition of deposit feeders and, conversely, the effect of deposit feeders on the decay of particulate material. As mentioned above, some of the controversy in the past devolves to an artificial dichotomy between the microbial stripping and the POM nutritional hypotheses. There is a wide range of POM types, ranging from very digestible to virtually indigestible. Similarly, there are strong habitat variations. It is unlikely that the POM raining down from the shallow water phytoplankton is equivalent in breakdown rate to material derived from marine seagrasses. We have to acknowledge that different systems will have different answers, depending upon properties of individual consumers and the source material for the POM. The deep sea adds an additional complication, as material becomes highly refractory after a long traverse from the sea surface to depths over 4000 m.

To acknowledge this diversity, it would be useful to devise a research plan that examines several systems, with the intent of studying comparatively everything from the feeding behavior of the dominant deposit feeders, to the source and seasonal cycle of the POM supply. At present, much information is available from *Spartina* salt marsh mud flats, although we are still ignorant of the relative proportions of POM in the sediment at different seasons, and the different rates of breakdown and nutritional importance to the consumers. It would be useful to compare this to shallow water embayments such as Long Island Sound, New York, the Baltic Sea, or other bodies of water that are known to have a classical seasonal phytoplankton cycle, with a concomitant POM supply to the bottom. While such bodies of water have been studied extensively, the team approach might be useful in integrating our knowledge of the system.

Literature Cited

Allen, J.A. and H.L. Sanders. 1966. Adaptations to abyssal life as shown by the bivalve *Abra profundorum Deep-Sea Res.* 13: 1175-1184.

Baker, J.H. and L.A. Bradnam. 1976. The role of bacteria in the nutrition of aquatic detritivores. *Oecologia (Berl.)* 24: 95-104.

Bianchi, T.S. and J.S. Levinton. 1981. Nutrition and food limitation of deposit feeders. II. Differential effects of *Hydrobia totteni* and *Ilyanassa obsoleta* on the microbial community. *J. Mar. Res.* 39: 547-556.

Bianchi, T.S. and J.S. Levinton. 1984. The importance of microalgae, bacteria, and particulate organic matter in the nutrition of *Hydrobia totteni. J. Mar. Res.* 39: 547-556.

Blegvad, H. 1914. Food and conditions of nourishment among the communities of invertebrate animals on the sea bottom in Danish waters. *Rep. Danish Biol. Stat.* 22: 41-78.

Calow, P. 1975a. The feeding strategies of two freshwater gastropods, *Ancylus fluviatilis* Mull. and *Planorbis contortus* Linn. (Pulmonata) in terms of ingestion rates and absorption efficiencies. *Oecologia (Berl.)* 20:33-49.

Calow, P. 1975b. Defaecation strategies of two freshwater gastropods, *Ancylus fluviatilis* Mull. and *Planorbis contortus* Linn. (Pulmonata) with a comparison of field and laboratory estimates of food absorption rate. *Oecologia (Berl.)* 20: 51-63.

Cammen, L.M. 1980a. The significance of microbial carbon in the nutrition of the deposit feeding polychaete *Nereis succinea*. *Mar. Biol.* 61:9-20.

Cammen, L.M. 1980b. Ingestion rate: an empirical model for aquatic deposit feeders and detritivores. *Oecologia* 44:303-310.

Cammen, L.M. 1982. Effect of particle size on organic content and microbial abundance within four marine sediments. *Mar. Ecol. Prog. Ser.* 9:273-280.

Carman, K.R. and D. Thistle. 1985. Microbial food partitioning by three species of benthic copepods. *Mar. Biol.* 88:143-148.

Christensen, H. and E. Kanneworff. 1986. Sedimentation of phytoplankton during a spring bloom in the Oresund. *Ophelia* 26: 109-122.

Connor, M.S., J.M. Teal, and I. Valiela. 1982. The effect of feeding by mud snails, *Ilyanassa obsoleta*, on the structure and metabolism of a laboratory benthic algal community. *J. Exp. Mar. Biol. Ecol.* 65: 29-45.

Crosby, N.D. and R.G.B. Reid. 1971. Relationships between food, phylogeny, and cellulose digestion in the bivalvia. *Can. J. Zool.* 49: 617-622.

Dale, N.G. 1974. Bacteria in intertidal sediments: factors related to their distribution. *Limnol. Oceanogr.* 19: 509-518.

Dauer, D.M. 1983. Functional morphology and feeding behavior of *Scolelepis squamata* (Polychaeta: Spionidae). *Mar. Biol.* 77: 279-285.

DeFlaun, M.F. and L.M. Mayer. 1983. Relationships between bacteria and grain surfaces in intertidal sediments. *Limnol. Oceanogr.* 28: 873-881.

Doris, V.E. 1984. Feeding selectivity in the deposit-feeding gastropod, *Hydrobia totteni* with regard to mineral grain surface area and sedimentary diatom abundance. Masters thesis, State Univ. of New York at Stony Brook, 51 pp.

Fenchel, T. 1970. Studies on the decomposition of organic detritus from the turtle grass *Thalassia testudinum*. *Limnol. Oceanogr.* 15: 14-20.

Fenchel, T., and L.H. Kofoed. 1976. Evidence for exploitative interspecific competition in mud snails (Hydrobiidae). *Oikos* 27:367-376.

Fenchel, T., C.P. McRoy, J.C. Ogden, P. Parker, and W.E. Rainey. 1979. Symbiotic cellulose degradation in green turtles. *Appl. Environ. Microbiol.* 37: 348-350.

Findlay, S. and J.L. Meyer. 1984. Significance of bacterial biomass and production as an organic carbon source in lotic detrital systems. *Bull. Mar. Sci.* 25: 318-325.

Findlay, S. and K.R. Tenore. 1982. Nitrogen source for a detritivore: detritus substrate vs. associated microbes. *Science* 218:371-373.

Gilbert, M.A. 1977. The behavior and functional morphology of deposit feeding in *Macoma balthica* (Linne 1758), in New England. *J. Moll. Stud.* 43: 18-27.

Grassle, J.F., J.P. Grassle, L.S. Brown-Leger, R.F. Petrecca and N.J. Copley. 1985. Subtidal macrobenthos of Narragansett Bay. Field and mesocosm studies of the effects of eutrophication and organic input on benthic populations. IN J.S. Gray and M.E. Christiansen, eds., *Marine Biology of Polar Regions and Effects of Stress on Marine Organisms.* pp. 421-434. New York: John Wiley and Sons.

Haines, E.B. 1975. Nutrient inputs to the coastal zone: the Georgia and South Carolina shelf. IN *Estuarine Research*, L.E. Cronin, ed., vol. 1, pp. 303-324. New York: Academic Press.

Haines, E.B. 1977. The origins of detritus in Georgia salt marsh estuaries. *Oikos* 29:254-260.

Hammond, L.S. 1982. Analysis of grain-size selection by deposit-feeding holothurians and echinoids (Echinodermata) from a shallow reef lagoon, Discovery Bay, Jamaica. *Mar. Ecol. Progr. Ser.* 8: 25-36.

Hargrave, B.T. 1970. The utilization of benthic microflora by *Hyalella azteca* (Amphipoda). *J. Anim. Ecol.* 39: 427-437.

Hargrave, B.T. 1976. The central role of invertebrate faeces in sediment decomposition. IN *The Role of Terrestrial and Aquatic Organisms in Decomposition Processes*, J.M. Anderson and A. MacFadyen, eds., pp. 301-321. Oxford, U.K.: Blackwell Scientific Publications.

Harrison, P.D. and K.H. Mann. 1975. Detritus formation from eelgrass (*Zostera marina*) the relative effects of fragmentation, leaching and decay. *Limnol. Oceanogr.* 20:924-934.

Holme, N.A. 1950. Population dispersion in *Tellina tenuis* da Costa. *J. Mar. Biol. Ass. U.K.* 29: 267-280.

Hughes, R.N. 1969. A study of feeding in *Scrobicularia plana*. *J. Mar. Biol. Ass. U.K.* 49: 805-823.

Hylleberg, J. 1976. Resource partitioning on basis of hydrolytic enzymes in deposit-feeding mud snails (Hydrobiidae). II. Studies on niche overlap. *Oecologia* (Berl.) 23: 115-125.

Hylleberg, J. and V. Gallucci. 1975. Selectivity in feeding by the deposit feeding bivalve *Macoma nasuta*. *Mar. Biol.* 32: 167-178.

Kermack, D.M. 1955. The anatomy and physiology of the gut of the polychaete *Arenicola marina* L.. *Proc. Zool. Soc. London* 125: 347-381.

Levinton, J.S. 1972a. Spatial distribution of *Nucula proxima* (Protobranchia): an experimental approach. *Biol. Bull.* 143: 175-183.

Levinton, J.S. 1972b. Stability and trophic structure in deposit-feeding and suspension-feeding communities. *Am. Nat.* 106: 472-486.

Levinton, J.S. 1977. The ecology of deposit-feeding communities: Quisset Harbor, Massachusetts. IN *Ecology of Marine Benthos*, B.C. Coull, ed., pp. 191-228. Columbia, S.C.: Univ. South Carolina Press.

Levinton, J.S. 1979. Particle feeding by deposit-feeders: models, data, and a prospectus. Pages 423-439 *in Marine Benthic Dynamics*, ed. B.C. Coull and K.R. Tenore, Univ. South Carolina Press, Columbia, South Carolina USA.

Levinton, J.S. 1985. Complex interactions of a deposit feeder with its resources: roles of density, a competitor, and detrital addition in the growth and survival of the mudsnail *Hydrobia totteni*. *Mar. Ecol. - Prog. Ser.* 22: 31-40.

Levinton, J.S. 1987. The body-size-prey-size hypothesis and *Hydrobia*. *Ecology* 68: 229-231.

Levinton, J.S., and T.S. Bianchi. 1981. Nutrition and food limitation of deposit feeders. I. The role of microbes in the growth of mud snails (Hydrobiidae). *J. Mar. Res.* 39: 531-545.

Levinton, J.S., T.S. Bianchi, and S. Stewart. 1984. What is the role particulate organic matter in benthic invertebrate nutrition? *Bull. Mar. Sci.* 35:270-282.

Levinton, J.S., and G.R. Lopez. 1977. A model of renewable resources and limitation of deposit-feeding benthic populations. *Oecologia* (Berl.) 31: 177-190.

Levinton, J.S. and S. Stewart. 1982. Marine succession: the effect of two deposit-feeding gastropod species on the population growth of *Paranais litoralis* Muller 1784 (Oligochaeta). *J. Exp. Mar. Biol. Ecol.* 59:231-241.

Levinton, J.S., and S. Stewart. 1988. Effects of sediment organics, detrital input, and temperature on demography, production, and body size of a deposit feeder. *Mar. Ecol. Prog. Ser.* in press.

Lewin, J.C., T. Hruby, and D. Mackas. 1975. Blooms of surf-zone diatoms along the coast of the Olympic peninsula, Washington. V. Environmental conditions associated with blooms (1971 and 1972). *Estuar. Coast. Mar. Sci.* 3: 229-242.

Lopez, G.R., and I-J. Cheng. 1982. Ingestion selectivity of sedimentary organic matter by the deposit-feeder *Nucula annulata* (Bivalvia: Nuculidae). *Mar. Ecol. Prog. Ser.* 8: 279-282.

Lopez, G.R., and L.H. Kofoed. 1980. Epipsammic browsing and deposit-feeding in mud snails (Hydrobiidae). *J. Mar. Res.* 38: 585-599.

Lopez, G.R., and J.S. Levinton. 1978. The availability of microorganisms attached to sediment particles as food for *Hydrobia ventrosa*. *Oecologia* (Berlin) 32: 263-275.

Lopez, G.R., and J.S. Levinton. 1987. Ecology of deposit-feeding animals in marine sediments. *Quart. Rev. Biol.* 62: 235-260.

Lopez, G.R., J.S. Levinton, and L.B. Slobodkin. 1977. The effects of grazing by the detritivore *Orchestia grillus* on Spartina litter and its associated microbial community. *Oecologia* (Berl.) 20: 111-127.

Mann, K.H. 1975. Relationship between morphometry and biological functioning in three coastal inlets of Nova Scotia. IN *Estuarine Research*, L.E. Cronin, ed., vol. 1, pp. 634-644. New York: Academic Press.

Marais, J.F.K. 1980. Aspects of food intake, food selection, and alimentary canal morphology of *Mugil cephalus* (Linnaeus, 1958). *Liza tricuspidens* (Smith, 1935), *L. richardsoni* (Smith, 1846), and *L. dumerili* (Steindachner, 1869). *J. Exp. Mar. Biol. Ecol.* 44:193-209.

Miller, D.C., P.A. Jumars, and A.R.M. Nowell. 1984. Effects of sediment transport on deposit feeding: scaling arguments. *Limnol. Oceanogr.* 29: 1202-1217.

Newell, R.C. 1965. The role of detritus in the nutrition of two marine deposit feeders, the prosobranch *Hydrobia ulvae* and the bivalve *Macoma balthica. Proc. Zool. Soc. Lond.* 144: 25-45.

Nixon, S. W. 1980. Between coastal marshes and coastal waters - a review of twenty years of speculation and research on the role of salt marshes in estuarine productivity and water chemistry. IN *Estuarine and Wetland Processes*, E. Hamilton and K.B. MacDonald, eds., pp. 437-525. New York: Plenum.

Nixon, S.W., C.W. Oviatt, and S.S. Hale. 1976. Nitrogen regeneration and the metabolism of coastal marine bottom communities. IN *The Role of Terrestrial and Aquatic Organisms in Decomposition Processes*, J.M. Anderson and A. MacFadyen, eds., pp. 269-283. Oxford, U.K.: Blackwell Scientific Publ.

Nowell, A.R.M., P.A. Jumars, and K. Fauchald. 1984. The foraging strategy of a subtidal and deep-sea deposit feeder. *Limnol. Oceanogr.* 25:645-649.

Odum, E.P. 1980. The status of three ecosystem-level hypotheses regarding salt marsh estuaries: tidal subsidy, outwelling, and detritus-based food chains. IN *Estuarine Perspectives*, V.S. Kennedy, ed., pp. 485-495. New York: Academic Press.

Odum, E.P. and A.A. De La Cruz. 1967. Particulate organic detritus in Georgia salt marsh-estuarine ecosystem. IN Estuaries, G.H. Lauff, ed., pp. 383-388. Washington D.C.: Amer. Assoc. Adv. Sci.

Olafsson, E.B. 1986. Density dependence in suspension-feeding and deposit-feeding populations of the bivalve *Macoma balthica*: a field experiment. *J. Animal Ecol.* 55:517-526.

Pace, M.L., S. Shimmel, and W.M. Darley. 1979. The effect of grazing by a gastropod, *Nassarius obsoletus*, on the benthic microbial community of a salt marsh. *Est. Coast. Mar. Sci.* 9: 121-134.

Peinert, R., A. Savre, P. Stegman, C. Stienen, H. Haardt, and V. Smetacek. 1982. Dynamics of primary production and sedimentation in a coastal ecosystem. *Neth. J. Sea Res.* 16: 276-289.

Petersen, C. G. J. 1918. The sea bottom and its production of fishfood. A survey of the work done in connection with the valuation of the Danish waters from 1883-1917. *Rept. Danish Biol. Stat.* 25: 1-62.

Petersen, C. G. J. and P. Boysen Jensen. 1911. Valuation of the sea. I. Animal life of the sea bottom, its food and quantity. *Rep. Danish Biol. Stat.* 20: 2-77.

Peterson, B.J., R.W. Howarth, and R.H. Garritt. 1986. Sulfur and carbon isotopes as tracers of salt-marsh organic matter flow. *Ecology* 67:865-874.

Peterson, C.H. 1982. The importance of predation and intra- and inter-specific competition in the population biology of two infaunal suspension-feeding bivalves, *Protothaca staminea* and *Chione undatella*. *Ecol. Monogr.* 52: 437-475.

Pohlo, R. 1969. Confusion concerning deposit-feeding in the Tellinacea. *Proc. Malacol. Soc. London* 38:361-364.

Race, M.S. 1982. Competitive displacement and predation between introduced and native mud snails. *Oecologia* (Berl.) 54: 337-347.

Rasmussen, E. 1973. Systematics and ecology of the Isefjord marine fauna (Denmark). With a survey of the eelgrass (*Zostera*) vegetation and its communities. *Ophelia* 11:1-495.

Reid, R.G.B., and K. Rauchert. 1972. Protein digestion in members of the genus *Macoma* (Mollusca: Bivalvia). *Comp. Biochem. Physiol.* 41A: 887-895.

Rhoads, D.C. 1967. Biogenic reworking of intertidal and subtidal sediments in Barnstable Harbor and Buzzards Bay, Massachusetts. *J. Geol.* 75: 461-474.

Rhoads, D.C. and D.K. Young. 1970. The influence of deposit-feeding organisms on sediment stability and community trophic structure. *J. Mar. Res.* 28: 150-178.

Rice, D.L., T.S. Bianchi, and E.H. Roper. 1986. Experimental studies of sediment reworking and growth of *Scoloplos* spp. (Orbiniidae: Polychaeta). *Mar. Ecol.–Progr. Ser.* 30: 9-19.

Riley, G.A. 1956. Oceanography of Long Island Sound. 1952-1954. IX. Production and utilization of organic matter. *Bull. Bingham Oceanogr. Coll.* 15: 324-344.

Rowe, G.T., S. Smith, P. Falkowski. T. Whitledge, R. Theroux, W. Phoel, and H.W. Ducklow. 1986. Do continental shelves export organic matter. *Nature* 325: 559-561.

Rudnick, D.T., R. Elmgren, and J.B. Frithsen. 1985. Meiofaunal prominence and benthic seasonality in a coastal marine ecosystem. *Oecologia* 67: 157-168.

Sanders, H.L. 1958. Benthic studies in Buzzards Bay. I. Animal-sediment relationships. *Limnol. Oceanogr.* 3: 245-258.

Self, R.F.L. and P.A. Jumars. 1978. New resource axes for deposit feeders? *J. Mar. Res.* 36: 627-641.

Taghon, G.L. 1981. Beyond selection: optimal ingestion rate as a function of food value. *Am. Nat.* 118: 202-214.

Taghon, G.L. 1982. Optimal foraging by deposit-feeding invertebrates: roles of particle size and organic coating. *Oecologia* (Berl.) 52: 295-304.

Taghon, G.L., and P.A. Jumars. 1984. Variable ingestion rate and its role in optimal foraging behavior of deposit feeders. *Ecology* 65: 549-558.

Taghon, G.L., A.R.M. Nowell, and P.A. Jumars. 1980. Induction of suspension feeding in spionid polychaetes by high particulate fluxes. *Science* 210:562-564.

Taghon, G.L., R.F.L. Self, and P.A. Jumars. 1978. Predicting particle selection by deposit-feeders: a model and predictions. *Limnol. Oceanogr.* 23: 752-759.

Tenore, K.R. 1977. Growth of *Capitella capitata* cultured on various levels of detritus derived from different sources. *Limnol. Oceanogr.* 22: 936-941.

Tenore, K.R., B.E. Dornseif, and C.N. Weiderhold. 1979. The effect of organic nitrogen supplement on the utilization of different sources of detritus. *Limnol. Oceanogr.* 24: 350-355.

Tenore, K.R. and D.L. Rice. 1980. A review of trophic factors affecting secondary production of deposit-feeders. IN *Marine Benthic Dynamics*, K.R. Tenore and B.C. C. Coull, eds., pp. 325-340. Columbia: Univ. South Carolina Press.

Trueman, E.R. 1971. The control of burrowing and the migratory behavior of *Donax denticulatus* (Bivalvia: Tellinacea). *J. Zool. London* 165: 453-469.

Valiela, I., J.M. Teal. 1979. The nitrogen budget of a salt marsh ecosystem. *Nature* 280: 652-656.

Vogel, S. 1978. Organisms that capture currents. *Sci. Am.* 239: 128-139.

Vogel, S. 1981. *Life in Moving Fluids*. Boston: Willard Grant Press.

Whitlatch, R.B. 1974. Food-resource partitioning in the deposit feeding polychaete *Pectinaria gouldii*. *Biol. Bull.* 147: 227-235.

Woodin, S.A. 1974. Polychaete abundance patterns in a marine soft-sediment environment: the importance of biological interactions. *Ecol. Monogr.* 44: 171-187.

Woodwell, G.M. D. E. Whitney, C.A. S. Hall, and R.A. Houghton. 1977. The Flax Pond ecosystem study: exchanges of carbon between a salt marsh and Long Island Sound. *Limnol. Oceanogr.* 22: 833-838.

Yamamoto, N. and G.R. Lopez. 1985. Bacterial abundance in relation to surface area and organic content of marine sediments. *J. Exp. Mar. Biol. Ecol.* 90: 209-220.

Yingst, J.Y. 1976. The utilization of organic matter in shallow marine sediments by an epibenthic deposit-feeding holothurian. *J. Exp. Mar. Biol. Ecol.* 23: 55-69.

Zobell, C.E. 1938. Studies on the bacterial flora of marine bottom sediments. *J. Sed. Pet.* 8: 10-18.

Zobell, C.E., and C.B. Feltham. 1938. Bacteria as food for certain marine invertebrates. *J. Mar. Res.* 1: 312-327.

Chapter 2

Examining Relationships Between Organic Carbon Flux and Deep-Sea Deposit Feeding

Robert S. Carney
Department of Marine Sciences
Louisiana State University
Baton Rouge, Louisiana 70803 USA

Introduction

The picture of a deep benthic environment subjected to fluctuating detritus supply and availability is now emerging from the convergence of geochemical, sedimentological, physical and ecological investigations. In the past decade there have been dramatic gains in organic carbon geochemistry contrasting to slower progress in ecology of deep-sea deposit feeding. Therefore, rather than reviewing the old question of, "what is the role of detritus feeding in the deep sea," it is the purpose of this chapter to outline a new perspective from which the question needs to be reassessed. We can already make two broad generalizations which point to the extreme importance of a variable food supply.

1. There is a relatively well described relationship between depth and the flux of organic carbon. In response to decreased carbon input with depth, we should expect to find in the fauna both a decreased overall abundance and species replacement determined by the efficiency of foraging.

2. Detritus flux varies in time on both ecological and evolutionary time scales. Therefore, both faunal abundances and the distribution of different foraging strategies should also vary on similar scales.

Considering the fact that the deep-sea has long been recognized as an environment dominated by deposit feeders, it is hard to understand why ideas about the rate and availability of detritus supply have played such a minor role in the development of deep- sea ecology. The view expressed by Bruun (1957) is illustrative. Brunn's review states that the rain of detrital food to bottom below 500m is too uniform with depth and meager to have much significant influence on deeper faunal patterns. In actuality, this critical flux had never been measured! Fortunately, there is movement to a more productive perspective typified by Jumars and Gallagher (1982), who reviewed deep-sea ecology from the optimal foraging theory perspective. In this approach, it is critically important that relative differences in rates and availability be known even if the absolute values are meager. Before proceeding to consider what is known about detritus rates and availability, it must be noted that few speculations about deep-sea ecology or detritus feeding can be altogether novel. Many if the ideas presented here can also be found in slightly different forms in recent reviews (Rowe, 1983; Ernst and Morin, 1982; Lopez and Levinton, 1987).

Making Critical Assumptions

In order to discuss the ecological significance of organic geochemistry, the problem of equating carbon with food must be resolved. I know of no convincing analysis that distinguishes labile (that fraction which can be digested directly by metazoans) from refractory organic carbon (that fraction not directly digestible by metazoans). As a result of our inability to directly measure labile detritus, we are severely limited in the ways which we can study its availability, distribution and foraging adaptations. While some studies attempt to use total organic carbon as indication of food, the more common method is to infer the nature of the detritus supply from faunal surveys (i.e., the presence of a detritivore is the best measure of detrital availability). Of the many problems associated with this approach, dangerous circularities can arise when the apparent utilization of a resource is the only means of assaying for that resource. This is particularly true in the deep-sea where there is extremely little natural history information about feeding. Geo-chemical efforts to determine the labile carbon fraction usually depend upon an indirect method as well. Typically, flux to bottom and burial rates are estimated. Since flux rates exceed burial, the difference is defined as la-bile carbon lost from the system due to biological consumption. Refractory carbon is that which is left after burial below biologically active sediment. There is considerable room for errors stemming from mixed scales, since flux rates involve measurements that average events over 10's of days and burial processes average events over thousands of years.

Newer attempts to more directly measure biological rates of consump-tion within the sediment mixed layer depend upon determination of oxygen gradients. With the development of microelectrode techniques (Reimers et al. 1986), we now have the ability to not only determine vertical patterns of diagenesis, but also to map horizontal labile carbon consumption.

Since there are neither good ecological or geochemical means of determin-ing the labile fraction of detritus, it is necessary to make certain assumption about how total carbon and labile carbon are related (Editorial comment: see chapters by Rice and Rhoads, Mayer, and Kofoed et al.). In this chapter I make three assumptions in which the relationship between total organic carbon and labile detritus are determined by the reservoir location and the length of time the total organic carbon pool has been subjected to animal foraging. Since less than 5% of the organic carbon falling to bottom is pre-served in the sediments as refractory carbon (see Bender and Heggie, 1984), the newly arriving detritus flux is considered to be virtually equivalent to labile carbon. Therefore, it is assumed that the dynamics which control total organic carbon flux at the sediment-water interface also control the availability of the labile fraction. Below this interface, the relationship be-tween total and labile carbon becomes more complex. Once detritus begins to be incorporated with the sediment of the mixed layer, it becomes ex-ceedingly difficult to distinguish between labile and refractory fractions. At the sediment water interface, it is assumed that recently arrived detritus is distinct from older sediments and is subject to different distributional pro-cesses. However, as the new material is consumed by animals and physically mixed with older sediments, it loses its distinct identity.

The Emerging Picture of Detritus Supply

McCave's works on the size spectra and flux of particles and aggregates in sea water (McCave, 1975) had a dramatic impact upon ideas about detritus supply in the deep-sea. These works made it quite obvious that the greatest volume of carbon transport to the deep bottom might be in the form of small material or larger aggregates of such material. Quickly, interest shifted from large food falls (Wiebe et al., 1976, Schoener and Rowe, 1970; Turner, 1977; Wolff, 1979) to the fall of detrital snow (Alldredge and Hartwig, 1987).

For our purposes, the key elements of detritus flux are sufficiently understood to discuss their ecological significance. The largest portion of biogenic particulate material generated in the euphotic zone is also consumed there (Knauer and Martin, 1981; Baker et al., 1985). Some material sinks below these depths as fecal pellets, aggregates, or fine particles. As it sinks the labile organic fraction decreases (Knauer et al, 1979; Rowe and Gardner, 1979; Honjo, 1980; Lee and Cronin, 1982; Knauer and Martin, 1981; Wakeham, 1982; Lorenzen et al., 1983; DeBaar et al., 1983; Matseuda and Handa, 1986; Naroki and Tsunogai, 1986), possibly due to microbial consumption (Fellows et al., 1981; Karl and Knauer, 1984; Karl et al., 1984; Naroki and Tsunogai, 1986; Gowing and Silver, 1983) or consumption by metazoans (Urrere and Knauer, 1981; Knauer and Martin, 1981). The decrease is quite regular with depth. Labile carbon undergoes an exponential decrease with depth, decreasing rapidly in shallow water and progressively slower as particles sink deeper.

Food Supply as a Function of Depth

Suess (1980) presented a compilation of available carbon flux data, surprisingly there was an unexpectedly clean relationship among depth, productivity, and carbon flux arriving at any particular depth (Figure 2.1). Due to the ubiquity of this relationship it can be used to produce a first approximation of the rate of food supply to the deep-sea.

Below the euphotic zone, the flux at any depth z was reasonably well ($r^2 = 0.79$) described by the equation

$$\frac{\log C_{flux}}{\log C_{prod}} = -\log(0.0238z + 0.212),$$

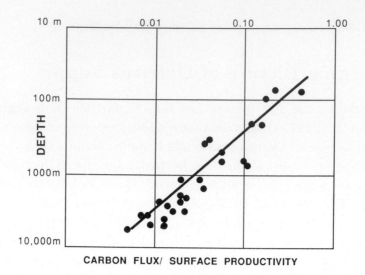

Figure 2.1: Depth associated decline in detritus influx. From a compilation of 12 studies Suess (1980) found a consistent relationship between depth and the percentage of surface productivity reaching bottom. Depth, which equates with time spent sinking, is a major determinant of the level of food input experienced by deep-sea deposit feeders in most regions of the world ocean. (Modified from Suess, 1980)

or

$$C_{flux} = \frac{C'_{prod}}{0.0238z + 0.212}.$$

This equation (the exact form of which is not important) suggests some interesting patterns. With respect to the depth associated change in carbon flux, a doubling of depth brings about a halving of influx. Thus, a population at 2000m experiences 1/2 the input experienced at 1000m and twice the input at 4000m. Changes in input due to variation in productivity, however, are felt equally across the entire depth range. A doubling of surface productivity produces a doubling of carbon input at all depths. If species distributions are restricted by the level of available detritus, then the depth-flux relationship suggests that ranges should respond to changes in surface productivity. A doubling of flux input would allow a species living at 2000m to survive at 4000m, while a halving of input would restrict distribution to only 1000m.

Depth as a Determinant of Nutrient Content

When the depth related change in nutritional content of detrital rain is considered, geochemical and ecological evidence appear to be in conflict. While the vertically changing chemistry of sinking detritus indicates that material becomes more refractory with depth, there is no evidence in the benthic biota that this is the case. Indeed, the detrital input appears to be rapidly consumed at all depths. Even though the nutritional content at 4000m may be less than at 1000m, the fauna still is able to utilize the material available.

Because net labile carbon input to the bottom decreases with depth, it is to be expected that the nutritional composition of this material will similarly vary as a function of depth. In a rather sketchy sense, this depth related nutrient change has been shown for amino acid content of detritus (Lee and Cronin, 1982), carbohydrates (Ittekot et al., 1984 a & b; Tanoue and Handa, 1987), lipids (Wakeham et al., 1980; Gagosian et al., 1982), and waxes and related compounds (Wakeham, 1982). Basically, the higher nutritional value and more labile organic components are consumed at relatively shallow depths, with more refractory components surviving to greater depths. These patterns also show regional variation (Lee and Cronin, 1982; Matsueda and Handa, 1986).

Matseuda and Handa (1986) introduced the "half depth", an interesting parameter, which illustrates the depth/sinking rate pattern of nutritional content. They studied the compositional change in organic matter with depth off the North and Central American Pacific coast. The observed changes were explained in terms of microbial and zooplankton consumption progressing at a rate that was approximately exponential with depth. By analogy to half life when dealing with decay in time, they calculated half depths for each component; the depth at which surface concentrations are reduced by 50% during sinking. Half depth for various components apparently varied regionally, an observation explained in terms of different sinking rates and mechanisms of remineralization.

Seasonal and Short-term Fluctuations of Detritus Input

The most exciting aspect of net labile carbon supply is the clear evidence that the depth gradients are highly variable on both the ecological and evolutionary time scales. This has been unequivocally shown in seasonal variation in sediment trap samples (Honjo,, 1982; Deuser and Ross, 1980; Cole et al., 1985; Deuser, 1986), and in time series deep-sea photo monitoring (Billett et al., 1983). Time series studies of detrital flux are at their earliest stages, and much more will be discovered after this writing. However, the following four examples establish the most critical points:

1. Seasonal variation is widespread in the deep-sea.

2. The annual range of detritus input may be on the order of 2x.

3. There is a faunal response to this seasonal input.

4. Local conditions may complicate general patterns.

Deuser's (1986) six year time series of particle flux at 3200m in the Sargasso Sea is the most fully analyzed study. During the six year interval, the range of seasonal high input to low was a factor of 2.3x. There was a distinct peak associated with surface phytoplankton productivity. Fully 1/3rd of the total variance was due to this periodicity with an additional 1/2 of the variance associated with longer periods of no obvious cycle. Deposit feeders can be expected to experience a marked seasonal variation and also experience longer period changes. Much like weather, there will be a regular pattern of good and bad years upon which is imposed longer-term climate trends.

Billett et al.'s (1983) observations confirmed that flux variation in the water are reflected on bottom. At bottom stations from 1,362 to 4,475m in the North Atlantic they photographed or detected in cores a rapid spring and early summer accumulation of diatomaceous deposits derived from the seasonal plankton blooms. Total pigment content decreased two orders of magnitude over this depth range. The material was markedly reduced in organic carbon and protein when compared with surface plankton, and the pigment content suggested bacterial and various consumer degradation prior to sampling. Unfortunately, their data does not support quantitative estimation of seasonal variation. There appears to be obvious response of the local benthos to increased detrital inputs (Gooday, 1988; Lochte and Turley, 1988). The best time-series evidence that the deep-sea fauna responds seasonally has been produced by Smith and Baldwin (1984) (Fig. 2.2). Using free vehicle respirometry, sediment community oxygen consumption was measured at a 5900m site in the oligotrophic Central North Pacific and at a 3815m site in the eutrophic Eastern North Pacific. Consistent with the exponential decrease in carbon flux and metabolic activity with depth, average oxygen consumption at 5900m was approximately an order of magnitude

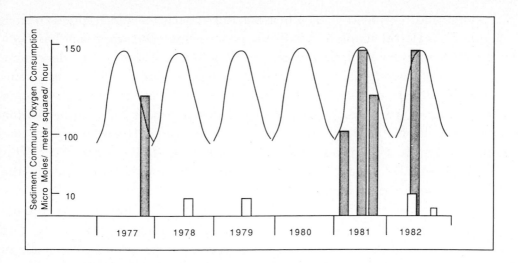

Figure 2.2: Response to seasonal peaks in detritus influx. Sediment community oxygen uptake at 3815m (solid bars) and 5900m (open bars) in the Pacific (Smith and Baldwin,1984) give some indications of an annual cycle. The most complete time series in 1981 at the shallower station showed the most convincing results, while less complete data in 1977-79 and in 1982 were consistent with this annual cycle of a late spring to early summer maximum. (Modified from Smith and Baldwin, 1984)

lower than at the shallower site. In spite of this between site difference, inter-month differences were quite similar. Each station showed a June maximum associated with known or suspected surface productivity patterns; flux and productivity were not actually measured as part of the project.

Long-Term and Geological Time Variation in Detritus Input

It can be argued that detrital flux to the deep-sea has varied considerably over long time periods (Eppley and Petersen, 1979). The case is quite simple. There are two components of primary productivity in the surface layer when nutrient sources are considered. First there is that productivity which utilizes nutrients recycled with the photic zone. Second, there is new productivity which utilizes nutrients being transported into the photic zone from some other source. In a steady state system, new productivity must balance the flux of material out of the photic zone. Therefore, flux should change in concert with many of the well documented paleo-oceanographic variations which alter nutrient availability to the surface layer.

Confirmation that the paleo-benthos did experience and respond to such changes in detrital supply is a difficult proposition. One approach has been to look at post-depositional carbon preservation, and then try to determine the nature of the original input signal. Mueller and Suess (1979) took an empirical relationship between bulk sedimentation rate and carbon preservation (preservation rate is proportional to the 1.4th power of bulk sedimentation rate) established by Heath et al. (1977) and then interpreted down core departures from this mean as evidence of high or low organic flux. This approach revealed an apparent cycle of high and low carbon input in the Atlantic associated with glacial cycles.

The more common attempt to identify variations in detritus flux in paleoenvironments is through the use of multivariate biological indicators. The benthic foraminifera complex *Uvigerina* spp. has been proposed as such an indicator of high nutrient input (Miller and Lohman, 1982). All of the proposed indicators remain unsatisfactory for the simple reason that the have been proposed only from correlational studies. They may have arisen from a spurious correlation among a multitude of factors and environmental parameters.

While none of the proposed indicators are especially convincing, it is reasonable to think that changes in flux might produce a faunal change preserved in the fossil record. However, rather than unique indicator species appearing and disappearing, we should expect vertical shifts in species distributions if the depth/flux relationship found by Suess (1980) holds true over geological time. If flux to the bottom doubles in one particular area, then that area will become nutritionally equal to the bottom at 1/2 that depth, and food limited species may successfully colonize deeper. If flux decreases by 1/2, then that area of bottom will become nutritionally equal to the benthos at twice that depth, and food limited species would become limited to shallower depths.

While it is doubtful if any direct evidence of benthic biomass can be preserved in the sediment record, there is a hint that biological feeding activity responds to flux variation on the geological time scale. When looking at biological blurring of down core paleotracers, Pisias (1983) found evidence that bioturbation mixing rate may be a function of sedimentation rate.

The Benthic Boundary Layer, the Sediment-Water Interface and the Sediment Mixed Layer

While the dynamics of the upper ocean and processes associated with detrital sinking determine the amount and variation of material reaching the deep-sea floor, it is the dynamics of the benthic boundary layer (BBL) and the sediment mixed layer (SML) which determine the pattern of detritus partitioning at the sea floor. On the gross scale, there are three reservoirs of detritus available to the benthic fauna (Figure 2.3). First, there is the detrital material suspended in and passing through the BBL. Second, there is the detrital material at the sediment-water interface. Thirdly, there is the material buried within the sediment mixed layer. A fourth reservoir, fossil carbon is buried deeper than animal activity and is not available. While the SML and deeper fossil layers show organic carbon gradients, such vertical decreases should reflect only very slow diagenetic processes acting on the refractory residue after removal of the labile fraction. It may be quite inappropriate to interpret such gradients as reflective of dominant trophic processes or as reflective of the pattern of detritus availability. Indeed, it is tempting to suggest that virtually no labile carbon persists more than a few millimeters into the sediment mixed layer. Rather, whether it arrives from above in labile form, or if postdepositional processes render it labile, it is consumed virtually instantaneously. In effect, biomass is the only significant labile carbon reservoir that persists for more than a few days.

Suspended in the BBL

The particulate material suspended in a bottom turbidity or nepheloid layer can be an important reservoir of detritus in regions that experience well developed benthic boundary layers (BBL). These are not static suspensions, but rather steady-state concentrations (Biscaye and Eittreim, 1977) made up of particles moving up and down under the opposing influences of gravity and boundary layer turbulence (Ludwick and Domurat, 1982). This suspended flux/reflux may be, on the average, younger detritus than that at the interface or buried within the biological mixed layer. As such, it is a richer food source although dilute and highly variable. An assessment of the size of the BBL detritus reservoir has not been made.

Labile carbon concentrations and residence times in the BBL have not determined. BBL particulates represent a mixture of flux and reflux sediment, therefore trap studies of flux carefully avoid deploying traps within

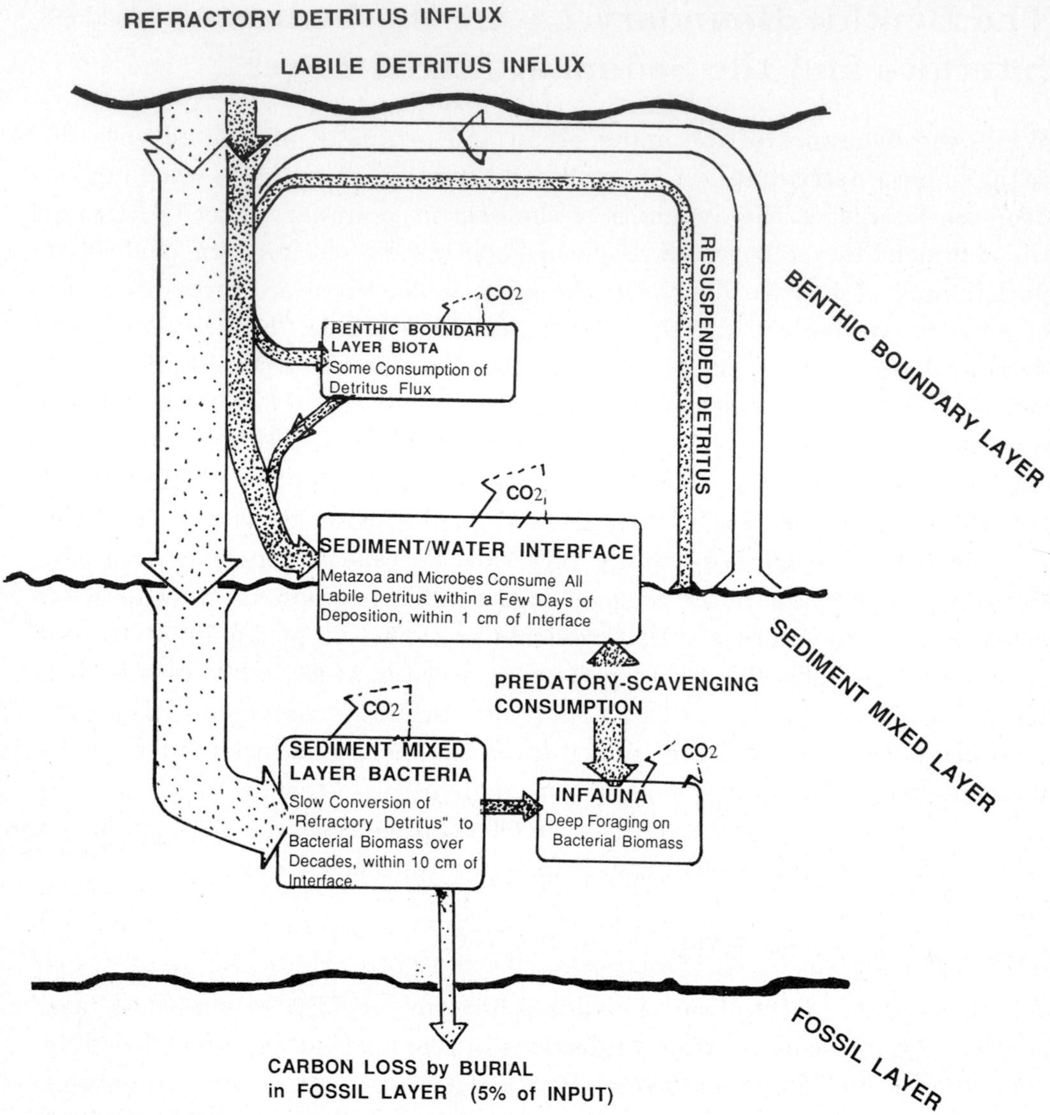

REFRACTORY DETRITUS INFLUX

LABILE DETRITUS INFLUX

CO_2

BENTHIC BOUNDARY LAYER BIOTA
Some Consumption of Detritus Flux

CO_2

SEDIMENT/WATER INTERFACE
Metazoa and Microbes Consume All Labile Detritus within a Few Days of Deposition, within 1 cm of Interface

RESUSPENDED DETRITUS

BENTHIC BOUNDARY LAYER

SEDIMENT MIXED LAYER

PREDATORY-SCAVENGING CONSUMPTION

CO_2

SEDIMENT MIXED LAYER BACTERIA
Slow Conversion of "Refractory Detritus" to Bacterial Biomass over Decades, within 10 cm of Interface.

CO_2

INFAUNA
Deep Foraging on Bacterial Biomass

FOSSIL LAYER

CARBON LOSS by BURIAL in FOSSIL LAYER (5% of INPUT)

Figure 2.3: Partitioning of detritus in the deep sea. As new detrital material enters the top of the BBL, refractory and labile fractions are tightly linked. However, once exposed to foraging benthic and benthopelagic fauna, separate routes are taken. Most labile material is consumed at or very near the sediment water interface in a matter of days. The refractory component is advected into the sediment mixed layer by bioturbation. Over decades 95% is converted to CO_2, and only 5% is preserved. Due to metabolic costs, only a small amount of bacterial biomass is produced and enters the labile carbon pool.

the BBL. As a result, less is known about particulate movement in the BBL than in the water above it. An exceptions is found in Richardson and Hollister (1987). From these studies it is clear that even very large and relatively dense detrital particles, including benthic foraminifera and fecal pellets, can be carried as high as 50 meters above bottom by BBL turbulence. In such an high energy region, large amounts of the total labile carbon pool may be in suspension in a very large volume of water and not at the sediment-water interface for extended periods.

While the BBL is seldom envisioned as a detritus reservoir, awareness of the ecological importance of BBL has increased due to joint ecological-physical studies of this system. The physical effects of bottom currents as an agent of disturbance have been examined as a component of the High Energy Benthic Boundary Layer Experiment (Nowell et al., 1982) which examined an environment at 4280m depth subject to benthic storms (Weatherly and Kelley, 1985) with erosional velocity currents. Most of the biological component was directed at questions of physical disturbance of the bottom (Carmen, et al., 1987; Thistle, 1983a and b, and references therein). Any process which redistributes surface sediments also redistributes detritus.

Sticking to the Bottom

The partitioning of sediment between the BBL and the bottom is found in H. Einstein's concept of sediment half life (discussed in Yalin, 1977, and applied to the abyssal BBL by McCave and Swift 1976). When a detrital particle sinks into the BBL, it becomes subject to turbulent transport. Whenever it strikes the interface, there is a probability (p) that it will be incorporated into the bottom and made available for benthic foraging, and there is a probability (1-p) that it will be resuspended. Therefore a pulse of detritus arriving at time zero will experience an exponential concentration decrease in the BBL. The equilibrium concentration and the average age of detritus in the BBL depend upon the dynamics of the particular detritus-BBL-interface system. Unfortunately, estimation of residence time of labile carbon in the BBL is not possible since so few of the critical parameters are known.

It is likely that recently arrived detritus is redistributed in a manner that produces spatial heterogeneity in availability at the sediment-water interface. This should be due to resuspension into the BBL followed by redeposition around topographic and microtopograhic features (Eckman, 1979). The scales of variation would be determined by the characteristics of the detritus, the BBL flow, and the scales of topography.

Mixing into the Mixed Layer

Once a particle of detritus adheres to the bottom, it immediately begins the process of incorporation into the SML. The processes of removal from the BBL and downward mixing are dependent on the dynamics of the BBL, physical reworking, and the degree of animal consumption at the interface. In quiescent areas, there will be minimal BBL turbulence, and material will sink directly to bottom and will be consumed by the benthos and mixed with underlying sediments.

It is unlikely that labile detritus is mixed by bioturbation in a manner similar to an inert tracer (see reviews by Matisoff, 1982; Carney, 1981; Boudreau, 1986a, 1986b, Boudreau and Imboden, 1987). Since detritus foraging is the main cause of deep-sea bioturbation, labile detritus must be rapidly stripped out of the sediment by selective mixing (Wheatcroft and Jumars, 1987). Due to the high rate and selectivity of consumption, readily available carbon can not be expected to be mixed more than a fraction of a centimeter in the sediment mixed layer (Fig. 2.4). Material being converted from the refractory to the labile pool, would similarly be consumed immediately wherever it occurs in the sediment mixed layer.

In deep-sea areas where biological reworking exceeds physical disturbance, the major process burying any labile carbon which escapes immediate consumption is the destruction and reconstruction of biological mounds, tubes, furrows, burrows, etc. (McCave et al., 1984) which can dominate microtopography on a scale of less than 2 cm (Swift et al, 1986). An example of this has been found by Aller and Aller (1986) who found chemical evidence that abandoned burrows served as miniature sediment traps, allowing recently arrived material to penetrate the length of a burrow into the sediments. It is these discrete deposits of potentially labile carbon that subsurface deposit feeders exploit. It is also these discrete structures which may produce the considerable place to place differences in apparent carbon utilization (oxygen profiles) found only a few centimeters apart in the deep-sea sediments (Reimers et al., 1986).

Ecological Partitioning of the BBL-Interface-Sediment Mixed Layer

Biological consumption of carbon is greater within the BBL than in the immediate overlying water (Hinga et al., 1979; Smith and Hinga, 1983; Wishner and Meise-Munns, 1984) and possibly the entire water column up to within

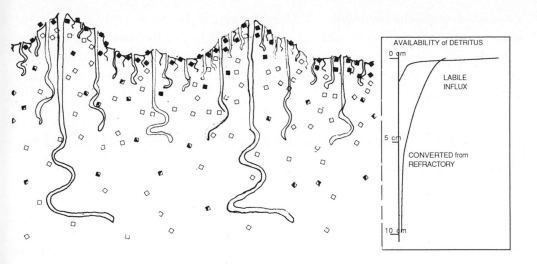

Figure 2.4: Effective carbon consumption at fast and slow rates. Microelectrode studies of oxygen gradients indicate that virtually all labile carbon is consumed in less than 1 cm of the sediment-water interface within days of arrival (Reimers et al., 1986). The distribution of most burrows and smaller fauna, in the top 1 cm is consistent with this observation. However, larger organisms and deeper burrows are present, suggesting some consumption deeper in the sediment mixed layer. Therefore, there may be a background of labile bacterial material being derived from refractory carbon. Exploitation of these two sources would require different detritus feeding strategies.

1000m of the surface (Jahnke and Jackson. ms). However, the extent of biological partitioning of organic detritus consumption in suspension, at the interface, and in the sediment mixed layer is known only in a rather preliminary sense.

In a series of papers K. Smith and his associates (Smith, 1982, 1987; Smith and Baldwin, 1984; Smith et al., 1986; Smith et al., 1987) have pieced together the general pattern of carbon consumption in the BBL, at the interface, and in the sediment mixed layer at a bathyal site off California and an abyssal site off Peru using oxygen consumption . Consistent with a short residence time and active consumption in the BBL, approximately 10% of the consumption occurred off bottom. Bacteria were found to be the primary consumers. However the techniques employed did not allow comparison to Wishner's work on benthopelagic plankton (Wishner, 1980; Wishner and Gowing, 1987; Wishner and Meise-Munns, 1984), and greater consumption is possible. The bulk of consumption, approximately 90% was associated with the sediment. Unfortunately, it is exceedingly difficult to separate the interface from the sediment mixed layer. However, populations of epifaunal ophiuroids and holothuroids could account for up to half the carbon consumed. This suggests that much of the carbon could be consumed at the interface.

Conflicts Between Geochemical and Ecologically Determined Rates of Carbon Utilization: A Variable Role for a Bacterial Intermediary?

Intriguing discrepancies from estimates of detritus flux and benthic consumption suggest that the linkage between detrital flux and consumption by a deposit feeding benthos may not be simple. There are four major problems to be resolved when suggesting a likely scenario.

1. As previously mentioned, studies of detrital flux show that material should become more refractory as it sinks deeper. However, the rapid loss of newly arrived materials at any depths suggests that it is highly labile.

2. When biologically determined rates of carbon consumption are compared to geochemically determined rates, the former may be orders of magnitude higher than the latter.

3. When biological needs are calculated, these may be greater than estimates of supply.

4. When isotopic composition of the fauna is considered, tissues are not predominantly new carbon.

Ecologically determined rates (biological half life of 10's to 100's of days) and geochemical rates (15 to 150 years biological half life, Emerson, et al., 1985) may be incomparable due to technical differences. The ecological approach (refer to any of the citations for K.L. Smith, Jr.) involves the *in situ* measurement of total sediment community oxygen demand for the SML supplemented by measurements typical of other community components. Organic carbon input is measured with sediment traps placed above the BBL so as to avoid contamination with resuspended material. The geochemical approach also employs measurement of flux above the BBL. However, biological consumption on and within the SML is not measured. Rather, carbon preservation below the SML is determined and then subtracted from the estimate of input. Rates derived in this manner may be of little ecological relevance since they are based on a very different time scale. (i.e., input measured over weeks versus burial averaged over 1000-10,000 years).

The most ecologically relevant geochemical rates are those based on short term organic carbon consumption. These use oxygen gradients within the SML in conjunction with relatively simple models of input, mixing by bioturbation, and first order reaction kinetics in which oxygen is the main electron acceptor (see Jahnke et al., 1982; Bender and Heggie, 1984; Emerson et al., 1985). These models allow estimation of carbon consumption as a function of depth in the sediment mixed layer. The distribution of the labile carbon pool is not measured directly but inferred from consumption. Input is measured above the BBL with a sediment trap.

In discussion of the unexpectedly slow (biological half life of 15 to 150 years) consumption rates in the sediment as compared to in the water column (Gardner et al., 1983), Emerson et al. (1985) made a strong argument that the estimates were reasonably accurate. Even if there is an unmeasured extremely fast consumption at and just below the interface, such consumption must not account for a significant portion of the total carbon budget, or there would be a major deficiency between input and longer term preservation rates; no such deficiency has been noted.

If there is a simple link between input and consumption one would expect that total community carbon demand would be less than or equal to total particulate organic carbon (POC) input. However, in a series of stations in the deep Pacific, Smith (1987) found a situation in which the apparent supply of POC ranged from equal to less than 10% the demand. This is in marked contrast to studies in the Atlantic (Smith, 1978; Smith and Hinga, 1983) in which POC supply was adequate to meet demands. In addition to the regional supply/demand imbalance, Smith found that POC variation explained less than 60% of the total variation in demand. In considering additional sources of carbon, Smith includes large detrital material not measured in traps, actively transported material in the tissue and guts of mobile organisms, and dissolved organic carbon.

A final bit of evidence that the linkage between organic carbon input and benthic consumption is not simple is the unexpectedly great ^{14}C depletion in megafaunal biomass across a wide range of deposit feeding organisms collected below 2800m off Oregon (Pearcy and Stuiver, 1983). Rather than determining apparent ages on the basis of ^{14}C decay, the rate of incorporation of fission product ^{14}C into deep-sea tissue was used to establish age. It was found that the average age of tissue carbon was 15 to 35 years!

Their results have raised a certain amount of controversy. Rau et al. (1986) reexamined the isotopic data in comparison with faunal abundance data, and found indication that the more abundant species, including epifaunal deposit feeding holothuroids, appeared to contain somewhat younger carbon, although appreciably older than that attributable to recently arrived detritus. In contrast, an infaunal deposit feeding holothuroid of the genus *Molpadia*, contained much older carbon. It was argued that ^{14}C depletion might result not only from slow turnover of an old organic pool of carbon, but rather by incorporation of old carbonate ions via anapleurotic carboxylation followed by foodchain amplification. Williams et al. (1987), also address the Pearcy and Stuiver results, arguing that neither an old organic carbon pool nor carboxylation are needed to explain the apparent age of midwater organism, but that the apparent age of benthic organisms might be attributed to partial incorporation of old organic matter.

A summary of the conflicting results might be phrased as follows. There is considerable good data from ecology and geochemistry which indicates rapid (10's of days) transport and consumption of detritus into the deepsea. There is also considerable good data from ecology and geochemistry which indicates that consumption is a slow (100's- 1000's days) process.

A possible resolution to the fast versus slow rates and the old versus new carbon tissues is the existence of a improperly measured microbial reservoir within the SML. Benthic bacteria might consume new detritus of any nutritional value converting it to a higher nutrition biomass. The low respiration of this microflora and associated microfauna would produce the interstitial oxygen gradients measured in the SML by geochemists. By contrast, the respiration of larger deposit feeders actively feeding upon this microflora and other labile material is less likely to influence the oxygen gradient in the sediments. The ventilation requirements of these organisms would result in effective venting to the overlying water. Their carbon consumption might be estimated by respirometers, but overlooked when gradients are employed.

However, if bacterial consumption is invoked, then the cost of bacterial consumption must be paid. Respiration losses due to bacterial consumption might leave less than 10% of the net input available for metazoan consumption. One possible scenario of detritus consumption would be for bacterial consumption to play a role that changes depending upon the nutritional content of detritus at the sediment-water interface. When rapidly sinking, high nutrient content pulses of detritus arrive, detritus feeding metazoans might consume this material directly and rapidly. This would result in rapid depletion of the labile fraction without appreciable loss to bacterial respiration and without creating an oxygen gradient in the SML. Between high nutrition pulses, bacterial biomass derived from more refractory detritus would be a more important part of the diet. During these periods, old carbon from the SML would be introduced into the diet via bacteria during subsistence feeding. The older carbon would produce an averaging of input and isotopic content.

This speculation must be concluded with a familiar lament; in spite of preliminary estimates of bacterial consumption (Rowe and Deming, 1985; Deming, 1986), the definitive study linking input, bacteria, and metazoan consumption has not been designed.

The Preliminary View of Larger Scale Patterns of Deposit Feeding

It would be extremely informative to produce maps of benthic fauna showing the distribution of animals on the basis of mobility, mode of ingestion, rates of digestion, and other aspects of foraging strategy.

Sokolova (summarized in English in Sokolova, 1972) synthesized a large body of data on the distribution of feeding types across a great depth and productivity range in the Pacific. Sokolova's patterns and their explanation are of interest because they invoke a relationship between detritus influx and availability. Near the continents detritus flux is high, and enough labile material is available on and in the SML to support high populations large deposit feeders (usually echinoderms in the data used). However, in deeper central oligotrophic areas influx is so low, that there is never a sufficient pool of labile carbon in and on the SML to support large deposit feeders, and suspension feeders predominate.

It does not seem reasonable that a detrital rain insufficient to support deposit feeders would be sufficient to support suspension feeders. There are two problems with Sokolova's scheme. First, it really deals almost exclusively with the larger fauna. When the smaller organisms collected by box corer are considered, deposit feeding still seems to predominate in central oligotrophic areas; Hessler and Jumars (1974) have considered this point in detail. It should be noted that Marshall (1979) considered both sides of the argument and tended to side with Sokolova discounting Hessler and Jumar's discussion of sampling differences. Second, in all benthic animals, the distinction between suspension and deposit feeding cannot be convincingly determined from preserved specimens.

As Sokolova envisions, in areas of low detritus input, the pool of labile material on and in the SML must be quite low. As a result, the effectiveness of ingestion of bulk sediments by large organisms should be prohibitively inefficient. More selective deposit feeding, if carried out with little cost, might be advantageous. In some taxa, the morphologies and behaviors associated with suspension feeding may be the most effective means of exploiting the limited detritus (either on bottom or during periods of resuspension). This would especially be the case if sessile suspension feeding was the lowest cost method of feeding.

When you look at holothuroid feeding mechanisms across the abyssal plain you can find the disappearance of epifaunal deposit feeders and the predominance of apparent suspension feeders . This is the case off the coast of Oregon (Carney, 1976; Carney and Carey, 1982) where at the most seaward and deepest stations *Abyssocucumis albatrossi* predominates. Species of this exclusively deep-sea genus possess tentacles typical of shallow water suspension feeders. However, gut contents suggest that they are deposit feeders.

An Inadequate View of Deposit Feeding Adaptations

It is no longer adequate to simply class most deep-sea animals as deposit feeders without consideration of ingestion/digestion mechanisms, morphologies and behaviors. The need to take a broader foraging-type rather than feeding-type perspective was aptly demonstrated when Jumars and Fauchald (1977) stressed that depth is more than a transition from suspension to deposit feeding. Rather, once this gross transition has occurred, there is a continuing species replacement of deposit feeders with depth.

At least in the case of deep-sea holothuroids, it is now clear that we have an inadequate view of the diversity of foraging strategies. Several of these morphologically complex deep-sea forms are benthopelagic and far. more mobile than previously anticipated (a good general account has been given by Billett, 1986). Two such taxonomic groups are actually quite common as shallow as 1000m and cosmopolitan, the *Peniagone-Scotoanassa* and the *Enypniastes-Psychropotes* complexes. While some swimming by deposit feeders must be temporary escape behavior, it is obvious from submersible observations that swimming and intermittent sediment ingestion is a common strategy. Pawson (1982) first reported the observation of *Enypniastes* dropping to the bottom for a few minutes, actively sweeping surface sediments with its tentacles, filling the gut and then swimming back into the water. Within the taxonomically complex group *Peniagone-Scotoanassa* there appears to be a full range of morphological types which may be completely benthic, intermittent bottom feeders, or even benthopelagic suspension feeders (Barnes et al., 1976).

Recent studies of deposit feeding of epifaunal holothuroids have produced fairly consistent results over a range of species and environments (see Hammond, 1983, for a review and discussion based largely upon the work of Moriarty, 1982; Massin, 1980; Webb et al., 1977; and Yingst, 1976). Simple comparisons between interface and gut sediments have shown preferential selection of smaller particles and relatively richer material. Non-living macrophyte detritus does not appear to be a major source of nutrition, while bacteria are (Yingst, 1976). In tropical coralline sands with low bacterial biomass and little macrophyte detritus, non-living mucous detritus is an important food source (Hammond, 1983). Similar results have been found for the few deep-sea epifaunal deposit feeders that have been examined (Khripounoff and Sibuet, 1980). When the sediment in the anterior portion of the gut was compared with interface sediments, that in the holothuroid had a greater organic content, a smaller size composition, and fewer meiofaunal organisms.

While studies of benthopelagic forms are just beginning, it can be suggested that slow, efficient swimming is a means of locating recently deposited detritus at the sediment water interface. Rather than trying to encounter patches rich in detritus by foraging over the surface, benthopelagic deposit feeders depend upon BBL currents and turbulence to transport them to areas where detritus is accumulating. In areas of erosion, these diaphanous animals would also be swept off bottom. In areas of still water, both detritus and holothuroids would be deposited.

What Can We Learn about Deep-Sea Foraging from Tracefossils?

Feeding traces are such a conspicuous part of the sediment-water interface that they are an obvious means of studying foraging. In an effort to find reliable paleobathymetry indicators, there have been several suggestions made as to how different trace fossil structures might reflect depth related gradients. Of special relevance to the topic of deposit feeding are the studies of Seilacher linking the complexity of foraging traces to the efficiency of detritus exploitation (see Seilacher, 1977, and Carney, 1981, for reviews). Conceptually, trace morphology could be used to study depth and geographic variation in modern foraging as well as paleoecological settings. This attractive idea, unfortunately, has not been supported by surveys of deep-sea foraging traces (Kitchell et. al., 1978). It is unrealistic to equate meanders and spirals (described by Seilacher and his associates) with efficient foraging when consuming a resource that is homogenous in two dimensions. Traces might provide a good record of foraging if we can identify the most appropriate parameters. As an example, if the availability of labile detritus is patchy in space, then we might examine traces for evidence of prolonged feeding in a restricted local and rapid transit across other areas.

Patches, Patterns, and High Diversity

If a temporally variable detritus influx is rapidly consumed at or near the sediment-water interface, while older, time averaged, refractory carbon is slowly converted to labile bacterial biomass within the SML, faunal elements may exist which are clearly adapted for either one or the other. The evidence that such specializations might occur should be found in spatial distributions on the scales of dominant topographic features.

Light weight detrital material is subject to redistribution by the currents and turbulence of the BBL interacting with bottom structures. Since these structures cover a considerable range of sizes and shapes, it can be anticipated that the bottom must contain areas swept clean of new detritus (e.g., the tops of small animal mounds, manganese nodule tops, upstream ridge faces and crests, abyssal hills, etc.) and areas which receive enhanced deposition (e.g., the lee of small animal structure, between nodules, ridge troughs, base of abyssal hills, etc.) which cover a considerable size range. Accordingly, benthic animals and/or their feeding tracks should reflect the resulting spatial pattern of labile detritus. Animals specialized for the consumption of this recently arrived carbon should be congregating in areas of enhanced detritus deposition, or trying to locate such an area.

If the major source of carbon is the SML pool converted to labile form via bacteria, then spatial distributions of foragers should reflect the distribution of the processes (bacterial productivity) which convert this standing stock. If this conversion takes place largely below the sediment-water interface, then physical processes of resuspension and deposition at the interface should have minimal influence on forager patterns. Due to the time averaging effects of bioturbation on refractory carbon, SML bacterial biomass might spatially homogenous. At the very least, the probability of finding higher bacterial biomass based upon refractory carbon should be more uniform over space than that of finding newly arrived labile material. Animals feeding on this refractory based source should show relatively uniform distribution.

We do not know if detritus foragers congregate in areas of enhanced sedimentation of detritus. Indeed, it is difficult to determine the significance of some of the observed patterns. Jumars and Eckman (1983) present a very thoughtful review of the available information on the spatial distribution of deep-sea fauna in the mega, macro, and meiofaunal size classes. One key point emerges from this review, with only a few exceptions which are easily explained in terms of specific organisms natural history, deep-sea faunal distributions can not be proven to depart from random. Therefore, the wide range of patch sizes that redistributed detritus should produce have not been found.

The study most relevant to the question of animal distributions was one based upon extensive spatial sampling by remote vehicle of a triangular area approximately 400 meters on a side (Expedition Quagmire, Jumars, 1976). The design of sediment core sampling allowed for analysis of spatial patterns on a scale of 0.1 to 500m. Of 13 species examined, only two showed distinct spatial autocorrelation. However, before we conclude that patches reflecting rapid consumption do not exist for most species we have to heed Jumars and Eckman's (1983) warning that the statistical power of the tests used to detect departures from randomness are extremely low. Patches may very well exist, but may be hard to detect. Published studies to date have not been designed to sample around structures that might influence detritus deposition.

There are congregations of large epifauna (holothuroids, ophiuroids, etc.) seen in the deep-sea during photosurveys or submersible transects (see Smith and Hamilton, 1983, and references therein). While some of these might be attributed to scavenging, others clearly involve deposit feeders. This is especially the case with dense aggregates of deposit feeding holothuroids. Perhaps, these aggregations reflect the foraging response of animals which specialize in the location and consumption of recently arrived detritus.

The deep-sea bottom is a striking exception to the generalization that a given community can not support a high diversity of deposit feeders (Fenchel et al., 1975). Unsatisfactory attempts to explain why this is so are a continuing theme in deep-sea ecology (see Rex, 1983 for review). Awareness that the deep-sea is a physically complex environment is leading to diversity maintenance schemes which require habitat heterogeneity and some form

of reduced competition through specialization. Grassle and Morse-Porteous
(1987) have argued that this heterogeneity is primarily in the form of a mo-
saic of succession triggered by larger food falls and/or associated disturbance
against a rather uniform background presumably fueled by general detritus
rain.

It may be an error to think of detritus flux as a monotonous background.
If there are processes which influence the distribution of labile carbon at
the sediment water interface, then variable food availability in space and
time can be an important source of environmental heterogeneity. Whatever the scales of variation are, these variations will be the major source of
environmental heterogeneity. If habitat heterogeneity prevents competitive
exclusion by some ecological/evolutionary mechanism, then the dynamics of
detritus redistribution should be important in allowing high diversity in the
deep-sea.

Trying to determine whether existing data reflect faunal patches on a
range of scales that might reflect detritus distributions is perplexing. Jumars'
argument (1976; Jumars and Eckman 1983) that the environmental grain of
the deep-sea benthos must be on a scale comparable in size to megafaunal
organisms, would seem to argue against the existence of larger detritus rich
patches associated with bottom topography on scales greater than a meter.
However, few sampling programs have been carried out with the appropriate
design and control of spatial sampling.

Diversity and Long-Time Period Variation of Detritus Influx

Since we have effectively abandoned the notion that the deep-sea is a stable environment due to its fluctuating detritus influx, we must examine the
longer-term consequences of a variable food supply that is controlled by
depth (i.e., sinking-associated processes) The benthic foraminifera record in
the North Atlantic is exciting evidence that major community change has
been experienced within the past 10,000 years. Caralp (1987) provides an
excellent introduction and complete bibliography. Unfortunately, the ecological importance of this literature has been ignored due to the emphasis upon
delineating water mass distributions. It has been shown, quite convincingly,
that the bathymetric and geographic distribution of contemporary benthic
foraminifera species and species assemblages have changed dramatically during and at the end of the Pleistocene.

It is tempting to ignore paleo-water masses and suggest a connection between detritus influx and the observed changing foram distribution zones. The bathymetric zones occupied by certain assemblages move about, expand and contract associated with Pleistocene climatic events. During one interval, a particular assemblage might be restricted to a relatively narrow zone on the continental slope. A subsequent time might see this same assemblage extended over the entire abyssal plain. This is the pattern expected if depth distributions reflect a fauna distributed in accordance to the minimal food requirement. If there was a net increase in detritus reaching bottom at all depths, species with higher food requirements could move into deeper water. If there were a net decrease, the species with lower food requirements would move into shallower water.

When an hypsographic curve of the ocean is examined, it is obvious that bathymetric range changes can cause tremendous changes in the geographic area occupied by a species, depending upon position on the continental slope. As species which live below 3000m undergo depth displacements, they should experience cyclic expansions out onto the abyssal plain followed by restriction to a much smaller area at the slope base. Shallower species whose range only moves up and down the slope would not experience such a dramatic range change.

This scenario of expanding and contracting ranges during the Pleistocene begs for a comparison with the Refuge hypothesis for tropical forest diversity proposed by Haeffer (1969) and extensively discussed in Prance (1982). While there are certain similarities, the deep-sea may be different. On the basis of paleoenvironmental pollen data and species distributions, allopatric speciation in isolated climatic refugia followed by cyclic reestablishment of a large homogeneous region has been proposed as the major process producing high species richness in the tropics. By contrast, the range changes seen in the deep-sea forams probably did not create isolated refuges. The deep-sea floor affords little opportunity for Mayr's isolation; it is, instead, the environment of Endler's clines (1977; 1982). As ranges expand across the abyssal plain, populations become subject to regional differentiation in the absence of physical barriers. As ranges contract, this genetic diversity is gathered into much smaller areas and conspecific competition increased. Through this process, a species rich fauna might be accumulated at the base of the continental slope. This position coincides with the maximum infaunal diversity for the North Atlantic (Sanders, 1969).

Concluding Comments

During the course of this chapter, I have tried to introduce scattered observations and ideas that suggest connections between the ecology of a fauna dominated by deposit feeders and a mode of detritus supply that results in time and space variations on many scales. While a more coherent body of findings is desirable, current evidence demonstrates the potential of the initial three suggestions. Slightly rephrased these are:

1. There is a relatively well described relationship between depth and the flux of organic carbon which should produce depth restricted adaptations in detritus foraging. Thus, the conspicuous species replacement found on the continental slope may be related to detrital influx more than other factors.

2. Detritus flux varies in time on both ecological and evolutionary time scales. Thus, variation in detrital influx rates should have a profound effect upon the ecology of the deposit feeding fauna; longer-term range changes may have contributed to high species diversity.

3. The spatial variation in availability of labile detritus, either newly arrived or via a bacterial intermediary, at the sediment-water interface may be a major source of environmental heterogeneity. Thus, the distribution of deep-sea deposit feedings organisms may be predominantly influenced by this food related patchiness.

Of course, I am safe in becoming an advocate for my own speculation. Traditional deep-sea ecological data, and even much of what we are now collecting, is not suitable for unequivocal answers. More than anything else, we must devise a means of effectively measuring the labile fraction of detritus and determining its availability to fauna. The most important questions all revolve around determining what the pattern of labile detritus availability is and how it varies in space and time on many scales. Clearly, we can not continue to use biological proxies due to the resulting circularities. Once labile carbon can be directly determined, a basis will exist for resolving the differences between biological demand and gradient based estimates of detritus partitioning and turnover.

Literature Cited

Alldredge, A., and E. Hartwig, eds., 1987, Office and Naval Research Aggregate Dynamics in the Sea Workshop Report.,

Aller, J.Y., and R.C. Aller. 1986. Evidence for localized enhancement of biological activity associated with tube and burrow structures in deep-sea sediments at the HEBBLE site, western North Atlantic. *Deep-Sea Res.* 33:755-790.

Baker, E.T., R.A. Feely, M.R. Landry and M. Lamb. 1985. Temporal variations in the concentration and settling flux of carbon and phytoplankton pigments in a deep fjordlike estuary. *Est. Coast. Shelf Sci.* 21:859-877.

Barnes, A.T., L.B. Quetin, J.J. Childress, and O.L. Pawson. 1976. Deep-sea macroplanktonic sea cucumbers: suspended sediment feeders captured from deep submergence vehicle. *Science* 194:1083-1085.

Bender, M.L., and D.T. Heggie. 1984. Fate of organic carbon reaching the deep-sea floor: a status report. *Geochim. Cosmochim. Acta* 48:977-986.

Billett, D.S.M. 1986. The rise and rise of the sea cucumber. *New Scientist* 109:48-51.

Billett, D.S.M., R.S. Lampitt, A.L. Rice, and R.F.C. Mantoura. 1983. Seasonal sedimentation of phytoplankton to the deep-sea benthos. *Nature* 302:520-522.

Biscaye, P.E, and S.L. Eittreim. 1977. Suspended particulate load and transport in the nepheloid layer and abyssal Atlantic ocean. *Mar. Geol.* 23:155-172.

Boudreau, B.P. 1986a. Mathematics of tracer mixing in sediments: I. spatially dependent, diffusive mixing. *Amer. J. Sci.* 286: 116-198.

Boudreau, B.P. 1986b. Mathematics of tracer mixing in sediments: II nonlocal mixing and biological conveyor-belt phenomena. *Amer. J. Sci.* 287, 693-719.

Boudreau, B.P., and D.M. Imboden. 1987. Mathematics of tracer mixing in sediments: III the theory of nonlocal mixing within sediments. *Amer. J. Sci.* 287: 693-719.

Bruun, A.F. 1957. Deep sea and abyssal depths. In: J.W. Hedgpeth (ed.) *Treatise on Marine Ecology and Paleoecology*. Vol. 1, Ecology. Memoir 67. Geological Soc. of Amer. pp. 641-672

Caralp, M.H. 1987. Deep-sea circulation in the northeastern Atlantic ocean in the past 30,000 years: the benthic foraminiferal record. *Oceanol. acta* 10:27-40.

Carmen, K.R., K.M. Sherman and D. Thistle. 1987. Evidence that sediment type influences the horizontal and vertical distribution of nematodes at a deep-sea site. *Deep-Sea Res.* 34:45-53.

Carney, R.S. 1976. Patterns of abundance and relative abundance of benthic holothuroids (Echinodermata: Holothuroidia) on Cascadia Basin and Tufts Abyssal Plain in the NE Pacific Ocean. PhD thesis. Oregon State University School of Oceanography, Corvallis Ore. 185p.

Carney, R.S. 1981. Bioturbation. **In** A. Boucot, *Principles of Benthic Marine paleoecology*. Academic Press, New York pp. 357-400.

Carney, R.S., and A.G. Carey, Jr. 1982. Distribution and diversity of holothurians on Cascadia Basin and Tufts Abyssal Plain. *Deep-Sea Res.* 29:597-607.

Carney, R.S., R.L. Haedrich and G.T. Rowe. 1983. Zonation in the deep sea. **In** Rowe (ed.) *The Sea*, vol. 8, Deep-Sea Biology. Wiley Interscience, New York. pp. 371-398.

Cole, J.J., S. Honjo and N. Caraco. 1985. Seasonal variation in the flux of algal pigments to a deep-water site in the Panama Basin. *Hydrobiologia* 122:193-197.

DeBaar, H.J.W., J.W. Farrington, and S.G. Wakeham. 1983. Vertical flux of fatty acids in the North Atlantic Ocean. *J. Mar. Res.* 41:19-41.

Deming, J.W. 1986. Ecological strategies of barophilic bacteria in the deep ocean. *Microbiol. Sci.* 3:205-212.

Deuser, W.G. 1986. Seasonal and interannual variations in deep-water particle fluxes in the Sargasso Sea and their relation to surface hydrology. *Deep-Sea Res.* 33:225-246.

Deuser, W.G., and E.H. Ross, 1980. Seasonal change in the flux of organic carbon to the Sargasso Sea. *Nature* 283:364-365.

Eckman, J.E. 1979. Small-scale patterns and processes in a soft-substratum benthic community. *J. Mar. Res.* 37:437-457.

Emerson, S., K. Fisher, C. Reimers, and D. Hedges. 1985. Organic carbon dynamics and preservation in deep-sea sediments. *Deep-Sea Res.* 32:1-21.

Endler, J. 1977. *Geographic Variation, Speciation and Clines.* Princeton University Press.

Endler, J. 1982. Pleistocene forest refuges. Fact or Fancy. In G.T. Prance (ed.) *Biological Diversification in the Tropics. Proceedings of the 5th International Symposium Association of Tropical Biologists. 1979.* Col. University Press pp. 641-657.

Eppley, R.W., and B.J. Petersen, 1979. Particulate organic matter flux and planktonic new production in the deep ocean. *Nature* 282:677-680.

Ernst, W.G., and J.G. Morin (eds.) 1982. *The Environment of the Deep Sea.* Prentice-Hall, Englewood Cliffs, New Jersey. pp. 217-255.

Fellows, D.A., D.M. Karl and G.A. Knauer. 1981. Large particle fluxes and the vertical transport of living carbon in the upper 1500m of the northeast Pacific Ocean. *Deep-Sea Res.* 28:921-936.

Fenchel, T.L., L.H. Kofoed, and A. Lappalainen. 1975. Particle size selection of two deposit feeders: the amphipod *Corophium volutator* and the prosobranch *Hydrobia ulvae. Mar. Biol.* 30:119-120.

Gagosian, R.B., S.O. Smith, and G.L. Nigrelli. 1982. Vertical transport of stero alcohols and ketones measured in a sediment trap experiment in the equatorial Atlantic Ocean. *Geochim. Cosmochim. Acta* 46:1163-1172.

Gardner, W.D., K.R. Hinga and J. Marra. 1983. Observations on the degradation of biogenic material in the deep ocean with implications on accuracy of sediment trap fluxes. *J. Mar. Res.* 41:195-214.

Gooday, A.J. 1988. A response by benthic foraminifera to the deposition of phytodetritus in the deep-sea. *Nature* 332:70-73.

Gowing, M.M., and M.W. Silver. 1983. Origins and microenvironments of bacteria mediated fecal pellet decomposition in the sea. *Mar. Biol.* 73: 7-16.

Grassle, J.F., and L.S. Morse-Porteous. 1987. Macrofaunal colonization of disturbed deep-sea environments and the structure of deep-sea benthic communities. *Deep-Sea Res.* 34: 1911-1950.

Haeffer, J. 1969. Speciation in Amazonian forest birds. *Science* 165:131-137.

Hammond, L.S. 1983. Nutrition of deposit feeding holothuroids and echinoids from a shallow reef lagoon, Discovery Bay, Jamaica. *Mar. Ecol. Prog. Ser.* 10: 297-305.

Heath, G.R., T.C. Moore, and J.P. Dauphine. 1977. Organic carbon in deep-sea sediments. **In** N.R. Anderson and A.J. Malahoff eds. *The Fate of Fossil Fuel CO_2 in the Oceans.* Plenum Press, pp. 605-625.

Hessler, R.R., and P.A. Jumars. 1974. Abyssal community analysis from replicate cores in the central North Pacific. *Deep-Sea Res.* 21:185-209.

Hinga, K.R., J.McN. Sieburth, and G.R. Heath. 1979. The supply and use of organic material at the deep-sea floor. *J. Mar. Res.* 37:557-579.

Honjo, S. 1980. Material fluxes and modes of sedimentation in the mesopelagic and bathypelagic zones. *J. Mar. Res.* 38:53-97.

Honjo, S. 1982. Seasonality and interaction of biogenic and lithogenic particulate flux at the Panama Basin. *Science* 218:883-884.

Ittekot V., E.T. Degens and S. Honjo. 1984a. Seasonality in the fluxes of sugars, amino acids, and amino sugars to the deep ocean: Panama Basin. *Deep-Sea Res.* 31:1071-1083.

Ittekot, V.E., W.G. Deuser, and E.T. Degens. 1984b. Seasonality in the fluxes of sugars, amino acids, and amino sugars to the deep ocean: Sargasso Sea. *Deep-Sea Res.* 31:1057-1069.

Jahnke, R.A., S.R. Emerson, and J.W. Murray. 1982. A model of oxygen reduction, denitrification, and organic matter mineralization in marine sediments. *Limnol. Oceanogr.* 27:610-623.

Jahnke, R.A. and G. Jackson. submitted ms. Oxygen consumption in the deep North Pacific: role of the seafloor.

Jumars, P.A. 1976. Deep-sea species diversity: does it have a characteristic scale? *J. Mar. Res.* 34:217-246.

Jumars, P.A., and J.E. Eckman. 1983. Spatial structure within deep-sea benthic communities. pp. 399-451, **In** G.T. Rowe, ed., *The Sea*, vol. 8, *Deep Sea Biology*, Wiley-Interscience, New York.

Jumars, P.A. and K. Fauchald, 1977. Between community contrasts in successful polychaete feeding strategies. B.C. Coull, ed., **In** Ecology of Marine Benthos, Univ. South Carolina Press, pp. 1-20.

Jumars, P.A., and E.D. Gallagher. 1982. Deep-sea community structure: Three play on the benthic proscenium. In: W.G. Ernst and J.G. Morin (eds.) *The Environment of the Deep Sea*. Prentice-Hall, Englewood Cliffs New Jersey. pp. 217-255.

Karl, D.M., and G.A. Knauer. 1984. Vertical distribution, transport and exchange of carbon in the northeast Pacific Ocean: evidence for multiple zones of biological activity. *Deep-Sea Res.* 31:221-243.

Karl, D.M., G.A. Knauer, J.H. Martin and B.B. Ward 1984. Bacterial chemolithotrophy in association with sinking particles. *Nature* 309:54-56.

Khirpounoff, A., and M. Sibuet. 1980. La nutrition d'echinodermes abbysaux I. Alimentation des holothuries. *Mar. Biol.* 60:17-26.

Kitchell, J.A., J.F. Kitchell, D.L.Clark and L. Dangeard. 1978. Deep-sea foraging behavior: its bathymetric potential in the fossil record. *Science* 200:1289-1291.

Knauer, G.A. and J.H. Martin. 1981. Primary production and carbon-nitrogen fluxes in the upper 1500m of the northeast Pacific. *Limnol. Oceanogr.* 26:181-186.

Knauer G.A., J. Martin, and K. Bruland. 1979. Fluxes of particulate carbon, nitrogen, and phosphorus in the upper water column of the northeast Pacific. *Deep-Sea Res.* 26:97-108.

Lee, C., and C. Cronin. 1982. The vertical flux of particulate organic nitrogen in the sea: decomposition of amino acids in the Peru upwelling area and the equatorial Atlantic. *J. Mar. Res.* 40:227-251.

Lochte, K., and C.M. Turley. 1988. Bacteria and cyanobacteria associated with phytodetritus in the deep sea. *Nature* 333:67-69.

Lopez, G.R., and J.S. Levinton. 1987. Ecology of deposit-feeding animals in marine sediments. *Quart. Rev. Biol.* 62:235-260.

Lorenzen, C.J., N.A. Welschmeyer and A.E. Copping. 1983. Particulate organic carbon flux in the subarctic Pacific. *Deep-Sea Res.* 30:639-643.

Ludwick, J.C., and G.W. Domurat. 1982. A deterministic model of the vertical component of sediment motion in a turbulent fluid. *Mar. Geol.* 45:1-15.

Marshall, N.B. 1979. *Developments in Deep-Sea Biology*. Blandford Press. Poole Dorset, Great Britain. 566p.

Massin, C. 1980. The sediments ingested by *Holothuria tubulosa* Gmelin (Holothuroidea:Echinodermata). **In** M. Jangoux, ed., *Echinoderms Present and Past, Proc. 2nd European Colloquium on Echinoderms, Brussels*. A.A. Balkema, Rotterdam, pp. 205-208.

Matisoff, G. 1982. Mathematical models of bioturbation. **In** P.L. McCall and M.J.S. Tevesz (eds.) *Animal-Sediment Relationships: The Biogenic Alteration of Sediments*. Plenum Press, N.Y. pp. 289-330.

Matseuda, H., and N. Handa. 1986. Vertical flux of hydrocarbons as measured in sediment traps in the eastern Pacific Ocean. *Mar. Chem.* 20:179-1 95.

McCave I.N., and S.A. Swift, 1976. A physical model for the rate of deposition of fine grained sediments in the deep-sea. *Geol. Soc. Amer. Bull.* 87:541-546.

McCave, I.N., C.D. Hollister, D.DeMaster, B. McKee, B. Nittrouer, C.A. Silva, and J. Yingst. 1984. Analysis of longitudinal ripple fronts on the Nova Scotian Rise. *Mar. Geol.* 58:275-286.

McCave, I.N. 1975. Vertical flux of particles in the ocean. *Deep-Sea Res.* 22:491-502.

Miller, K.G., and G.P. Lohmann. 1982. Environment and distribution of recent benthic foraminifera on the northeast U.S. continental slope. *Geol. Soc. Amer. Bull.* 93:200-206.

Miller, T.E. 1982. Community diversity and interactions between the size and frequency of disturbance. *Am. Nat.* 120:533-536.

Moriarty, D. 1982. Feeding in *Holothuria atra* and *Stichopus chloronotus* on bacteria, organic carbon and organic nitrogen in sediments of the Great Barrier Reef. *Aust. J. mar. freshw. Res.* 33:255-264.

Mueller, P.J. and E. Suess. 1979. Productivity, sedimentation rate, and sediment organic matter in the oceans- I. Organic carbon preservation. *Deep-Sea Res.* 26A: 1347-1362.

Naroki, S., and S. Tsunogai. 1986. Particulate fluxes and major components of settling particles from sediment trap experiments in the Pacific Ocean. *Deep-Sea Res.* 33:903-912.

Nowell, A.R.M., C.D. Hollister and P.A. Jumars. 1982. High Energy Benthic Boundary Layer Experiment: HEBBLE. *EOS* 63:594-595.

Pawson, D.L. 1982. Deep-sea echinoderms in the Tongue of the Ocean, Bahama Islands: a survey using the research submersible ALVIN. *Australian Museum Mem.* 16:129-145.

Pearcy, W.G., and M. Stuiver. 1983. Vertical transport of carbon-14 into deep-sea food webs. *Deep-Sea Res.* 30:427-440.

Pisias, N. 1983. Geological time series from deep-sea sediment. *Mar. Geol.* 51:77-98.

Prance, T. 1982. *Biological Diversification in the Tropics. Proceedings 5th International Symposium Tropical Biology 1979.* Columbia Univ. Press

Rau, G.H., D.M. Karl and R.S. Carney. 1986. Does inorganic carbon assimilation cause ^{14}C depletion in deep-sea organisms. *Deep-Sea Res.* 33:349-357.

Reimers, C.E., K.M. Fisher, R. Merewether, K.L. Smiths Jr, and R.A. Jahnke 1986. Oxygen microprofiles measured in situ in deep ocean sediments. *Nature* 320:741-744.

Rex, M.A. 1983. Geographic patterns of species diversity in the deep-sea. **In** G.Rowe (ed.) *The Sea, vol. 8, Deep-Sea Biology.* Wiley Interscience, New York. pp. 453-472.

Richardson, M.J., and C.D. Hollister. 1987. Compositional changes in particulate matter on the Iceland Rise through the water column and at the sea floor. *J. Mar. Res.* 45:175-200.

Rowe, G.T. (ed.) 1983. *The Sea, vol. 8, Deep-Sea Biology.* Wiley Interscience, New York. pp. 371-398.

Rowe, G.T., and W.D. Gardner, 1979. Sedimentation rates in the slope water of the northwest Atlantic Ocean measured directly with sediment trap. *J. Mar. Res.* 37:581-600.

Rowe., G.T. and J.W. Deming. 1985. The role of bacteria in the turnover of organ carbon in deep-sea sediments. *J. Mar. Res.* 43:925-950.

Sanders, H.L. 1969. Benthic marine diversity and the stability-time hypothesis. *Brookhaven Symp. Biol.* 22: 71-81.

Schoener, A. and G.T. Rowe, 1970. Pelagic sargassum and its presence among the deep-sea benthos. *Deep-Sea Res.* 17:923-925.

Seilacher, A. 1977. Evolution of trace fossil communities. In A. Hallam (ed.) *Patterns of Evolution as Illustrated in the Fossil Record*, pp. 359-379. Elsevier, Amsterdam.

Smith, C.R. and S.C. Hamilton. 1983. Epibenthic megafauna of a bathyal basin off southern California: patterns of abundance, biomass and dispersion. *Deep-Sea Res.* 30:907-928.

Smith, K.L., Jr. 1982. Zooplankton of a bathyal benthic boundary layer: In situ rates of oxygen consumption and ammonium excretion. *Limnol. Oceanogr.* 27:461-471.

Smith, K.L., Jr. 1987. Food energy supply and demand: A discrepancy between particulate organic carbon flux and sediment community oxygen consumption in the deep ocean. *Limnol. Oceanogr..* 32:201-220.

Smith, K.L., Jr., and R.J. Baldwin. 1984. Vertical distribution of the necrophagous amphipod, *Eurythenes gryllus,* in the North Pacific: spatial and temporal variation. *Deep-Sea Res.* 31:1179-1196.

Smith, K.L., Jr., A.F. Carlucci, R.A. Jahnke and D.B. Craven. 1987. Organic carbon mineralization in the Santa Catalina Basin: benthic boundary layer metabolism. *Deep-Sea Res.* 34:185-211.

Smith, K.L., Jr., A.F. Carlucci, P.M. Williams, S.M. Henrichs, R.J. Baldwin, and D.B. Graven. 1986. Zooplankton and bacterioplankton of an abyssal benthic boundary layer: in situ rates of metabolism. *Oceanologica acta* 9:47-55.

Smith, K.L. and K.R. Hinga. 1983. Sediment community respiration in the deep sea. In *The Sea*, G.T. Rowe editor, J. Wiley and Sons Inc. New York, New York. pp. 331-370.

Sokolova, M.N. 1972. Trophic structure of deep-sea macrobenthos. *Mar. Biol.* 16:1-12.

Suess, E. 1980. Particulate organic carbon flux in the ocean: surface productivity and oxygen utilization. *Nature* 288:260-263.

Swift, S.A., C.D. Hollister and R.S. Chandler. 1986. Close-up stereophotographs of abyssal bedforms on the Nova Scotian continental rise. *Mar. Geol.* 66:303-322.

Tanoue, E., and N. Handa. 1987. Monosaccharide composition of marine particles and sediments from the Bering Sea and North Pacific. *Oceanologica Acta* 10:91-99.

Thistle, D. 1983a. The role of biologically produced habitat heterogeneity in deep-sea diversity maintenance. *Deep-Sea Res.* 30:1235-1245.

Thistle, D. 1983b. The stability-time hypothesis as a predictor of diversity in the deep-sea soft bottom communities: a test. *Deep-Sea Res.* 30:267-277.

Thistle, D., and K.M. Sherman, 1985. The nematode fauna of a deep-sea site exposed to strong near-bottom currents. *Deep-Sea Res.* 32:1077-1088.

Turner, R.D. 1977. Wood, mollusks and deep-sea food chains. *Bull. Amer. Malacol. Un.* 1877:13-19.

Urrere, M.A. and G.A. Knauer, 1981. Zooplankton fecal pellet flux and vertical transport of particulate organic material in the pelagic environment. *J. Plankton Res.* 3:369-387.

Wakeham, S.G. 1982. Organic matter from a sediment trap experiment in the equatorial North Atlantic: wax esters, steryl esters, triacyglycerols and alkyldiacylglycerols. *Geochim. Cosmochim. Acta* 46:2239-2257.

Wakeham, S.G., J.W. Farrington, R.B. Gagosian., C. Lee, H. DeBaar, G.L. Nigrelli, B.W. Tripp, S.O. Smith and N.M. Frew. 1980. Organic matter fluxes from sediment traps in the equatorial Atlantic Ocean. *Nature* 286:798-800.

Weatherly, G.L., and E.A. Kelley, Jr. 1985. Storms and flow reversals at the HEBBLE site. *Mar. Geol.* 66:205-218.

Webb, K.L., DuPaul, W.D., C.F. D'Elia. 1977. Biomass and nutrient flux measurements on *Holothuria atra* populations at Enewetak, Marshall Islands. *Proc. 3rd Int. Symp. Coral Reefs* 2:409-416.

Weibe P., S. Boyd, and C. Winget. 1976. Particulate matter sinking to the deep-sea floor at 2000m in the Tongue of the ocean, Bahamas, with a description of a new sediment trap. *J. Mar. Res.* 34:341-354.

Wheatcroft, R.A., and P.A. Jumars. 1987. Statistical reanalysis for size dependency in deep-sea mixing. *Mar. Geol.* 77:157-163.

Williams, P.M., E.R.M. Druffel, and K.L. Smith, Jr. 1987. Dietary carbon sources for deep-sea organisms as inferred from their organic radiocarbon activities. *Deep-Sea Res.* 34:253-266.

Wishner, K.F. 1980. The biomass of the deep-sea benthopelagic plankton. *Deep-Sea Res.* 27:203-216.

Wishner, K.F., and M.M. Gowing. 1987. In situ filtering rates of deep-sea benthic boundary-layer zooplankton in the Santa Catalina Basin. *Mar. Biol.* 94:357-366.

Wishner, K.F. and C.J. Meise-Munns. 1984. In situ grazing rates of deep-sea benthic boundary layer zooplankton. *Mar. Biol.* 84:65-74.

Wolff, T. 1979. Macrofaunal utilization of plant remains in the deep-sea. *Sarsia* 64:117-136.

Yalin, M.S. 1977. *Mechanics of Sediment Transport*. Pergamon, New York.

Yingst, J.Y. 1976. The utilization of organic matter in shallow marine sediments by an epibenthic deposit-feeding holothuroid. *J. Exp. Mar. Biol. Ecol.* 23:55-69.

Chapter 3

Early Diagenesis of Organic Matter and the Nutritional Value of Sediment

Donald L. Rice
Chesapeake Biological Laboratory
University of Maryland
Solomons, Maryland 20688 USA
and
Donald C. Rhoads
Science Applications International Corp.
Newport, Rhode Island 02840

Introduction

The quantity, quality, and spatial distribution of particulate organic matter (POM) in the bioturbated zone of a sedimentary deposit are intimately related to the size and composition of the deposit-feeding community. Fresh allochthonous POM from the water column and autochthonous POM from epibenthic primary production are incorporated into the deposit by burial and through geophysical and biological mixing. Although the quality   and quantity of organic materials produced at or settling onto the sediment surface determine benthic secondary production, subsurface particle transport determines how metabolizable POM is distributed within the deposit. Inasmuch as particle transport itself is often dominated by the mechanical activities of deposit-feeding macrofauna (Rhoads 1974; Aller 1982; Rice 1986), the biomass, species composition, and feeding depths of the deposit-feeding community and the standing crop and vertical distribution of metabolizable organic matter are fundamentally interdependent.

The kinetics of POM decomposition in the bioturbated zone reflects to a great extent the nutritional value of the POM to macroconsumers as well as its susceptibility to attack by microbial enzymes. In the absence of chemical feeding inhibitors and antibiotics (Sieburth and Conover 1965; Valiela et al, 1979), organic detritus that is rapidly decomposed by microheterotrophs is generally also readily available to macroconsumers (Tenore and Rice 1980). Deposit feeders possess a limited suite of digestive enzymes and may depend to some extent upon gut and sediment microbes for the conversion of macromolecular POM into simpler, assimilable units (Tenore and Rice 1980). In a sense, the deposit can function as an external rumen for deposit feeders. In this regard, it is important to bear in mind that mineralization is only the final step in a complex, enzymatically orchestrated process that converts complex organic polymers to progressively simpler (and more assimilable) organic substrates.

In this paper we use general diagenetic theory to discuss some relationships between bulk nutritional value of sediment and subsurface transport and decomposition of POM. For convenience, discussion is restricted to bulk particulate organic carbon (POC) and nitrogen (PON) although many of the concepts may be applied to specific organic moieties. Because diagenetic transformation is of special importance to the nutrition of subsurface deposit feeders, a portion of the discussion is centered around vertical gradients in the chemistry of a specific deposit and the growth and feeding of a subsurface deposit feeder cultured on sediment from that deposit. We do not include a treatment of pelletization and pellet decomposition. These two biophysical aspects of diagenesis, which may be important to POM preservation and availability (Self and Jumars 1978), are discussed elsewhere in this volume (Levinton, this volume).

Readers unacquainted with either the geochemical or the nutritional concepts presented here will find five review works especially helpful. General summaries of diagenetic processes in the bioturbated zone are given in Rhoads (1974) and Aller (1982). A good conceptual foundation in early diagenesis and deposit feeder nutrition may be obtained from reviews by Berner (1980a), Tenore and Rice (1980), and Lopez and Levinton (1987). Many of the concepts developed in this paper are related to ideas and hypotheses presented in Rhoads (1974).

Theoretical Relationships

Regardless of whether a given animal derives its nutrition principally from detrital POM or from the associated detrital microflora, it is clear that deposit feeder nutrition is fundamentally related to POM diagenesis. Although this concept is generally valid, it is perhaps most apparent, if not most critical, for subsurface feeders and bulk sediment ingesters in comparison to highly-selective near-surface microbe grazers (e.g., some hydrobiid gastropods). Transport and decompositional processes in the benthic environment affect both the total inventory and the spatial distribution of reactive POM (Aller, 1982). Except in high energy environments, macrobenthic infauna, especially deposit feeders, are the major agents of particle "mixing" (Rhoads and Boyer 1982). Together with the meiofauna, they may also stimulate microbial activity (Hargrave 1972; Hylleberg 1975; Yingst and Rhoads 1980). Consequently, it is not surprising that vigorous burrowers are usually associated with organic muds (Rhoads 1974).

Usually, only a fraction of the POM in a deposit is sufficiently reactive (enzymatically labile, or metabolizable) to be readily available either to microbes or to macroconsumers(see Mayer, this volume). Typically (but not always), the concentration-depth profile of POC or PON in the bioturbated zone (g POM . g dry sediment^{-1}) can be approximated by an exponential function $G(x)$ that decreases with depth x from a surface maximum concentration G_0 to a non-zero asymptotic concentration G^*:

$$G(x) = G^* + G_0 e^{-ax} \tag{3.1}$$

The attenuation factor a can often be regarded as constant. At any depth, the quantity $[G - G^*]$ is nutritionally significant because, over the stratigraphic time scale represented by the depth of the bioturbated zone, it represents the *maximum* amount of metabolizable POM available to benthic heterotrophs foraging at that depth (Fig. 3.1). This concentration-depth profile is generated by the combined effects of biological (and geophysical) sediment mixing and decomposition. Because the intensity and spatial distribution of biogenic mixing is related to vertical distributions and population densities of the bioturbating deposit-feeding community, secondary production of those deposit feeders is influenced by the amount of available POM in the deposit (Rhoads 1974). Therefore, one should be able to relate the abundance and nutritional dynamics of the bioturbating deposit-feeding community to POM decomposition rates and vertical transport phenomena.

If depositional inputs, transport within the deposit (e.g., bioturbation, mixing by currents, burial), and decomposition are in steady-state balance, the concentration of some POM moiety at a given depth below the surface will not change with time. It is clear that in real benthic systems such steady-state balance is rare as each of these dynamic components may experience regular (diel and seasonal) oscillations as well as novel or even catastrophic changes with time (Berner 1980); however, for the purposes of this discussion we will assume that the steady-state assumption is adequate. Under these conditions the steady-state balance of mixing, burial, and decomposition rates within a laterally homogeneous deposit may be described by the one-dimensional general diagenetic equation (Berner 1980):

$$\frac{\delta(\hat{G} - \hat{G}^*)}{\delta t} = \frac{\delta}{\delta x} D_B \frac{\delta(\hat{G} - \hat{G}^*)}{\delta x} - w[\hat{G} - \hat{G}^*) - k[\hat{G} - \hat{G}^*] = 0 \qquad (3.2)$$

where t = time, x = sediment depth relative to the ambient sediment surface ($x = 0$), $\hat{G} = \hat{G}(x)$ = steady-state total POM concentration (mass/sediment volume) at depth x, G^* = concentration of unreactive POM (assumed here to be a constant), D_B = random mixing coefficient for particulates (analogous to an eddy mixing coefficient), w = rate of burial due to input of particles at the sediment surface, and k = apparent first-order decay constant of labile POM such that

$$\frac{d\hat{G}}{dt} = \frac{d(\hat{G} - \hat{G}^*)}{dt} = -k[\hat{G} - \hat{G}^*] \qquad (3.3)$$

In Eqn. 2 mixing is taken to be a random process (Goldberg and Koide 1962) and includes both geophysical mixing and bioturbation. Volumetric concentration $\hat{G}$ is related to mass concentration G (Eqn. 3.1) by the simple relationship

$$\hat{G} = \rho[1 - \phi]G \qquad (3.4)$$

in which ρ = average density of sediment particles, and ϕ = porosity (volume fraction of interconnected pore space). Although the steady-state model is an obvious simplification, similar approaches have proven to be useful in the interpretation of "snapshot" concentration-depth profiles of a variety of reactive substances decomposing by first-order kinetics in the bioturbated zone (Berner, 1980).

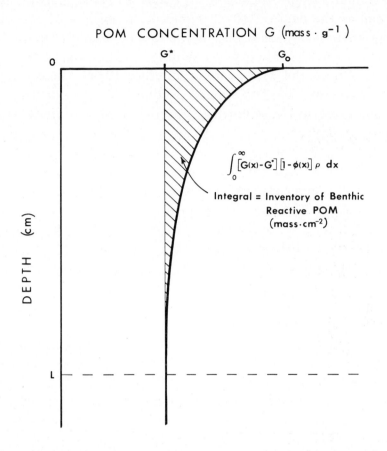

Figure 3.1: Ideal Concentration-Depth Profile of Particulate Organic Matter (POM) in Deposit Mixed to Depth L. Surface concentration G_0 decreases exponentially with depth to a non-zero asymptotic value G^*. At steady-state, POM at any depth in excess of G^* represents POM metabolizable on the time scale represented by the depth of the mixed layer. The benthic inventory of metabolizable POM (crosshatched region) is determined by integrating over depth after accounting for vertical variations in particle density ρ and porosity ϕ.

The development of the POM-depth profile in the bioturbated zone is also dependent upon compositional and/or transport constraints at the sediment surface and at the depth limit of faunal occurence. An important natural constraint at the sediment surface is the rate of supply of POM. In the case of organic matter, the rate is often assumed to be equal to the depositional flux of POM from the water column (Berner 1980). However, in shallow water environments *in situ* primary production by epibenthic microalgae may be important in the sedimentary carbon budget (Valiela 1984). Unless an explicit productivity term is included in the governing equation (Eqn. 3.2), *in situ* primary production should be included as an input along with depositional flux (the physical dimensions of flux and areal production are identical) in the description of the surface boundary constraint on POM (see Eqn. 3.5 below). Also, in most sedimentary environments, resuspension and lateral exchange of surficial particulate matter within a basin exert a buffering effect on local surface concentrations.

For a steady-state system one can envision two ideal end-member surface constraints that bracket the condition in real sediments: constant rate of surface supply and constant surface concentration (Aller 1982). Boundary conditions for these two end-member systems may be stated explicitly. If there is an constant flux (J_0) of POM to the sediment surface and if all of the incoming POM is incorporated into the deposit, then the surface boundary condition constraining Eqn. 3.2 is given by

$$x = 0, -D_B[\delta \hat{G}/\delta x] + w\hat{G} = J_0 \tag{3.5}$$

Condition 5 indicates that POM depositional flux and/or *in situ* surface production is exactly balanced by mixing and burial into the deposit. On the other hand, if the surface concentration is buffered at some constant value Go by particle resuspension and lateral dispersion, the appropriate surface condition would be

$$x = 0, \hat{G} = \hat{G}_0 \tag{3.6}$$

For present purposes, an *a priori* limit to the depth of the bioturbated zone will not be specified. Aller (1982) has previously developed an analogous mixing model for radiotracers which specifies a depth limit for the mixed layer. Here, we require only that labile POM eventually decay away to an infinitely small concentration; i.e.,

$$x = \infty, \delta \hat{G}/\delta x = 0 \tag{3.7}$$

For constant (i.e., depth-averaged) D_B, w, and k, the solutions to the systems of equations 3.2, 3.3, 3.4, 3.5, 3.7 (constant rate of supply) and 3.2, 3.3, 3.4, 3.6, 3.7 (constant surface concentration) have the same form:

$$\hat{G}(x) = \hat{G}^* + \hat{G}(0)e^{\lambda x} \tag{3.8}$$

where

$$\lambda = \frac{w}{2D_B} - \sqrt{(\frac{w}{2D_B})^2 + \frac{k}{D_\beta}} \tag{3.9}$$

and $G(0)$ is the concentration at the sediment surface given by

Constant surface rate of supply: $\hat{G}(0) = J_0/[w - D_B\lambda]$ (3.10)

Constant surface concentration: $\hat{G}(0) = \hat{G}_0$ (3.11)

Note that because w, D_β, and k are positive constants, the attenuation factor λ (Eqn. 3.9) is always negative and the solution (Eqn. 3.8) is bounded. For interpretive purposes, Eqn. 3.8 may be compared term by term to the empirical relationship in Eqn. 3.1 after correcting for porosity (Eqn. 3.4).

The end-member relationships between the steady-state POM inventory and partitioning of POM between near-surface and deep portions of the deposit, POM decomposability, mixing rate, and POM flux across the sediment surface are summarized in Table 3.1. In order to keep the algebraic expressions simple, entries in Table 3.1 are given assuming the effects of burial are insignificant compared to mixing; this is generally a valid assumption for sediments that are moderately well mixed (see below). The following important points should be noted:

1. High decomposability and slow mixing cause the concentration of reactive POM to attenuate rapidly with depth. Resistance to decay and rapid mixing enhance the concentration of reactive POM found at a given depth.

2. In the absence of surface buffering by external mechanisms, the surface concentration of reactive POM is enhanced by increasing rate of supply and depressed by increasing POM decomposability and mixing.

3. The total benthic inventory of reactive POM is directly proportional to the flux across the surface and indirectly proportional to decomposability. If the surface concentration is buffered, higher rates of mixing lead to higher subsurface inventories.

Model Surface Condition	Surface * Concentration G_0	Benthic** Inventory
CONSTANT RATE OF SUPPLY (Total of rates of depositional flux and surface production fixed; Eqns. 2 and 5b)	$J_0/\sqrt{k/D_B}$	J_0/k
SURFACE BUFFERING (Surface concentration fixed; Eqns. 2 and 5a)	G_0	$G_0/\sqrt{k/D_B}$

Table 3.1: Surface Concentration and Total Benthic Inventory of Reactive POM According to Two End-member Steady-State Diagenetic Models. For simplicity, burial rate is assumed to contribute negligibly to subsurface transport ($w = 0$) so that the attenuation constant $= k/D_B$. $k =$ first-order decay constant for reactive POM; $D =$ random mixing coefficient (assumed constant); $J_0 =$ depositional flux of POM to sediment surface; $G_0 =$ concentration of POM in particulate matter at sediment surface. * Dimensions of surface concentration are, e.g., g cm^{-3}. ** The benthic inventory is equal to $\int_0^\infty G(x) - G^* dx$, with dimensions of, e.g., g cm^{-2}.

All three of these relationships are important to the nutrition of deposit feeders. The first two are directly related to the spatial distribution of food resources. As far as long-term stability of a food supply is concerned, the most important difference between the two end-member models is described in the third item above: namely, that flux into the deposit may be controlled by the macrofauna responsible for mixing if the surface is buffered. As Aller (1982) has pointed out, this means that zones of high macrofaunal activity can be "hotspots" of geochemical activity because of high inventories of reactive organic matter. The persistence of characteristic densities of a conveyor-belt deposit-feeding polychaete in isolated patches on a New England mudflat has been attributed to that organism's population density-dependent control of local downmixing of POM (Rice 1986). Generally the sediment surface condition can be considered to be a hybrid of the two extremes. In deep calm water the situation may be closer to the flux control end-member (Eqn. 3.5), while in higher energy shallow-water environments the surface may be well buffered (Eqn. 3.6).

In the following discussion, both surface conditions have been used, but for different types of problems. First, the flux-controlled surface model is used to compare reactive POM-depth distributions under sediment mixing regimes characteristic of the deep sea and nearshore environments. Then, to discuss the important problem of differential depth distributions of reactive POM of different decomposabilities, the buffered surface model is used to represent shallow-water systems which commonly receive a variety of terrestrial, estuarine, and oceanic detrital organic matter.

Model of Reactive POM-Depth Distributions

The deposition rate of detrital POM and *in situ* primary production are the primary determinants of benthic secondary production. Even for shallow water environments where epibenthic POM concentrations may be buffered somewhat (as discussed in the next section), available evidence indicates that secondary production of deposit feeders is directly linked to production and sedimentation in the overlying water column (Parsons et al. 1984). However, as shown above for the ideal one-dimensional (depth) model, vertical partitioning of reactive POM available to the benthos depends upon the decomposability of the POM and the intensity of sediment mixing by waves, currents, and bioturbation.

The influence of decomposability and mixing rate on the benthic inven-

tory and vertical distribution of reactive POM is illustrated for a hypothetical case of constant rate of supply (Eqns. 3.8 and 3.10) in Figure 3.2. For
simplicity, epibenthic primary production is considered insignificant here,
although it does not have to be. The benthic inventory (area bounded by
each curve and the coordinate axes) in each case depends only upon the
rate of POM deposition and the decomposition constant. For a given rate
of POM deposition, the more decay-resistant material will persist in higher
standing amounts and to greater depths than the more easily decomposable POM. Theoretically some POM resides at any depth because of the
exponential nature of first-order decomposition. In reality however, for a
particular combination of J_0, w, D_B, and k there is necessarily some depth
below which the standing concentration of metabolizable POM is too low to
support secondary production.

Although mixing does not influence the influx or the benthic inventory
of POM in the hypothetical sediments of Fig. 3.2, mixing does influence
the steady-state depth distribution of POM of a given decomposability. The
overall effect of increased mixing, either biological or geophysical, is to spread
out the POM over a greater depth range. This means that increased mixing
tends to lower standing amounts of reactive POM at the sediment surface.
Basically, bioturbation is a mechanism by which subsurface feeders can compete with surface feeders for fresh detritus. Surface concentration of reactive
POM also decreases with increasing burial rate provided the rate of POM
supply to the benthos is not coupled to sedimentation of clastics (as, for
example, in the diagenesis of detritus derived from autochthonous epibenthic algae in a shallow-water deposit). The effect of burial rate on surface
concentration is exactly opposite when sedimentation of inert particles and
POM are coupled. This latter point can be demonstrated easily with Eqns.
3.8 and 3.11 by setting $J_o = G_i \rho w[1 - \phi(0)]$ where G_i is the concentration of
POM in incoming particles. In most deposits inhabited by deposit-feeding
macrofauna, for a given deposition rate of reactive POM, the effects of decomposition and sediment mixing overshadow the effects of burial rate on
the steady-state POM concentration at the surface and at depth. Burial rate
by physical sedimentation (w) becomes quantitatively unimportant when it
is substantially less than $\sqrt{4kD_B}$ (Eqn. 3.7).

The constant deposition rate model can generate profiles of concentration versus depth for metabolizable POC in deep sea and nearshore-estuarine
sediments. By not placing an *a priori* restriction on the depth of the bioturbated zone (Eqn. 3.7), these profiles should yield theoretical guidelines
on the comparative depth distributions and depth limits of deposit-feeding

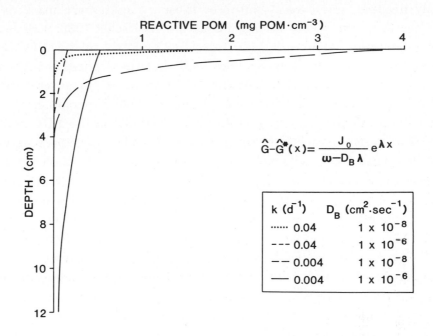

Figure 3.2: Influence of Decomposability and Sediment Mixing Rate on the Steady-state Depth Distribution of Reactive POM (Eqns. 3.6, 3.7, and 3.8b). For this hypothetical case, constant depositional flux of POM to the sediment surface is $J_0 = 100$ mg POM m^{-2} d^{-1}; sedimentation rate $w = 0.5$ cm y^{-1}; mixing rate $D_B = 1 \times 10^{-6}$ (representing highly productive nearshore sediments) or 1×10^{-8} cm^2 sec^{-2} (deep ocean); first-order decay constant $k = 0.04$ (for algal detritus) or 0.004 d^{-1} (for older algal material or vascular plant detritus). Values for D_B were selected from the compilation by Aller (1982); values for k were taken from Rice and Tenore (1981).

activity. Estimates of the deposition rate of metabolizable POC are obviously needed. For present purposes these estimates are made as follows: For the deep sea, it was assumed that 2% (Zeitschel 1980; Valiela 1984) of the annual phytoplankton production of 125 g POM m^{-2} y^{-1} (Valiela 1984) eventually falls to the deep sea floor, and that the detritus is 50% carbon by weight. By comparing depth profiles of POC in the top several cm of cores from MANOP sites (Emerson and Dymond 1984; Emerson et al. 1984) to the ideal profile in Fig. 3.1, we estimated that 33% of the POC reaching the sediment surface is metabolizable (Table 3.2). For nearshore input, it was assumed that 50% (Zeitschel 1980) of annual phytoplankton production of 1500 g POM m^{-2} y^{-1} reaches the benthos, where it is further processed by suspension feeders with an assimilation efficiency of 55% (estimated from the data compilation of Valiela 1984). As before, the detrital POM was assumed to be 50% carbon by weight and 33% of the deposited POC was assumed to be metabolizable (Table 3.2). The rounded deposition rates are 40 and 5500 μg metabolizable C cm^{-2} x y^{-1} for deep ocean and nearshore/estuarine sediments respectively.

The predicted steady-state depth profiles of metabolizable POC $(G - G_*)$ in these two model sediments (using Eqns. 3.8 and 3.10) are shown in Fig. 3.3. The predictions assume an average decay rate of 60% per year for metabolizable POM; this value corresponds to the first-order decay constant of POM in the bioturbated zone at the FOAM site in Long Island Sound, USA (Berner 1980b) and of well-leached and diminutized scenescent leaf detritus derived from *Spartina alterniflora* decomposing under simulated epibenthic conditions (Rice and Tenore 1982). Estimates of burial and mixing rates were taken from recent data compilations (Berner 1980; Aller 1982; Valiela 1984). For POM having k values similar to or greater than 0.60 y^{-1}, typical magnitudes of sedimentation rate w and the mixing coefficient D_B in abyssal and neritic environments (Fig. 3.3 caption) are such that w is much less than $\sqrt{4kD_B}$. Consequently, attenuation of these profiles is due primarily to the relative magnitudes of POM decomposability and particle mixing. Because these values are not extreme, Fig. 3.3 should portray a reasonably fair comparison of the standing crop and depth distribution of *metabolizable* POM in abyssal and neritic benthic environments. Surface concentrations and subsurface inventories actually found may vary broadly from place to place; however, the general features of Fig. 3.3 appear to be borne out by data in several recent studies (Aller 1980; Emerson et al. 1984; Barbaro 1985). The potentially important input of relatively fresh, highly decomposable detritus in the nearshore case has been ignored here but will be considered below.

The results shown in Fig. 3.3 indicate that the feeding zone for deposit feeders in nearshore deposits should naturally be able to develop to a depth of at least several cm, while in the model abyssal sediment feeding must be oriented toward the most labile surface material. Although the relative depths of the deposit-feeding zones in the two environments can be surmised from Fig. 3.3, the actual depth limit for energetically efficient foraging will depend strongly upon how a particular subsurface feeder partitions its energy. Inasmuch as burrowing and searching activities require a relatively large expenditure of energy (Eds.-but see chapters by T. Forbes and G. Taghon), it would probably not be an overgeneralization to assert that in nearshore deposits macrofauna that feed at depths greater than a few cm consist of relatively stable populations of comparatively large, slow-growing, relatively sedentary conveyor-belt feeders. Conversely, in the top few cm metabolizable POM may be sufficiently plentiful that deposit feeders that forage in that zone are more likely to be smaller, faster growing, and mobile. Although this generalization is by no means perfect, common experience would suggest that it holds most of the time (c.f., Levinton 1972).

The constant flux steady-state model provides some quantitative insight into how deep deposit-feeding assemblages may develop from a near-surface assemblage in a successional paradigm (Rhoads et al. 1978). Surface and near-surface feeders initially exploiting POM resources near the sediment surface gradually cause a mixing downward of less labile POM and promote oxidation of slightly deeper layers. Subsequently, new deeper feeding species may become established to exploit the reservoir of less decomposable POM. The depth limit of feeding should represent a energetic trade-off between the amount of energy obtainable from reactive POM at depth and metabolic expenditure in foraging and processing the material. One consequently would expect biogenic downmixing of reactive POM, colonization by large subsurface deposit-feeders (especially conveyor-belt species), and the establishment of subsurface feeding niches to progress together naturally over time (Rhoads et al. 1978).

At steady-state then, in both deep-sea and nearshore deposits bioturbational mixing is a primary determinant of the vertical distribution of enzymatically labile POM. Although the rate of supply of nutritious POM (J_0) is the *sine qua non* for benthic secondary production, larger standing crops of deep-bioturbating macrofauna should incorporate proportionally greater amounts of food to a given depth in the deposit. Except when mixing by currents and waves is more important than bioturbation, as it certainly is in

LOCATION and DEPTH INTERVAL	G_0 (%)	G_* (%)	$G_0 - G_*$ (%)	$(G_0 - G_*)/$ G_0	Ref.
Long Island Sound (estuary)					
0–15 cm	2.0	1.3	0.7	.35	(1)
0–15 cm	1.8	1.2	0.6	.33	(1)
0–5 cm	1.5	1.1	0.4	.27	(1)
0–25 cm	2.6	1.8	0.8	.31	(2)
Lowes Cove, Maine (mudflat)					
0–10 cm	1.0	0.6	0.4	.40	(3)
0–10 cm	1.7	1.1	0.6	.35	(3)
0–10 cm	1.6	1.0	0.6	.38	(4)
MANOP Sites (deep sea)					
0–5 cm: Range	0.4–1.7	0.2–1.3	0.2-1.3		(5)
0–5 cm: Average	0.9	0.6	0.3	.33	

Table 3.2: Estimates of the Metabolizable Fraction of Particulate Organic Carbon in Surface Sediments from Several Marine Environments. ** References: (1) Berner 1982; (2) Rosenfeld 1981; (3) Barbaro (1985); (4) This paper; (5) Emerson and Dymond 1984; Emerson et al. 1984.

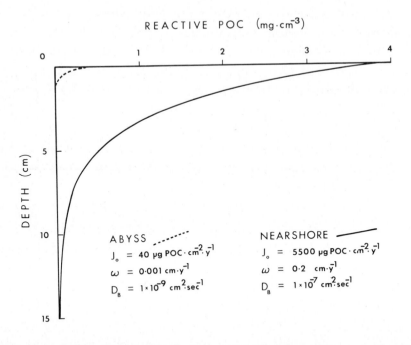

Figure 3.3: Model Steady-State Depth Distributions of Metabolizable POM in Deep Sea and Nearshore Sediments. Decomposition constant k = 0.60 y^{-1} is assumed for "average" sedimentary POM (see text for details).

some nearshore environments, populations of deep-feeding macrofauna are to a great extent instrumental in stabilizing their food supply at a rate proportional to population density. Even when food supply and mixing are not constant, this effect should be most apparent for conveyor-belt deposit feeders since they are often the major agents of deep particle bioturbation (Rhoads 1974; Rice 1986). Downmixing of POM into a deposit does not necessarily occur by continuous transport, nor does it necessarily occur only *via* bioturbation. Some subsurface deposit feeders may short-circuit the relatively slow process of diffusive downmixing in the sediment continuum by actively pulling relatively fresh surface material into their burrows (Gerlach 1971; Hylleberg 1975; Dobbs and Whitlatch 1982). Another type of "non-local mixing" (i.e., transfer between two non-adjacent points; see, e.g., Boudreau 1986) that may be of importance to the nutrition of subsurface feeders is avalanching of surface particulates into burrows during periods of epibenthic turbulence. Geophysical downmixing (e.g., "sifting" of fines through coarse sands, wave activity, rapid dune migration) may also be important in the rapid transport of fresh POM to depth, especially in high-energy sandy environments.

Spatial Distribution of Food Quality

Owing to the heterogeneous chemical origins of the benthic detrital pool (Tenore et al. 1982; Lopez and Levinton 1987), potential particulate food resources of dissimilar reactivity and nutritional value are distributed differently in the bioturbated zone. Consequently, the relative amounts of different types of food vary with location in the deposit. Moreover, the relative importance of those food types to deposit feeders foraging in different zones may also vary.

Spatial variation of POM quality is most apparent in nearshore sediments. In these systems, the bioturbated zone is relatively deep and contains a mixture of highly reactive (e.g., living and recently dead algal cells) and less reactive (vascular plant detritus and reworked algal material) POM (Mann 1972; Tenore and Rice 1980; Valiela 1984). Conditions at the sediment-water interface in these shallow-water environments are often buffered by resuspension and lateral mixing (Aller 1982; Rice 1986). Then, one can assume that surface concentration of the particulate material of interest is set at some constant value as in Eqn. 3.6. Assuming for present purposes that burial rate is negligibly small ($w = 0$; see above) the general steady-state solution

(Eqns. 3.8 and 3.11) becomes

$$G(\hat{x}) = \hat{G}_* + [\hat{G}_0 - \hat{G}_*]exp(-\frac{k}{D_B}x) \tag{3.12}$$

Predicted concentration-depth profiles are shown for fresh, highly decomposable, high-nitrogen algal POC ($k = 0.04$ $d^{-1} = 14.6$ y^{-1}) (Rice and Tenore 1982) and for bulk, depth-averaged POC in an inshore mud ($k = 0.60$ y^{-1} as above) (Berner 1980a) in Figure 3.4. The mixing coefficient ($D_B = 1$ x 10^{-7} cm^2 sec^{-1}) is a reasonable estimate for a productive inshore shelf or estuarine mud (Berner 1980; Aller 1982). For illustrative purposes, $w = 0$ and a constant surface concentration of 4 mg POC cm^{-3} were selected (c.f., Fig. 3.3). For siliciclastic sediments with surface porosity of 75%, this concentration corresponds to a reactive carbon content of about 0.6% on a dry weight basis. The overall impact of decomposability on attenuation of the POC-depth profile is the same as in Fig. 3.3. However, in this case, for POM of a given decomposability, the total benthic inventory increases with increasing mixing rate; in Fig. 3.3, subsurface inventory depends only upon J_0 and is unaffected by mixing rate. This phenomenon has been previously illustrated using models for the diagenesis of the particle-bound radionuclides Th-234 (half-life = 24 days) and Pb-210 (half-life = 22 years) in similar hypothetical situations (Aller 1982).

Organic reactivity and particle mixing rate limit the depth at which subsurface bulk deposit feeders can derive utilizable carbon (available calories). The reservoir of "average" reactive POC drops precipitously with depth so that deposit-feeding activity below 10 cm may be severely restricted in the "typical" nearshore muds depicted in Fig. 3.4. High quality algal detritus is probably inaccessible to deposit feeders foraging below about 2 cm unless surface material is actively pulled down by the animal or is injected directly to depth because of physical disturbance. Without "non-local" injection of surface material, deposit feeders utilizing the highest quality organic matter in these deposits must feed on or near the surface.

Inasmuch as the magnitude of the decomposition parameter k actually decreases with depth (as POM becomes more refractory) (Berner 1980), higher densities of bioturbating macrofauna may not only increase the total benthic inventory of reactive POM as discussed above, but may also increase the overall quality of the POM in the deposit. This would suggest that for subsurface deposit feeders there is some advantage in dense colonization vis à vis the ability of denser populations to increase the rate of downmixing. Conveyor-belt feeders may especially benefit from such a strategy (Rice and

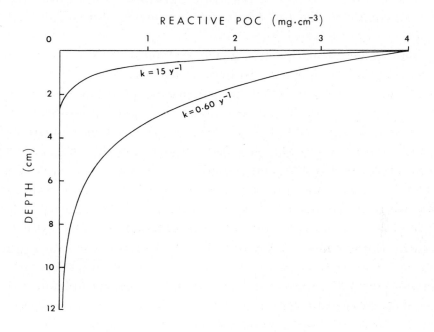

Figure 3.4: Model Steady-State Depth Distributions of "Highly- Decompos-able" and "Average" Metabolizable POC in Nearshore Sediments. Surface concentration of metabolizable POC is assumed to be buffered at a value of 4 mg C cm^{-3}.

Whitlow 1985a,b; Rice 1986). This is in marked contrast to the situation for surface deposit feeders where competition for food can increase greatly with increasing population density. However, dense colonization by burrowers can also increase sediment redox potential and stimulate decomposer activity (Rhoads 1974; Yingst and Rhoads 1980), thereby increasing the proportion of POM respired by the microbial community. The kinetic relationship between population density of bioturbating subsurface deposit feeders and their food supply should prove to be an interesting and challenging area of research.

In some cases, rapid injection and *in situ* subsurface primary production may be of central importance to deposit feeder nutrition. In the organic-poor, clean sands of Cape Henlopen, Delaware, populations of the orbiniid polychaete *Scoloplos fragilis* thrive year-round, apparently by feeding at a depth of 3 to 4 cm on living benthic diatoms and other sources of POM (Brown 1982; T. S. Bianchi, personal communication). Cape Henlopen is representative of a benthic environment in which the importance of geophysical mixing exceeds that of bioturbation. In this case, rapid downmixing of high-quality POM may occur via the sinking of small particles (including non-motile microalgae) through an open network of coarse sand grains as well as by shifting of sand dunes. Even in relatively quiescent muddy deposits, resuspension, surface disturbance, and direct injection via burrows may be responsible for the appearance of substantial amounts of surface material at depth (Bembia 1985; Rice 1986), although the overall significance to the nutrition of deep deposit feeders is not known. In any event, it is clear that below the top few centimeters, subsurface feeders cannot take advantage of the highest quality surface POM without rapid bioturbation (driven by high densities of key macrofauna, probably conveyor-belt feeders (Rice 1986)), intense and regular physical disturbance, and/or some sort of non-local injection mechanism.

An important corollary of the POC-depth profiles of Fig. 3.4 is that the concentration of enzymatically labile PON may become very low below a depth of about 2 cm in nearshore muds. A typical non-aromatic C-N bond is about 20 kcal mol^{-1} less stable than a C-C single bond; consequently, fresh PON and associated POC (to a good approximation, protein) are utilized rapidly near the sediment-water interface. The diagenesis of the highly-reactive POC ($k = 15$ y^{-1}) shown in Fig. 3.4 should mirror that of primary algal PON as well. Although there may be enough labile POC to support the carbon requirements of bulk sediment ingesters (see below), PON availability appears to be problematic for deposit feeders that forage at depth, unless rapid "injection" mechanisms (see above) and/or *in situ* production of labile PON (localized microbial production) are operative. This is especially provocative in light of theoretical arguments and laboratory studies suggesting that non-selective deposit feeders may generally be nitrogen-limited (Russell-Hunter 1970; Tenore et al. 1979; Tenore and Chesney, 1985).

Nutritional Potential of Sediment and Secondary Production

The nutritional potential or richness of a given volume of sediment depends on the quantity and quality of potential food items in that volume. For some component of available POC or PON, one can estimate nutritional potential of an arbitrarily small volume of sediment as volumetric reactivity (see Eqn. 3.3); i.e.,

$$\text{Nutritional Potential} = -d\hat{G}/dt = k[\hat{G} - \hat{G}^*] \tag{3.13}$$

Defined in this way, nutritional potential is analogous to activity of a radioactive source; that is radioactivity of a sample is the product of the decay constant and the ambient amount of radionuclide. For some particular component of POM, "quality" is represented by k and quantity by $(\hat{G} - \hat{G}^*)$. From Eqn. 3.2, at steady-state the depth-integrated nutritional potential (INP) of a layer of sediment in the depth interval $x1 \leq x \leq x2$ is equal to the net flux of metabolizable POM into the interval

$$\text{INP}(x1, x2) = \text{Flux }(x1) \text{ - Flux }(x2) \tag{3.14}$$

That is, metabolizable POM which enters the layer at depth x1 but does not exit at depth x2 is expended in heterotrophy. Note that the physical dimensions for INP, flux, and production are identical (mass area^{-1} time^{-1}). For the model nearshore system described above in which $w = 0$ (Eqn. 3.12), one can easily demonstrate that

$$\text{INP}(x1, x2) = ([\hat{G} - \hat{G}^*]_{x1}) - ([\hat{G} - \hat{G}^*]_{x2})\sqrt{kD_B}; \tag{3.15}$$

$$\text{Total Benthic INP} = \text{Surface Flux of Reactive POM} \tag{3.16}$$

$$\text{Total Benthic INP} = x = b = [\hat{G} - \hat{G}^*]_{x=0}\sqrt{kD_B} \tag{3.17}$$

The Total Benthic INP deeper than $x = b$ equals the Flux of Reactive POM across $x = b$.

$$\text{Flux}_{x=b} = [\hat{G} - \hat{G}*]_{x=b}\sqrt{kD_B} \qquad (3.18)$$

INP's for the two model nearshore POC diagenetic schemes (Fig. 3.3) are calculated for several depth horizons in Table 3.2. For fresh algal POC ($k = 15$ y^{-1}), almost 89% of the nutritional potential is concentrated in the topmost 1 cm; only 1% of the total benthic nutritional inventory is below 2 cm. For average reworked POC ($k = 0.60$ y^{-1}), about 65% of INP is below 1 cm; nevertheless, if the bioturbated zone were 15 cm deep, a disproportionately large fraction of this INP (35%) would be concentrated in the top 1 cm.

The calculations in Table 3.2 illustrate the importance of decay resistance to the nutrition of subsurface bulk sediment ingesters. For the same surface concentration of both types of end-member POC, the total benthic INP would be 5 times greater if the detritus were high-quality algal rather than reworked material; however, the great majority of the fresh algal POC would be partitioned spatially into surface heterotrophy. Conversely, most of the reworked POC is utilized at depth. For example in the 4 to 10 cm depth interval 16% of the total benthic INP of the $k = 0.60$ y^{-1} POC remains while less than 0.04% of that of the $k = 15$ y^{-1} POC remains. In the absence of *in situ* subsurface primary production or mechanisms for rapid non-local injection of surface material, inputs of highly decomposable POM at the sediment surface probably cannot support a subsurface deposit-feeding community below the top few centimeters. The fact that deep-feeding species do exist attests to the potential importance of less assimilable organic matter in their nutrition. As discussed above, utilization by deposit feeders of the "slow" reservoir of potential nutrition probably depends upon depolymerization (as opposed to mineralization) activities of microbial decomposers as well as "repackaging" into microbial biomass (living and non-living).

Assuming some average ecological efficiency, nutritional potential can be used to estimate the secondary production potential (SPP) of a deposit. At the detrital trophic level, ecological, trophic transfer, and gross growth efficiencies, etc. calculated on the basis of total detrital (organic) carbon are small and obviously meaningless because a large fraction of the organic matter is resistant to enzymatic attack. However, assuming that *reactive* detrital POC is transferred to deposit feeder biomass (meiofauna + macrofauna) with 10% efficiency as in a grazing food chain (Valiela 1984), we can estimate that

$$SPP \simeq 0.1 \text{ INP} \qquad (3.19)$$

Although 10% efficiency based on enzymatically reactive carbon does not seem unreasonable, it may be a maximum value. Reactive components in primary organic matter are probably more accessible to enzymatic attack than relics of the same components in organic detritus that has undergone various degrees of depolymerization and rearrangement (Rice 1982). The availability to deposit feeders of relic primary components, especially carbohydrates and proteins, merits future study.

The SPP's of the two "end-member" POC systems described in Fig. 3.4 and Table 3.3 and of three "hybrid" systems are described in Table 3.4. The "hybrids" are hypothetical systems in which the surface POC contains 60% to 10% fresh algal POC (average 35%). The 60%/40% and 10%/90% proportions bracket the range of the relative amounts of phytoplankton and "detritus" components in suspended POC in estuarine and nearshore waters (Valiela 1984). For a total surface concentration of metabolizable POM of 4 mg . cm^{-3}, estimated SPP ranges from ca. 6 to 28 g C m^{-2} y^{-1}. However, because of grazing of the phytoplankton by pelagic zooplankton and benthic suspension feeders, the actual reactive POC composition of surface sediment is probably better bracketed by the 35%/65% and 0%/100%. On this basis, one would expect the total production of deposit-feeding meio- and macrofauna to be between 5 and 14 g C m^{-2} y^{-1}; if the upper limit of surface composition were 10%/90%, the corresponding heterotrophic production would be 8 to 5 g C m^{-2} y^{-1}. The range of values of benthic secondary production reported by Valiela (1984) is 5 - 17 g C m^{-2} y^{-1}. Inasmuch as the range reported by Valiela (1984) is principally for muddy bottom estuaries in which deposit feeders dominate the benthos, the agreement is good.

A relatively small amount of algal detritus can greatly affect secondary production. In the 0%/100% system, all SPP is obviously derived from the more decay-resistant end-member POC. But if 10% of the reactive POC on the sediment surface were fresh algal POC, that 10% alone would support 36% of the total SPP, which itself would increase by 40% (Table 3.4). It should be noted however that almost 90% of the increased secondary production would be realized by surface feeders (the topmost 1 cm). Episodic pulses of fresh plankton detritus may boost benthic secondary production of surface feeders, but without rapid transport methods, there will be little benefit for subsurface deposit feeders.

Secondary production of subsurface deposit feeders in the model estuarine sediment is remarkably stable despite wide oscillations in the amount of fresh algal material at the sediment surface. The results in Table 3.4 indi-

	Fresh Algal Detritus*			Average Sediment Detritus**		
	POM Conc. at Depth x mg C cm^{-3}	INP Below Depth x mg C cm^{-2}y^{-1}	INP in Depth Interval x1, x2 mg C cm^{-2}y^{-1}	POM Conc. at Depth x mg C cm^{-3}	INP Below Depth x mg C cm^{-2}y^{-1}	INP in Depth Interval x1, x2 mg C cm^{-2}y^{-1}
0	4.0000	27.54		4.0000	5.51	
			24.42			1.95
1	0.4530	3.12		2.5871	3.56	
			2.77			1.26
2	0.0510	0.35		1.6733	2.30	
			0.34			1.34
4	0.0006	0.004		0.7000	0.96	
			< 0.01			0.89
10	10^{-8}	10^{-7}		0.0512	0.07	
			-			0.06
15	.	.		0.0058	0.008	
20	.	.		0.007	0.001	

* Assumes k=15 y^{-1}, D_B = 3.16 cm^2 y^{-1} ** Assumes k = 0.60 y^{-1}, D_B = 3.16 cm^{2}y^{-1}

Table 3.3: Nutritional Potential of Model End-Member Estuarine Sediments (Eqn. 3.9 and Fig. 3.3).

	Composition of POC at Sediment Surface (Wt. % Fresh Algal POC/ Wt % Avg. Detr. POC)				
	100 / 0	60 / 40	35 / 65	10 / 90	0 / 100
Total Spp.	27.54	18.72	13.22	7.71	5.51
Spatial distr.					
Total 0 - 1 cm	24.42	15.43	9.82	4.20	1.95
Total Below 1 cm	3.12	3.29	3.40	3.51	3.56
Source of spp.					
From Fresh Algal POC	27.54	16.52	9.64	2.75	0.00
From Average Detritus	0.00	2.20	3.58	4.96	5.51

Table 3.4: Secondary Production Potential (SPP) (g C . m^{-2} . y^{-1}) of Deposit-feeding Benthos in Model Estuarine Sediments. End-member sediments from Table 3.2 are included along with three intermediate "hybrids". Total surface concentration of metabolizable carbon is assumed to be 4 mg C cm^{-3}. Ecological efficiency for conversion of reactive POC to deposit-feeder carbon assumed to be 10%.

cate that while production of surface deposit feeders may increase as much as 1100% or decrease as much as 92% because of episodic inputs of high-quality detritus, production of subsurface feeders should vary no more than about 13%. Provided there is a steady supply of average reworked POC (k = 0.60 y^{-1}) to the benthos, oscillations in the supply of highly reactive POC may cause surface-feeding populations to boom and stagnate or crash while subsurface feeders are almost unaffected (Levinton 1972). This result is consistent with the general concept of spatial feeding patterns of opportunistic surface feeders (primarily r-strategists) and deep-feeding K-strategists in a benthic successional paradigm. That is, deep-deposit feeders are characteristic of the equilibrium benthic assemblage (Rhoads et al. 1978; Rhoads and Boyer 1982).

These applications of diagenetic theory to deposit-feeding ecology lead us to the provocative possibility of using POC/PON depth profiles to estimate secondary production of deposit feeders in a given benthic environment. Simultaneous analysis of the depth profiles of POC/PON and appropriate particle-bound radionuclides (for determination of burial and mixing rates) with appropriate diagenetic models such as the ones used here could provide useful checks on other methods of estimating secondary production (e.g., the Allen curve approach). At present, one drawback to this method is that concentration-depth profiles actually found do not necessarily resemble the one in Fig. 3.1. Sometimes the concentration-depth profile may clearly demonstrate that sediment dynamics are far from steady-state. Another major contributor to this problem is the inadequacy of the diffusion analogy (Eqn. 3.2) as a representation of sediment mixing. Recently, more realistic models for mixing, including "non-local" injection mechanisms, have been developed (Boudreau 1986; Rice 1986) and may eventually help overcome this obstacle.

Nutritional Value of Sedimentary Organic Matter: A Case Study

Field POC/PON-depth profiles have recently been used to interpret the results of laboratory feeding experiments with conveyor-belt deposit-feeding polychaetes, *Scoloplos* spp. (Rice et al., 1986). The polychaetes were cultured in sediment (sandy mud) from a site where the vertical distribution of POC and PON were known and for which the content of available POC and PON (in the sense of Fig. 3.1) could be estimated.

The POC and PON depth profiles in an undisturbed core taken from the collection site at Lowes Cove, Maine (USA) in 1982 illustrate some of the classical features of simple "2-G" (Berner 1980) burial diagenesis (Table 3.5). Both POC and PON decrease steadily from maximum values near the sediment surface to non-zero asymptotic values. Because of the more rapid decay of nitrogenous components, the PON-depth profile attenuates more rapidly and reaches an asymptotic value at a shallower depth than the POC profile. Consequently the C:N ratio increases slightly and then decreases with increasing depth. The fraction of POC in the top 10 cm that is metabolizable should be equal to the fraction of total POC that is above the asymptotic value (Fig. 3.1 and Eqn. 3.12). Assuming that particle density does not vary with depth, this asymptotic value is approximately

$$(\%POC \text{ asymp}) = \frac{\int_{10}^{20}(\%POC)(1-\phi)dx}{\int_{10}^{20}(1-\phi)dx} = 0.97\% \qquad (3.20)$$

of the total dry sediment mass. Note that vertical variation in the volume fraction of particulates (i.e., $1 - \phi$) must be taken into account in this calculation. The depth-averaged total POC concentration in the top 10 cm is

$$(\%POC \text{ total}) = \frac{\int_0^{10}(\%POC)(1-\phi)dx}{\int_0^{10}(1-\phi)dx} = 1.36\% \qquad (3.21)$$

Therefore, 0.39% of the dry sediment weight is metabolizable carbon. Consequently, about 29% of the POC in the 0 - 10 cm depth region is metabolizable. From the PON data, one can likewise estimate that about 6% of the total PON is metabolizable.

Similarly, by subtracting asymptotic values and correcting for porosity changes with depth, one can demonstrate that in the topmost 10 cm the molar C:N ratio of metabolizable organic matter is about 50. This means that for every gram of available nitrogen there are 44 g of available carbon. Assuming that all of the nitrogen is proteinaceous and that the molar C:N ratio of average protein is 3.2 (Russell-Hunter 1970), more than 90% of the available carbon is non-proteinaceous. Inasmuch as one can assume that proteolytic enzymes cleave polymeric units no smaller than individual amino acids, protein carbon must be utilized stoichiometrically with protein nitrogen. Proceeding as above (Eqns. 3.19 and 3.20), one can demonstrate that in the top 2.5 cm depth interval, the molar C:N ratio of metabolizable POM is about 28. Comparing this value to the 10-cm average underscores the potential of highly degradable protein as a source of readily available carbon (as well as nitrogen) near the sediment surface.

Depth Interval (cm)	Porosity (%)	%POC**	%PON**	Molar C:N Ratio
0 - 2.5	72	1.65	0.136	14.2
2.5 - 5.0	64	1.45	0.114	14.8
5.0 - 7.5	60	1.43	0.111	15.0
7.5 - 10	58	1.03	0.109	11.0
10 - 15	56	0.95	0.108	10.3
15 - 20	58	1.00	0.109	10.7

** Weight percent of dry sediment

Table 3.5: Vertical profiles of porosity (% pore volume), particulate organic carbon and nitrogen, and particulate organic C:N ratio in a core from Lowes Cove, Maine. Sediment from the top 10 cm at the collection site from which this cores was taken was used in a feeding and growth study with the orbiniid polychaetes *Scoloplos* spp. (Rice et al. 1986).

Nevertheless, most of the available carbon in these shallow sediments is not proteinaceous. In all probability, the "extra" carbon is mostly algal carbohydrate, although some fraction may be the long-term decomposition products of vascular plant detritus (Rice et al. 1986). The rather high C:N ratios in surface material at this site (14 - 15 compared to typical sediment C:N ratios of 9 - 11) suggests a relatively high input to the subsurface of organic carbon compared to organic nitrogen.

However, the values of %POC are not extraordinary, suggesting that the high nearsurface C:N ratio is due to a rapid loss of organic nitrogen from newly deposited material. Because preferential loss of nitrogen occurs only during the very early phase of decomposition of labile, nitrogen-rich detritus (Rice and Tenore 1982), the relative POC enrichment probably occurred just before or just after deposition. In the case of Lowes Cove, new POM input to the sediment surface is principally phytoplankton detritus biodeposited by macrobenthic suspension-feeders and to a lesser extent *in situ* primary production by benthic diatoms (Anderson et al. 1981; Mayer et al. 1985).

The vertical profile of POM chemistry described here is quite similar to the general theoretical relationship depicted in Fig. 3.4 for a nearshore deposit. Using Be-7 as a mixing rate tracer (to estimate the mixing coefficient) for the top 5 cm of Lowes Cove sediments (Rice 1986), Eqn. 3.12 can be applied to the data in Table 3.5 to bracket the decay constant for metabolizable POC in the top 10 cm:

$$0.5y^{-1} \leq k(POC \text{ react}) \leq 1.2y^{-1}. \tag{3.22}$$

This range brackets the value of 0.60 y^{-1} calculated by Berner (1980) for metabolizable POC in the bioturbated zone of the FOAM site and also used for modeling purposes above. Assuming that POC and PON are mixed by the same mechanism, Eqn. 3.12 requires that for any two depths x1 and x2

$$\frac{k(POC \text{ react})}{k(PON \text{ react})} = (\frac{\ln(C(\text{x1})/C(\text{x2}))}{\ln(N(\text{x1})/N(\text{x2}))})^2 \tag{3.23}$$

where $C(x)$ and $N(x)$ are the concentrations of reactive POC and reactive PON respectively. From data for the two topmost intervals in Table 3.2 and the estimates of unreactive POC and PON calculated above, one can estimate this ratio to be about 20. Then from the bracketed range of values for k(POC react), the first-order decay constant for reactive PON in this deposit is

$$9y^{-1} \leq k(PON \text{ react}) \leq 24y^{-1}, \tag{3.24}$$

which is a range of values characteristic of seawater-leached, high-nitrogen, fresh algal detritus decaying under simulated epibenthic conditions (Rice and Tenore 1982), obviously bracketing the value of ca. 15 y^{-1} used above to construct Fig. 3.4. This simple calculation underscores the high nutritional potential of relatively fresh, nitrogen-rich POM as well as the tendency for such material to be preferentially utilized in heterotrophy near the sediment surface (Valiela 1984).

On the basis of these calculations and estimates of the carbon- nitrogen nutritional requirements of invertebrates, organic nitrogen rather than carbon/calorific value should be the limiting macronutrient in these sediments, at least in the subsurface. To the extent that the sediments used in this case study are typical of nearshore deposits, as suggested by the foregoing calculation, this is also a reasonable hypothesis for nearshore fine-grained sediments in general. Assuming that deposit feeders require metabolizable organic carbon and nitrogen in a molar ratio of 17:1 (Russell-Hunter 1970), there is almost a 200% excess of carbon in the top 10 cm of these sediments. In the vicinity of the sediment surface the C:N ratio of available

POM is closer to the Russell-Hunter estimate, and precisely at the sediment surface the ratio may even be lower, approaching that of epibenthic diatoms (C:N = 5 to 6) and recently deposited (and relatively fresh) organic material. Consequently, in this deposit and similar sediments, we expect deposit feeders that more or less nonselectively ingest bulk sediment to be nitrogen-limited as suggested by laboratory nutritional studies with the polychaete *Capitella capitata* (Type 1) (Tenore and Chesney 1985), providing, of course, that essential micronutrients are available (Phillips 1984). Highly selective, herbivorous surface "deposit-feeding" gastropods and to a lesser extent true epibenthic deposit feeders, may be more limited by metabolizable POC (available calories) or the abundance of suitable food items than by food quality *per se.* Indeed, a fresh macroalgal nitrogen supplement has been shown to have no discernible effect on somatic growth of the surface grazing gastropod *Hydrobia totteni*, when diatoms were readily available (Bianchi and Levinton 1984).

The nutritional value of Lowes Cove sediment to a subsurface deposit feeder was evaluated through feeding experiments (Rice et al. 1986). Growth and feeding of *Scoloplos* spp. (family Orbiniidae) in homogenized sediment from the top 10 cm were followed for 16 days. Using a Conover ratio approach based on total sediment POC of ingestible size, assimilation efficiency was about 24% (see Cammen, this volume). From the above estimate that 29% of the total POC in these sediments is metabolizable, it is evident that this worm assimilated labile POC with better than 80% efficiency. Gross growth efficiency was about 8% based on available POC and 63% based on available PON, reflecting both the carbon respiratory requirement and the organic nitrogen limitation predicted by Tenore and Chesney (1985) and suggested by the geochemical evidence above (Rice et al. 1986). Availability of food resources in this experiment was not limited by particle size (Rice 1986; Rice et al. 1986). Microbial POM, living and nonliving, is almost certainly an important component of the pool of PON utilized by deposit feeders. Inasmuch as microbial material is more susceptible to enzymatic attack and utilization by deposit-feeders than refractory sedimentary POM (Newell 1965; Lopez and Levinton 1987), the vertical distribution of microbial biomass contributes to the depth distribution of labile POC and PON and affects the spatial availability of food. In muddy deposits, microbes probably contribute little to the total pool of metabolizable POC (Cammen 1980; Rice et al. 1986). However, because most of the nitrogen remaining in POM during prolonged decay is tightly bound in refractory geopolymeric structures (Rice 1982; Rice and Hansen 1984; Mayer, this volume), microbial decomposers may sequester nitrogen from the surroundings (e.g., pore water ammonia and nitrate) to meet physiological requirements (Lopez et al. 1977; Fenchel and Blackburn 1979). Although POC moves from the detrital pool to the microbial pool during decomposition, there must be substantial metabolic loss of carbon as well. Conversely, by nitrogen sequestering, relatively labile organic nitrogen in the form of living microbes, their exudates (Rice, 1979; Hobbie and Lee 1980; Rice 1982), and perhaps their carcasses is added to the pool of relatively labile PON. At least two studies have indicated that living microbes may provide most or all of the organic nitrogen required by deposit- feeding polychaetes (Cammen 1980; Rice 1986). Overall, one would expect microbial sequestering of nitrogen to become quantitatively more significant in the breakdown of POM at progressively greater distances from the sites of fresh organic input, such as the sediment surface and subsurface "microbial gardens" (Hylleberg 1975). Despite observations that sediment bacteria are probably unimportant as sources of organic carbon for deposit feeders (Christian and Wetzel 1978), the importance of living and non-living microbial material as sources of organic nitrogen may explain in part why the deposit-feeding activity of benthic macrofauna tends to be concentrated at two zones of high microbial activity – the sediment surface and the redoxocline (Rhoads 1974; Rhoads and Boyer 1982).

A Summary Perspective on Nutrition

Although the the rate of supply of organic matter to the benthic environment and in situ primary production are the fundamental determinants of deposit feeder production, bioturbating fauna are themselves important agents affecting the spatial distribution of the quantity and quality of detrital food. Diagenetic modeling of organic matter in sediments indicates that subsurface deposit-feeding infauna can increase the nutritional value of the sediment at depth but that they feed in an "oligotrophic" environment relative to near-surface conditions. This conclusion supports Levinton's (1972) observations that the differences in trophic regimes between the epifaunal and infaunal environment may explain differences in adaptive strategies and population dynamics between those species which feed above and below the sediment surface. Bioturbational downmixing is a mechanism by which subsurface feeders may compete with surface feeders for new food resources introduced to or produced at the sediment surface. To some extent populations of subsurface feeders, especially conveyor-belt feeders, may stabilize their food supply by virtue of their ability to affect mixing rate in proportion to their abundance.

Inputs of high-quality organic detritus to the sediment surface may benefit surface and nearsurface deposit feeders, but in the absence of rapid injection mechanisms there is little direct nutritional impact on consumers foraging below the top one or two cm. Bioturbational downmixing through the sediment continuum cannot bring high quality organic matter into subsurface feeding zones fast enough to sustain secondary production of subsurface deposit feeders. The energetic requirements of subsurface feeders must be met by utilizing organic carbon of inferior quality and which is present in deep feeding zones at low concentrations. The common characteristics of subsurface deposit feeding fauna – slow-growing, sedentary, K-strategists that process large amounts of sediment – are consistent with an implied energetic requirement to partition a large amount of energy into processing this dilute food resource (but see Taghon, this volume).

If subsurface deposit feeders have evolved for feeding in a relatively oligotrophic sediment, are they capable of feeding on organically enriched sediments? Research on this topic is wanting. However, Falk (in preparation) has shown that the orbiniid polychaete *Leitoscoloplos* sp., a head-down deposit feeder, has a higher assimilation efficiency and higher ontogenetic growth rate when feeding in a relatively carbon-poor sediment (ca. 1% by weight) as compared to an organic carbon-rich sediment (ca. 3%). Reciprocal transplants of worms from one sediment to the other gave the same results; i.e., assimilation efficiency and growth rates were higher in the oligotrophic (with respect to carbon only) sediment. Field data on the mapped distributions of head-down or conveyor-belt species suggests that they are not as successful in enriched sediments. The second author (DCR) has mapped the distributions of conveyor-belt species in a wide range of coastal and inner shelf environments in New England, Chesapeake Bay, Florida, the Gulf Coast, and Puget Sound. This mapping was done by means of *in situ* sediment-profile imaging (Rhoads and Germano 1986). Recognition of this biofacies from sediment-profile images is done by identifying the presence of subsurface feeding voids which develop around the anterior ends of conveyor-belt species. Large areas of the seafloor in these environments are populated by subsurface feeders but they appear to be limited to sediments (muds or sands) which have high optical reflectance (low, or no, associated sulfides). The perimeters of their distributions are commonly sharply demarked, especially when these distributions are adjacent to organically enriched sediments.

These distributions have prompted us to erect the following hypotheses:

1. Assemblages of subsurface deposit feeders may be best developed where the input of labile organic matter is more or less balanced with its respiration.

2. Deep bioturbational processing of sediment may prevent the accumulation of labile organic matter in sediments. At a given loading rate of labile organic matter, these bottom types should then have lower biological and chemical oxygen demands than bottoms which are unmixed or are only shallowly bioturbated.

3. The sharp margins of populations of conveyor belt species suggest that the success of these species is density dependent and that, above a critical loading rate of labile organic matter, these populations become locally extinct.

4. In oligotrophic conditions, the carrying capacity of subsurface conveyor-belt species may be higher than that for near- surface or suspension feeders.

5. In intermediate levels of labile organic input, net annual secondary production of deep infaunal bioturbators may generally be less than that of near-surface feeding deposit- feeders or suspension feeders (other factors being equal).

Other causal interpretations and hypotheses might be offered to explain these same field distribution data. Nevertheless, the above hypotheses would seem to raise some first-order questions for future research. The question of critical loading rates for deep conveyor-belt species is particularly important if we are to understand the importance of this phenomenon to the function of the overall ecosystem, specifically the potential relationships among eutrophication, changing depths and rates of bioturbation, and the subsequent development of high levels of BOD and COD in sediments.

The success of subsurface "gardening" is probably also dependent on the ability of the infauna to maintain pore water profiles in an advected state. This maintainence can be compromised by physical disturbance. The scale and frequency of the disturbance is important. If the depth of the disturbance is greater than the mean feeding depth and the average time lapse between disturbances is less than the generation time of the population, head-down feeders may have difficulty in establishing themselves and their "garden". Surficial disturbance by water turbulence which is much less than the mean feeding depth may actually benefit head-down feeders by providing an additional injection mechanism for high-quality POM into the bottom. The thriving populations of *Heteromastus filiformis* and *Scoloplos fragilis* in the coarse intertidal sands of Cape Henlopen, Delaware, are examples (T. Bianchi, personal communication). Despite the obvious physical instability of such environments, these communities are essentially the "equilibrium" communities of Rhoads et al. (1978) except that surface feeders cannot survive because of extreme turbulence and a concomitant absence of food items (diatoms); nevertheless, diatoms do accumulate at depth in the relatively quiescent subsurface feeding zone of *S. fragilis*.

The evidence from diagenetic modeling and nutritional studies with minimally modified sediments (Cammen 1980; Rice et al. 1986) suggests that the trophic relationship between the detrital heterotrophic microflora and deposit feeders that nonselectively ingest bulk sediment depends on the food substrate. In the case of organic carbon, the microbe-macroconsumer association is primarily one of interspecific competition. Conversely, in the case of nitrogen, there is a clear predator-prey relationship. These ideas are entirely consistent with the Newell-Frankenberg hypothesis of protein (*not* nitrogen) enrichment by bacterial colonization (Newell 1965; Frankenberg and Smith 1967; Rice 1982) and with the fact that the detrital microflora is generally unimportant as an organic carbon reservoir (Christian and Wetzel 1978). The corresponding nutritional problem for highly selective surface browsers that utilize diatoms and fresh macroalgal detritus is trivial by comparison. Given the relatively high caloric content and favorable C:N ratio of such food, it makes more sense to regard such consumers as facultative herbivores limited by the number of suitable food items rather than as classical deposit feeders (Rice et al., 1986), although the distinction is frustratingly semantic.

Perhaps the major obstacle to advancing our current understanding of deposit feeder nutrition is the lack of data on the organic chemistry of productive muds – specifically, the standing amounts and rates of production of enzymatically labile carbohydrates, amino acids and polypeptides, and, to a lesser extent lipids. R. G. Johnson realized the importance of this problem in the early 1970's (Johnson 1974; 1977), but his work was cut short by his untimely death. Given the ubiquity of microbes in sediments, the question of availability of organic micronutrients (Phillips 1984) is of secondary importance. Simultaneous studies of the organic components of natural muds and the assimilability of those components by *bulk sediment feeders* should be given very high priority. Simple organic analyses and immunochemical assays coupled with radiotracer labeling techniques (Lopez and Crenshaw,

1982) appear to be promising approaches (see Lopez et al., this volume). There is little to be gained from several more rounds of gross C:N measurements on consumers, food, and feces.

It is also worth noting that, despite the evidence for nitrogen limitation in the production of nonselective deposit feeders, the organic carbon source is still not understood. Sediment microbes may provide nitrogen at a limiting rate, but the great reservoir of nonliving sedimentary organic carbon cannot be ignored since that is where most of the available carbon is. There may also be a small amount of assimilable organic nitrogen in the nonliving organic pool (Rice and Hansen 1986; Mayer, this volume), although it is probably of secondary importance compared to living microbial nitrogen. Carbon availability is just as much a factor in the quality of detritus as (protein) nitrogen availability, even when the latter is limiting.

Paleobiology has an important role to play in documenting the evolution of subsurface deposit feeding. The evolution of deep bioturbation may be preserved in the sedimentary fabrics of Paleozoic marine sediments. Larson and Rhoads (1982) suggest that bioturbation depths increased from 2–3 cm in the Ordovician to about double this depth by the Devonian. They speculate that this progressive infaunalization may have been related to increased feeding competition among deposit feeders. Thayer (1979) further suggests that enhanced bioturbation at this time was an important factor for excluding attached or immobile epifauna from surfaces of physically unstable bioturbated muds. The change in mean bioturbation depths in the early Paleozoic is poorly documented. A habitat-by-habitat analysis of this phenomenon may prove fruitful. Did this infaunalization begin in nearshore environments and move offshore, or did the phenomenon begin offshore and progress inshore? Perhaps there was no discernible pattern, or did it develop synchronously in a wide range of environments? Can this phenomenon be related to the appearance of vascular plant detritus in the Silurian? Answers to these questions would provide important insights into the phenomenon as it is observed today.

Acknowledgments

We thank T. S. Bianchi, G. R. Lopez, L. M. Mayer, and K. R. Tenore for helpful discussions and criticism before and during the production of this manuscript. Financial support was provided by National Science Foundation grant numbers OCE-8442759 and OCE-8511383.

Literature Cited

Aller, R. C. 1980. Diagenetic processes near the sediment-water interface of Long Island Sound. I. Decomposition and nutrient element geochemistry (S,N,P). *Adv. Geophys.* 22: 237-350.

Aller, R. C. 1982. The effects of macrobenthos on chemical properties of marine sediment and overlying water. In: McCall, P. L. and M. J. S. Tevesz (eds.), *Animal-Sediment Relations*, Plenum Press, New York. pp. 53-102.

Anderson, F. E., L. Black, L. E. Watling, W. Mook, and L. M. Mayer. 1982. A temporal and spatial study of mudflat erosion and deposition. *J. Sed. Pet.* 51: 729-736.

Barbaro, J. R. 1985. Early Diagenesis of Particulate Organic Matter in Bioadvective Sediments, Lowes Cove, Maine. Master of Arts Thesis, State University of New York, Binghamton. 78 pp.

Bembia, P. J. 1985. Bioadvective Sediment Mixing and Beryllium-7 Diagenesis in Intertidal Sediments, Lowes Cove, Maine. Master of Arts Thesis, State University of New York, Binghamton. 61 pp.

Berner, R. A. 1980. *Early Diagenesis.* Princeton Univ. Press, Princeton. 214 pp.

Berner, R. A. 1982. Burial of organic carbon and pyritic sulfur in the modern ocean: its geochemical and environmental significance. *Am. J. Sci.* 282: 451-473.

Bianchi, T. S. and J. S. Levinton. 1984. The importance of microalgae, bacteria, and particulate organic matter in the somatic growth of *Hydrobia totteni* (Gastropoda). *J. Mar. Res.* 42: 431-443.

Boudreau, B. P. 1986. Mathematics of tracer mixing in sediments: II. Nonlocal mixing and the biological conveyor-belt phenomenon. *Am. J. Sci.* 286: 199-238.

Brown, B. 1982. Spatial and temporal distributions of a deposit-feeding polychaete on a heterogeneous tidal flat. *J. Exp. Mar. Biol. Ecol.* 65: 213-227.

Cammen, L. M. 1980. The significance of microbial carbon in the nutrition of the deposit-feeding polychaete *Nereis succinea. Mar. Biol.* 61: 9-20.

Christian, R. R. and R. L. Wetzel. 1978. Interaction between substrate, microbes, and consumers of *Spartina* detritus in estuaries. In: M. L. Wiley (ed.), *Estuarine Interactions.* Academic Press, New York. pp. 93-114.

Dobbs, F. C. and R. B. Whitlatch. 1982. Aspects of deposit-feeding by the polychaete *Clymenella torquata. Ophelia* 21: 159-166.

Emerson, S. and J. Dymond. 1984. Benthic organic carbon cycling: Toward a balance of fluxes from particle settling and pore water gradients. In: *Global Ocean Flux Study.* National Academy Press, Washington, D. C. pp. 283-305.

Emerson, S., K. Fischer, C. Reimers, and D. Heggie. 1984. Organic carbon dynamics and preservation in deep-sea sediments. *Deep Sea Res.*

Falk, K. In Preparation. Experimental studies of the feeding ecology of *Leitoscoloplos* sp. (Orbiniidae: Polychaeta) from Barnstable Harbor and Boston Harbor.

Fenchel, T. and T. H. Blackburn. 1979. *Bacteria and Mineral Cycling.* Academic Press, New York. 225 pp.

Frankenberg, D. and K. L. Smith. 1967. Coprophagy in marine animals. *Limnol. Oceanogr.* 12: 443-450.

Gerlach, S. A. 1971. On the importance of marine meiofauna for benthos communities. *Oecologia* 6: 176-190.

Hargrave, B. T. 1972. Prediction of egestion by the deposit-feeding amphipod *Hyalella azteca. Oikos* 23: 116-124.

Hobbie, J. E. and C. Lee. 1980. Microbial production of extracellular material: importance in benthic ecology. In: Tenore, K. R. and B. C. Coull (eds.), *Marine Benthic Dynamics.* Univ. of S. Carolina Press, Columbia. pp. 341-346.

Hylleberg, J. 1975. Selective feeding by *Abarenicola pacifica* with selective notes on *Abarenicola vagabunda* and a concept of gardening in lugworms. *Ophelia* 14: 113-137.

Johnson, R. G. 1974. Particulate matter at the sediment-water interface in coastal environments. *J. Mar. Res.* 33: 313- 330.

Johnson, R. G. 1977. Vertical variation in particulate matter in the upper twenty centimeters of marine sediment. *J. Mar. Res.* 35: 273-282.

Larson and D. C. Rhoads. 1983. The evolution of infaunal communities and sedimentary fabrics. In: M. J. S. Tevesz and P. L. McCall (eds.), *Biotic Interactions in Recent and Fossil Benthic Communities.* Plenum Press, New York. pp. 627-648.

Levinton, J. S. 1972. Stability and trophic structure in deposit-feeding and suspension-feeding communities. *Am. Nat.* 106: 472-486.

Lopez, G. R. and M. A. Crenshaw. 1982. Radiolabelling of sedimentary organic matter with ^{14}C-formaldehyde: preliminary evaluation of a new technique for use in deposit-feeding studies. *Mar. Ecol. Prog. Ser.* 8: 283-289.

Lopez, G. R., J. S. Levinton, and L. B. Slobodkin. 1977. The effect of grazing by the detritivore *Orchestia grillus* on *Spartina* litter and its associated microbial community. *Oecologia* (Berl.) 30: 111-127.

Lopez, G. R. and J. S. Levinton. 1987. Ecology of deposit-feeding animals in marine sediments. *Quart. Rev. Biol.* 62: 235-260.

Mann, K. H. 1972. Macrophyte production and detritus food chains in coastal waters. *Mem. Ist. Ital. Idrobiol.* 29 (Suppl): 353-383.

Mayer, L. M. (This Volume)

Mayer, L. M., P. T. Rahaim, W. Guerin, S. A. Macko, L. Watling, and F. E. Anderson. 1985. Biological and granulometric controls on sedimentary organic matter of an intertidal mudflat. *Estuar. Coastal. Shelf Sci.* 20: 491-503.

Newell, R. C. 1965. The role of detritus in the nutrition of two marine deposit-feeders, the prosobranch *Hydrobia ulvae* and the bivalve *Macoma balthica. Proc. Zool. Soc. Lond.* 4: 25-45.

Parsons, T. R, M. Takahashi, and B. Hargrave. 1984. *Biological Oceanographic Processes*, 3d Edition. Pergamon Press, Oxford. 330 pp.

Phillips, N. W. 1984. Role of different microbes and substrates as potential suppliers of specific, essential nutrients to marine detritivores. *Bull. Mar. Sci.* 35: 283-298.

Rhoads, D. C. 1974. Organism-sediment relations on the muddy sea floor. *Oceanogr. Mar. Biol.* 12: 263-300.

Rhoads, D. C. and L. F. Boyer. 1982. The effects of marine benthos on physical properties of sediments: A successinal perspective. In: McCall, P. L. and M. J. S. Tevesz (eds.), *Animal-Sediment Relations*, Plenum Press, New York. pp. 3-43.

Rhoads, D. C. and J. D. Germano. 1986. Interpreting long-term change in benthic communities: a new protocol. *Hydrobiologia*.

Rhoads, D. C., P. L. McCall, and J. Y. Yingst. 1978. Disturbance and production on the estuarine sea floor. *Amer. Sci.* 66: 577-586.

Rice, D. L. 1979. Trace element chemistry of aging marine detritus derived from coastal macrophytes. Ph.D. Dissertation, Georgia Institute of Technology, Atlanta. 144 pp.

Rice, D. L. 1982. The detritus nitrogen problem: new observations and perspectives from organic geochemistry. *Mar. Ecol. Prog. Ser.* 9: 153-162.

Rice, D. L. 1986. Early diagenesis in bioadvective sediments: relationships between the diagenesis of beryllium-7, sediment reworking rates, and the abundance of conveyor-belt deposit- feeders. *J. Mar. Res.* 44: 149-184.

Rice, D. L. and Hanson, R. B. 1984. A kinetic model for detritus nitrogen: role of the associated bacteria in nitrogen accumulation. *Bull. Mar. Sci.* 35: 326-340.

Rice, D. L. and K. R. Tenore. 1982. Dynamics of carbon and nitrogen during the decomposition of detritus derived from estuarine macrophytes. *Estuar. Coastal Shelf Sci.* 13: 681-690.

Rice, D. L. and S. I. Whitlow. 1985a. Early diagenesis of transition metals: a study of metal partitioning between macrofaunal populations and shallow sediments. In: *The Fate and Effects of Pollutants*. Maryland Seagrant Office, College Park. pp. 21-30.

Rice, D. L. and S. I. Whitlow. 1985b. Diagenesis of transition metals in bioadvective marine sediments. In: *Heavy Metals in the Environment, Vol. 2.* C. E. C. Consultants, Ltd., Edinburgh. pp. 353-355.

Rice, D. L., T. S. Bianchi, and E. H. Roper. 1986. Experimental studies of sediment reworking and growth of *Scoloplos* spp. (Orbiniidae: Polychaeta). *Mar. Ecol. Prog. Ser.* 30: 9-19.

Rosenfeld, J. K. 1981. Nitrogen diagenesis in Long Island Sound sediments. *Am. J. Sci.* 281: 436-462.

Russell-Hunter, W. D. 1970. *Aquatic Productivity.* Macmillan Publ., New York. 306 pp.

Sieburth, J. McN., and J. T. Conover. 1965. *Sargassum* tannin, an antibiotic that retards fouling. *Nature* 208: 52-53.

Tenore, K. R. and E. J. Chesney. 1985. The effects of interaction of rate of food supply and population density on the bioenergetics of the opportunistic polychaete *Capitella capitata* (type 1). *Limnol. Oceanogr.* 30: 1188-1195.

Tenore, K. R. and D. L. Rice. 1980. A review of trophic factors affecting secondary production of deposit-feeders. In: Tenore, K. R. and B. C. Coull (eds.), *Marine Benthic Dynamics.* Univ. of S. Carolina Press, Columbia. pp. 325-340.

Tenore, K. R., R. B. Hansen, B. E. Dornseif, and C. N. Wiederhold. 1979. The effect of organic nitrogen supplement on the utilization of different sources of detritus. *Limnol. Oceanogr.* 84: 350-355.

Tenore, K. R., L. Cammen, S. E. G. Findlay, and N. Phillips. 1982. Perspectives of research on detritus: Do factors controlling the availability of detritus to macroconsumers depend on its source? *J. Mar. Res.* 40: 473-490.

Thayer, C. W. 1979. Biological bulldozing and the evolution of marine benthic communities. *Science* 203: 458-461.

Valiela, I., L. Koumjian, T. Swain, J. M. Teal, and J. E. Hobbie. 1979. Cinnamic acid inhibition of detritus feeding. *Nature* 280: 55-57.

Valiela, I. 1984. *Marine Ecological Processes*. Springer-Verlag, New York. 546 pp.

Yingst, J. Y. and D. C. Rhoads. 1980. The role of bioturbation in the enhancement of bacterial growth rates in marine sediments. In: *Marine Benthic Dynamics*, K. R. Tenore and B. C. Coull, eds. Univ. of South Carolina Press, Columbia. pp. 407-421.

Zeitschel, B. 1980. Sediment-water interactions in nutrient dynamics. In: *Marine Benthic Dynamics*, K. R. Tenore and B. C. Coull, eds. Univ. of S. Carolina Press, Columbia. pp. 195- 218.

Chapter 4

The Nature and Determination of Non-Living Sedimentary Organic Matter as a Food Source for Deposit Feeders

Lawrence M. Mayer
Oceanography Program
Ira C. Darling Center
University of Maine
Walpole ME 04573

Introduction

Several lines of evidence imply that deposit feeders can and do use non-living food resources in marine sediments. Indeed, non-living food may comprise the bulk of the food for many species. The ability to use such food is indicated by feeding experiments which have shown ingestion selectivity by deposit feeders for protein-coated beads (Taghon 1982; Taghon and Jumars 1984) and demonstrated an ability to absorb non-living organic matter (Lopez et al., this volume). Tenore and coworkers (e.g. Tenore 1983) have also demonstrated the ability of polychaetes to utilize non-living detrital material. The actual use of non-living material *in situ* has been implied primarily via budgetary calculations (e.g. Cammen 1980; Rice et al. 1986), which show that the required assimilation efficiency of sedimentary organic matter indicates a bioavailable organic pool larger than can be provided by the living component.

The purpose of this Chapter is to discuss some constraints upon, and the determination of, the non-living component of sedimentary organic matter that serves as food for deposit feeders. This Chapter emphasizes sediments in coastal and shelf ecosystems. Calculations of the depth distribution of benthic biomass (e.g. Menzies et al. 1973) indicate that the vast bulk of the world's macrobenthos live in estuarine and shelf sediments. Assuming that these macrofauna are dominated by deposit feeders (Parsons et al. 1977), it is fair to infer that the bulk of the world's benthic deposit feeder production occurs in shallow-water habitats.

Concentrations and Nature of Sedimentary Organic Matter

The concentrations of organic carbon in the surface sediments of unpolluted estuarine and shelf environments generally lie in the range of 10^{-1} to 10^1 percent organic carbon (e.g. Bordovskiy, 1965; Premuzic et al. 1982; Berner 1982). For the "typical" case of aluminosilicate sediments away from strong upwelling or polluted areas, values usually fall into the range 0.5 to 3 percent organic carbon.

Sediments generally show a strong dependence of organic matter concentration on grain size, with finer grained sediments containing higher concentrations. A data set that illustrates this generalization is shown in Figure 4.1, representing data of Mayer et al. (1981) from estuarine and shelf environments of the Gulf of Maine. The organic carbon concentrations show a roughly linear, proportional dependence on sediment surface area for each

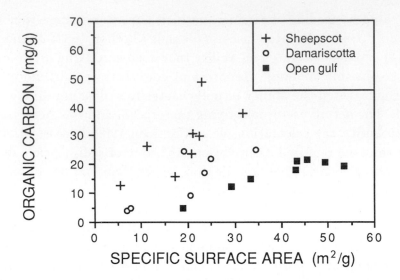

Figure 4.1: Concentrations of sedimentary organic carbon in two estuaries and the open shelf of the Gulf of Maine plotted against mineral-specific surface area as determined from monolayer adsorption of cetyl pyridinium bromide. Data are from Mayer et al. (1981).

of the three provinces plotted. This type of grain size dependence has indicated to a variety of investigators that sedimentary organic matter is present mainly as adsorbed material on mineral surfaces (e.g. Weiler and Mills 1965; Suess 1973; Tanoue and Handa 1979; Mayer et al. 1985). Indeed, the slopes of the relationships between organic carbon and surface area indicate organic carbon concentrations on the order of 0.5 to 1 mg organic carbon per square meter of mineral surface area. Such values are similar to adsorption densities of materials such as proteins at an air-water interface (e.g. Neurath and Bull 1938; Arnold and Pak 1962) in which roughly monolayer coverage of the molecules (on the order of 5 to 10 Å thick) is obtained.

It is important, however, to consider that at least part of the explanation for the correlation between organic matter and specific surface area is due to the hydrodynamic equivalence between organic matter and finer grained minerals. In other words, large particles of organic detritus, with low specific gravity, will behave sedimentologically like much smaller mineral grains, with higher specific gravity. This equivalence will also lead to an accumulation of organic detritus in finer grained sediments that may result in the same linear plots. Estuarine and continental shelf sediments have been found to contain up to 30% of their organic matter in a low density, discrete fraction, separable by heavy liquids of density 1.9 g cc^{-1} (Prahl and Carpenter 1983; Ertel and Hedges 1985; Mayer, unpub. data). This material is likely not absorbed to mineral surfaces.

The issue of the physical state of organic matter in sediments is poorly understood primarily because of lack of attention paid to the problem. The chemical nature of sedimentary organic matter is hardly better resolved, in spite of comparatively intense efforts at chemical analyses over the past several decades. One feature of particulate organic matter in sediments that is clear is its largely polymeric nature. This polymeric material can be divided into an artificially sharp dichotomy of two endmember classes: Biopolymers and geopolymers.

Biopolymers consist largely of the polysaccharides and proteins that are synthesized by all organisms. Biopolymers are generally relatively labile in sediments. There are of course well-known variations in lability associated with different polymers; for example, cellulose is less digestible than many other polysaccharides, such as glycogen. The geopolymeric material, often further classified into operationally defined fractions such as humic or fulvic acids and humins, is not well understood. Marine geopolymeric material is largely aliphatic, acidic, old, colored, and contains constituents from the major biopolymeric compound classes. However, the actual structural chemistry in terms of quantitative constituent concentrations and modes of linkage among them is very poorly known. The typically great age of bulk sedimentary organic matter (Benoit et al. 1979) indicates its general unavailability to benthic heterotrophs. Biogenic, monomeric molecules are generally all metabolizable by at least some heterotrophic organisms; it is in the geopolymerization of monomers that they become kinetically, and perhaps absolutely, refractory to utilization. Geopolymeric material is presumably composed of biogenic monomers that have undergone a form of polymerization resulting in a product with connections that are not hydrolyzable by benthic organisms. One common explanation for the inability of organisms to depolymerize this material derives from the likely extraordinary variety of types and geometries of chemical linkages connecting the monomers. Hydrolytic enzymes are generally rather specific in terms of the types of bonds they can break and in the geometric conditions necessary for them to act. It would therefore be energetically inefficient for an organism to generate the wide variety of enzymes necessary to obtain much nutritive value from such a complex material.

The cycle of organic matter incorporation into sediments can be expressed in terms of a change in physical and chemical state which encompasses the two dichotomies described above. Fresh organic inputs to sediments appear to be dominated by material which is (1) from a physical standpoint dominated by discrete, particulate, organic detritus, rather than a monolayer of organic material adsorbed on mineral surfaces, and (2) relatively rich in biopolymers and hence relatively labile. This material is almost completely metabolized within a few years after delivery to the sediments, with a small fraction participating in (as yet unidentified) humification reactions. In the process of humification, the remaining fraction is incorporated into what appears to be a monolayer of adsorbed organic material, which is largely unavailable to sedimentary biota. There is a relatively high turnover rate of the biopolymeric material which likely comprises a small portion of the total organic matter. These two dichotomies suggest the hypothesis that the organic matter which is available to deposit feeders is likely relatively rich in biopolymeric material and in a relatively discrete form relative to mineral particles (Figure 4.2).

It is important to note that the dichotomies as described above present an artificially sharp and separate picture. Partial humification of biopolymeric material likely occurs, with subsequent (perhaps kinetically inhibited) uptake by the biota. In addition, some biopolymeric material is likely not as labile as some partially humified material.

Chemical humification may not be the only means by which organic matter is rendered unavailable to biota. Organo-mineral interactions, such as the adsorption of organic molecules into the lattices of clays, may also play a role in preventing heterotrophic utilization (e.g., Marshman and Marshall 1981).

Constraints on the Nature of the Bioavailable Fraction

In order to determine the nature of the component(s) of sedimentary organic matter actually utilized by deposit feeders, it is necessary first to estimate

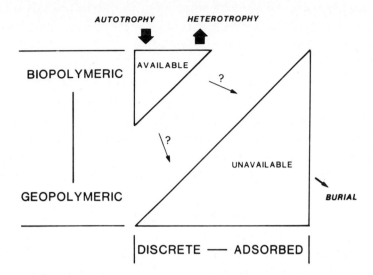

Figure 4.2: Diagram of available and unavailable organic matter pools in sediments, according the chemical and physical dichotomies discussed in the text. The relative sizes of triangles approximate relative pool sizes of the two pools. Relative sizes of arrows approximate mass flow among pools.

the size of the fraction of interest. One way to make this estimate is to determine the magnitude of the maintenance ration required by deposit feeders for their normal metabolic processes, and compare it to the amount of sedimentary organic matter actually ingested. This type of calculation has rarely been attempted. Cammen (1980) calculated that *Nereis succinea* could supplement microbial organic matter with an assimilation efficiency of 5.2 % of the non-living organic matter it ingested. Rice et al. (1986) calculated that *Scoloplos* spp. likely subsist on no more than 24 % of the ingested organic carbon and 4 % of ingested organic nitrogen. Experimental approaches have also been taken.

George (1964) estimated the assimilation efficiency of sedimentary organic matter by *Cirriformia tentaculata* to be 8 %, based on a comparison of fecal pellet with bulk sediment organic matter, an approach which is subject to error if particle selection occurs during feeding. Lopez (this vol. and pers. comm.) has found, in a number of experiments, *Nucula* and *Hydrobia* to absorb 5–30 % of ingested organic matter, using sedimentary organic matter that was nonspecifically labeled with radioactive formaldehyde. Cammen (this volume) has generalized the relationship among organism size, organic content of sediment, and feeding rate to conclude that between 8–20 % of ingested organic matter must be assimilated.

The general conclusion from these studies is that but a minor fraction of sedimentary organic matter, probably in the range of 5–30 %, is in a form utilizable by deposit feeders. It is worth noting that some early workers (e.g., Waksman and Hodgkiss 1938) made similar estimates, from oxygen consumption experiments, of the fraction of total organic matter available for benthic metabolism. This conclusion is of course an overgeneralized one, which applies to overall nutritional requirements for deposit feeders. Clearly the need for the various components of nutrition (gross calories for metabolism, amino acids for protein synthesis, essential fatty acids, etc.) will be met by varying fractions of the bulk organic matter. In addition, many specific nutritional requirements may well be satisfied by the living fraction of the sedimentary organic matter (Phillips 1984).

Although the bulk of sedimentary organic matter is clearly in a polymeric form, it is worth considering the possibility that adsorbed monomeric material comprises the minor bioavailable fraction. This possibility can be examined by assuming that adsorbed monomeric organic compounds are in sorption equilibrium with the dissolved phase. From known concentrations of representative monomers in the dissolved phase, and known sorption partition coefficients, we can calculate the maximum concentrations of adsorbed monomeric material as follows: Assume a sample case of a typical silty sediment with total organic carbon (OC) concentration of 2 %. If we require an assimilation efficiency of 15 %, we need 3 mg OC g^{-1} dry weight sediment to be biologically available. Given a porosity of 0.7, this concentration is equivalent to 2.25 mg OC ml^{-1} wet sediment. The pore water of this sediment is likely to have no more than 10 mg-dissolved OC l^{-1} (Krom and Westrich, 1980), which we can liberally assume to be completely monomeric organic compounds. This concentration is equivalent to 0.007 mg dissolved OC ml^{-1} wet sediment, which of course precludes the dissolved material itself from being the primary source of nutrition in deposit feeding. In order for the 2.25 mg OC ml^{-1} wet sediment to consist of adsorbed monomers, sorption partition coefficients (defined as the mass adsorbed to mass dissolved ratio in a wet sediment volume) of on the order of $2.25/0.007 = 320$ are necessary for the monomers of interest. Relatively few such partition coefficients for such monomers in natural sediments have been determined, and partition

Compound	Partition Coefficient (Mass on Sediment/ Mass in Pore Water)	Reference
Adenine	$10^{-1}-10^{1}$	Craven and Karl (1984)
Acetate	$10^{-1}-10^{0}$	Christensen and Blackburn (1982)
Alanine	$10^{-1}-10^{0}$	Christensen and Blackburn (1980)
Acetate, Butyrate	10^{-1}	Sansone et al. (1987)
Stearate	10^{2}	Sansone et al. (1987)
Lactate	$< 10^{-1}$	Sansone et al. (1987)
Glucose	$< 10^{0}$	Meyer-Reil (1978)

Table 4.1: Partitioning of various organic monomers between solid phase and pore water in sediments.

coefficients using pure mineral substrates only are inapplicable. Table 4.1 provides some order-of-magnitude estimates for several representative compounds. It is seen that only for the large fatty acid stearate is a sufficient partition coefficient observed. The lower partition coefficients imply that the adsorbed monomers in equilibrium with the measured concentrations of low molecular weight material, which was liberally assumed to be completely monomeric material and more likely has but a small component of monomers, are in concentrations much lower than the 3 mg OC g^{-1} dry weight sediment needed for sustenance. It can therefore be concluded that even adsorbed monomeric material does not significantly contribute to the bulk organic matter needed by deposit feeders.

Quantification and Identification of the Bioavailable Fraction

The questions of identification and quantification of bioavailable material are related, but may also be quite separate. Identification relates to the issue of the nature of the material assimilable by deposit feeders. For example, questions can be posed in the context of the dichotomies employed above;

e.g., is food in a discrete or adsorbed form relative to the mineral matrix? Quantification issues can be concerned with no more than the amount of nutrient in a given sediment available to a given deposit feeder; e.g., is enough assimilable protein present? It need not be concerned with the form of the nutrient. Identification and quantification of potential food resources can utilize both experimental and analytical methods.

Quantification

From the discussion above, it is clear that a technique designed to measure assimilable bulk nutrients must "see" a polymeric fraction that comprises about 5–30 % of the total sedimentary organic matter in typical coastal and shelf sediments. The fact that the technique must be able to detect a subset of the overall polymeric pool argues that the hydrolytic capability of the organisms of interest must be taken into account in the design of the technique.

In the opinion of this author, there is no better way to simulate the hydrolytic capability of an organism than the use of the same hydrolytic apparatus available to that organism - specifically, the hydrolytic enzymes. A truly accurate assessment of the ability of a given deposit feeder should use the actual enzymes manufactured by that organism. However, it is probably a reasonable first step to utilize enzymes similar in function to those known to be present in an organism's gut, preferably delivered in a physico-chemical context similar to that in the organism's gut. Such analogous enzymes are now commercially available, at reasonable cost, for a variety of polymer hydrolyses. The literature on the enzymatic apparatus possessed by various deposit feeders is far from complete, but the general outlines of hydrolytic capabilities are known for many animals. For example, Hylleberg Kristensen (1972) showed that a variety of macrobenthos are able to hydrolyze storage polysaccharides while showing little ability to hydrolyze structural polysaccharides.

This enzymatic approach has received some attention, with results that are promising with respect to the need to obtain analyses of 5–30 % of the total sedimentary organic matter. Boysen-Jensen (1914) incubated sediment with pancreatic extract, and found a small but measurable amount of nitrogen liberated from bottom sediments. George (1964) quantified the organic carbon liberated by a mixture of protease, amylase, and lipase, and found 14 % of the total organic carbon released. This amount was twice that apparently utilized by the deposit feeder under study by him, but results within a factor of two are promising.

Mayer et al. (1986) developed a method for measuring the enzymatically available protein content of sediments. This technique used dye-binding, with Coomassie Blue (CB) dye, which measures only larger polypeptides (i.e., protein). A protease incubation allows separation of the CB signal due to sedimentary proteins from that due to reaction with other interfering substances in the sediment. This technique allows measurement of the proteinaceous material that is available to protease hydrolysis. Values typically range about 10–20 % of the total hydrolyzable amino acids that are found with strong acid hydrolysis followed by amino acid detection (Mayer and Macko, unpublished data), demonstrating that acid hydrolysis is a very poor simulator of enzymatic hydrolysis. Protein nitrogen accounts for 5–20 % of the total sedimentary nitrogen. The method was developed in order to measure total bioavailable protein rather than that available to a specific deposit feeder. However, the data for Rice et al. (1986) on *Scoloplos* spp. nutrition suggest that this method is also applicable to an assessment of nutritionally available protein for deposit feeders. In the depth zone where a large population of *Scoloplos* feeds on an intertidal mudflat in Maine, the measured protein concentration was about twice the level that was calculated by Rice et al. to be necessary for maintenance. This factor of two overestimation is similar to that of George (1964) discussed above, and is likely due in our case to two factors. First, protein is extracted from the sediment with a strong base, providing a stronger removal mechanism that is likely available to *Scoloplos*. Second, the use of two nonspecific proteases may provide a more potent hydrolytic capability than is available to this animal. It should be possible to vary the analytical conditions of this assay to more closely approximate the actual hydrolytic capability of a given organism, once that capability is determined.

Analogous methodologies could be developed for nutritionally available polysaccharides. The case for carbohydrates is likely to be somewhat more complicated than for proteins, because of the wide variety of polymer types that require very different enzymes. Development of measurements of nutritional quality should be calibrated against deposit feeder utilization of the food sources. For example, nutritional measurements of food source and fecal material should show a high absorption efficiency.

Identification

A wide variety of questions exist concerning the nature of the non-living food sources used by deposit feeders; an even larger variety of potential methodologies could be suggested to answer them. To this author three questions seem particularly important.

First, what is the importance of discrete organic particulates as compared with adsorbed organic material? This question could be addressed analytically by performing measurements of nutritional quality on sediments before and after physical separation of the low density detritus. It could be studied experimentally by feeding studies before and after these physical separations. Preliminary measurements indicate that the low density fraction (< 1.9 g/cc, separated by centrifugation in a sodium polytungstate solution) has a protein concentration of more than 50 times (on a volumetric concentration basis) that of the high density mineral fraction (unpublished data). This finding provides some justification for the observed preferential selection for low density materials observed for a deposit feeder by Self and Jumars (1978). A recent study on the nutrition of *Corophium volutator*, however, showed that discrete organic particulates likely comprise a minor fraction of that animal's nutritional needs (Murdoch et al. 1986).

Second, what is the role of partially humified organic matter in deposit feeder nutrition? The chemical pathways that humify detritus and their ability to render organic matter unavailable to assimilation need far more attention than they have received to date. Tracer studies using stable and radiolabeled isotopes could be quite valuable; for example, labeled material could easily be partially humified and used in feeding studies. The application of this approach to whole habitats, in microcosm or field (e.g., Garber 1984), seems a particularly valuable approach, particularly in collaboration with organic geochemists and microbial biogeochemists.

Third, the role of microbial exudates in deposit feeder nutrition needs further attention. Little work on this problem has followed the stimulating hypothesis of Hobbie and Lee (1980) that the exudates might comprise a significant nutritional pool in sediments. Conflicting results have been obtained on the digestibility of mucus exopolymers (Harvey and Luoma 1984; Baird and Thistle 1986). While the focus of attention on these polymers has been their carbohydrate content, it is likely that proteinaceous material is also exuded in significant quantities, e.g. as exoenzymes (Rice and Hanson 1984).

Conclusions

The use of non-living food resources in sediments by deposit feeders has been implied by several studies; unclear, however, are the identity and amounts of this food resource in various sedimentary regimes. For shallow water environments, which contain the bulk of the world's deposit feeders, the bioavailable organic matter is likely polymeric and probably comprises 5–30 % of the total organic matter. The physical nature of non-living food resources has received little attention; it may be composed of either discrete particulate organic detritus or material adsorbed onto mineral grains. Identification of this fraction seems a high priority goal for deposit feeder ecologists; a variety of analytical and experimental approaches are possible. Measurement of the amounts of bioavailable organic matter may profit from duplication of the means by which deposit feeders themselves depolymerize sedimentary organic matter in order to gain its nutritive value.

Acknowledgments

This paper benefited from reviews by D. Rice, G. King, C. Lee and L. Cammen. Partial support for this research was provided by NSF ISP 8011448, the Petroleum Research Fund (Am. Chem. Soc.), and NOAA Sea Grant (R/LRF-45).

Literature Cited

Arnold, J.D. and C.Y.C. Pak. 1962. Protein-protein interaction at the air-water interface. *J. Coll. Sci.* 17: 348-362.

Baird, B.H. and D. Thistle. 1986. Uptake of bacterial extracellular polymer by a deposit-feeding holothurian (*Isostichopus badionotus*). *Mar. Biol.* 92: 183-187.

Benoit, G.J., K.K. Turekian, and L.K. Benninger. 1979. Radiocarbon dating of a core from Long Island Sound. *Est. Coastal Mar. Sci.* 9: 171-180.

Berner, R.A. 1982. Burial of organic carbon and pyrite sulfur in the modern ocean: its geochemical and environmental significance. *Am. J. Sci.* 282: 451-473.

Bordovskiy, O.K. 1965. Accumulation and transformation of organic substance in marine sediments. 3. Accumulation of organic matter in bottom sediments. *Mar. Geol.* 3: 33-82.

Boysen-Jensen, P. 1914. Studies concerning the organic matter of the sea bottom. *Rept. Danish Biol. Sta.* 22: 5-49.

Cammen, L.M. 1980. The significance of microbial carbon in the nutrition of the deposit feeding polychaete *Nereis succinea*. *Mar. Biol.* 61: 9-20.

Christensen, D. and T.H. Blackburn. 1980. Turnover of tracer (^{14}C, ^{3}H labeled) alanine in inshore marine sediments. *Mar. Biol.* 58: 97-103.

Christensen, D. and T.H. Blackburn. 1982. Turnover of ^{14}C-labeled acetate in marine sediments. *Mar. Biol.* 71: 113-119.

Craven, D.B. and D. M. Karl. 1984. Microbial RNA and DNA synthesis in marine sediments. *Mar. Biol.* 83: 129-139.

Ertel, J.R. and J.I. Hedges. 1985. Sources of sedimentary humic substances: vascular plant debris. *Geochim. Cosmochim. Acta* 49: 2097-2107.

Garber, J. 1984. ^{15}N tracer study of the short-term fate of particulate organic nitrogen at the surface of coastal marine sediments. *Mar. Ecol. Prog. Ser.* 16: 89-104.

George, J.D. 1964. Organic matter available to the polychaete *Cirriformia tentaculata* (Montagu) living in an intertidal mud flat. *Limnol. Oceanogr.* 9: 453-455.

Harvey, R.W. and S.N. Luoma. 1984. The role of bacterial exopolymer and suspended bacteria in the nutrition of the deposit-feeding clam, *Macoma balthica*. *J. Mar. Res.* 42: 957-968.

Hobbie, J.E. and C. Lee. 1980. Microbial production of extracellular material: importance in benthic ecology. In: *Marine Benthic Dynamics* (Tenore, K.R. and B.C. Coull, Eds.) Univ. So. Carolina Press, pp. 341-346.

Hylleberg Kristensen, J. 1972. Carbohydrases of marine invertebrates with notes on their food and on the natural occurrence of the carbohydrates studied. *Mar. Biol.* 14: 130-142.

Krom, M.D. and J.T. Westrich. 1980. Dissolved organic matter in the pore waters of recent marine sediments; a review. *Colloques Internationaux du C.N.R.S.* 294: 103-111.

Marshman, N.A. and K.C. Marshall. 1981. Bacterial growth on proteins in the presence of clay minerals. *Soil Biol. Biochem.* 13: 127-134.

Mayer, L.M., S.A. Macko, W.H. Mook, and S. Murray. 1981. The distribution of bromine in coastal sediments and its use as a source indicator for organic matter. *Org. Geochem.* 3: 37-42.

Mayer, L.M., P.T. Rahaim, W. Guerin, S.A. Macko, L. Watling, and F.E. Anderson. 1985. Biological and granulometric controls on sedimentary organic matter of an intertidal mudflat. *Est. Coast. Shelf Sci.* 20: 491-503.

Mayer, L.M., L.L. Schick, and F.W. Setchell. 1986. Measurement of protein in nearshore marine sediments. *Mar. Ecol.–Prog. Ser.* 30: 159-165.

Menzies, R.J., R.Y. George, and G.T. Rowe. 1973. *Abyssal Environment, and Ecology of the World Oceans*. Wiley-Interscience, 488 pp..

Meyer-Reil, L.-A. 1978. Uptake of glucose by bacteria in the sediment. *Mar. Biol.* 44: 293-298.

Murdoch, M.H., F. Bärlocher, and M.L. Laltoo. 1986. Population dynamics and nutrition of *Corophium volutator* (Pallas) in the Cumberland Basin (Bay of Fundy). *J. Exp. Mar. Biol. Ecol.* 103: 235-249.

Neurath, H. and H.B. Bull. 1938. The surface activity of proteins. *Chem. Rev.* 23: 391-435.

Parsons, R.T., M.N. Takahashi, and B. Hargrave. 1977. *Biological Oceanographic Processes.* Pergamon Press, 332 pp.

Phillips, N. 1984. Role of different microbes and substrates as potential suppliers of specific, essential nutrients to marine detritivores. *Bull. Mar. Sci.* 35:283-298.

Prahl, F.G. and R. Carpenter. 1983. Polycyclic aromatic hydrocarbon (PAH)-phase associations in Washington coastal sediment. *Geochim. Cosmochim. Acta* 47: 1013-1023.

Premuzic, E.T., C.M. Benkovitz, J.S. Gaffney, and J.J. Walsh. 1982. The nature and distribution of organic matter in the surface sediments of world oceans and seas. *Org. Geochem.* 4: 63-77.

Rice, D.L. and R.B. Hanson. 1984. A kinetic model for detritus nitrogen: Role of the associated bacteria in nitrogen accumulation. *Bull. Mar. Sci.* 35: 326-340.

Rice, D.L., T.S. Bianchi, and E.H. Roper. 1986. Experimental studies of sediment reworking and growth of *Scoloplos* spp. (Orbiniidae: Polychaeta). *Mar. Ecol. Prog. Ser.* 30: 9-19.

Sansone, F.J., C.C. Andrews, and M.Y. Okamoto. 1987. Adsorption of short-chain organic acids onto nearshore marine sediments. *Geochim. Cosmochim. Acta* 51: 1889-1896.

Self, R.F.L. and P.A. Jumars. 1978. New resource axes for deposit feeders? *J. Mar. Res.* 36: 627-641.

Suess, E. 1973. Interaction of organic compounds with calcium carbonate. II. Organo-carbonate association in Recent sediments. *Geochim. Cosmochim. Acta* 37: 2435-2447.

Taghon, G.L. 1982. Optimal foraging by deposit-feeding invertebrates: roles of particle size and organic coating. *Oecologia* 52: 295-304.

Taghon, G.L. and P.A. Jumars. 1984. Variable ingestion rate and its role in optimal foraging behavior of marine deposit feeders. *Ecology* 65: 549-558.

Tanoue, E. and N. Handa. 1979. Differential sorption of organic matter by various sized sediment particles in recent sediment from the Bering Sea. *J. Oceanogr. Soc. Japan* 35: 199-208.

Tenore, K.R. 1983. Organic nitrogen and caloric content of detritus III. Effect on growth of a deposit-feeding polychaete, *Capitella capitata*. *Est. Coast. Shelf Sci.* 17: 733-742.

Waksman, S.A. and M. Hotchkiss. 1938. On the oxidation of organic matter in marine sediments by bacteria. *J. Mar. Res.* 1: 101-118.

Weiler, R.R. and A. A. Mills. 1965. Surface properties and pore structure of marine sediments. *Deep-Sea Res.* 12: 511-529.

Chapter 5

Digestion Theory Applied to Deposit Feeding

Peter A. Jumars and Deborah L. Penry
School of Oceanography, WB-10
University of Washington, Seattle, WA 98195

Introduction

As many of the contributions to this volume show, consideration of deposit feeding leads quickly to questions of digestion. There are spectacular variations in feeding rate both among species (Cammen, 1980) and within individuals (Taghon and Jumars, 1984), respectively demanding digestive diversity and flexibility. Intuitively, it seems likely that organisms eating sand and mud might more often be limited by processing ability and food quality – i.e., by the rate at which digestive products can be formed – than by acquisition rate. When one looks for theoretical guidance to design measurements and experiments regarding this interspecific diversity and intraspecific flexibility, comparatively little is available (Milton, 1981; Sibly, 1981; Taghon, 1981; Troyer, 1984). Theories of how an organism should forage and what it should ingest are abundant, but comparably general optimization approaches to predict how it ought to digest what it captures are not. The need is clear for animals in general and for deposit feeders in particular: Variations in fitness can result from variations in digestion just as readily as they can from differences in acquisition.

While browsing in a bookstore, one of us stumbled across remarkable parallels between chemical reactor design approaches for maximizing production rate (or efficiency) of a given chemical product (Froment and Bischoff, 1979) and the problem of maximizing rate (or efficiency) of digestive product formation. We pursued this analogy far enough to find that digestion in guts is homologous with conversion in chemical reactors (Penry and Jumars, 1986, 1987). Just as with early applications of foraging theory, however, the costs of digestion and subsequent utilization appear difficult to parameterize and difficult to measure – certainly more so than the costs of building, maintaining, and operating commercial chemical reactors. Net profit in fitness terms of incorporation into somatic growth or reproductive output depends on digestion, on absorption, and on synthesis of new tissues (Kiørboe et al., 1985), including both gross costs and gross gains. To maximize fitness, both foraging and digestion must be optimized, and theory clearly is not yet well enough developed to couple all costs and benefits in a realistic way.

These latter sentences are intended to give an impression of the level of development of this theoretical approach. It is too soon to make apologies, however, because no data can yet be found to contradict the theory's predictions. More to the point, the theory both identifies important digestive variables and links them together in a functional, mechanistic way that allows prediction. It is unfair to use old data to "test" these predictions because the theory is moderately complex; past data can be fitted to predictions simply by allowing those model variables not simultaneously measured to vary. We consequently will not rummage through the deposit-feeding literature for hollow demonstrations of adequate fits.

A major benefit of an explicit digestive theory is the specification of what needs to be measured, how well, and in what time sequence to provide a strong test. At the present level of development it seems most appropriate to make such predictions for gross gains in digestive product formation rate under mild constraints of volume and time. Until they are better parameterized and measured, we will implicitly assume that fixed, unavoidable digestive costs (present even with an empty gut) scale roughly linearly with gut volume and time and that the other costs of digestion (accounting for "specific dynamic action" sensu Kiørboe et al., 1985) scale with processing rate (vol time^{-1}) to some small exponent (greater than or equal to 1). If these assumptions are roughly correct, then gross rate of gain from digestion can give substantial insight into net gain.

Because it permits explicit solution without formulation of any cost functions, the most convenient premise against which to compare alternatives is that of digestive homeostasis. By analogy with the among-species, among-environment trends he observed, Cammen (1980) suggested that individual deposit feeders would maintain constant rates of organic matter intake. We translate Cammen's original idea of foraging homeostasis or constant rate of intake into digestive homeostasis or constant rate of digestive product formation (mol $s^{-1}cm^{-3}$ of gut). We thus do not suggest that the homeostasis premise we examine is identical to that proposed by Cammen. We pose two alternatives, those of rate (mol s^{-1} cm^{-3} of gut) and conversion efficiency (mol product mol^{-1} of reactant) maximization. The former is the digestive analog of energy optimization in optimal foraging, while the latter is an alternative approach used in chemical engineering when reactants are expensive or difficult to obtain. By analogy, the latter might apply where food abundance (not quality) has been severely limiting over the evolutionary history of the organism.

Our intent in this paper is to provide explicit parameterizations, based on reactor theory, of measurable features of digestion in deposit feeders and then to make predictions under each of the three alternative premises of production-rate maximization, homeostasis, and efficiency maximization. In other words, our goal is to take our previously developed theory (Penry and Jumars 1986, 1987) and put it in the form that we believe will be the most useful in designing and interpreting experiments. We hope that others will join us in testing both the parameterizations and the predictions.

As a byproduct, the reactor-theory approach provides a useful mechanism for systematizing both the formation of (digestive) functional groups and the study of microbial (digestive) symbioses of deposit feeders. The bewildering diversity of deposit feeders appears to fall into three distinct classes of reactor types and along one axis of mean particle residence time in the gut. As chauvinists of the study of deposit feeding, we point out that deposit feeders turn out to be fortunate choices for application of reactor theory to digestion: The governing equations can be simplified substantially by assuming that digesta volume does not change significantly during digestion. If structural and kinematic similarity with chemical reactors is found to reflect functional similarity, then seemingly esoteric reactor theory has immediate applications beyond feeding ecology. It should be useful in choosing species and generalizing results for evaluation of geochemical transformations occurring in animal guts. In an applied context it could provide an objective way to choose model systems for examining dietary pathways of pollutants.

A Classification of Chemical Reactors

Chemical reactors are classified on the bases both of time variation of reactant input (continuous or discontinuous) or throughput and of the pattern or method in which reactants are brought together (with or without mixing) (e.g., Levenspiel, 1972). In terms of time variation there are batch, continuous-flow, and semi-batch reactors. In a batch reactor, all reactants are added instantaneously, the reaction is allowed to proceed for a set period, and then products and unreacted material are all removed. The empty batch reactor then can remain idle for a period or be refilled. In continuous flow, reactants are continuously introduced and products, removed. Anything in between is referred to as semi-batch.

One kind of batch reactor and two kinds of continuous-flow reactors are recognized as ideal (in the sense of being described accurately by simple equations) on the basis of patterns of reactant mixing. In ideal batch reactors, contents are instantaneously and continuously mixed, so that concentrations are spatially uniform and vary only in time.

In continuous, plug-flow reactors (hereafter PFRs), material does not mix along the flow axis, so that at steady state (no variation at any point in the reactor over time) concentrations vary in a continuous gradient from inlet to outlet of the reactor. In continuous-flow, stirred-tank reactors (hereafter CSTRs), material is continuously and completely mixed, such that concentrations vary neither in space nor in time and are the same at the inlet as at the outlet. Reactions go on, of course, but products are mixed instantaneously with newly introduced reactants, while the volume of newly introduced material displaces an equivalent volume of material from the outlet. A familiar oceanographic application of the CSTR is the chemostat, the theory of which comes directly from the literature of reactor analysis and design.

In the ideal batch reactor reactant concentration is constant in space and varies in time, in the ideal PFR concentration varies in space and is constant (at any point along the flow path) in time, and in the ideal CSTR concentration is constant in both space and time. In the gut of the real deposit feeder, however, food reactant concentration most likely varies in both space and time as digestive enzymes and products diffuse into and out of sediments passing through the gut. In short, the situation may well not be ideal in the sense of producing simple, general equations. Some insight into non-ideal and unsteady behavior can be gained nonetheless by using ideal batch- and continuous-processing models to define end members. Further, to

$$\text{Batch Reactor and PFR} \qquad \text{CSTR}$$
$$t = \tau = C_{AO} \int_0^{X_{Af}} \frac{dX_A}{-r_A} \qquad \tau = \frac{C_{AO} X_{Af}}{-r_A}$$

t = holding time (batch reactor) (time)

τ = throughput time (PFR and CSTR) (time)

C_{AO} = initial concentration of reactant A in ingested food (mol volume^{-1})

X_A = conversion of reactant A into products (dimensionless fraction)

X_{Af} = final conversion of reactant A after holding or throughput time

$-r_A$ = reaction rate, given as the disappearance rate of reactant A (mol volume^{-1} time^{-1})

Table 5.1: Reactor-theory solutions for digestive equations in batch reactors, plug-flow reactors (PFRs), and continuous-flow stirred-tank reactors (CSTRs), assuming insignificant change in volume of gut contents during digestion.

make testing of predictions as easy as possible, we give the simplest models that cannot yet be refuted by observations.

We give the most compact and general (assuming no volume reduction during digestion) forms of the reactor equations for the three ideal reactor types in Table 1. We will not give derivations here, for they are available elsewhere (Levenspiel, 1972; Penry and Jumars, 1987). We note that the solution for batch-reactor holding time when there are no idle periods between batches is identical to the solution for the throughput in a PFR of equivalent volume. For the remainder of this chapter, we will describe these two reactors with the same equation, implying that the batch reactor is instantaneously emptied and refilled. Graphical solutions for batch reactors with varying idle periods (search times between meals) are given by Penry and Jumars (1986).

We also will not give the more general formulations in which volume can change during digestion. Tests of predictions resulting from the formulations given here should thus focus on animals that do not digest an appreciable proportion of the volume they ingest; i.e., they should avoid the smaller species or life stages that may verge on macrophagy and avoid any species that succeed in being so selective that they ingest primarily digestible material. Such species fall outside our intentionally narrow definition of deposit feeding.

There are some other inherent assumptions, however, that bear close scrutiny, specifically, the mixing patterns of digesta during throughput. If predictions are not met, it is worth knowing whether the approach as a whole lacks merit, or whether the assumptions need modification. We thus will try to point out sensitive assumptions as they are made.

A Gut Reactor Classification of Deposit Feeders

Where (if anywhere) among deposit feeders are guts that may operate as these varieties of ideal chemical reactors seen? We often have to rely on morphology because patterns of digesta throughput have been so little studied. Guts with one opening are suggestive of batch processing, though the converse need not be true. Among the Ophiuroidea and Asteroidea, members have been classed as deposit feeders (e.g., Shick et al., 1981), although we do not know the extent to which volume reduction due to selective ingestion of digestible material (e.g., Scheibling, 1981) occurs. If the gut is filled in one event (rather than as a series of smaller meals), if the contents are mixed upon filling and continually thereafter, and if, after some period of digestion, the gut is completely emptied, ophiuroid and asteroid guts can be modeled as batch reactors. It is obvious, in this case, that the patterns of gut filling, mixing and emptying need to be described. The literature is virtually silent on this issue because the need for such information was not apparent prior to digestive modeling. The most common kind of deposit-feeder gut is a straight tube in which little axial mixing occurs. Evidence of good fit to plug flow is given by Cammen (1980) for *Nereis succinea*, by Miller (1984) for *Corophium* spp. and by Jumars and Self (1986) for *Pseudopolydora kempi japonica*. Our unpublished tracer experiments add *Abarenicola pacifica*, *Parastichopus californicus*, and *Pygospio elegans* to the list. We expect this pattern to be found frequently because, under most conditions, plug flow provides the greatest rate of digestive product formation in minima of time and volume (Penry and Jumars, 1987). Peristalsis, so long as it produces mixing cells of small axial extent, does not substantially affect the predictions from pure plug flow (Penry and Jumars, 1987).

We have found via tracer experiments, however, that mixing is much more substantial in some deposit feeders. In *Amphicteis scaphobranchiata* (Penry, in prep.) and *Hobsonia florida* (Jumars and Self, 1986) substantial mixing goes on in an expanded anterior portion of the gut. We assume that similar mixing goes on in the expanded anterior chambers of other terebellimorph polychaetes (e.g.: Dales, 1955; Dales and Pell, 1970). We have suggested (Penry and Jumars, 1987) that these animals' guts can be modeled as CSTR-PFR series, as is clearly the case with ruminants (Penry and Jumars, 1986). We have suggested that the mixing chamber serves to overcome problems of diffusing enzymes into food when food is of low porosity or gut diameter is large (Penry and Jumars, 1987). If microbial fermentation does prove to be important in digestion, then these mixing chambers would be more likely places to look for unattached symbiotic microbes than would tubular PFR segments of guts. Degree of mixing in both batch reactor and CSTR-PFR guts must be quantified. If it is incomplete as it is in some commercial reactors, the actual degree of mixing can be quite easily incorporated into models (e.g.: Bailey and Ollis, 1977; Smith, 1981) when making predictions. At this point, we assume that mixing is complete in batch reactor guts and the CSTR portions of CSTR-PFR guts and use the unmodified, ideal reactor equations. Similarly, we do not deal here with complications such as digestive caeca. Again, the models can be easily modified (Penry and Jumars, 1987), should early results indicate that it is necessary.

Predictions

To make predictions explicit, one must stipulate reaction kinetics. In the continuing spirit of choosing the simplest model that cannot be discredited with existing data, we use the Michaelis-Menten model for digestive-enzyme reaction kinetics:

$$-r_A = \frac{V_{max} C_A}{K_m + C_A}, \text{where}$$

V_{max} is the maximal rate of reaction, C_A is the concentration of substrate, and K_m is the concentration when the rate of reaction is one half its maximal value. Enzyme concentration is assumed constant, and reaction rate reaches V_{max} when all available enzyme is saturated with substrate. Substituting this expression for $-r_A$ in the equations of Table 1, the ideal reactor performance equations can be solved for throughput time in terms of the Michaelis-Menten parameters and the extent of conversion (X_A) of reactant into product (Table 2A).

In designing experiments to test the predictions derived from the three premises, homeostasis, energy maximization, and efficiency maximization, the most straightforward approach we have envisioned proceeds as follows: First, an animal ingests a food substance with a well defined initial concentration (C_{A0}) of some component. To avoid semantic difficulties later, we call this food concentration the "conditioning" concentration. The extent of conversion is measured as the concentration of food remaining ($[1 - X_A]C_{A0}$) in the fecal material and, perhaps, at various points along the gut. Measurements are carried out until it is established that feeding rate and conversion no longer change with time (constant V_{max} and K_m). Concentration of the food component is then altered from the conditioning concentration to a new level (C'_{A0}), and measurements are made again.

There is one unique solution for digestive homeostasis (Table 2B), both in terms of the expected conversion and of throughput time under the new food condition (C'_{A0}), assuming that enzyme kinetics (i.e., V_{max} and K_m) remain constant over the short-term course of the perturbation experiment. For the CSTR neither V_{max} nor K_m is required to specify the predicted extent of conversion (X'_{Af}) or the relative throughput time (τ'/τ). For the PFR and batch reactor, the same is true of conversion, but the value of K_m is required to solve for relative holding (t'/t) or throughput (τ'/τ) time (see Table 2B). The solution for a batch reactor that is not immediately refilled upon emptying is obtained by adding the amount of time the gut remains idle to the holding time that appears in the denominator for the instantaneously refilled batch-reactor equation (equivalent to the PFR equation) of Table 2B.

To better illustrate the behaviors of both PFRs and CSTRs and to allow comparison between them, we present (Fig. 1) graphs of absolute conversion and of relative throughput time, both plotted against relative concentration of substrate in the ingested food (C'_{A0}/C_{A0}). Only the relative throughput-time curve for the PFR ($=$ the holding-time curve for a batch reactor with no idle periods) requires stipulation of absolute conditioning and new substrate concentrations (rather than simply their ratios). Since we must stipulate these absolute concentrations, we express them in the way that is least restrictive, as concentrations relative to (i.e., divided by) K_m. For purposes of illustration, we take the conditioning concentration of substrate (C_{A0}) as equal to K_m. Again, this restriction is necessary only for the throughput curves for PFRs (and holding times for batch reactors). The curves drawn in Fig. 1 are explicitly for the premise of digestive homeostasis, and describe how conversion and relative throughput time should change in response to the conditioning concentration if an animal is to maintain a constant rate of digestive product formation (mol s^{-1} cm^{-3}). Departures that fall below the curves (assuming unchanged enzyme kinetics) suggest that the animal is achieving a greater rate of digestive product formation on the new food concentration (C'_{A0}) than it was on the conditioning concentration, and de-

A. Solutions for holding time (batch reactor) or throughput time in terms of X_{Af} and C_{AO}.

Batch reactor and PFR:

$$t = \tau = \frac{k_m}{V_{\max}}[-\ln(1-X_{Af}) + \frac{C_{AO}X_{Af}}{K_m}]$$

CSTR:

$$\tau = \frac{K_m}{V_{\max}}(\frac{X_{Af}}{1-X_{Af}} + \frac{C_{AO}X_{Af}}{K_m})$$

B. Solutions for homeostasis (mol product produced time^{-1} = constant) with varying C'_{AO}, where V = volume of gut contents = constant.

$$\frac{X_{Af}C_{AO}V}{t \text{ or } \tau} = \text{constant} = \frac{(\text{dimensionless fraction})(\text{mol volume}^{-1})(\text{volume})}{\text{time}}$$

$$\text{Therefore} \frac{X'_{Af}C'_{AO}V}{t' \text{ or } \tau'} = \frac{X_{Af}C_{AO}V}{t' \text{ or } \tau'}, \text{and}$$

1. X'_{Af} in terms of C_{AO}, C'_{AO} and X_{Af}:

Batch reactor and PFR (solved iteratively): $(1-X'_{Af})^{X_{Af}} = (1-X_{Af})^{\frac{C'_{AO}X'_{Af}}{C_{AO}}}$

$$\text{CSTR:} \quad X'_{Af} = [\frac{C_{AO}}{C'_{AO}}(X_{Af} - 1)] + 1$$

2. t'/t or τ'/τ in terms of $C_{AO}, X_{Af}, C'_{AO}, X'_{Af}$, and K_m:

$$\text{Batch reactor and PFR:} \quad t'/t = \tau'/\tau = \frac{-\ln(1 - X'_{Af}) + \frac{C'_{AO}X'_{Af}}{K_m}}{-\ln(1 - X_{Af}) + \frac{C_{AO}X_{Af}}{K_m}}$$

$$\text{CSTR:} \quad \tau'/\tau = \frac{C'_{AO}C'_{Af}}{C_{AO}X_{Af}}$$

Table 5.2: Experimentally useful solutions of the digestive equations, assuming that Michaelis-Menton kinetics limit the rate of digestion. Unprimed variables refer to the conditioning period, while primed (′) variables refer to expectations under the new initial food concentration (C'_{AO}). See Table 1 and text for explanation of other symbols.

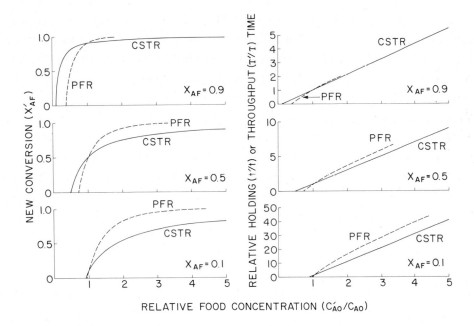

Figure 5.1: Predicted new conversion (X'_{Af}) and relative holding (t'/t) or throughput (τ'/τ) times for digestive homeostasis with three different conditioning conversions (X_{Af}). Predicted new conversions are independent of kinetic parameters of the digestive enzymes; CSTR holding times are as well. Batch reactor relative holding times and PFR relative throughput times, however, depend upon the ratios of both C_{A0} and C'_{A0} to K_m; for purposes of illustration, the case where $C_{A0} = K_m$ is shown. See text and Tables 1 and 2 for symbols, mathematical solutions and explanations. Dashed lines (PFR and batch reactor) terminate at values of X'_{Af} greater than 0.99 because they appear unrealistic.

partures that fall above suggest the converse. It is extremely important to note that throughput time and conversion can not be varied independently and one is readily calculable from the other if V_{max} and K_m are invariant (Table 2). Thus, when an animal varies its throughput time, it also changes its conversion in a predictable fashion. We give the homeostasis solutions for three specified states characterized by widely different conversion efficiencies ($X_{Af} = 0.9, 0.5, 0.1$) achieved on the conditioning substrate concentration.

There is no explicit solution based only on gross digestive gains for either of the other two premises, since inspection of the equations for Tables 1 and 2 shows that rate maximization should drive throughput times (and conversions) toward zero, while efficiency maximization should push throughput times and conversions very high. Exactly how low or high will be determined by the associated costs, which remain unparameterized. If rate of digestive product formation is an important determinant of net mass or energy gain in a fitness context, however, and if short-term variations of food quality are frequent in the animal's natural environment, one would expect systematic departure downward from the homeostasis curves. If, alternatively, the amount of food (as opposed to the concentration of digestible substrate in it) has frequently been limiting in an organism's evolutionary history, one might expect conversion efficiency to remain high, even at those low food concentrations where both the homeostasis premise and the production-rate maximization premise predict decreased conversion in order to maintain or to increase, respectively, the rate of product formation.

Discussion and Conclusions

An immediate advantage of these very explicit models for digestion is that predictions are made in terms of measurable parameters. The models allow the idea of digestive homeostasis, for example, to be tested through the measurement of both conversion and throughput time. Without this explicit formulation the extent of conversion necessary to maintain digestive homeostasis with increasing food concentration would not be obvious. Likewise, it would not be apparent that increasing throughput times (decreasing feeding rate) with increasing food concentration produce greater rates of digestive conversion (mol s^{-1} cm^{-3} of gut), as long as the throughput times increase more slowly than the homeostasis solution curve. More obviously, Michaelis-Menten kinetics assure that unchanging throughput times with increasing food concentration result in increasing rates of digestive conversion.

We have eliminated those segments of the curves that require conversions above 0.99, because they are likely to be unattainable. Should we be wrong, the solutions are easily generated and visualized by extending the present curves. Since we are dealing with organisms of unspecified absolute size, we cannot similarly eliminate segments of the relative throughput time curves for requiring unrealistically fast throughput rates. At some low throughput time, diffusion of digestive products to absorptive surfaces will not have time to occur. Conversion will occur so long as our kinetic reaction description is accurate, but products will go out with the feces. The relevant diffusion times will depend upon absolute gut diameters and the geometries of absorptive sites, so we are unable to specify minimal retention times on the more general (relative retention-time) plots of Fig. 1.

Since we know of no deposit feeder which operates entirely as a CSTR, the degree to which the CSTR curve is the better (or worse) descriptor of a deposit feeder using a CSTR-PFR series will depend on the relative volume of the CSTR portion of its gut. Note also that the PFR will not receive a concentration of C_{A0} or C'_{A0}, but rather a concentration reduced by both mixing and digestive reaction in the CSTR portion of the gut. The curves might also suggest that CSTRs are the more flexible in situations of rapidly and widely varying food concentration, since the homeostasis solutions do not require as great a range of either conversion or relative throughput time, and since the homeostasis is possible at lower concentrations in CSTRs as compared to PFRs or batch reactors. The reason is simple: Food concentration is reduced immediately to the gut average concentration by mixing. This seeming advantage in a homeostatic sense becomes a disadvantage under the rate-maximization premise, since at the same C_{A0} and total gut volume a PFR can outproduce a CSTR (Penry and Jumars, 1986).

We again emphasize that the solutions of Fig. 1 are for short-term experiments only. It is very likely, for example, that increasing substrate concentration will induce increased enzyme secretion, increasing V_{max}, and thus changing the homeostasis solution for longer time scales in a manner predictable from the equations of Table 2. Increasing V_{max} with time of exposure to high substrate concentrations (relative to K_m) seems more compatible, however, with the premise of maximizing rate of digestive conversion than with either of the other two premises. Further, such increase is compatible with field data collected to date (Stuart et al., 1985). With two of three species in the laboratory, Taghon and Jumars (1984) found slowing of feeding from initially high rates. Their results would be consistent with induction of enzyme secretion in these two species but not in the third.

An implicit assumption throughout is that the concentration of the limiting nutrient or energy source (or at least of some component well correlated with it) is being measured. For deposit feeders in particular and detritivores in general, either the rate of supply of assimilable nitrogen or the rate of supply of chemical energy can be limiting (Bowen, 1984). If one measures concentrations and conversions of non-limiting food substances in heterogeneous resources when making plots of the sort put forth in Fig. 1, the results may well be uninterpretable. Application of digestion theory emphasizes the need to identify the limiting resource, as pointed out amply in this book.

Lastly, we repeat (Penry and Jumars, 1986, 1987) the caution that digestion is only one phase of the problem of acquiring and utilizing energy and nutrients. Digestion is a phase that can now be attacked with explicit, mechanistic models to determine gross gains, to put useful constraints on the subsequent steps of absorption and assimilation and to balance against costs. There might, for example, be two alternate means of achieving net homeostasis via digestion, one (close to that we have shown in Fig. 1) with comparatively long throughput times balanced against low costs, and one with comparatively shorter throughput times (with higher gross formation rate of product) and consequently higher costs. If digestion is indeed an energetically cheap process (Kiørboe et al., 1985) and if little energy is needed to vary throughput times substantially in deposit feeders (Taghon, this volume), then there is good reason to suspect that of our three premises the idea of conversion-rate maximization is the most likely to be supported by experiment.

Unless an argument firmly grounded in Darwinian selection could be found to contradict it (Calow, 1982) for deposit feeders, we would favor the premise of digestive rate maximization as an a priori hypothesis, even if there were strong selective pressure for a constant rate of energy or nutrient supply for growth. If food concentration varies in nature from time to time for any given individual, then a much more reliable way (than digestive homeostasis) of assuring a constant energy or nutrient supply for growth is achievement of conversion in excess of immediate requirements—with absorption and transfer to a storage organ. The storage organ can then supply energy or nutrients at the required rate independent of short-term, external variation. Such arguments, however, can go on ad nauseam without any clear scientific benefit. We hope that, rather than fueling continuing debate, our explicit formulation in terms of measurable variables will be used experimentally to extinguish it.

Acknowledgements

This work was supported by contract N00014-84-C-0111 from the Office of Naval Research and by grant OCE-81-17397 from the National Science Foundation. Contribution number 1742 from the School of Oceanography, University of Washington

Literature Cited

Bailey, J.E., and D.F. Ollis. 1977. *Biochemical engineering fundamentals.* McGraw-Hill, N.Y.

Bowen, S.H. 1984. Detrital amino acids and the growth of *Sarotherodon mossambicus*–A reply to Dabrowski. *Acta Hydrochim. Hydrobiol.* 12: 55- 59.

Calow, P. 1982. Homeostasis and fitness. *Am. Nat.* 120: 416-419.

Cammen, L.M. 1980. Ingestion rate: an empirical model for aquatic deposit feeders and detritivores. *Oecologia* 44: 303-310.

Dales, R.P. 1955. Feeding and digestion in terebellid polychaetes. *J. Mar. Biol. Assoc. U.K.* 34: 55-79.

Dales, R.P. and J.S. Pell 1970. The nature of the peritrophic membrane in the gut of the terebellid polychaete *Neoamphitrite figulus. Comp. Biochem. Physiol.* 34: 819-826.

Froment, G.E. and K.B. Bischoff 1979. *Chemical reactor analysis and design.* Wiley, New York.

Jumars, P.A. and R.F.L. Self 1986. Gut-marker and gut-fullness methods for estimating field and laboratory effects of sediment transport on ingestion rates of deposit feeders. *J. Exp. Mar. Biol. Ecol.* 98: 293-310.

Kiørboe, T., F. Møhlenberg and K. Hamburger 1985. Bioenergetics of the planktonic copepod *Acartia tonsa*: relation between feeding, egg production and respiration, and composition of specific dynamic action. *Mar. Ecol. Prog. Ser.* 26: 85-97.

Levenspiel, O. 1972. *Chemical reaction engineering,* 2nd ed. Wiley, New York.

Miller, D.C. 1984. Mechanical post-capture selection by suspension- and deposit-feeding *Corophium*. *J. Exp. Mar. Biol. Ecol.* 82: 59-76.

Milton, K. 1981. Food choice and digestive strategies of two sympatric primate species. *Am. Nat.* 117: 496-505.

Penry, D.L. and P.A. Jumars 1986. Chemical reactor analysis and optimal digestion theory. *BioScience* 36: 310-315.

Penry, D.L. and P.A. Jumars 1987. Modeling animal guts as chemical reactors. *Am. Nat.* 129: 69-96.

Scheibling, R.E. 1981. Optimal foraging movements of *Oreaster reticulatus* (L.) (Echinodermata: Asteroidea). *J. Exp. Mar. Biol. Ecol.* 44: 67-83.

Shick, J.M., K.C. Edwards and J.H. Dearborn. 1981. Physiological ecology of the deposit-feeding sea star *Ctenodiscus crispatus*: Ciliated surfaces and animal-sediment interactions. *Mar. Ecol. Prog. Ser.* 5: 165-184.

Sibly, R.M. 1981. Strategies of digestion and defecation. In: C.R. Townsend and P. Calow (eds.), *Physiological ecology: An evolutionary approach to resource use*, pp. 109-139. Sinauer Associates, Sunderland, Massachusetts.

Smith, J.M. 1981. *Chemical engineering kinetics*, 3rd ed. McGraw-Hill, N.Y.

Stuart, V., E.J.H. Head and K.H. Mann 1985. Seasonal changes in the digestive enzyme levels of the amphipod *Corophium volutator* (Pallas) in relation to diet. *J. Exp. Mar. Biol. Ecol.* 88: 243-256.

Taghon, G.L. 1981. Beyond selection: optimal ingestion rate as a function of food value. *Am. Nat.* 118: 202-214.

Taghon, G.L. 1988. Modeling deposit feeding. In G.R. Lopez and G.L. Taghon, Ecology of marine deposit feeding. This volume.

Taghon, G.L. and P.A. Jumars 1984. Variable ingestion rate and its role in optimal foraging behavior of marine deposit feeders. *Ecology* 65: 5449- 558.

Troyer, K. 1984. Diet selection and digestion in *Iguana iguana*: the importance of age and nutrient requirements. *Oecologia* 61: 201-207.

Chapter 6

Time-Dependent Absorption in Deposit Feeders

Lars Kofoed[1], Valery Forbes[1], and Glenn Lopez[2]
Biology Institute[1], Odense University,
DK 5230 Odense M, Denmark, and Marine Sciences Research
Center[2], State University of New York, Stony Brook, NY 11794

Identifying the Problem

Deposit feeders obtain food from sediments consisting mostly of indigestible mineral grains. In order to procure the required energy and nutrients, these animals must process enormous quantities of sediment (Cammen 1980b). The necessarily rapid processing rates limit the amount of time material may remain in the gut. Many deposit feeders have gut residence times of 30 minutes or less. Juvenile *Streblospio benedicti* can have gut residence times as low as 4 minutes (T. Forbes, pers. com.). Since digestion is a time-dependent process, gut residence time is likely to control absorption of ingested food, particularly when the food is difficult to digest. While the amount of material absorbed will increase with increasing gut residence time, it is likely to do so at a reducing rate (Sibly and Calow 1986). Therefore there will be a tradeoff between the efficiency and speed of digestion.

Determining the specific components of the sedimentary food matrix that are the most critical to deposit feeder nutrition has been the focus of much research in this field (Lopez and Levinton 1987). It is becoming evident that deposit feeders most likely utilize a suite of food types depending on availability and on their immediate dietary needs. A variety of foods of widely differing digestibility are ingested simultaneously; there is evidence that easily digested bacteria provide most of the protein, while less readily digestible detritus is the primary energy source (Cammen 1980a; see Rice and Rhoads; Mayer, this volume). Understanding the food resources of deposit feeders is essential to interpreting their morphologies, life history strategies, and population dynamics. Additionally, characterization of the food resources and investigation of digestive functioning in this group of animals are critical to the development of foraging theory and to an understanding of biologically mediated sedimentary processes.

Defining the Model

Dietary components can be defined and categorized in a variety of ways (i.e. C:N, percent protein, caloric content, etc.). A simple and straightforward means of characterizing given food types is in terms of their digestibility. Digestion is a time-dependent process, and the digestibility of a food can thus be described by a rate constant. Since we are interested primarily in that fraction of the ingested food that is absorbed across the gut wall (ingested - feces), we can define an absorption rate constant, K_a, which has the units of time^{-1}. K_a describes the digestive environment for a particular food. It will be a function of the species and temperature. Absorption efficiency will be determined by the K_a of the food as well as by the amount of time that material remains in the gut. Gut residence time, in turn, is inversely related to ingestion rate and positively related to gut volume.

If gut volume is constant, the change in concentration of food in the gut is a function of ingestion, egestion, and absorption such that:

$$\text{change in concentration} = \text{ingestion - egestion - absorption}$$

or

$$dC/dt = (I/V)C_0 - (I/V)C - K_aC. \tag{6.1}$$

C = concentration of food in the gut (mass vol^{-1})
C_0 = concentration of food in ingested material (mass vol^{-1})
I = volumetric feeding rate (vol time^{-1})
V = gut volume (vol)
K_a = absorption rate constant (time^{-1})

At steady state, $dC/dt = 0$ and $C = C_{eq}$, thus

$$C_{eq} = (C_0 I/V)/(K_a + I/V)$$

Absorption efficiency as a proportion can be expressed by

$$A = (C_0 - C_{eq})/C_0$$

and by substituting C_{eq} from above and rearranging

$$A = K_a/(K_a + I/V) \qquad (6.2)$$

Gut turnover time, T, is inversely related to ingestion rate such that

$$T = 1/(I/V)$$

Substituting for I/V in equation 2, above, gives

$$A = K_a/(K_a + 1/T) \qquad (6.3)$$

From equation 6.3, it can be shown that at very low gut turnover times, absorption efficiency will be nearly proportional to the amount of time available for digestion (1st order). As gut turnover time increases, absorption efficiency will approach its maximum value and will be nearly independent of gut turnover time (0 order). This type of relationship between gut turnover time and absorption efficiency (eqn. 6.3) is graphically represented by a rectangular hyperbola (Fig. 6.1). If maximum absorption efficiency is taken as 1 (100%), then at 50% absorption ($A = 0.5$), $T = 1/K_a$.

Equation 6.3 defines absorption efficiency of a food in terms of its absorption rate constant and gut residence time. Both of these variables are particular to a given species of deposit feeder. The novelty of this approach is that the animal itself is used to characterize the digestibility of the components of its diet. In addition, K_a can be measured ontogenetically to investigate potential shifts in the digestive environment as an animal grows. The utility of this model is that K_a can be measured directly from a curve relating absorption efficiency to gut turnover time. By necessity, gut turnover is the independent variable and successful estimation of K_a lies in the ability to manipulate gut turnover without introducing substantial artifacts. We know that gut residence time varies with animal size (see T. Forbes, this volume), physiological state (i.e. starvation, Calow 1975b; see below), and sediment type (see below). We have begun with these manipulations in our first tests of absorption rate constants.

Experimental Protocol

Ingestion, absorption, and gut residence time were measured by one of two methods as follows:

A) In the first technique, food items were homogeneously labeled by culturing them in the presence of ^{14}C (i.e. $^{14}CO_2$ for barley hay, $H^{14}CO_3$ for diatoms, ^{14}C-glucose for bacteria) (Kofoed 1975a,b). The labeled food was collected on a filter upon which animals were allowed to feed for a time period short enough to insure no loss of label in the feces. The fate of the labeled food was traced by placing animals in respiration chambers and collecting ^{14}C given off as CO_2, DOC, and POC (see Kofoed 1975a,b for details). Thus

$$^{14}C_{ingested} = {}^{14}C_{animals} + {}^{14}C_{feces} + {}^{14}C_{dissolved} + {}^{14}C_{gas}$$

and

$$\text{Absorption Efficiency} = ({}^{14}C_{ingested} - {}^{14}C_{feces})/{}^{14}C_{ingested}$$

Gut turnover time (T) was estimated by measuring the recovery of ^{14}C in the feces at appropriate intervals until complete emptiness of the gut could be assumed. Percent ^{14}C remaining in the animals over time was calculated by the difference between total ^{14}C recovered in the feces $(= 100\%)$ and the cumulative recovery of ^{14}C summed for each time interval. Logarithmic transformation of the residue curve indicated the number of compartments involved and allowed calculation of $T_{1/2}$ $(=\ln_2 T)$ (see below).

B) In the second method, (Calow and Fletcher 1972; Lopez and Crenshaw 1982), a potential food type was labeled with ^{14}C (i.e. ^{14}C-bicarbonate for microalgae, ^{14}C-formaldehyde for non-living organic matter, ^{14}C-amino acids for bacteria). The material was additionally labeled with ^{51}Cr which acts as an unabsorbed marker and is recovered in the feces. The absorption efficiency of a labeled food was measured by the change in the ratio of $^{14}C/^{51}Cr$ between ingested and defecated material:

$$\text{Absorption Efficiency} = [1 - (^{14}C/^{51}Cr_{\text{feces}})/(^{14}C/^{51}Cr_{\text{ing}})]$$

Ingestion rate as well as the isotope ratio of ingested material was measured in a group of animals sacrificed after a short ingestion period. The length of the ingestion period was chosen to be shorter in duration than the gut passage time of the animal. Feces were collected at periodic intervals from a parallel group of animals that were repeatedly transferred to unlabeled sediment after the ingestion period.

Gut turnover time of the two isotopes was estimated from the cumulative % recovery rates of unabsorbed isotope in the feces over time (as in method A). ^{51}Cr and ^{14}C may in some cases exhibit different recovery curves. At this time it is not known which of these provides the 'better' estimate of gut turnover, however, since ^{51}Cr labels the surfaces of all particles while ^{14}C labels only specific dietary components it is likely that ^{51}Cr will give a better estimate of total gut turnover. Also, since much of the ingested ^{14}C is absorbed, the loss rate of unabsorbed ^{14}C may not be as representative a measure of the passage of ingested material as ^{51}Cr. The pattern of egestion was measured by the change in radioactivity in an animal following a labeled meal. For an animal fed a labeled pulse of food and then transferred to a nonlabeled food, the egestion of radioisotope can be described by the exponential equation

$$A_t = A_0 e^{-\lambda t}. \tag{6.4}$$

A_0 = radioactivity at time zero
A_t = radioactivity at time t
t = time since ingestion
λ = loss rate constant ($= I/V$).

Since the isotope was not administered instantaneously, time since ingestion was estimated by adding half of the amount of time the animal fed on a labeled food to the amount of time since transfer to unlabeled food. For example, an animal fed 30 min on labeled food followed by transfer to unlabeled food for 60 min would have $t=15+60=75$ min. The half time for ingested material is given by

$$T_{1/2} = \ln 2/\lambda.$$

The shape of the isotope loss rate curve will indicate the number of compartments involved in the digestive process (Shipley and Clark 1972). If the cumulative loss rate of unabsorbed tracer is linearized by a logarithmic transformation of equation 6.4, the gut contents behave as a single compartment. Nonlinearity of the loss rate curve indicates a system behaving as two or more compartments which can be expressed by a series of exponential functions. Using a process called curve peeling or curve stripping (Shipley and Clark 1972; Cameron 1986) the separate exponential functions can be determined. For a two compartment system, such as that shown in Figure 6.2, the fraction of initial tracer present in pool 1 is

$$A_1/A_0 = Be^{-gt} + Ce^{-ht}$$

and that for pool 2 is

$$A_2/A_0 = De^{-gt} - De^{-ht}$$

The rate constants for each compartment are $k_{11} = Bg + Ch$ and $k_{22} = g+h-k_{11}$. The half-time for compartment 1 is $\ln 2/k_{11}$ and for compartment 2 is $\ln 2/k_{22}$ (corrected for half the ingestion period, see above). Since the turnover times for the individual compartments are additive, turnover times for separate compartments or for the system as a whole can be obtained for an individual or group and can be plotted against absorption efficiency measured in the same animal or group.

The relationship between gut turnover time and absorption given by equation 6.3 was tested by plotting $T_{1/2}/A$ vs. $T_{1/2}$. In theory, a line of slope $= 1$ and y-intercept $= 1/K_a$ would be expected if the above model were valid. Another means of testing

equation 6.3 is to plot $1/A$ vs. $1/T$ (or $T_{1/2}$). This double reciprocal plot is analogous to the Lineweaver-Burk transformation of the Michaelis-Menten rate equation for a one–substrate enzyme–catalyzed reaction, also a rectangular hyperbola (Lehninger 1975). A line of slope $1/K_a$ and y-intercept of 1 would be expected for a good fit of the data to the model.

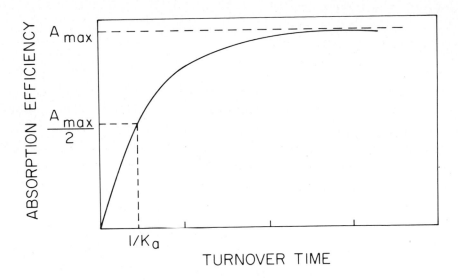

Figure 6.1: Model hyperbolic relationship between absorption efficiency and gut turnover time.

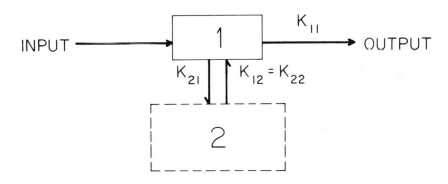

Figure 6.2: Diagram of 2 compartment system with input into compartment 1. K's are rate constants for each compartment.

Animal	Food	T°C	S(°/oo)	K_a
Littorina littorea	Ulva	20	20	.046
Littorina littorea	Enteromorpha	20	20	.046
Hydrobia ulvae	Bacteria	20	20	.036
Hydrobia ulvae	Diatoms	20	20	.023
Neoepisesarma versicolor	Barley Hay	30	35	.0013
Chiromanthes dussumieri	Barley Hay	30	35	.0013
Strongylocentrotus purpuratus	Ceramium	8	30	.0008

Table 6.1: K_a values obtained for different species on a variety of food types.

Such graphical transformations of equation 6.3 will determine the goodness of fit of the data to model curves, the reasonableness of estimates of K_a, and in effect whether the model offers an appropriate description of time–dependent digestive processes in deposit feeders.

Preliminary Results

1. Absorption rate constants obtained for a variety of species and food types are given in Table 6.1.

2. Comparison of time–dependent absorption of diatoms and bacteria by *Hydrobia ulvae* demonstrated more rapid saturation of the latter (Figure 6.3a). Linear transformation of the hyperbolic relationship yielded K_a values of 0.036 min^{-1} for bacteria and 0.023 min^{-1} for diatoms (Table 6.1 and Figure 6.3b).

3. Loss of ^{14}C from the gut of *Hydrobia ulvae* involved a single compartment when the labeled diet consisted of diatoms and two compartments when the labeled food was bacteria. Starvation following a labeled meal resulted in a decreased loss rate of ^{14}C (=increased $T_{1/2}$) for both food types compared to non-starved snails. When loss of ^{14}C

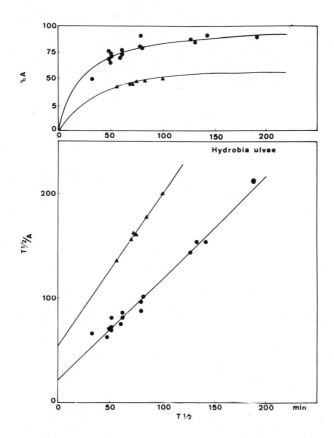

Figure 6.3: a) Absorption efficiency as a function of $T_{1/2}$ in *Hydrobia ulvae*. b) Linear transformation of hyperbolic equation. Y-intercept is equal to $1/K_a$. Circles are for bacteria, triangles are for diatoms.

Food		Starved	Not Starved
Diatoms	Compartment 1		
	Half-time	55	37
	Size	1	1
Bacteria	Compartment 1		
	Half-time	31	17
	Size	.80	.89
	Compartment 2		
	Half-time	515	77
	Size	.20	.11

Table 6.2: Compartment size and half-time (min) for *Hydrobia ulvae* fed continuously or starved following a labeled pulse of food.

occurred via two compartments (i.e. for bacteria), the relative size of the second compartment was larger when snails were starved following the labeled meal (Table 6.2).

4. Absorption efficiency of ^{14}C-labeled microalgae by *Hydrobia totteni* was found to be high and relatively constant (67-85%) over the range of gut turnover times measured. Analysis of loss rate curves of ^{51}Cr indicated that ingested material was partitioned into at least two compartments. Compartment 1 was observed to be fairly constant in size and had a mean half-time of 44 min. Compartment 2 was generally larger in size than compartment 1 and demonstrated much greater variability in size. Mean half-time for compartment 2 was 5 hours. Since input to the system was into the first compartment, and since turnover times for compartment 1 were much shorter than compartment 2, turnover time of compartment 1 would be the more likely of the two to impose a time constraint upon absorption.

5. For *Hydrobia totteni*, the effects of starvation prior to or following a labeled pulse of food were as follows:

(a) Absorption efficiency: For snails feeding on sand, starvation preceding a labeled meal had no effect on absorption efficiency. For animals feeding on silt-clay, the effect of starvation prior to a labeled meal was to decrease absorption efficiency (Kruskal-Wallis test, $P=0.05$).

		Starved Before	Starved After	Not Starved
Sand	% Absorption	77.5(2.4)	69.2(7.7)	79.5(2.8)
	Compartment 1			
	Half-Time	28	110	33
	Size	.14	.35	.20
	Compartment 2			
	Half-Time	141	1519	118
	Size	.86	.65	.80
Silt-Clay	% Absorption	74.0(1.8)	65.3(11.5)	81.4(1.3)
	Compartment 1			
	Half-Time	60	60	58
	Size	.39	.33	.33
	Compartment 2			
	Half-Time	107	143	135
	Size	.61	.67	.67

Table 6.3: Absorption efficiency (N=3; mean (s.d.)), compartment size, and half-time (min.) for *Hydrobia totteni* fed labeled diatoms. Snails were continuously fed, starved prior to, or starved following the labeled pulse of food. Substrate consisted of either the sand or silt-clay fraction of sediment.

Absorption efficiency of microalgae from both sediment types was significantly decreased if starvation occurred following a labeled meal (P = 0.05, Table 6.3).

(b) $T_{1/2}$ of compartment 1: On sand, the loss rate of ^{51}Cr from compartment 1 was more rapid when starvation occurred before a labeled meal and slower when starvation occurred after a labeled meal compared to snails that were not starved. On silt-clay, loss of ^{51}Cr from compartment 1 was slower whether starvation occurred prior to or following a meal, compared to non-starved snails (Table 6.3).

(c) $T_{1/2}$ of compartment 2: On sand, the loss rate of ^{51}Cr from compartment 2 was slower when starvation occurred prior to or following a labeled meal. On silt-clay, the loss rate of ^{51}Cr from compartment 2 was more rapid when starvation occurred prior to a meal, but decreased with starvation following a labeled meal (Table 6.3).

	SC-SC	SC-SA	SA-SA	SA-SC
% Absorption	77.3(3.2)	80.9(1.3)	65.6(3.2)	85.9(1.1)
Compartment 1				
Half-Time	17	37	49	22
Size	.12	.15	.12	.07
Compartment 2				
Half-Time	71	252	522	216
Size	.88	.85	.88	.93

Table 6.4: Effect of changing sediment particle size on absorption efficiency (N = 3; mean(s.d.)), compartment size, and half-time (min.) in *Hydrobia totteni*. SC-SA=Labeled food on silt-clay, transferred for egestion period to unlabeled sand, etc.

(d) Compartment size: Starvation prior to a labeled meal was associated with a decrease in the relative size of compartment 1 for sand and an increase in the relative size of compartment 1 for silt-clay. Starvation following a labeled meal resulted in an increase in the relative size of compartment 1 for snails feeding on sand and had no effect on relative compartment size for snails feeding on silt-clay (Table 6.3).

6. The effects of changing sediment type between the ingestion and egestion periods were as follows:

(a) Transfer from silt-clay to sand did not significantly affect absorption efficiency but resulted in an increase in the half-time of both compartments and an increase in the relative size of compartment 1 compared to snails transferred from silt–clay to silt–clay (Table 6.4).

(b) Transfer from sand to silt-clay resulted in an increase in absorption efficiency (Kruskal-Wallis, P = 0.05), a decrease in the half-time of both compartments, and a decrease in the relative size of compartment 1 compared to snails transferred from sand to sand (Table 6.4).

7. There was a positive relationship between the chl-a content of offered sediment (μg chl-a mg^{-1} dry sediment) and chl-a ingestion rate chl-a ingested hr^{-1}) by *Hydrobia totteni*. This was true for both sand (r=.604, N=21, P < 0.01) and silt-clay (r=0.663, N=21, P < 0.01)

(Figure 6.4).

Discussion and Implications

Since it is technically more feasible to artificially lengthen gut turnover time than shorten it, adult deposit feeders may not readily provide information on the first order portion of the absorption-time curve. In other words, as a result of natural selection, gut turnover rate may be under tight control. The inability to shorten gut residence time may prove the strongest test for the importance of gut turnover rate to deposit feeder physiology. If this is the case, observations on juveniles and starved individuals may be especially significant since they may exhibit gut turnover times shorter than required for saturation. Another method of artificially shortening gut residence might consist of 'tail ablation' (D. Carey, pers. comm.). While this method would not be appropriate for all types of deposit feeders, some animals (i.e. maldanid polychaetes and enteropneusts) are known to lose and regenerate posterior segments in nature and thus might be amenable to this technique.

Rapid saturation of absorption is likely to occur with certain food types that are digested and absorbed easily, such as bacteria and some diatoms. For these food groups, absorption efficiency should not change very much over a wide range of gut turnover times. Absorption efficiency of diatoms by *H. totteni* was found to be nearly independent of turnover time over the range of times measured. Rapid saturation of absorption efficiency suggests that the rate of absorption of such easily digested foods is limited by constraints on ingestion rate rather than by the amount of time spent in the gut. Forbes and Lopez (1986) found no change in pellet production rate with increasing sediment chlorophyll-a content, but Figure 4 (above) shows a positive relationship between sediment chl-a content and chl-a ingestion rate for this species. This implies that sediment processing rate may be inflexible, and that ingestion rate (and hence absorption) of digestible material by this species will be limited by the nutritional content of the sediment.

For animals that simultaneously ingest foods of widely varying digestibility, compartmentalization of the digestive tract may provide an effective mechanism for efficient digestion of the ingested mixture. Utilization of several dietary components can be optimized independently by subjecting each to different periods and types of digestion (Sibly and Calow 1986).

Many deposit feeders, mollusks in particular, have complex digestive tracts which allow partitioning of food particles within the gut. Relatively indigestible material passes quickly to the intestine while more nutritious matter is diverted to the digestive gland where it undergoes intracellular digestion (Calow 1975; Purchon 1977; Bricelj, et al. 1984). Calow (1975) analyzed the defecation pattern of ^{51}Cr-labeled food in the gastropods, *Ancylus fluviatilis*, primarily an algal feeder, and *Planorbis contortus*, a detritivore. Isotope loss indicated a three–compartment system in which the initial rapid phase represented emptying of the gizzard-stomach complex; the second less rapid phase represented loss from the digestive gland; the third and slowest phase represented caecal string production (=excretion). Additionally, the rates of loss varied with the nutritional state of the animal such that loss rate from the digestive gland decreased with starvation either prior to or following the labeled meal.

Using curves of the loss rate of unabsorbed ^{51}Cr, the digestive system of *Hydrobia totteni* could be partitioned into at least two compartments. Based on Calow's (1975) results (above) and on analysis of fecal samples produced by *H. totteni*, compartment 1 was hypothesized to represent material subjected to extracellular digestion which is transported directly to the intestine. Compartment 2 was considered to consist of material diverted to the digestive gland for intracellular digestion. This type of two–compartment system is diagrammatically represented by Figure 6.2. In comparison to Calow's (1975) results, starvation following a labeled meal resulted in a decrease in the turnover rate of both intestinal and digestive gland material. The effect of starvation prior to a labeled meal on turnover rate of ingested material was more complex, however, and seemed to be sediment specific. The proportion of material diverted to the digestive gland was generally larger for snails fed sand compared to snails fed silt-clay. This may indicate that intracellular digestion becomes relatively more important as particle size increases and *Hydrobia* switches from deposit feeding to browsing modes of feeding.

By studying time–dependent feeding and digestion processes, it may be possible to determine the relevant constraints on foraging behavior in order to discern whether these behaviors comprise coherent foraging strategies (Taghon et al. 1978; Taghon 1981; Phillips 1984). Analysis of digestive functioning can be utilized to investigate the physiological energetics of deposit feeders and to predict growth and feeding rates under varying conditions by extension of the above model to include a cost term. Gross absorption rate (GRA) is the product of ingestion rate and absorption efficiency.

$$GRA = IC_0A$$

Gross absorption rate is positively related to ingestion rate (and therefore inversely related to turnover time). However, increasing energetic costs accompany an increase in the rate of food intake, and as discussed above, the efficiency of absorption will decrease with increasing ingestion as well. For these reasons net absorption rate is expected to show a maximum at intermediate levels of gut turnover. Net growth is a function of absorption rate minus the cost of metabolism (independent of feeding rate) minus the feeding-rate-dependent cost of feeding such that

$$G/B = (IC_0/B)[K_a/(K_a + 1/T)] - M/B - LI/B \qquad (6.5)$$

where
G = growth rate (mass/time)
B = body carbon content (or tissue dry wt) (mass)
M = rate-dependent cost of metabolism (mass/time)
L = feeding-rate-dependent cost of feeding (mass/vol)

The concentration of food in the ingested material is defined as

$$C_0 = k_1B/V,$$

the ingestion rate given as
$$I = k_2V/t$$

(where t is not turnover time, but real time), and the rate-dependent cost of feeding as
$$L = k_3B/V$$

where k_1, k_2, and k_3 are proportionality constants, with $k_2/t = I/V = 1/T$. By substitution, we obtain

$$G/B = k_2k_1/t[K_a/(K_a + 1/T)] - M/B - k_2k_3/t.$$

$$G/B = [(C_0V/B)/T]/[(K_a + 1/T)/K_a] - M/B - LV/BT.$$

$$G/B = (C_0V/B)/(T + 1/K_a) - LV/BT - M/B \qquad (6.6)$$

which predicts growth rate as a function of feeding rate, concentration of sedimentary food, and food quality. Predictions based on the extended model can be demonstrated by substituting appropriate values for the model parameters. As an example, let $M/B = 1\%$ day^{-1}, $K_a = .03$ min^{-1}, and $B = 500$ μg carbon. Set gut volume, V, equivalent to 100 μg sediment and $L = 5.25 \times 10^{-4}$ μg carbon/μg sediment (or $LV/BT = 0.5\%$ day^{-1} at $T = 30$ min). Simulation of the model leads to the following predictions:

1. For a given feeding rate and food type (i.e. K_a), growth rate will increase with increasing food concentration (Figure 6.5).

2. Based on fitness arguments, optimum feeding rate can be defined as that which maximizes growth. For a given food concentration, maximum growth rate occurs at intermediate rates of feeding. Optimum feeding rate will increase with increasing food concentration (Figure 6.5).

3. If cost and benefit sides of equation 6.6 are set equal, lines of zero growth can be generated for foods of differing quality (Figure 6.6). Optimum feeding rate is given by the minima of the isogrowths. As the quality of food increases, the minimum food concentration needed to maintain a given growth rate decreases and optimum feeding rate increases.

The discussion above emphasizes the importance of distinguishing food quality from food quantity. While the direction of the feeding rate response to changes in both of these parameters may be the same, the magnitude of the response may differ. Using this formulation, feeding rate predictions can be made for various combinations of food quality and quantity. Once k_a values have been calculated for individual food types, the model can be expanded to incorporate mixtures of foods of varying digestibility and relative concentration. One advantage of this approach is that all of the relevant variables, namely growth rate, feeding rate, and concentration and type of food in the sediment, are measurable parameters, thus the predictions of the model can be rigorously tested.

It has been suggested that deposit feeders obtain different components of the diet from different food sources, for example calories from detritus and protein from bacteria (Rice, et al., 1986). Are ingestion rate and gut turnover time adjusted to maximize the absorption of one food type, or do they vary with the mixture or the immediate dietary needs of the animal? Do animals sort material in the gut to optimize absorption of each component in

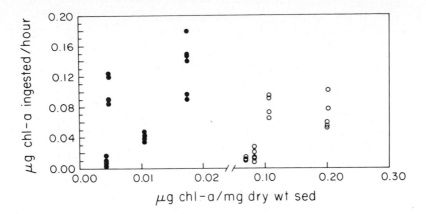

Figure 6.4: Chlorophyll-*a* ingestion rate by *H. totteni* as a function of sedimentary chl-*a* concentration. Filled circles represent sand and open circles represent silt-clay.

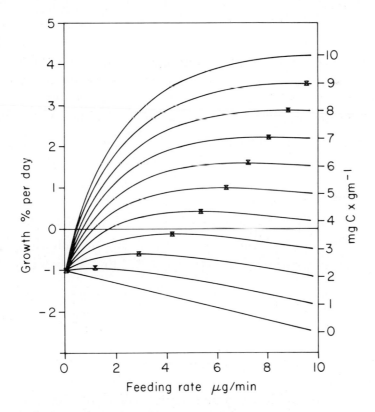

Figure 6.5: Optimal yield model. Growth rate as a function of feeding rate and food concentration. K_a, B, V, M, and L are given (see text).

146

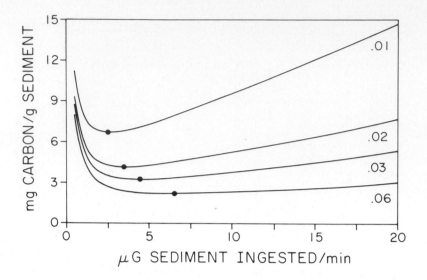

Figure 6.6: Zero-growth curves for variable quality foods (K_a = 0.01, 0.02, 0.03, 0.06) as a function of feeding rate and food concentration.

the mixture? Study of the digestive course of material is likely to reveal long awaited information regarding the nature of the sedimentary food sources of deposit feeders. Detailed analysis of the time–dependent processes of digestion and absorption will provide a framework within which studies of foraging behavior can be meaningfully applied.

Summary

1. Digestion is a time-dependent process, and due to high sediment processing rates, gut turnover time is likely to limit digestion in deposit feeders.

2. Absorption rate constants can be used to characterize the food sources of deposit feeders. Determination of these constants relies on the ability to manipulate gut turnover time.

3. Characterization of digestive functioning in deposit feeders, in terms of absorption rate constants, is critical to an understanding of bioenergetics and energy allocation patterns (and associated ontogenetic shifts), and to the development of appropriate foraging models.

4. The next step is to attempt manipulations of gut turnover time with concurrent measurements of absorption efficiency for a variety of foods and deposit-feeding species. In addition to estimates of absorption rate constants, measurements of physiological cost (both metabolic and feeding-rate-dependent) are needed to fully test any digestion model.

Acknowledgements

We thank D. Carey, T. Forbes, J. Levinton, D. Rice, and G. Taghon for stimulating discussions and critical comments on these ideas. Facilities for this work were provided by Odense University, Denmark and State University of New York at Stony Brook. This research was partially supported by NSF grant OCE8711619. This is contribution 628 from the Marine Sciences Research Center, SUNY Stony Brook.

Literature Cited

Bricelj, V. M., A. E. Bass, and G. R. Lopez. 1984. Absorption and gut passage time of microalgae in a suspension feeder: an evaluation of the ^{51}Cr:^{14}C twin tracer technique. *Mar. Ecol. Prog. Ser.* 17: 57-63.

Calow, P. 1975. Defaecation strategies of two freshwater gastropods, *Ancylus fluviatilis* Mull. and *Planorbis contortus* Linn. (Pulmonata) with a comparison of field and laboratory estimates of food absorption rate. *Oecologia* (Berl.), 20: 51-63.

Calow, P. and C. R. Fletcher. 1972. A new radiotracer technique involving ^{14}C and ^{51}Cr for estimating the assimilation efficiency of aquatic primary producers. *Oecologia* (Berl.), 9: 155-170.

Cameron, J. N. 1986. *Principles of Physiological Measurement.* Academic Press, New York.

Cammen, L. M. 1980a. The significance of microbial carbon in the nutrition of the deposit feeding polychaete *Nereis succinea*. *Mar. Biol.*, 61: 9-20.

Cammen, L. M. 1980b. Ingestion rate: an empirical model for aquatic deposit feeders and detritivores. *Oecologia* (Berl.), 44: 303-310.

148

Forbes, V. E. and G. R. Lopez. 1986. Changes in feeding and crawling rates of *Hydrobia truncata* (Prosobranchia: Hydrobiidae) in response to sedimentary chlorophyll-*a* and recently egested sediment. *Mar. Ecol. Prog. Ser.* 33: 287-294.

Kofoed, L. H. 1975a. The feeding biology of *Hydrobia ventrosa* (Montague). I. The assimilation of different components of food. *J. Exp. Mar. Biol. Ecol.* 19: 233-241.

Kofoed, L. H. 1975b. The feeding biology of *Hydrobia ventrosa* (Montague). II. Allocation of the components of the carbon budget and the significance of the secretion of dissolved organic material. *J. Exp. Mar. Biol. Ecol.* 19:

Lehninger, A. L. 1975. *Biochemistry*, 2nd ed. Worth Publishers Inc. New York.

Lopez, G. R. and J. S. Levinton. 1987. Ecology of deposit-feeding animals in marine sediments. *Quart. Rev. Biol.*, 62: 235-260.

Lopez, G. R. and M. A. Crenshaw. 1982. Radiolabelling of sedimentary organic matter with ^{14}C-formaldehyde: preliminary evaluation of a new technique for use in deposit-feeding studies. *Mar. Ecol. Prog. Ser.*, 8: 283-289.

Phillips, N.W. 1984. Compensatory intake can be consistent with an optimal foraging model. *Am. Nat.* 123: 867-872.

Purchon, R. D. 1977. *The Biology of the Mollusca*, 2nd ed. Pergamon Press, Oxford.

Rice, D. L., T. S. Bianchi, and E. H. Roper. 1986. Experimental studies of sediment reworking and growth of *Scoloplos* spp. (Orbiniidae: Polychaeta). *Mar. Ecol. Prog. Ser.* 30: 9-19.

Shipley, R. A. and R. E. Clark. 1972. *Tracer Methods for In Vivo Kinetics*. Academic Press, New York.

Sibly, R. M. and P. Calow. 1986. *Physiological Ecology of Animals: An Evolutionary Approach*. Blackwell Scientific Publications, London.

Taghon, G. L. 1981. Beyond selection: optimal ingestion rate as a function of food value. *Am. Nat.*, 118: 202-214.

Taghon, G. L., R. F. L. Self, and P. A. Jumars. 1978. Predicting particle selection by deposit feeders: a model and predictions. *Limnol. Oceanogr.*, 23: 752-759.

Chapter 7

Radiotracer Methods For Determining Utilization of Sedimentary Organic Matter by Deposit Feeders

Glenn Lopez, Pitiwong Tantichodok, and I-Jiunn Cheng
Marine Sciences Research Center
State University of New York
Stony Brook, New York 11794

Introduction

The purposes of this chapter are to evaluate methods to measure ingestion and absorption by deposit feeders of sedimentary organic matter, to consider the assumptions underlying these methods, and to recommend approaches to develop better methods. Deposit feeders acquire food by ingesting large volumes of sediment and absorbing some fraction of the organic matter. Particle-associated microorganisms are generally absorbed well but are not abundant enough in sediment to account for very much of the absorbed organic matter (Cammen, 1980a and this volume; Lopez and Levinton 1987).

Deposit feeders are therefore digesting and absorbing some fraction of the detrital sedimentary organic matter. The refractory nature of much of the sedimentary organic matter results in low absorption efficiency. Gravimetric and chemical methods of estimating organic absorption reach their limits of resolution at the lower range of absorption; it is very difficult to distinguish 5% from 0% absorption, although it is obviously of great consequence to the animal. The difficulty in accurately measuring organic absorption by deposit feeders is compounded by selective ingestion of the organic fraction of sediment. Therefore the study of the utilization of sedimentary organic matter by deposit feeders should include methods for accurately determining absorption efficiency and ingestion selectivity.

Calow and Fletcher (1972) discussed gravimetric, indicator, and radio-tracer methods available for estimating assimilation efficiencies. They noted that a major advantage of radiotracer methods is that they do not require the implicit assumption of gravimetric and indicator methods that all material in feces is derived from food. This assumption may not generally hold for deposit feeders because secreted mucus may enrich considerably the organic content of egested sediment.

Gravimetric Methods

The most direct way to estimate absorption of some dietary component is to compare the amount of that component that was ingested during a given meal with the amount egested from that meal. Gravimetric methods are thus based on mass balance. This straightforward approach is used widely in the study of animals that feed on discrete food items that can be enumerated or weighed easily. Unfortunately, the method is not readily applicable to the study of deposit feeders because it is generally difficult to measure the amount ingested because they are not feeding on easily counted food items.

Indicator Methods

The basic approach of an indicator method is to measure the change upon gut passage of an assimilated component of food relative to a nonassimilated component. Because indicator methods are based on measuring the change in a ratio, they do not require a mass budget. Ivlev (1939) estimated organic assimilation by *Tubifex* by measuring the ratio of organic matter to added platinum black in sediment and feces. Tande and Slagsted (1985) used the ^{14}C:silica ratio of labelled diatoms to investigate assimilation by a copepod.

Conover (1966) developed a simple and elegant method to estimate organic assimilation, calculated as:

$$U = 100[(F - E)/(1 - E)F]$$

where U is assimilation efficiency, F is fraction (ash-free dry weight/dry weight) of organic matter in ingested food, and E is the organic fraction in a representative feces sample.

This "ash ratio" method is the most widely used indicator method in the study of assimilation of organic matter by aquatic animals. One of its main virtues is that natural foods such as seston and sediment can be used. This method is based on the assumption that the mineral fraction passes unassimilated through the gut, and was developed "primarily for use with natural foods containing a large proportion of ash in insoluble form" (Conover, et al., 1986). Because the diet of deposit feeders is defined by its high proportion of insoluble ash (the mineral particles of sediment), it is safe to assume that the mineral fraction of the ingested sediment passes unaltered through the digestive tract.

The ash ratio method requires the measurement of organic content of ingested food and feces. Because deposit feeders have high feeding rates, it is generally a simple task to collect enough fecal pellets for analysis, but the small size of most deposit feeders precludes collection of ingested material. Conover (1966) faced a similar difficulty in applying the method to herbivorous zooplankton, and found it necessary to assume that there was no particle selection by organic content, so that F, the organic content of ingested food, is equal to the organic content of the available food. Given this assumption, organic assimilation can be estimated from measuring weight loss upon ashing in representative samples of the uneaten food and feces, but "if particulate matter was selected on the basis of its organic content, a serious error would be introduced into the calculation of assimilation" (Conover, 1966).

The sources of organic matter in a fecal pellet are the nonassimilated organic fraction of the ingested sediment and metabolic losses from the animal (mucus, sloughed cells, etc.). Because an animal cannot continually be losing more organic matter than it is absorbing, production of organically enriched pellets is indicative of selective ingestion. Because many deposit feeders produce fecal pellets that are slightly enriched in organic matter relative to the available sediment (Cammen, 1980b), a primary requirement for applying the ash ratio method to the study of organic assimilation by deposit feeders is an accurate estimation of ingestion selectivity of organic matter. This has proven to be a difficult problem.

This problem has been neatly solved in the study of suspension-feeding bivalves, many of which are capable of sorting and rejecting the organic-poor fraction from filtered seston (Kiørboe and Møhlenberg, 1981; Newell and Jordan, 1983; Bricelj and Malouf, 1984). For those animals that produce separable pseudofeces, the ash ratio method can be applied because the organic fraction of the ingested material can be calculated from the organic fractions of the total seston and pseudofeces (Bricelj and Malouf, 1984). Unfortunately, most deposit feeders do not produce pseudofeces that can be distinguished and separated from the uneaten sediment.

Radiotracer Methods

Another major approach to the study of assimilation of natural foods by deposit feeders is through the use of radioactive tracers. Radiotracer techniques can greatly improve sensitivity in measuring absorption in small animals, but generally suffer in that food particles must be handled during labelling (Conover, et al. 1986). ^{14}C labelling of food allows measurement of absorption and allocation of the absorbed food (e.g. Kofoed, 1975a,b). Radiotracer techniques have been successfully applied to the study of absorption of sedimentary microalgae and bacteria by deposit feeders, because microbes can be specifically labelled with appropriate metabolic substrates (Kofoed, 1975a,b; Cammen, 1980a; Lopez and Cheng, 1983).

Radiotracer methods have also been applied to specific components of sedimentary organic matter. Some compounds, such as cellulose and lignin, are commercially available in radioactive form (Hargrave, 1970; Foulds and Mann, 1978). Synthetic detritus can be prepared by growing plants in a labelled medium. After harvesting, this labelled plant material can be subjected to microbial decay, chemical fractionation, etc., to produce a variety of complex organic substrates labelled for feeding studies (e.g. Tenore and Hanson, 1980; Kemp, 1986). These methods have the advantage of allowing investigation of availability of particular types of organic substrates, or differential use of detritus from different sources (Tenore and Hanson, 1980). Potential foods can be uniformly labelled, which is a critical assumption in the use of radiotracers for absorption estimates, although preparing uniformly labelled vascular plants can be expensive and time-consuming. Two recently developed methods allow much more rapid labelling of plant detritus (Banks and Wolfinbarger, 1981; Wolfinbarger and Crosby, 1983).

A Radiotracer Indicator Technique: the ^{14}C:^{51}Cr Method

^{14}C-labelled foods can be additionally labeled by adsorption of ^{51}Cr, allowing estimation of ^{14}C absorption by the change in ^{14}C:^{51}Cr upon gut passage (Calow and Fletcher, 1972; Lopez and Cheng, 1983). Absorption efficiency is estimated as:

$$100x[1 - (^{14}C/^{51}Cr,\text{feces}/^{14}C/^{51}Cr,\text{ingested})].$$

Biological membranes are nearly impermeable to the trivalent form of chromium, so ^{51}Cr serves as an unabsorbed marker, a radioactive equivalent to the ash content in the ash ratio method. The ^{14}C:^{51}Cr dual tracer method combines the advantages of indicator methods (no quantitative sampling of feces) and radiotracer methods (no interference from carbon lost from animal). Like other radiotracer methods, the method suffers from the necessity of considerable particle handling during labelling.

Lopez and Cheng (1982, 1983) modified the dual tracer method to measure ingestion selectivity in addition to absorption efficiency. Selectivity measurements are based on comparison of the relative abundance of a particular food in the offered sediment with that ingested. To compute ingestion selectivity of organic matter, one must estimate the proportion of organic matter ingested relative to the total amount (inorganic + organic) of sediment ingested. Organic matter in sediment was labeled with ^{14}C-formaldehyde (Lopez and Crenshaw, 1982). (See below.) The amount of organic matter ingested was calculated by dividing ^{14}C ingested by the specific activity of the sedimentary organic matter, assuming that animals were not able to select organic matter by specific activity. The ^{51}Cr adsorbed to the sediment was used as to estimate the amount of inorganic matter ingested by dividing ^{51}Cr ingested by the ^{51}Cr/ash ratio in feces. Adsorbed ^{51}Cr does not in any sense "label" the inorganic fraction of sediment, but because neither Cr^{3+} nor the mineral fraction is absorbed upon gut passage, their ratio should not change after ingestion. In fact, most animals do absorb a small fraction of ingested Cr, but this is easily measured directly by gamma counting and thus can be taken into account.

Radiolabelling of Sedimentary Organic Matter

The ability to specifically label particular foods is usually a major advantage of radiotracer techniques in feeding studies, but it creates a difficult problem in developing a method to trace ingestion and absorption of natural sedimentary organic matter. This requires a radiotracer technique that is specific for organic matter in sediment, but nonspecific for different types of organic matter. ^{14}C-dimethyl sulfate has been used to label the various organic components of *Spartina* detritus, but it has not been applied to sedimentary organic matter (Wolfinbarger and Crosby, 1983; Crosby, 1985). We have examined the use of ^{14}C-formaldehyde to label sedimentary organic matter, initially choosing this compound because of its broad reactivity with a wide variety of functional groups (Lopez and Crenshaw, 1982). The goal was to develop a technique to tackle both of the critical problems described above, namely estimation of ingestion selectivity and absorption of sedimentary organic matter (Lopez and Crenshaw, 1982; Lopez and Cheng, 1983).

The two critical assumptions for the use of ^{14}C- formaldehyde (or any other) labelling technique to study ingestion of sedimentary organic matter deal with labelling specificity and selection by specific activity. The first (labelling specificity) assumes that ^{14}C activity is incorporated into the organic and not the inorganic fraction of the sediment after incubation with ^{14}C-formaldehyde. The second assumption states that animals do not select sedimentary organic matter by specific activity.

Lopez and Crenshaw (1982) demonstrated that uptake of ^{14}C- formaldehyde by sediment incubated in 30% NaCl was directly correlated to the organic content of the sediment. The concentrated NaCl solution reversibly inhibited microbial activity (Brock, 1978).

Removal of the organic fraction from sediments by ashing at 500°C reduced ^{14}C uptake to 2.2-6.4% of the control sediments (Lopez and Crenshaw, 1982). This suggests that most of the ^{14}C uptake was due to the organic fraction, but the prolonged high temperature of ashing may have altered the physical state of clay minerals and so reduce their adsorptive capacity. This problem has been investigated more recently by examining the effect of peroxide removal of organic matter on ^{14}C-formaldehyde uptake. Peroxide treatment is a standard procedure for preparing sediment samples for surface area analysis (i.e. DeFlaun and Mayer, 1983). Samples were heated only to 70-80°C, so mineral alteration did not occur. Peroxide treated sediment took up only 9.5% of the ^{14}C activity of non-treated sediment. This experiment probably overestimated ^{14}C uptake by adsorption to inorganic surfaces because removal of organic matter generally increases specific surface area of sediments (Sequi and Arenghieri, 1977; L. Mayer, pers. comm.). In this experiment, we determined that peroxide treatment doubled the specific surface area of the sediment. Peroxide treatment is not completely efficient in oxidizing sedimentary organic matter. Carbon content was reduced here from 2.57% C to 0.45%, so 17.5% of the organic carbon survived peroxide treatment.

Our tentative conclusion based on these results is that most ^{14}C becomes associated with the organic and not the inorganic fraction of sediment following incubation with ^{14}C-formaldehyde. These experiments do not give any clue regarding the nature of the association of ^{14}C with sedimentary organic matter.

The second assumption required for ingestion measurements states that the specific activity of the labelled organic matter is preserved upon ingestion (dpm/mg C ingested = dpm/mg C in sediment). Montagna (1984) found it necessary to make a similar assumption to study utilization of sedimentary microbes by meiofauna. This assumption has not been tested.

The validity of using the ^{14}C-formaldehyde method to estimate absorption of sedimentary organic matter is based on the assumption that the organic matter is uniformly labelled. If this is the case, then animals cannot select by specific activity.

We present here a series of experiments conducted to characterize the association of ^{14}C with organic matter incubated with ^{14}C-formaldehyde, and to test the assumptions of preservation of specific activity and labelling uniformity.

Materials and Methods

Several experiments were conducted to examine the nature of the uptake and subsequent loss of ^{14}C from sediment labelled with ^{14}C-formaldehyde.

A. Uptake/Loss Experiments

Effect of incubation temperature on ^{14}C and ^{3}H uptake by sediment incubated with ^{14}C- and ^{3}H-formaldehyde.

Experiment 1:

Ten ml subsamples of a sediment suspension in 30% NaCl (approx. 50 mg x ml^{-1}) were dispensed into glass scintillation vials and preincubated at experimental temperatures (-20, 5, 9, 16, 24, 38, 62 and 85°C). Duplicate vials were prepared for each temperature. After the suspensions had equilibrated to the experimental temperatures, 0.125 μCi ^{14}C-formaldehyde (52 mCi/mmol, New England Nuclear) and 0.500 μCi ^{3}H-formaldehyde (85 mCi/mmol, New England Nuclear) were added to each vial. Samples were incubated for 41 hours, then the entire contents of each vial was filtered (24 mm Whatman GF/C). The filter was then rinsed 6 times with 10 ml distilled water to remove unincorporated isotopes. Samples were then prepared for scintillation counting by solubilization. Activities of ^{14}C and ^{3}H were estimated by dual channel counting. For all possible temperature intervals, the Q_{10} ($Q_{10} = (k_2/k_1)(10/t_2-t_1$) was calculated.

Experiment 2:

Several experimental trials were conducted to determine the susceptibility to loss of ^{14}C by rinsing of labelled sediment. In trial no. 1, sediment (4 gm) was incubated for 48 hr in 30% NaCl with 70 μCi ^{14}C-formaldehyde (52 mCi/mmol). A one ml subsample (approx. 150 mg sediment) was filtered onto a Nuclepore filter (0.2 μm, 25mm diameter) in a glass filtration apparatus. The filtered sample was then subjected to 50 sequential rinses of 1 ml distilled water. Filtrates were collected and prepared for liquid scintillation counting.

In trial no. 2, similarly labelled sediment, filtered onto a glass fiber filter (Whatman GF/A, 25 mm) was subjected to 32 sequential rinses of 5 ml distilled water. In all rinses except the 16th, the water was kept in the funnel for 1 minute before being pulled through the filter; that sample was allowed to incubate for one hour.

Trial no. 3 consisted of subjecting labelled sediment to a first rinse of 100 ml distilled water, followed by 4 sequential rinses of 50 ml.

Experiment 3: Net ^{14}C loss from ^{14}C-formaldehyde labelled sediment

This experiment was conducted to measure net loss under equilibrium conditions of ^{14}C from labelled sediment. A slurry of <63 μm sediment (2 ml settled sediment diluted with 15 ml 30% NaCl) was labelled with ^{14}C-formaldehyde (10 μCi) for 2 days at 38° C. Sediment was then centrifuged, rinsed twice with filtered seawater, then resuspended in either 30% NaCl or filtered seawater. Subsamples were taken every day for ten days by filtering subsamples onto weighed filters (Nuclepore, 0.2 μm).

Absorption Experiments

Several experiments were conducted to test the validity of the labelling specificity and uniformity assumptions of the ^{14}C- formaldehyde method applied to ingestion and absorption studies.

Experiment 4: Absorption of labelled algae and algal detritus.

We have conducted four trials comparing absorption of uniformly labelled and formaldehyde labelled algae and algal detritus by *Hydrobia totteni*, and three additional trials with *Mytilus edulis*. For the first *Hydrobia* trial, fresh algae was used. In trials no. 2 and no. 3, cultures were autoclaved before being offered to animals. In trial no. 4, autoclaved algae was inoculated with raw seawater and incubated for 7 days. In trials no. 5 and no. 6, *M. edulis* was fed autoclaved algae. Trial no. 7 used algae that had been autoclaved, inoculated with raw seawater, and incubated in the dark for 8 days. Uniformly labelled algae was prepared by growing an algal culture (*Isochrysis* sp., Tahitian strain) in a closed container for 7 days with 40 μCi ^{14}C bicarbonate x l^{-1}. Unlabelled but otherwise identical cultures were grown alongside the labelled cultures. Cells from both cultures were harvested by centrifugation.

Following the treatment for the given trials (autoclaving, etc.), the unlabelled culture was then labelled with ^{14}C-formaldehyde, and simultaneously both cultures were labelled by adsorption with ^{51}Cr, (Calow and Fletcher, 1972). Following a 48 hour labelling period and 2 centrifuge rinsings, algae was presented to animals. Filters were placed in small dishes containing filtered seawater. For the deposit-feeding gastropod *Hydrobia totteni*, algae was filtered onto Nuclepore filters (0.6 μm, 47 mm); these snails readily ingest algae from a filter surface (Kofoed, 1975a). For each treatment, 3 bowls of 15 animals each were used for estimating ingestion. Parallel groups were allowed to ingest labelled algae, then were transferred onto unlabelled algae. Fecal pellets were collected at 2, 4 and 8 hours after transfer. Absorption efficiencies were calculated by the modified ^{14}C:^{51}Cr technique (Lopez and Cheng, 1983).

Mytilus edulis were fed with labelled algae suspended with fresh algae (to induce feeding). After 30 minutes groups of animals were either sampled for ingestion or transferred to unlabelled suspensions for fecal collection at 1, 2, 4, 8, and 12 hours.

Experiment 5: Comparison of organic absorption estimates using the dual tracer (^{14}C-formaldehyde: ^{51}Cr) and the ash ratio techniques.

A series of 6 ingestion/absorption trials have been conducted with the protobranch bivalve *Nucula proxima*. A modified ^{14}C:^{51}Cr method was used to estimate absorption of sedimentary organic matter (Calow and Fletcher, 1972; Lopez and Cheng, 1983). Absorption was also estimated by a modified ash- ratio method, which was based on estimating the forage ratio, a measure of ingestion selectivity. Lopez and Cheng (1983) should be consulted for details of the methods.

The organic forage ratio (FR_{org}) is a measure of the enrichment of organic matter in ingested sediment relative to offered sediment. FR_{org} is calculated as r/p, where r = proportion by weight of organic matter in the ingested sediment, and p = proportion in the available sediment. Because selectivity is an attribute of ingestion, the validity of a selectivity estimate is based on the assumptions of labelling specificity and preservation of specific activity, but not on the labelling uniformity assumption. Assuming for the moment that specific activity is preserved, the amount of organic matter ingested is estimated by ^{14}C ingested/(^{14}C/organic matter in sediment). The amount of inorganic matter ingested is estimated by ^{51}Cr ingested/(^{51}Cr/inorganic matter in feces); this calculation is based on the assumption that neither inorganic matter in sediment nor ^{51}Cr is absorbed upon gut passage (Lopez and Cheng, 1983). The product of FR_{org} and the organic content of the sediment estimates the organic content of ingested sediment, which is difficult to measure directly. Given this and the measured organic content in feces, absorption of sedimentary organic matter can be estimated by the ash ratio method (Conover, 1966), corrected for selective ingestion.

Results

A. Uptake/Loss Experiments

Experiment 1: Effect of incubation temperature on ^{14}C and ^{3}H uptake by sediment incubated with ^{14}C- and ^{3}H- formaldehyde.

^{14}C and ^{3}H uptake by sediment incubated with ^{14}C and ^{3}H formaldehyde increased with increasing incubation temperature to a maximum at 62°C (Fig. 7.1). Patterns of temperature-dependent uptake were very similar for

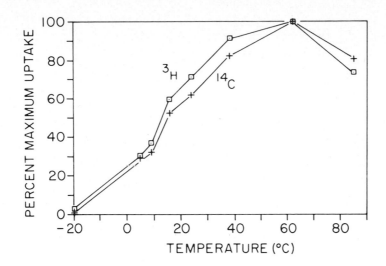

Figure 7.1: Effect of incubation temperature on uptake of ^{3}H- and ^{14}C-formaldehyde by sediment.

the two isotopes.

The matrix of Q_{10} values for all temperature intervals is shown graphically in Fig. 7.2. The Q_{10} of isotope uptake decreases with increasing temperature; this applies to either an increase in the lower or the upper limit of the temperature range. Q_{10} values ranged from a high of 2.56 (^{3}H, -20 to 5°C) to a low of 0.88 (^{3}H, 62 to 85°). At less extreme temperature ranges, most values were between 1.2 and 1.7.

Experiment 2: ^{14}C loss due to washing of ^{14}C- formaldehyde labelled sediment.

In trial no. 1, the amount of ^{14}C removed with each rinse was high for the first several rinses (undoubtedly unincorporated formaldehyde), followed by a steadily decreasing amount loss for each subsequent rinse (Fig. 7.3). Because the results are graphed on log-linear axes, the constant slope from the 6th to the 50th rinse indicates a constant fractional loss per rinse over this entire interval.

Similar results were obtained in trial no. 2, except for the effect of rinsing volume. The 16th rinse was incubated for 1 hour, demonstrating the effect of incubation time on fractional loss. Trial no. 3 corroborated the effect of rinsing volume.

Experiment 3: Net ^{14}C loss from ^{14}C-formaldehyde labelled sediment.

There was no net loss of adsorbed ^{14}C during the first 6 days (Fig. 7.4), and even after 8 days, over 90% of the ^{14}C was still particle-associated. Loss rates were similar in seawater and 30% NaCl, suggesting that microbial

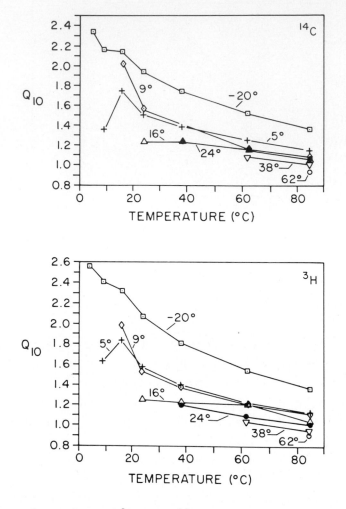

Figure 7.2: Q_{10} values of ^{3}H- and ^{14}C-formaldehyde uptake by sediment.

mineralization of formaldehyde was not a major cause of ^{14}C loss.

B. Absorption Experiments

Experiment 4: Absorption of uniformly labelled and ^{14}C- formaldehyde labelled algae and algal detritus.

The absorption efficiency of *Hydrobia totteni* feeding upon fresh *Isochrysis* was estimated at 75% with both ^{14}C labelling techniques (Table 1). In the other three absorption trials, the agreement between the two estimates was within 10%. Algae that had been autoclaved, which presumably resulted in loss of soluble material, was absorbed less efficiently than fresh algae.

Experiment	Absorption Efficiency	
	Uniform-^{14}C	Formaldehyde-^{14}C
Hydrobia totteni:		
1. Fresh algae	76.0	74.0
2. Autoclaved, sterile	48.8	40.1
3. Autoclaved, sterile	63.2	70.0
4. Expt. 3, nonsterile and aged 7 days	51.3	43.0
Mytilus edulis:		
5. Autoclaved, sterile	18.4	20.3
6. Autoclaved, sterile sterile	19.2	18.3
7. Autoclaved, nonsterile aged	26.1	28.2

Table 7.1: Comparison of absorption of uniformly labelled and formaldehyde labelled algae and algal detritus.

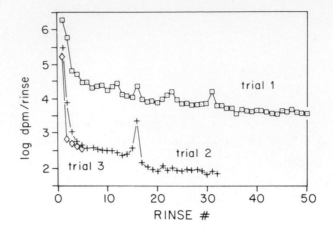

Figure 7.3: The effect of repeated rinsing of ^{14}C-formaldehyde labelled sediment on 14 removal.

In the three absorption trials using *Mytilus edulis*, absorption estimates using formaldehyde and uniform labelling were very similar.

Experiment 5: Comparison of organic absorption estimates using the dual tracer (^{14}C-formaldehyde: ^{51}Cr) and the ash ratio techniques.

Estimates of absorption of sedimentary organic matter by *Nucula proxima* ranged from -8.0% to 42.4% for the dual tracer method, and from 4.4 to 49.3% for the ash ratio method (Table 2). In 5 of the 6 trials, the ash ratio method gave the higher estimate. The agreement of the two estimates appeared to be better in those trials (2, 3, and 6) exhibiting higher absorption. FR_{org} ranged from 1.39 to 2.16, although none of the values were statistically different from 1.0. Nevertheless, the organic content of feces was always significantly higher then the sediment content. In trial 3, fecal organic content was anomolously high. An overestimate of fecal organic content would result in underestimating absorption by the ash ratio method.

Discussion

The results of experiment 1 corroborate an earlier experiment by Lopez and Crenshaw (1982). The rate of abiotic uptake of ^{14}C- and ^{3}H-formaldehyde by sediment is temperature dependent, with Q_{10} values for most intervals falling between 1.1 and 1.7. The decline in Q_{10} with increasing temperature may be due to the decreased solubility of formaldehyde as temperature is raised. Such values are too low for typical thermochemical reactions (Q_{10} of

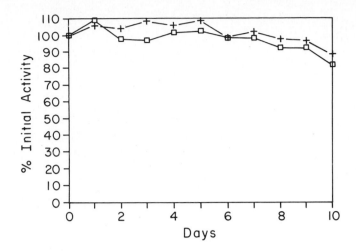

Figure 7.4: Net loss of ^{14}C from ^{14}C-formaldehyde labelled sediment. Following initial incubation in 30% NaCl, sediment was incubated in either filtered seawater or filtered 30% NaCl.

at least 2 is expected). They fall in the range typical for chemisorption.

Experiment 2 demonstrated that there was a constant percentage of ^{14}C lost during sequential rinsing of ^{14}C-formaldehyde labelled sediment. Thus, most of the sediment-associated ^{14}C was in one pool that could be removed by simple rinsing. These results also suggest that most of the ^{14}C that becomes associated with sedimentary organic matter during incubation with ^{14}C-formaldehyde does so by chemisorption, and not by thermochemical bonding, as suggested in an earlier paper (Lopez and Crenshaw, 1982).

Testing the Uniformity Assumption

There is no reason to believe that ^{14}C-formaldehyde would uniformly label sedimentary organic matter, but the results of experiment 4 demonstrated good agreement between the behavior in absorption trials of uniformly labelled and formaldehyde labelled algae and algal detritus. On the basis of these results, the labelling uniformity assumption should not be rejected. The agreement between uniform labelling and formaldehyde labelling may not hold for more refractory types of organic matter. We are presently investigating the preparation of uniformly labelled melanoidin as a model of poorly utilizable material (Hedges, 1978).

The inference that ^{14}C-formaldehyde labels organic matter by chemisorption is consistent with the results of these absorption experiments. If the

Trial no.	1	2	3	4	5	6
date	10-82	12-82	8-85	10-85	5-86	8-86
AFDW/DW,						
sediment	.1290	.0891	.1048	.0947	.0726	.1026
feces	.1581	.1239	.1870	.1144	.1313	.1173
FR_{org}	1.42	1.68	1.85	2.16	2.03	1.39
% Absorption,						
dual tracer	10.1	1.4	21.6	42.4	-8.0	16.3
ash ratio	15.7	19.6	4.4	49.3	12.5	20.4

Table 7.2: Experiment 5: Comparison of organic absorption estimates by *Nucula proxima*, using the dual tracer (^{14}C-formaldehyde: [51]Cr) and the ash ratio techniques.

ligand or ligands to which formaldehyde chemisorbs are common in all types of organic matter, then the ^{14}C should be evenly dispersed through all organic classes. We predict that formaldehyde labelling will track uniform labelling in absorption experiments investigating refractory substrates.

Paradoxically, labelling by chemisorption also may limit the utility of the ^{14}C-formaldehyde method, because the label is easily lost during rinsing. The error in absorption estimates due to desorption is small when absorption is high, but even if rinsing protocol is very carefully controlled, accurate estimation of low absorption efficiencies may be beyond the limits of this method.

Perhaps the most useful aspect of this interpretation is the guidance it can provide in the future development of methods to label sedimentary organic matter. We suggest that the ideal label would chemisorb strongly to organic matter, and would not desorb easily. A gamma emitting isotope would be especially useful because it can be counted in living animals.

Preservation of Specific Activity

To our knowledge, the validity of this assumption has not been rigorously tested. It can be confused easily with the uniformity assumption, because uniform labelling precludes selection by specific activity. For animals large enough to allow gut dissection, quantitative analysis of organic carbon and

[14]C of gut contents could be conducted. For smaller animals, it may be possible to measure total carbon ingested and total ^{14}C ingested by mass balance. Such approaches have not been reported in the literature.

Calculation of forage ratio in experiment 5 was based on the *ad hoc* acceptance of this assumption. What are the consequences of its rejection? If there was positive selection, a given amount of ingested ^{14}C would then represent a smaller amount of organic matter. Thus, the estimate of FR_{org} would be too high. Consider an example in which the specific activity of the ingested sediment was double that of the offered sediment. In trial 4 of experiment 5, the FR_{org} for *Nucula proxima* would be lowered from the original estimate of 2.16 to approximately 1.0. The ash ratio absorption estimate based on $FR_{org} = 1$ yields a value of -23.5%, instead of 49.3%. Absorption estimates based on the ash ratio method are thus very sensitive to the validity of this assumption.

While it is perfectly plausible (and intriguing) that animals may select organic matter by specific activity, experiment 5 provides an interesting consequence to rejecting this assumption. Because selection by specific activity reduces the estimate of organic ingestion, there is a problem in explaining the sources of organic matter in the feces. Organic matter in feces can come only from the ingested sediment or from the animal. If the FR_{org} estimate was too high due to selection by specific activity, a higher fraction of the fecal organic matter must come from the animal tissue, and not from nonabsorbed sedimentary organic matter. In trial 4, if *Nucula proxima* fed nonselectively ($FR_{org} = 1$), it would have suffered a net loss from its tissue of at least 0.0197 mg organic matter for each mg of sediment ingested. This loss would not include additional respiratory losses. Given the measured ingestion rate of 0.378 mg x animal-1 x hr^{-1} (Cheng, unpubl.), it would lose daily 0.179 mg of its tissue. Small animals such as this protobranch bivalve (1 to 11 mg dry tissue weight) could not withstand such losses for long.

We cannot prove that animals did not lose weight in these particular experiments, although we have no trouble maintaining *Nucula proxima* in the laboratory. In all 6 trials of experiment 5, fecal pellets were organically enriched over sediment (Table 2). These are direct gravimetric measurements that are independent of radiotracer measurements. Organically enriched feces can only be explained by selective ingestion ($FR_{org} > 1$) or by net weight loss from the animal. We regard organic enrichment in feces as best explained by selective ingestion (i.e. Cammen, 1980b). Because rejection of the assumption of preservation of specific activity precludes selective ingestion, acceptance of this assumption is warranted.

In experiment 5 the ash ratio calculation of absorption efficiency is based on acceptance of this assumption, while the dual tracer estimate is additionally dependent upon the uniformity assumption. Therefore, a comparison of the estimates from these two methods is essentially a test of the uniformity assumption. It is not a completely independent test because some data (^{14}C and ^{51}Cr ingested) is used in both calculations. The rest of the data is independent.

The greatest divergence between the estimates of absorption efficiency occurred in the trials exhibiting lowest absorption. Because the dual label method gave the lower estimate 5 of 6 times, ^{14}C desorption during rinsing is the probable explanation for this divergence. The negative absorption estimate of the dual tracer method in trial 5 may have resulted from ^{14}C desorption during sediment sampling. The low ash ratio estimate in trial 3 appeared to be due to curiously high organic content in feces.

It is interesting that, in most of the trials, both methods estimate substantial absorption of sedimentary organic matter. It appears that *Nucula proxima* obtains most of its energy from absorption of sedimentary detritus during the late spring and summer (Cheng, unpubl). Our results, therefore, are in good agreement with the assertion that deposit feeders must absorb 5- 20% of sedimentary organic matter to meet their caloric demands (see chapters in this volume by Cammen; Mayer; Rice and Rhoads).

Summary

Radiotracer methods applied to measure ingestion of sedimentary organic matter by deposit feeders are based on the assumptions that only the organic fraction is labelled and that specific activity is preserved upon ingestion. Absorption measurements require the assumption that the organic fraction is uniformly labelled. These assumptions appear to hold for the ^{14}C-formaldehyde method. The second assumption could not be tested directly, but it is not possible to account for fecal organic content without accepting it. We suggest that ^{14}C adsorbs to the organic fraction in sediment. The ligands to which it adsorbs are probably common enough that the labelling is not highly dependent on the composition of the organic fraction, so that ^{14}C becomes widely dispersed throughout it. This is probably why it behaves like a uniform marker in absorption experiments. We predict that the uniformity assumption would not hold in assimilation/allocation experiments.

Desorption of ^{14}C from ^{14}C-formaldehyde labelled sediment appears to be the major drawback of this method. The development of better techniques for radiolabelling sedimentary organic matter should take into account the advantages of labelling by chemisorption.

Because each ingestion/absorption experiments allows two ways of calculating absorption, the assumptions are tested each time. This is a particularly nice way to detect either methodological errors or real characteristics of sediment or animals for which the assumptions do not hold.

The series of experiments on *Nucula proxima* demonstrated that they selectively ingest the organic fraction of sediment, such that feces are always organically enriched. (They are also selective on sedimentary bacteria (Cheng, unpub.)). Organic absorption can be surprisingly high. Absorption estimates agree well with required estimates based on respiratory budgets (Cammen, this volume). This deposit feeder appears to obtain most of its energy from absorption of sedimentary organic matter.

Acknowledgements

We thank Doug Capone, Don Rice and Larry Mayer for their advice and critical comments. This work has been partly supported by NSF grants OCE8501140 and OCE8711619 to G. Lopez. This is contribution 629 from the Marine Sciences Research Center, SUNY at Stony Brook.

Literature Cited

Banks, C. W., and L. Wolfinbarger, Jr. 1981. A rapid and convenient method for radiolabelling detritus with [^{14}C]acetic anhydride. *J. Exp. Mar. Biol. Ecol.* 53: 115-123.

Bricelj, V.M. and R. E. Malouf. 1984. The influence of algal and suspended sediment concentrations on the feeding physiology of the hard clam *Mercenaria* L. *Mar. Biol.* 84: 155-162.

Brock, T.D. 1978. The poisoned control in biogeochemical investigations. pp. 717-725, IN W.G. Krumbein, ed., *Environmental Biogeochemistry and Geomicrobiology* vol. 3. Ann Arbor Sci., Ann Arbor.

Calow, P. and C. R. Fletcher 1972. An new radiotracer technique involving ^{14}C and ^{51}Cr for estimating the assimilation efficiency of aquatic primary producers. *Oecologia* (Berl.), 9: 155-170.

Cammen, L. M. 1980a. The significance of microbial carbon in the nutrition of the deposit feeding polychaete *Nereis succinea*. *Mar. Biol.* 61: 9-20.

Cammen, L. M. 1980b. Ingestion rate: An empirical model for aquatic deposit feeders and detritivores. *Oecologia* (Berl.) 44: 303-310.

Conover, R. J. 1966. Assimilation of organic matter by zooplankton. *Limnol. Oceanogr.*, 11: 338-345.

Conover, R. J., R. Durvasula, S. Roy and R. Wang. 1986. Probable loss of chlorophyll-derived pigments during passage through the gut of zooplankton, and some of the consequences. *Limnol. Oceanogr.* 31: 878-887.

Crosby, M.P. 1985. The use of a rapid radiolabeling method for measuring ingestion rates for detritivores. *J. Exp. Mar. Biol. Ecol.* 93: 273-283.

DeFlaun, M.F. and L.M. Mayer. 1983. Relationships between bacteria and grain surfaces in intertidal sediments. *Limnol. Oceanogr.* 28: 873-881.

Foulds, J. B., and K. H. Mann. 1978. Cellulose digestion in *Mysis stenolepis* and its ecological implications. *Limnol. Oceanogr.* 23: 760-766.

Hargrave, B. T. 1970. The utilization of benthic microflora by *Hyalella azteca* (Amphipoda). *J. Anim. Ecol.*, 39: 427-437.

Hedges, J.I. 1978. The formation and clay mineral reactions of melanoidins. *Geochim. Cosmochim. Acta* 42: 69-76.

Ivlev, V.S. 1939. Transformation of energy by aquatic animals. *Int. Rev. den Gesam. Hydrobiol. Hydrograph.* 38: 449-458.

Kemp, P.F. 1986. Direct uptake of detrital carbon by the deposit-feeding polychaete *Euzonus mucronata* (Treadwell). *J. Exp. Mar. Biol. Ecol.* 99: 49-61.

Kiørboe, T. and M. Møhlenberg. 1981. Particle selection in suspension-feeding bivalves. *Mar. Ecol. Prog. Ser.* 4: 43-55.

Kofoed, L. H. 1975a. The feeding biology of *Hydrobia ventrosa* (Montague). I. The assimilation of different components of food. *J. exp. mar. Biol. Ecol.* 19: 233-241.

Kofoed, L. H. 1975b. The feeding biology of *Hydrobia ventrosa* (Montague). II. Allocation of the components of the carbon budget and the significance of the secretion of dissolved organic material. *J. Exp. Mar. Biol. Ecol.* 19: 243-256.

Lopez, G.R. and I-J. Cheng. 1982. Ingestion selectivity of sedimentary organic matter by the deposit-feeder *Nucula annulata* (Bivalvia: Nuculidae). *Mar. Ecol. Prog. Ser.* 8: 279-282.

Lopez, G.R. and I-J. Cheng. 1983. Synoptic measurements of ingestion rate, ingestion selectivity, and absorption efficiency of natural foods in the deposit-feeding molluscs *Nucula annulata* (Bivalvia) and *Hydrobia totteni* (Gastropoda). *Mar. Ecol. Prog. Ser.* 11: 55-62.

Lopez, G.R. and M. A. Crenshaw. 1982. Radiolabelling of sedimentary organic matter with ^{14}C-formaldehyde: Preliminary evaluation of a new technique for use in deposit-feeding studies. *Mar. Ecol. Prog. Ser.* 8: 283-289.

Lopez, G.R. and J.S. Levinton. 1987. Ecology of deposit-feeding animals in marine sediments. *Quart. Rev. Biol.* 62: 235- 260.

Montagna, P.A. 1984. In situ measurement of meiobenthic grazing rates on sediment bacteria and edaphic diatoms. *Mar. Ecol. Prog. Ser.* 18: 119-130.

Newell, R.I.E. and S.J. Jordan. 1983. Preferential ingestion of organic material by the American oyster *Crassostrea virginica*. *Mar. Ecol. Prog. Ser.* 13: 47-53.

Sequi, P. and R. Arenghieri 1977. Destruction of organic matter by hydrogen peroxide in the presence of pyrophosphate and its effects on soil specific surface area. *Soil Sci. Soc. Am. J.* 41: 340-342.

Tande, K.S. and D. Slagsted. 1985. Assimilation efficiency in herbivorous aquatic organisms—The potential of the ratio method using ^{14}C and biogenic silica as markers. *Limnol. Oceanogr.* 30: 1093-1099.

Tenore, K.R. and R.B. Hanson. 1980. Availability of detritus of different types and ages to a polychaete macroconsumer, *Capitella capitata*. *Limnol. Oceanogr.* 25: 553-558.

Wolfinbarger, Jr., L., and M. P. Crosby. 1983. A convenient procedure for radiolabelling detritus with [^{14}C]dimethylsulfate. *J. Exp. Mar. Biol. Ecol.* 67: 185-198.

Chapter 8

The Importance of Size-Dependent Processes in the Ecology of Deposit-Feeding Benthos

Thomas L. Forbes
Marine Sciences Research Center
State University of New York
Stony Brook, NY 11794

Introduction

> Whenever we look at the functions of living organisms, we find
> that size is important and that a change in size has consequences
> that require appropriate adjustments or changes. ... When ani-
> mals meet constraints that set limits to further change in scale,
> discontinuities in design may solve the problem (Schmidt-Nielsen,
> 1984, p. 209).

What are the environmental and ontogenetic constraints that control the
size-scaling of form and function, and therefore energy gain and expenditure,
in deposit-feeding invertebrates? How do these constraints interact to shape
the ontogeny of an organism from larval recruit to reproductive adult? Evo-

lutionary theory predicts that natural selection can act at any point within the life cycle of an organism in order to increase the fitness of the individual (Calow, 1978). The comprehensive study of developmental changes in functional morphology and critical physiological rate processes should therefore provide valuable insights into the adaptation and design of deposit-feeding benthos.

The research strategy described here is derived from that of classical comparative physiology, a field which explores the ways in which diverse organisms perform similar functions or solve similar problems. Questions of this type have traditionally been investigated using a species or animal type (e.g., functional group) as an experimental variable. This use has not only led to important biological generalizations, but has also aided in discovery of the diverse mechanisms by which different animals have solved identical functional problems (Prosser, 1973, 1986; Schmidt-Nielsen, 1983).

In the present study, body size during growth is used as an experimental variable. I will attempt to show that the study of size-related changes in vital physiological rate processes during growth can be very effective in identifying important environmental or morphological constraints as well as critical life-history thresholds or discontinuities (e.g., Forbes and Lopez, 1987).

The principal focus of the work described here is the size- scaling of feeding and metabolic carbon loss rates in individual *Capitella* species I (see Grassle and Grassle, 1976, 1977, 1978; Grassle, 1979 for background concerning the *Capitella* sibling species complex). The methodology of ontogenetic allometry was employed as a tool to investigate morphological and functional changes, and thus potential critical periods, occurring in individual animals during growth and development (e.g., Teissier, 1960; Cock, 1966; Gould, 1966; Fleagle, 1985). For the purpose of this discussion, allometry is defined in the broad sense as "the study of size and its consequences" (Gould, 1966).

The data on the scaling of egestion rate and total metabolic carbon loss presented below indicate that adult *Capitella* sp. I are not geometrically scaled-up versions of juveniles. Relative form and function changes during growth have very important consequences for development in *Capitella* species I. Preliminary results from metabolic carbon loss experiments indicate that smaller animals have relatively greater loss rates than larger animals. Sharp discontinuities were also found in the scaling relationships between feeding rate (and the parameters that combine to produce feeding rate) and body size. This indicates that the representation of the scaling of egestion rate as a single power curve can obscure important biological processes (Smith, 1984). The ontogeny of egestion rate in *Capitella* sp. I appears to be more accurately modeled by two allometric (i.e., power) functions in series.

In addition to giving direct answers to specific questions concerning relative changes that occur during growth, the information obtained from studies of the size-scaling of important rate processes during the development of individual animals can be used to generate testable hypotheses concerning the factors that may limit growth and fitness.

Materials and Methods

Metabolic carbon loss experiments

Worms and culture conditions.

Worms were collected from the low intertidal region of Setauket Harbor, New York in May 1985. Electrophoretic analyses indicated that the collected individuals were *Capitella* species I (J.P. Grassle, pers. comm.). The worms were maintained until use in the experiments in static culture at room temperature (21-24°C) under constant aeration in circular glass culture dishes (1l). The culture dishes were layered with 1-2 cm of azoic sediment (<250 μm) which was prepared by heating moist sediment to 85°C in a water bath for 2-3 h. Animals were fed a twice-weekly ration of Gerber's Mixed Cereal (7.0 g m^{-2}; Tenore, 1981). The culture water was changed every 2 days using fresh, glass fiber filtered (GFF) seawater (26-28 o/oo).

Uniform labeling of animals.

Uniform labeling of animals in metabolic studies of aquatic invertebrates has recently been developed by Famme and Kofoed (1982), in their study of *Mytilus edulis*; and by Cammen (1985), who employed this method with *Capitella* species I. I have adapted the methods of Cammen (1985) and scaled them so that carbon loss rates could be measured in very small, individual animals while they are actively feeding on sediment. Once worms have been labeled uniformly, very precise measurements can be made of their metabolic carbon loss rates.

Worms were removed from mass culture (200-300 individuals) and added to freshly collected intertidal sediment (< 250 μm) contained in a 1l glass culture dish. GFF seawater (28 o/oo, pH 8.4) and 150 μCi of ^{14}C bicarbonate (New England Nuclear) were then added and the culture dish sealed with vacuum grease and placed under constant illumination at room temperature.

The culture was incubated until all animals became uniformly labeled (until ^{14}C:^{12}C was constant among all carbon pools). Under these conditions, uniform labeling required approximately 2 months at 24^0C. A labeling period of at least 2 months allowed the rearing of two or more generations of worms in closed, radioactive culture conditions. The animals reproduced quite readily as indicated by the fact that juveniles, adults, and larvae were always present in culture. Worms were considered to be uniformly labeled if there was no correlation between worm specific activity [DPM (mm^3 worm)$^{-1}$] and body size (mm^3) over the experimental size range of worms. Periodic additions of NaOH solution were made to the radioactive culture in order to maintain the seawater pH at 8.0 or above, and prevent excessive loss of $H^{14}CO_3^-$ from the water phase.

For this study, particulate carbon was defined to be that radioactive label retained on a 61 μm mesh screen.

Determination of worm body volume.

Worm volumes were determined using methods outlined in Forbes and Lopez (1987). Briefly, a video camera was mounted on a dissecting microscope and used to videotape live animals. Individual body volumes (BV) could then be estimated from measurements of projected area and length under the assumption that the animals are circular at any cross section. Replicate measurements of individual animals indicated that the precision of BV estimates was ±15%.

Experimental protocol.

A total of 3 separate experiments were performed to measure the size-scaling of particulate carbon (PC) loss rates. Experiments I, II, and III were run at 22^0, 24^0, and 22^0C respectively. In experiments I and II only PC loss rates were measured. In experiment III, however, both dissolved (DC) and PC rates were measured. DC and PC values were then summed to provide a measure of total carbon (TC) loss rate. The worms in experiments I to III ranged in size from 0.009 to 3.02 mm^3 BV. This range covers worms from larval metamorphosis (< 0.01 mm^3, 0.2 mm length, Forbes and Lopez, unpubl.) to small, reproductively mature adults.

I converted carbon loss rates to mm^3 worm lost hr^{-1} by calculating the ratio of the carbon loss rate to the worm specific activity [(DPM ^{14}C lost h^{-1})/(DPM/mm^{3}worm^{-1}]. These data were then fit to power functions via log-log transformations and Model II regression.

Prior to each experiment, chloramphenicol (2-3 mg l^{-1}) was added to 2-3 l of filtered (0.2 μm), autoclaved, seawater. Chloramphenicol was chosen for these experiments because it is a specific and reversible inhibitor of prokaryotic protein synthesis (Vogel et al, 1969). pH was maintained at 8.4±0.1 for all experiments. Approximately 20 ml of moist, silt-clay sediment was also autoclaved, and to this was added enough of the seawater prepared above to form a slurry that could be easily pipetted.

Egestion rate experiment

To obtain egestion rate data, living animals were sized every two days for three weeks. Acclimation and experimental temperatures were maintained at 15^{0}C. Worm body size was measured as described for the carbon loss experiments. Total pellet number, individual fecal pellet weight, and individual pellet volume were measured for the same 2 day intervals as well. Animals were kept individually in small glass dishes and fed a mixture of silt-clay sediment that was enriched with Gerber's Mixed Cereal (approx. 1 cereal:3 sediment, V:V). The egestion rate experiment began with 10 individuals ranging in initial size from 0.12 mm^3 to 1.00 mm^3 and was conducted for 28 days.

Fecal pellet volumes were estimated from length and width measurements. Pellets were assumed to be ellipsoidal in shape and their volumes were calculated as ellipsoids of revolution (Protter and Morrey, 1964).

In order to determine whether a relationship existed between the number of fecal pellets per gut and worm size (for worms less than 1.00 mm^3) a single cohort of larvae was sampled from mass culture. The cohort was grown on silt-clay sediment; pellet standing stocks and worm body sizes were measured every two or three days (Forbes and Lopez, 1987).

Data analysis

Asymmetrical confidence limits for the allometric exponents were calculated and compared according to methods described in Clarke (1980) and Ricker (1984). Geometric mean (reduced major axis) regressions were calculated for all allometric functions (see Jolicoeur, 1975; Kuhry and Marcus, 1977; Rayner, 1985; Ricker, 1973, 1975, 1984; Smith, 1980, 1984; Zar, 1968; for discussion of allometric curve fitting methods and assumptions). Geometric mean regressions were chosen for the fitting of log-log transformed data for four reasons: (1) log-log transformation homogenized the variance in egestion rate as a function of BV, (2) functional rather than predictive relationships were sought between the dependent and independent variables, (3) the measurement error for body size is relatively large ($\leq$15%) and violates one of the assumptions of standard least mean square regressions, and (4) for this analysis, the exact value of the allometric exponent obtained is less important than its variation during ontogeny. However, for comparison with other studies, the scaling exponents obtained with GM regression techniques can be converted to standard regression slopes by multiplying them by the correlation coefficient (r) of the log transformed bivariate distribution (Ricker, 1984).

Based on dimensional criteria, an allometric exponent (α) equal to 1.0 indicates that a physiological rate process or morphological parameter is directly proportional to body volume, indicating that the rate per unit volume is constant over the size range of animals examined. That is, if

$$\text{Rate} = k(\text{Volume})^{\alpha},$$

$$\text{Volume–specific Rate} = k(\text{Volume})^{\alpha - 1}$$

where k is an empirically determined constant. If α is less than 1.0, α-1 will be negative, and the volume-specific rate will decrease as a function of increasing body size. Cleveland's (1979) LOWESS algorithm was applied to the log-log transformed data of feeding rate (mm^3h^{-1}) versus body size (mm^3) to examine the data for deviations from a simple straight-line relationship. LOWESS is a robust, locally-weighted scatter plot smoother that can be used to aid in visualizing trends in bivariate data plots. In order to examine deviations from simple allometry during development by estimating changes in α, a moving regression program (ALPHA) was developed. The use of a moving regression technique allows one to determine whether the size-scaling of a process can be adequately described as a single power curve, and if not, to determine the direction and degree of the changes occurring during ontogeny. This greatly aids in the rapid determination of potential critical periods in the scaling of functional processes. If a relationship can be described by a simple power function, then consecutive estimates of the allometric exponent will not change in a systematic fashion, but will tend to fluctuate randomly about a particular value. In this way, one can readily depict the rate of change of the exponent, and note the body sizes over which the change occurs. Computational details for each ALPHA run are given in the appropriate figure captions.

Since both LOWESS and ALPHA indicated that the relationship between feeding rate and body size might best be described by two allometric curves in ontogenetic sequence. A nonlinear, piecewise, least squares regression model using a geometric mean loss function was used to fit the log-log transformed data. This model allowed simultaneous fitting of two power functions while estimating the breakpoint (X_0) between them (Neter et al. 1985).

Results

Metabolic carbon loss experiments

Allometric exponents, power curve coefficients, scaling null hypotheses, and animal size ranges for experiments I, II, and III are summarized in Table 8.1. The projected areas of the worms in experiments I-III scaled as BV to the 0.74 power. Therefore, carbon loss scaling in these experiments was compared to the null hypotheses of H_0: $\alpha = 0.74$ and H_0: $\alpha = 1.00$ to test for ontogenetic correlations between projected area and BV. This comparison was made because a loss rate with an exponent indistinguishable from 0.74 might indicate a functional coupling with external surface area (Von Bertalanffy, 1960; Hargrave, 1972; Calow, 1981; Pauly, 1981).

The size-scaling of PC loss for the first three experiments indicates that loss rate is isometrically related to worm volume. None of the power curves had an allometric exponent different from 1.0, nor were any of the PC loss rate exponents significantly different from any of the others. Two out of three of the exponents (experiments I and II) were significantly greater than 0.74.

DC loss was also measured in experiment III (Table 8.1). This includes respiratory and anaerobic CO_2 production as well as any forms of dissolved organic carbon (DOC) that were lost. DC loss rate was found to be a function of body size to the 0.76 power and was ontogenetically correlated with projected area. TC loss rate for each individual was calculated for experiment III by summing the particulate and dissolved rate for each worm. The TC loss rate scales as body size to the 0.80 power (Table 8.1). Analysis of the combined data set for metabolic carbon loss in experiments I, II, and III indicates that DC and PC loss rates accounted for 54 percent and 46 percent of the total daily loss, respectively. Carbon loss rate in per cent per day partitioned among the three fractions reveals that DC and PC losses amounted to 4.21% and 3.60% d^{-1}, respectively. Total loss was therefore 7.81% d^{-1}. Loss rate measurements for the individual worms in experiment III (Table 8.2) indicated that there was no relationship between body size

Expt.	T°C	Type	α	95% CL (n)(r)	Sizes (mm³)	b(x10³)	H₀:=1.0	H₀:=0.74
I	23	PC	1.19	0.970-1.460 (11)(.96)	0.28-3.02	1.01	yes	no
II	24	PC	1.03	0.924-1.148 (14)(.98)	0.01-1.19	1.21	yes	no
III	22	PC	0.88	0.702-1.104 (12)(.95)	0.02-1.26	1.22	yes	yes
III	22	DC	0.76	0.657-0.880 (12)(.98)	0.02-1.26	1.18	no	yes
III	22	TC	0.80	0.677-0.946 (12)(.97)	0.02-1.26	2.36	no	yes

Where:

Loss Rate $(mm^3h^{-1}) = b(\text{Worm volume})^{\alpha}$

n = number of individuals

r = Product-moment correlation coefficient

Loss rate $(mm^3h^{-1}) = [(\text{DPM } 14C \text{ lost } h^{-1})/(\text{DPM } (mm^3 \text{ worm})^{-1})]$

Table 8.1: Allometric exponent (α), power curve coefficient (b), and *Capitella* species I size ranges for metabolic carbon loss experiments.

Worm	TC ($\times 10^4$)(mm^3h^{-1})	PC ($\times 10^4$)(mm^3h^{-1})	DC ($\times 10^4$)(mm^3h^{-1})	Worm volume (mm^3)
1	15.59	7.30	8.29	0.59
2	5.22	2.26	2.96	0.28
3	8.76	5.19	3.56	0.17
4	7.53	3.45	4.08	0.24
5	13.45	5.95	7.50	0.77
6	9.36	5.16	4.20	0.31
7	3.14	1.16	1.98	0.05
8	14.62	5.73	8.89	0.42
9	1.11	0.58	0.53	0.02
10	0.76	0.23	0.53	0.02
11	28.42	15.03	13.38	0.26
12	15.56	7.48	8.08	0.56

Table 8.2: Carbon loss rates (TC,PC,DC) in mm^3 h^{-1} for individual worms in Experiment III.

and the predominant form of carbon loss (DC or PC). In 1/3 of the animals, particulate loss was the greatest, whereas 2/3 of the worms had greater rates of carbon loss in dissolved form.

Egestion rate experiment

The relationship between body size and egestion rate (mm^3 h^{-1}) is plotted in Figure 8.1. This curve spans the development of *Capitella* species I from early post-settlement juveniles to reproductively mature adults. The allometric exponent for the entire curve is 0.98, and it is highly significant ($P < 0.001$). Serial autocorrelation analysis indicated that the scaling of egestion rate (mm^3 h^{-1}) was not significantly different from a linear log-log relationship ($P = 0.15$) (Box and Pierce, 1970). This suggests that egestion rate is directly proportional to worm body volume throughout growth and development. However, if one compares the functional relationships for animals smaller and larger than 1-2 mm^3, using both curve smoothing and moving regression analysis, one finds that the exponent changes (Fig. 8.1 and Fig. 8.2) fairly abruptly as worms grow through a body size of approximately 1-2 mm^3. These data can then be fit as consecutive power functions using nonlinear methods, and the best breakpoint (X_0) estimated iteratively (Neter et al. 1985). This analysis indicates that the exponent changes from 1.21 for animals less than or equal to 1.72 mm^3 (X_0) to 0.78 for animals greater than 1.72 mm^3. Fitted equations and the approximate standard errors of the allometric exponents are given in Figure 8.1.

The relationship between pellet production rate (FP h^{-1}) and worm volume indicates that very small worms increase their pellet production rate during growth until a body volume of approximately 1.00 - 2.00 mm^3 is reached (Fig. 8.3). As the worms continue to grow above sizes greater than 1 - 2 mm^3, average pellet production rate becomes quite variable, but remains at approximately 35 pellets animal^{-1} h^{-1} at 15^{0}C.

Application of the moving regression analysis to worms that show an increasing pellet production rate with increasing body size, that is, worms less than approximately 2.00 mm^3, reveals a negative linear relationship (Fig. 8.4). Estimated values decline in a linear fashion and are always less than one. GM estimates of the allometric exponent of feeding rate (FP h^{-1}) as a function of body size decrease in a linear fashion from 0.8 to 0.6 as worm size increases to approximately 1.5 mm^3 (Fig. 8.4). This indicates that this relationship should not be modeled as a simple allometric power function, even though doing so yields a statistically significant result.

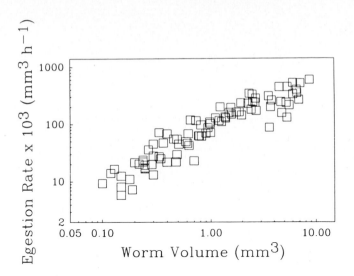

Figure 8.1: Log-log plot of changes in egestion rate (ER) (mm^3 h^{-1}) versus body size (S) (mm^3) for all worms in the egestion rate experiment. Individual worm allometries have been pooled. Where $X_0 = 1.72$ mm^3 and ER $\propto$ S$^{1.21}$ for worms ≤ 1.72 mm^3; ER $\propto$ S$^{0.78}$ for worms > 1.72 mm^3.

Changes in fecal pellet volume as a function of worm body volume are shown in Figure 8.5. The change in the allometric exponents as a function of increasing body size is shown in Figure 8.6. As is the case for the size-scaling of egestion rate, the allometric exponent of fecal pellet volume as a function of body size drops abruptly as the worms grow through the sizes of approximately 1 - 2 mm^3.

Changes in the number of fecal pellets per gut as a function of worm body size are shown in Figure 8.7. The number of pellets per gut increases with body size up to worm volumes of approximately 3-4 mm^3.

Moving regression estimates of the allometric exponent of the number of fecal pellets per gut as a function of size for worms less than 2.00 mm^3 in body volume are plotted in Figure 8.8. The exponent remains constant at approximately 0.3 from larval settlement to a body size of approximately 0.1 mm^3. This indicates that in these very small worms pellet number is related to total length of the animal. Qualitative visual observations of the guts of the small worms always revealed them to be completely packed with fecal pellets, while this was not true for larger worms (> 1.00 mm^3). At body sizes between 0.1 and 0.2 mm^3 there is a sharp peak in the estimated scaling exponent.

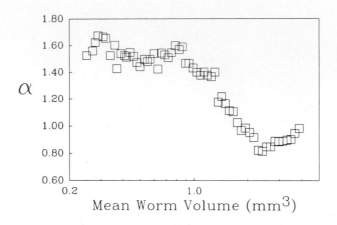

Figure 8.2: Plot of the allometric exponent (α) versus log mean body size for moving regression analysis by ALPHA on log egestion rate ($mm^3\,h^{-1}$) versus log body size (mm^3). GM regressions were calculated. The number of variate pairs per regression (L) which were used to calculate each separate exponent was determined according to one of two criteria: (1) the minimum number necessary to achieve significance ($P < 0.05$) for every calculated exponent over the entire range of worm sizes in the relationship, or (2) the minimum necessary to achieve significance to a point after which all calculated values were not significant ($P > 0.05$). Consecutive regressions were calculated for I=1 to L, I=2 to L+1,..., I=N-L+1 to N. Where N=the total number of variate pairs in the analysis (86) and L=the number of pairs used to calculate each value of α (29). I=index variable.

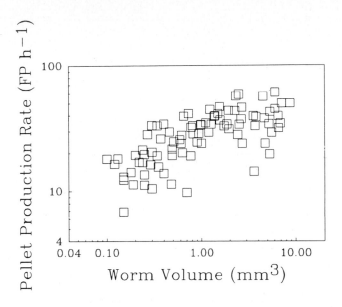

Figure 8.3: Relationship between worm body volume and fecal pellet (FP) production rate.

Discussion

Metabolic carbon loss experiments

Total carbon loss rates measured for *Capitella* species I scale as body size to a power less than one. This suggests that total carbon loss rate per unit volume or 'cost of living' is relatively greater in smaller animals, and is in the range of previously measured exponents for *Capitella* sp. I (Cammen, 1985; (0.93-1.25)) and other marine invertebrates measured as weight loss on starvation (Sebens, 1981; 1982; (0.77-1.08)). For the experiments reported here, cost, measured as total carbon loss rate, should reflect an integration of both aerobic and anaerobic metabolic processes in feeding animals. These preliminary data suggest that smaller worms have greater total carbon (i.e., energy) turnover rates. Recent experimental evidence from studies by Cammen (1985) and Forbes and Lopez (1987) indicates that individuals of *Capitella* sp. I, especially the smallest worms, show very low metabolic and feeding rate compensatory abilities under changing temperature regimes. An exponential increase in metabolic carbon loss rate as a function of increasing temperature occurs in *Capitella* sp. I, even when the worms are acclimated to the experimental temperature for 11 to 16 days (Forbes and Lopez, 1987; calculated from data in Cammen, 1985). While feeding rate appears to

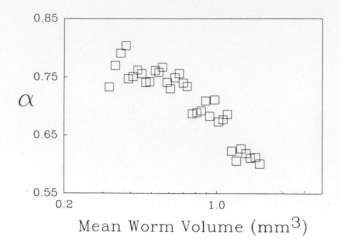

Figure 8.4: Changes in α versus mean body volume for moving regression analysis of egestion rate (FP h^{-1}) as a function of worm size. Where N=40 and L=6. See legend of Figure 1 and text for explanation.

be correlated with measurements of carbon loss rate as a function of temperature (Forbes and Lopez, 1987), energy intake or food absorption rates across the gut wall as a function of temperature and body size are unknown. The total metabolic carbon loss rate of 7.8 %/day measured in the present study agrees quite well with the value of 8 - 9 %/day found by Cammen (1985) at a similar temperature (22^0 versus 20^{0}C, respectively). Cammen's data was based on weight loss of starved animals. This agreement suggests that non-metabolic forms of radioactive carbon loss (e.g., carboxyl-group exchange reactions) did not pose a significant problem in these experiments. It is surprising that the metabolic carbon loss rates in feeding and starved worms were so similar. This suggests that *Capitella* sp. I may have a relatively poor ability to compensate metabolically for decreases in food level. This will compound the metabolic stress already implied by *Capitella* sp. I's inability to make compensatory adjustments in feeding or metabolic rate in response to temperature increases, particularly evident in small worms (Cammen, 1985; Forbes and Lopez, 1987). These data further suggest that the cost of deposit feeding (ingesting, processing and defecating sediment) in *Capitella* sp. I is relatively low compared to other costs associated with an infaunal, burrowing existence (see Taghon, this volume).

The metabolic carbon loss rates from both the present study and that of Cammen (1985) are somewhat higher than the previously reported values of 1 to 5 per cent per day for weight loss in polychaetes (Kay and Brafield,

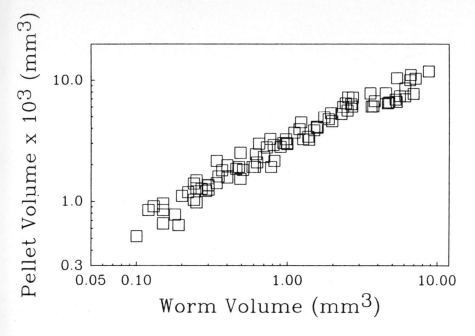

Figure 8.5: Relationship between fecal pellet (FP) volume (mm^3) and worm body size (mm^3).

1973; Tenore and Gopalan, 1974; Neuhoff, 1979). One can estimate, using well established allometric relationships for aerobic metabolism (20^{0}C) and average energy content of dry animal tissue, that the 'average' 200 μg DW poikilotherm burns approximately 2.6% of its total energy content per day (Peters, 1983). This suggests that, for *Capitella* sp. I, there is a significant anaerobic component to metabolism and/or *Capitella* sp.I turns over energy at a higher rate than a 'typical' 200 μg poikilotherm.

Previous measurements on other polychaetes were made on larger worms (e.g., *Nereis* spp.), where lower rates would be expected based on knowledge of size-scaling of aerobic respiration in polychaetes and other small invertebrates (Shumway, 1979; Banse, 1982). Also, only oxygen uptake is typically measured and is often taken as an estimate of the total energy or maintenance requirement (Duncan and Klekowski, 1975). While this may be adequate in many situations, for infaunal deposit feeders, particularly those which dwell in the low oxygen environment of organic-rich muds, oxygen uptake may be a poor estimate of total metabolic requirements (Famme and Knudsen, 1984, 1985). Anaerobic CO_2 production has been shown to correlate positively with aerobic respiration in *Mytilus edulis* (Famme and Kofoed, 1982). Approaches utilizing direct calorimetry (Gnaiger, 1980; Pamatmat, 1980; Pamatmat and Findlay, 1983) and carbon loss rates in uniformly-labeled

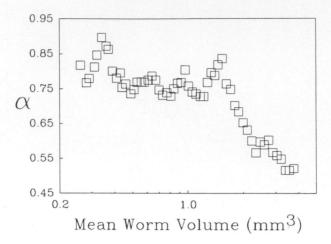

Figure 8.6: Changes in versus mean body volume for moving regression analysis of fecal pellet volume (mm^3) as a function of worm size, where N=85 and L=31. See legend of Figure 1 and text for explanation.

animals (Famme and Kofoed, 1982; this study), may prove useful in determining both the size-scaling and partitioning of aerobic and anaerobic metabolism.

For this study, particulate carbon was defined to be that radioactive label retained on a 61 μm mesh screen. This material includes all fecal pellets, tube fragments, and other sedimentary accretions produced by *Capitella* sp. I during normal feeding and burrowing activity. The major fraction of the particulate losses consisted of mucus in the form of secretions for the construction of tube walls and membranes around fecal pellets.

The finding that PC loss scales as body volume to the first power is surprising. *A priori* one might expect the amount of mucus secretion to be related to worm surface area. However, the scaling exponent of 1.0 indicates that particulate losses are directly proportional to body volume throughout growth, unlike those of dissolved carbon.

The loss rate of 3.6 percent per day for carbon in particulate form is much greater than any previously reported for a marine deposit feeder. The percentage of the total carbon pool within the animal that is lost in particulate form (40%) is also extremely high. Tenore and Gopalan (1974) report that individuals of *Nereis virens* lost only 4-5 % week^{-1} of their total carbon in the form of mucus. The freshwater pulmonates *Ancylus fluviatilis* and *Planorbis contortus* lose between 13 and 32 % of the energy absorbed across the gut wall as mucus (Calow, 1974).

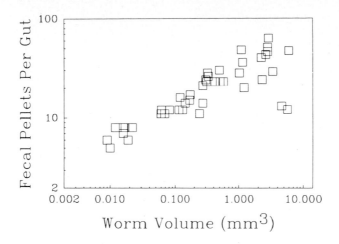

Figure 8.7: Relationship between the number of fecal pellets counted within the gut and worm body size.

Egestion rate experiment

The available studies allowing estimation of the size-scaling of egestion or reworking rates for polychaetes (some of which include pseudofeces production) reveal a wide range of allometric exponents (Hobson, 1967; Nichols, 1974; Cadée, 1979; Kudenov, 1982; Dobbs and Scholly, 1986; Forbes and Lopez, 1987). Forbes and Lopez (1987) found that egestion rate scaled as body volume to the 0.70 power for *Capitella* sp. I with volumes of 0.27 - 2.62 mm^3, and modeled it as a single power curve. Their curve was calculated using data on fecal pellet weight, worm body volume, and average pellet production rate. This earlier work suggested that steady-state fecal pellet standing stocks within smaller individuals of *Capitella* species I (< 1.0 mm^3) might be less than those of larger worms, although the overall correlation between the number of fecal pellets per gut and body size was insignificant. Forbes and Lopez (1987) used a constant pellet production rate as a function of body size to calculate their feeding rate curves. The present study was designed to investigate this relationship in greater detail by combining feeding rate data (FP h^{-1}) with counts of fecal pellets within the guts of small worms. In addition to measuring feeding rate on individual animals directly, one can also calculate the scaling of average gut residence time (FP gut $^{-1}$/FP h^{-1}. These more recent data show that average particulate gut residence time increases in a curvilinear fashion from <30 minutes in recently metamorphosed worms (0.01 mm^3) to slightly greater than one hour as worms reach a body size of 0.5 mm^3, and remains constant thereafter.

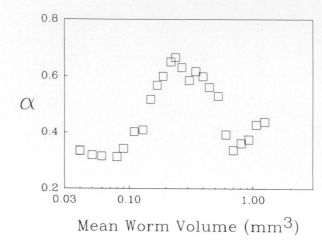

Figure 8.8: Changes in α versus mean body volume for moving regression analysis of the number of fecal pellets per gut as a function of worm size, where N=29 and L=13. See legend of Figure 8.2 and text for explanation.

The results of both studies indicate that for worms greater than approximately 1-2 mm^3 in body volume, egestion rate scales to a power less than one.

The scaling of the absorption process itself will depend on the time food remains within the gut, but may also be influenced by the scaling of the suite of enzymes available for digestion, gut surface area, and possibly other factors (see Kofoed et al. this volume). Smaller *Capitella* sp. I process a relatively greater amount of sediment, but hold that sediment within the gut for a shorter period of time. In addition, the observations that small animals (< 1.0 mm^3) maintain constantly packed guts in which pellets are added to gut standing stocks as soon as there is enough growth in length to accommodate them (whereas larger animals do not), and average gut residence time increases with size in this region, all suggest that smaller animals may tend to be more easily limited by low food levels than larger worms.

The concomitant abrupt shifts in several of the measured scaling exponents as a function of body volume suggest important ontogenetic changes in energy acquisition and growth processes. Egestion rate (measured either as volume of sediment processed or fecal pellet number per hour), relative fecal pellet volume versus size, and the number of pellets maintained within the gut of individual worms all show fairly sharp shifts in size-scaling exponents at worm body volumes of between 0.1 and 2.0 mm^3. Referring to earlier studies on morphometric changes in crustaceans during growth, Teissier (1960) stated that it "is a very important fact that the abrupt changes in slope and the discontinuities which mark the growth curves for different organs of the same animal are not distributed at random. On the contrary, they appear simultaneously in various structures, thus defining the critical stages of growth."

The size-related changes that act in concert to determine the rate of change of egestion rate during growth in *Capitella* sp. I clearly show the type of breaks referred to by Teissier. In contrast to the commonly reported scaling breaks in morphometric measurements, the results of the present study show an ontogenetic change in the allometry of a physiological rate process. This is especially interesting in light of the fact that *Capitella* sp. I appears to grow in a continuous fashion (i.e., does not undergo molting or metamorphosis) after larval settlement. 'Critical stages' in the relative growth of body parts have been suggested by Teissier (1960) and others (Reeve and Huxley, 1945 and references therein) to correspond to biochemical shifts in the ontogeny of endocrine function and metabolic states. Earlier work on *Cancer pagurus* revealed sharp breaks in the log-log relationships of several morphological measurements at sexual maturity (MacKay, 1942, 1943a,b).

More recently, crustacean fisheries biologists have utilized computer programs to estimate the sizes of various morphometric parameters at 50% maturity (Somerton, 1980; 1981). These programs were developed to distinguish distinct but overlapping power function relationships. However, for *Capitella* sp. I, the scaling of the allometric feeding relationships appears to be a strictly sequential, rather than a sequential- overlapping one. It is also interesting to note that the initial macroscopic appearance of copulatory setae and onset of vitellogenesis in *Capitella* sp. I occurs at approximately 1.00 mm^3 (males) and 3.00 mm^3 (females) respectively (Forbes and Lopez, unpub.). The ontogenetic shifts in the allometric exponents are quite closely correlated with, and possibly functionally related to, the onset of sexual maturity.

While there have been many instances of both smooth log-log curvature and discontinuities in the scaling of morphological relationships in both invertebrates and vertebrates (Reeve and Huxley, 1945; Count, 1947; Teissier, 1960; Ford and Horn, 1959; Gould, 1966; MacKay, 1942; 1943a,b; Harel et al., 1972; Martin and Harvey, 1985); there have been few reports of shifts in the scaling exponent of a physiological rate process during ontogeny (but see Hamburger et al., 1983). It is clear in this case of the *Capitella* data

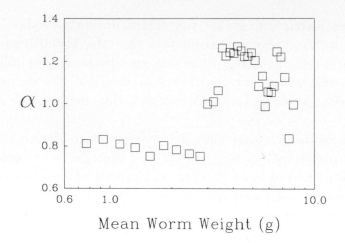

Figure 8.9: Changes in α versus mean body weight (g) for moving regression analysis of oxygen uptake rate (ml O_2 g^{-1} h^{-1}) as a function of worm size. Data from Krüger (1964) for *Arenicola marina*. Where N=50 and L=18. See legend of Figure 8.2 and text for explanation.

that a fit to a single power function masks biologically important changes occurring during ontogeny.

The *Capitella* data are not an isolated example. Inspection of metabolic rate data for *Arenicola marina*, previously reported as conforming to a single power function, reveals an abrupt change in the scaling exponent. Using ALPHA and the raw data provided by Krüger (1964) it is possible to analyze the changes in the allometric exponent of oxygen uptake as a function of body weight in this species. Krüger (1964) provides data for the size-scaling of O_2 uptake rate at 15^0C (Table 2, p. 43). Krüger fitted a simple continuous power curve to his data, where oxygen uptake rate was proportional to worm weight (g) to the 0.77 power. Use of the moving regression analysis reveals a shift in the exponent from between 0.7-0.8 to slightly greater than 1.0 at a body weight of 3.0 g (Fig. 8.9). This provides further evidence of an ontogenetic break in a physiological process that has previously only been modeled by a single power function, with the shift occurring at approximately the weight at which worms spawn (De Wilde and Berghuis, 1979). This analysis reveals that metabolic rate (ml O_2 g^{-1} h^{-1}) in *A. marina* decreases as a function of size until the worm reaches 3 grams, and hereafter remains relatively constant as worms continue to grow, in contrast to what has been reported previously.

For the egestion rate data of *Capitella* sp. I and the metabolic rate data of

A. marina, a simple power curve does not adequately describe the ontogeny of any of the parameters or rate processes examined (FP gut^{-1}, FP h^{-1}, (mm^3 sediment) h^{-1}, (ml O$_2$ h^{-1}). For some processes (metabolic rate in *A. marina*, egestion rate in *Capitella* sp. I) there is an abrupt change preceded and followed by a relatively constant scaling, whereas in others (FP h^{-1}, Fig. 8.4) there is a continuous change in the size-scaling exponent. These data are significant in that they document changes in the *rate of change* (with respect to size) in the ontogeny of physiological rate processes.

A theoretical framework for the allometric development of morphological characters during individual growth has been developed by Lande (1985). An interesting aspect of Lande's formulation is that it allows for departures from simple allometry (i.e., single power curve scaling). At any point in development, the slope of the allometric relation (from the log- log linearized bivariate distribution) between two characters is the ratio of weighted averages of the specific growth rates of their parts (Lande, 1985). Unfortunately, our ignorance concerning the mechanisms which underlie ontogenetic changes in physiological rate processes currently prevent an analogous theoretical development.

The scaling of constraints on energy acquisition

One of the most valuable aspects of an approach that outlines scaling changes during ontogeny (e.g., departures from simple allometry) lies in the hypotheses that can be generated concerning possible constraints on growth and energy intake, and the body sizes at which they can be expected to become important. Inferences from scaling relationships can then be combined with experimental manipulations to determine the underlying mechanisms behind form and function changes during development. For example, estimates of external surface area in *Capitella* sp. I reveal that body surface scales as worm volume to approximately the 0.7-0.8 power (Forbes and Lopez, 1987; this study). The similarity between the exponent for external surface area and that of egestion rate (0.78) for worms larger than 1.7 mm^3 suggests a possible functional coupling of feeding rate with the available respiratory surface in larger animals. In contrast, the scaling exponent for egestion rate in worms less than 1.7 mm^3 is 1.21 and shows no correlation with external surface scaling.

The high specific egestion rates, short gut throughput times and the worm length-related gut packing all combine to suggest that processes of anabolism and net energy intake rate of smaller worms may be more readily affected by food availability than those same processes in larger worms. Carbon loss and egestion rates also appear to show a greater response to temperature in smaller *Capitella* sp. I (Cammen, 1985; Forbes and Lopez, 1987).

Based on the scaling data outlined above, the two parameters most likely to influence growth and anabolism appear to be food and oxygen level, and their interaction with body form and physiological rate processes during ontogeny. One hypothesis suggested by the data for *Capitella* sp. I is that small worms, due to relatively favorable surface to volume ratios, tend to be food rather than oxygen limited (Forbes and Lopez, 1987). This hypothesis states that larger animals feed at lower relative rates because the ability to digest and absorb food is greater than the ability to procure oxygen to efficiently metabolize that food. This hypothesis can be rigorously tested by experiments that manipulate food densities, animal body sizes, and oxygen tensions. An alternative, but not mutually exclusive, hypothesis for the scaling of egestion rate ($mm^3 h^{-1}$) in animals greater than 1.7 mm^3 is that total gut volume is prevented from increasing in direct proportion to body size by the requirement for coelomic space for the production of eggs (Forbes and Lopez, 1987). Under typical conditions, the oocytes of gravid female polychaetes tend to completely fill the available coelomic space (Olive, 1983), suggesting a possible 'competition for space' between the opposing functional demands of egg production and food processing. Calculations based on data presented in Grassle and Grassle (1974) show that egg number scales as worm length squared for *Capitella*. This is in contrast to that of brooding bivalves (e.g., Kabat, 1985) where egg number scales as shell length cubed. The data of Grassle and Grassle (1974) reflect an intrinsic constraint on the reproductive biology of polychaetes possibly due to the tube-within-a-tube morphology or brooding strategy. The potential restriction on total gut volume related to the need to provide space for egg production and development would be expected to operate on all animals because even functioning males retain the potential to become hermaphrodites in the absence of females (Petraitis, 1985).

Summary and Conclusions

1. The scaling of carbon loss rate in individual worms is dependent upon the type of loss being measured. Preliminary results indicate that total carbon loss rate is relatively greater in smaller worms. Total dissolved

carbon loss rate in *Capitella* sp. I is also proportional to estimates of external surface area, suggesting a possible functional relationship. The loss rate of 7.8% d^{-1} measured here agrees with that of 8-9% found by Cammen (1985), calculated from data on weight loss during starvation. These loss rates are higher than those reported for other deposit feeders and may reflect a high metabolic rate related to *Capitella* sp. I's small size and opportunistic life history.

2. The similarity in total carbon loss estimates for feeding, uniformly labeled worms (this study) and estimates based on weight loss during starvation (Cammen 1985) is striking. This similarity suggests that the costs of feeding are relatively minor compared to costs associated with other aspects of a burrowing infaunal existence. Factors tending to increase metabolic expenditure, such as an increase in temperature, should have a relatively greater impact on smaller worms.

3. Due to small sample size, the carbon loss rate data could not be subjected to a moving regression analysis. Given the results obtained for the scaling of egestion rate, caution should be exercised in modeling and interpreting the carbon loss data as simple power curves.

4. Unfortunately, no meaningful comparison between the egestion rate (mm^3 h^{-1}) and carbon loss data is possible without a measure of the scaling of absorption efficiency or some other measure of actual energy intake rate. Methods currently being developed for work on absorption rate constants, combined with the methods of ontogenetic allometry, hold real promise in this regard (see Kofoed et al., this volume).

5. Several factors interact to produce the ontogenetic scaling of egestion rate in *Capitella* sp. I. They are: (a) the size-scaling of fecal pellet production rate, (b) relative fecal pellet volume, and (c) the average number of fecal pellets maintained within the gut. Relative pellet volume is a function of changes of pellet dimensions during growth. Recent data indicate that the ontogeny of relative pellet volume in *Capitella* sp. I is primarily a function of a decreasing pellet width to length ratio (T. Forbes and G. Lopez, unpub.).

6. Most importantly, analysis of scaling and size-dependent processes identifies potential 'critical stages' (Teissier, 1960) and leads to the development of hypotheses concerning the constraints operating on

growth and energy gain during ontogeny. These hypotheses can then be rigorously tested by controlled experimental manipulation.

Acknowledgments

Special thanks go to my advisor, Dr. Glenn Lopez, for his comments on the material in this manuscript, and for many insights and fruitful discussions about deposit feeder organismal biology, without which these ideas could never have developed. Dr. William Jungers very generously made available his substantial expertise in the biology of size and scaling. Dr. Judith Grassle identified the Setauket Harbor *Capitella* to sibling species and Dr. F. James Rohlf helped debug ALPHA. Critiques by Dr. M. Bricelj, Dr. F.C. Dobbs, Dr. P. Lawton, and V. Forbes were instrumental in improving earlier versions of the manuscript. This work was supported by NSF grants OCE8501140 and OCE8711619 to G. Lopez. This is contribution 627 from the Marine Sciences Research Center, SUNY at Stony Brook.

Literature Cited

Banse, K. 1982. Mass-scaled rates of respiration and intrinsic growth in very small invertebrates. *Mar. Ecol. Prog. Ser.* 9:281-297.

Bertalanffy, L. Von. 1960. Principles and theory of growth. Pp. 137-259 in *Fundamental Aspects of Normal and Malignant Growth*, W.W. Nowinski, ed. Amsterdam.

Bertalanffy, L. Von. 1964. Basic concepts in the quantitative biology of metabolism. *Helgolander Wiss. Meeresunters.* 9: 5- 37.

Box, G.E.P. and D.A. Pierce. 1970. Distribution of residual autocorrelation in autoregressive - integrated moving average time series models. *J. Am. Stat. Assoc.* 65: 1509- 1526.

Cadée, G.C. 1979. Sediment reworking by the polychaete *Arenicola marina* in the Dutch Wadden Sea. *Neth. J. Sea Res.* 13: 441-456.

Calow, P. 1974. Some observations on locomotory strategies and their metabolic effects in two species of freshwater gastropods, *Ancylus fluviatilis* Mull. and *Planorbis contortus* Linn. *Oecologia* 16: 149-161.

Calow, P. 1978. Life's logic. Pp. 1-18 in *Life Cycles: An Evolutionary Approach to the Physiology of Reproduction, Development and Aging.* John Wiley and Sons, New York. 164 pp.

Calow, P. 1981. Respiration. Pp. 63-91 in *Invertebrate Zoology: A Functional Approach.* John Wiley and Sons, New York. 183 pp.

Cammen, L.M. 1985. Metabolic loss of organic carbon by the polychaete *Capitella capitata* (Fabricius) estimated from initial weight decrease during starvation, oxygen uptake, and release of 14-C by uniformly labeled animals. *Mar. Ecol. Prog. Ser.* 21: 163-167.

Clarke, M.R.B. 1980. The reduced major axis of a bivariate sample. *Biometrika* 67: 441-446.

Cleveland, W. S. 1979. Robust locally weighted regression and smoothing scatterplots. *J. Am. Stat. Assoc.* 74: 829-836.

Cock, A.G. 1966. Genetical aspects of metrical growth and form in animals. *Quart. Rev. Biol.* 41: 131-190.

Count, E.W. 1947. Brain and body weight in man: Their antecedents in growth and evolution. *Ann. N.Y. Acad. Sci.* 46: 993-1122.

Dobbs, F.C., and T. Scholly. 1986. Sediment processing and selective feeding by *Pectinaria koreni* (Polychaeta: Pectinariidae). *Mar. Ecol. Prog. Ser.* 29: 165- 176.

Duncan, A. and R.R. Klekowski. 1975. Parameters of an energy budget. Pp. 97-147 in *Methods For Ecological Energetics.* IBP Handbook No. 24, W. Grodzinski and A. Duncan, eds. Blackwell Scientific, Oxford. 367 pp.

Famme, P., and L. Kofoed. 1982. Rates of carbon release and oxygen uptake by the mussel, *Mytilus edulis* L., in response to starvation and oxygen. *Mar. Biol. Lett.* 3: 241-256.

Famme, P., and J. Knudsen. 1984. Total heat balance study of anaerobiosis in *Tubifex* (Muller). *J. Comp. Physiol.* 154(B): 587-591.

Famme, P., and J. Knudsen. 1985. Anoxic survival, growth and reproduction by the freshwater annelid, *Tubifex* sp., demonstrated using a new simple anoxic chemostat. *Comp. Biochem. Physiol.* 81(A): 251-253.

Fleagle, J.G. 1985. Size and adaptation in primates. Pp. 1-19 in *Size and Scaling in Primate Biology*, W.L. Jungers, ed. Plenum Press, New York. 491 pp.

Forbes, T.L., and G.R. Lopez. 1987. The allometry of deposit feeding in *Capitella* species I (Polychaeta:Capitellidae): The role of temperature and pellet weight in the control of egestion. *Biol. Bull.* 172: 187-201.

Ford, E.H.R., and G. Horn. 1959. Some problems in the evaluation of differential growth in the rat's skull. *Growth* 23: 191- 203.

Gnaiger, E. 1980. Energetics of invertebrate anoxibiosis: Direct calorimetry in aquatic oligochaetes. *FEBS* Letters 112: 239- 242.

Grassle, J.F. and J.P. Grassle. 1974. Opportunistic life histories and genetic systems in marine benthic polychaetes. *J. Mar. Res.* 32: 253-284.

Grassle, J.F., and J.P. Grassle. 1977. Temporal adaptations in sibling species of *Capitella*. Pp. 177-189 in *Ecology of Marine Benthos*, B.C. Coull, ed. Belle Baruch Library of Marine Science No. 6., University of South Carolina Press, Columbia, South Carolina.

Grassle, J.F., and J.P. Grassle. 1978. Life histories and genetic variation in marine invertebrates. Pp. 347-364 in *Marine Organisms: Genetics, Ecology, and Evolution*, B. Battaglia and J.A. Beardmore, eds. Plenum Press, New York.

Grassle, J.P. 1979. Polychaete sibling species. Pp. 25-32 in *Aquatic Oligochaete Biology*, R.O. Brinkhurst and D.G. Cook eds. Plenum Press, New York.

Grassle, J.P., and J.F. Grassle. 1976. Sibling species of the marine pollution indicator *Capitella* (Polychaeta). *Science* 192: 567-569.

Gould, S.J. 1966. Allometry and size in ontogeny and phylogeny. *Biol. Rev.* 41: 587-640.

Hamburger, K., F. Møhlenberg, H. Randløv, and H. U. Riisgaard. 1983. Size, O_2 consumption, and growth in the mussel *Mytilus edulis*. *Mar. Biol.* 75: 303-306.

Harel, S., K. Watanabe, I. Linke, and R.J. Schain. 1972. Growth and development of the rabbit brain. *Biol. Neonate* 21: 381- 399.

Hargrave, B.T. 1972. Prediction of egestion by the deposit- feeding amphipod *Hyalella azteca*. *Oikos* 23: 116-124.

Hobson, K.D. 1967. The feeding ecology of two North Pacific *Abarenicola* species (Arenicolidae,Polychaeta). *Biol. Bull.* 133: 343-354.

Huxley, J.S. 1932. *Problems of Relative Growth.* 2nd ed. Dover Publications, Inc. New York. 312 pp.

Jolicoeur, P. 1975. Linear regressions in fishery research: Some comments. *J. Fish. Res. Board Can.* 32: 1491-1494.

Kabat, A.R. 1985. The allometry of brooding in *Transenella tantilla* (Gould) (Mollusca:Bivalvia). *J. Exp. Mar. Biol. Ecol.* 91: 271-279.

Kay, D.G., and A.E. Brafield. 1973. The energy relations of the polychaete *Neanthes (=Nereis) virens* (Sars). *J. Anim. Ecol.* 42: 673-692.

Krüger, F. 1964. Versuche über die Abhängigkeit der Atmung von *Arenicola marina* (Annelides Polychaeta) von Grosse und Temperatur. *Helgolander wiss. Meeresunters.* 10: 38-63.

Kudenov, J.D. 1982. Rates of seasonal sediment reworking in *Axiothella rubrocincta* (Polychaeta:Maldanidae). *Mar. Biol.* 70: 181-186.

Kuhry, B., and L.F. Marcus. 1977. Bivariate linear models in biometry. *Syst. Zool.* 26: 201-209.

Lande, R. 1985. Genetic and evolutionary aspects of allometry, Pp. 21-32 in *Size and Scaling in Primate Biology*, W.L. Jungers, ed. Plenum Press, New York. 491 pp.

Mackay, D.C.G. 1942. Relative growth of the European edible crab, *Cancer pagurus*. I. Growth of the carapace. *Growth* 6: 251-258.

Mackay, D.C.G. 1943a. Relative growth of the European edible crab, *Cancer pagurus*. II. Growth of the abdomen. *Growth* 7: 217-226.

Mackay, D.C.G. 1943b. Relative growth of the European edible crab, *Cancer pagurus*. III. Growth of the sternum and appendages. *Growth* 7: 401-412.

Martin, R.D., and P.H. Harvey. 1985. Brain size allometry: Ontogeny and phylogeny, Pp. 147-173 in *Size and Scaling in Primate Biology*, W.L. Jungers, ed. Plenum Press, New York. 491 pp.

Neter, J., W. Wasserman, W., and M.H. Kutner. 1985. *Applied Linear Statistical Models.* 2nd. ed., Richard D. Irwin, Inc., Homewood, Illinois.

Neuhoff, H.-G. 1979. Influence of temperature and salinity on food conversion and growth of different *Nereis* species (Polychaeta, Annelida). *Mar. Ecol. Prog. Ser.* 1: 255-262.

Nichols, F.H. 1974. Sediment turnover by a deposit-feeding polychaete. *Limnol. Oceanogr.* 19: 945-950.

Olive, P.J.W. 1983. Annelida-Polychaeta, Pp. 357-422 in *Reproductive Biology of Invertebrates: Oogenesis, Oviposition, and Oosorption*. Vol. I, K.G. and R.G. Adiyodi, eds. John Wiley and Sons, New York. 770 pp.

Pamatmat, M.M. 1980. Facultative anaerobiosis of benthos, Pp. 69-90 in *Marine Benthic Dynamics*, K.R. Tenore and B.C. Coull, eds. Belle Baruch Library of Marine Science No. 11., University of South Carolina Press, Columbia, South Carolina.

Pamatmat, M.M., and S. Findlay. 1983. Metabolism of microbes, nematodes, polychaetes, and their interactions in sediment, as detected by heat flow measurements. *Mar. Ecol. Prog. Ser.* 11: 31-38.

Pauly, D. 1981. The relationships between gill surface area and growth performance in fish: A generalization of von Bertalanffy's theory of growth. *Meeresforschung* 28:251-282.

Peters, R.H. 1983. Metabolism. Pp. 24-44 in *The Ecological Implications of Body Size*. Cambridge Univ. Press, New York. 329 pp.

Petraitis, P.S. 1985. Females inhibit males propensity to develop into simultaneous hermaphrodites in *Capitella* species I (Polychaeta). *Biol. Bull.* 168: 395-402.

Prosser, C.L. 1973. Introduction. Pp. xv-xxii in *Comparative Animal Physiology*, C.L. Prosser, ed. Saunders, Philadelphia. 456 pp.

Prosser, C.L. 1986. *Adaptational Biology: Molecules to Organisms*. John Wiley and Sons, New York. 784 pp.

Protter, M.H., and C.B. Morrey Jr. 1964. Volumes of solids of revolution. Pp. 245-247 in *Modern Mathematical Analysis*. Addison-Wesley, Reading, Massachusetts. 790 pp.

Rayner, J.M.V. 1985. Linear relations in biomechanics: The statistics of scaling functions. *J. Zool.*, Lond.(A) 206: 415-439.

Reeve, E.C.R., and J.S. Huxley. 1945. Some problems in the study of allometric growth. Pp. 121-156 in *Essays on Growth and Form*, W.E. le Gros Clark and P.B. Medawar eds. Oxford Univ. Press, London.

Ricker, W.E. 1973. Linear regressions in fishery research. *J. Fish. Res. Board Can.* 30: 409-434.

Ricker, W.E. 1975. A note concerning Professor Jolicoeur's comments. *J. Fish. Res. Board Can.* 32: 1494-1498.

Ricker, W.E. 1984. Computation and uses of central trend lines. *Can. J. Zool.* 62: 1897-1905.

Schmidt-Nielsen, K. 1983. What is physiology? Pp. 1-2 in *Animal Physiology*. Cambridge University Press, New York. 619 pp.

Sebens, K.P. 1981. The allometry of feeding, energetics, and body size in three sea anemone species. *Biol. Bull.* 161: 152-171.

Sebens, K.P. 1982. The limits to indeterminate growth: An optimal size model applied to passive suspension feeders. *Ecology* 63: 209-222.

Shumway, S.E. 1979. The effects of body size, oxygen tension, and mode of life on the oxygen uptake rates of polychaetes. *Comp. Biochem. Physiol.* 64(A): 273-278.

Smith, R.J. 1980. Rethinking allometry. *J. theor. Biol.* 87: 97-111.

Smith, R.J. 1984. Allometric scaling in comparative biology: Problems of concept and method. *Am. J. Physiol.* 246: R152- R160.

Somerton, D.A. 1980. A computer technique for estimating the size of sexual maturity in crabs. *Can. J. Fish. Aquat. Sci.* 37: 1488-1494.

Somerton, D.A. 1981. Regional variation in the size of maturity of two species of Tanner crab (*Chionoecetes bairdi* and *C. opilio*) in the Eastern Bering Sea, and its use in defining management subareas. *Can. J. Fish. Aquat. Sci.* 38: 163-174.

Teissier, G. 1960. Relative growth. Pp. 537-560 in *The Physiology of Crustacea: Metabolism and Growth*, Vol. I, T.H. Waterman, ed. Academic Press, New York. 670 pp.

Tenore, K.R. 1981. Organic nitrogen and the caloric content of detritus: I. Utilization by the deposit-feeding polychaete *Capitella capitata*. *Estuarine Coastal Shelf Sci.* 12: 39-47.

Tenore, K.R., and U.K. Gopalan. 1974. Feeding efficiencies of the polychaete *Nereis virens* cultured on hard-clam tissue and oyster detritus. *J. Fish. Res. Board Can.* 31: 1675-7678.

Vogel, Z., A. Zamir, and D. Elson. 1969. The possible involvement of peptidyl transferase in the termination step of protein biosynthesis. *Biochemistry* 12: 5161-5168.

Wilde, P.A.J.W. De and E.M. Berghuis. 1979. Laboratory experiments on growth of juvenile lugworms, *Arenicola marina*. *Neth. J. Sea Res.* 13: 487-502.

Zar, J.H. 1968. Calculation and miscalculation of the allometric equation as a model in biological data. *Bioscience* 18: 1118- 1120.

Chapter 9

The Relationship Between Ingestion Rate of Deposit Feeders and Sediment Nutritional Value

Leon M. Cammen
Bigelow Laboratory for Ocean Sciences
West Boothbay Harbor, Maine 04575

Introduction

Food resources of marine deposit feeders have been a subject of intense investigation for many years, but it has been only recently that some of the details have become apparent. Two general hypotheses have dominated research in this field: first, non-living organic carbon including detritus cannot be utilized directly by deposit feeders, but must first be transformed into microbial biomass by bacteria, fungi, and other microbes; and second, the resulting microbial biomass represents a major food resource for the deposit feeders (for example, Newell 1965; Fenchel 1970; Hargrave 1976; Lopez et al, 1977; Gerlach 1978). These two hypotheses are by no means independent and each has been used to support the other. However, as I have pointed out previously (Cammen 1980a), in order to evaluate the importance of a potential food resource it is necessary to consider both the rate at which it is ingested and the efficiency with which it is assimilated. In terms of non-living organic carbon, we have an abundance of data for deposit feeders on ingestion rates (Cammen 1980b), but very little quantitative data on assimilation efficiencies; the situation for microbial carbon is exactly the inverse, with numerous studies of deposit feeder assimilation efficiencies (for example, Zhukhova 1963; Hargrave 1970; Kofoed 1975; Yingst 1976; Lopez et al. 1977; Cammen 1980a), but very few of ingestion rates (Wetzel 1977; Jensen and Siegismund 1980; Cammen 1980a). Yet, somehow the qualitative data showing that assimilation efficiency is generally low for non-living organic carbon or detritus and the data showing high assimilation efficiencies for microbes have been combined to suggest that the major food source for marine deposit feeders must be the microbes—the information on ingestion rates has been largely ignored. Recently, however, several studies have taken into account the ingestion rates of microbes by the deposit feeders (Wetzel 1977; concluded that bacteria can be only of minor importance in the carbon budgets of the animals. In fact, no one has ever shown that any deposit feeder uses bacteria for a major fraction of its nutritional requirements. Thus, the question of how much non- living organic matter contributes to deposit feeder nutrition has become much more important. Unfortunately, it is a difficult question to address since the high ingestion rates make even a low assimilation efficiency significant (Cammen 1980a; Levinton 1980) and with current methods we cannot measure a low assimilation efficiency with any degree of accuracy.

How Much of the Organic Matter in Sediments is Available to Deposit Feeders?

In view of the variety of potential food sources available to deposit feeders in marine sediments, it may actually be preferable to evaluate their importance by concentrating on the animals themselves, rather than on the sediment; the question, then, would be how much of the ingested organic carbon needs to be assimilated in order to satisfy the animal's carbon requirement. Since the largest fraction of an animal's carbon budget usually goes to satisfy the requirement for respiration, those data are a good place to begin. Table 9.1 represents a compilation of data for deposit feeders where ingestion rates in terms of organic carbon are available along with respiration rates. The data set was limited to those species where similar temperatures and body weights were used for both measurements; where possible, the ingestion data have

Species	Dry body weight (mg)	Organic carbon ingestion (μg h^{-1})	Carbon respired (μg h^{-1})	M	Temperature, Source Notes
P1	340	1491	47.7	3.2	10-14°C; 1,a
P2	340	961	31.8	3.3	10-14°C; 1,b
A	0.3	5	0.2	4.1	15°C; 2
D	63	223	9.4	4.2	20°C; 3,c
G	0.5	9	0.4	4.5	20°C; 4
P3	5.8	30	1.5	5.0	15°C; 5
B	5.1	20	1.1	5.5	6°; 6,d

Table 9.1: Calculation of minimum assimilation, M required by deposit feeders. Species are: P1 *Abarenicola vagabunda* (polychaete); P2 *A. pacifica*; A *Hyalella azteca* (amphipod); D *Uca pugnax* (decapod); G *Potamopyrgus jenkinsi* (gastropod); P3 *Nereis succinea* (polychaete); and B *Macoma balthica* (bivalve). Organic matter concentrations were converted to organic carbon by dividing by 1.9 (Bader 1954), and a respiratory quotient of 0.9 has been assumed; body weight is as close as possible to the geometric mean of the size range considered in each study. Experimental temperatures varied from 6–20 °C, but were the same for ingestion and respiration for each species. Sources of the data are: 1) Hobson 1967; 2) Hargrave 1970, 1972; 3) Krebs 1976, Shanholtzer 1973; 4) Heywood and Edwards 1962; 5) Cammen 1980a; and 6) Bubnova 1972, Kennedy and Mihursky 1972. Notes: (a) Ingestion of organic matter multiplied by 1.52 to account for selection (Hylleberg 1975). (b) Ingestion of organic matter multiplied by 1.03 to account for selection (Hylleberg 1975). (c) Organic matter concentration of the sediment from Valiela et al. (1974), multiplied by 2.15 to account for selection (Teal 1962; Shanholtzer 1973). (d) Respiration predicted from Q_{10} calculated from Kennedy and Mihursky (1972).

Required for:	Estimated by:	Percent of total ingested C
Respiration	Measurement	3.2–5.5
Growth	25% growth efficiency	1.1–1.8
Release of DOC	Magnitude of respiration	0–5.5
Total		4.3–12.8
Assuming a 60% assimilation efficiency		7–21

Table 9.2: Estimated percentage of organic carbon in ingested material needed to satisfy the carbon requirement of a typical deposit feeder.

been corrected to take into account selection for organic matter. At first glance, the percentage of ingested organic carbon that must be assimilated to satisfy respiration is remarkably similar for such a diverse group of animals and body sizes. However, we must remember that there are strong, species-independent, exponential relationships between body size and respiration rate (e.g. Zeuthen 1953) and body size and ingestion rate (Cammen 1980b) and that in both cases the exponent for body size is about 0.7; thus, it is not surprising that the ratio of respiration rate to ingestion rate is relatively constant.

Respiration is only one aspect of the overall carbon budget of an animal, though, and if we make the budget more complete, the percentage assimilation required is increased (Table 9.2). For purposes of this calculation, an average growth efficiency (P/A) of 25% has been used, representing a conservative value for many species (Conover 1978; Cammen 1987). Release of dissolved organic carbon varies greatly from species to species, but the highest values can be greater than the respiratory loss of carbon; in this calculation the maximum release rate has been assumed to equal the respiratory loss of carbon. Thus, the total percentage of organic carbon in the sediment that must be assimilated might be on the order of 4 to 13%. However, animals cannot assimilate 100% of even the most available sources of carbon such as bacteria or microalgae; if we assume an assimilation efficiency of 60% (typical for sediment microbes) for the "available carbon," then this simple model suggests that from 7 to 21% of the organic carbon in the sediment must be "available" if the animals are to be able to satisfy their carbon requirements. With that limitation in mind, we can begin to examine the sediment in order to identify which organic matter fractions might be abundant enough to make up this "available" pool.

As discussed earlier, most of the speculation regarding food resources available to deposit feeders has focused on microbes in general and on bacteria, specifically. But just how abundant are the microbes in marine sediments? This question has been addressed for bacteria in marine sediments in general (Rublee 1982) and in specific size-fractions within sediments (Cammen 1982) and the conclusion was the same: Bacteria usually make up only a minor fraction of sediment organic carbon, that is, less that 2%. That means that if an animal actually needs 10 or 20% of the sediment organic carbon to be "available," some organic pool other than just bacteria must be included. The presence of microalgae in the sediments offers another potentially abundant food resource. Microalgal biomass can be an order of magnitude greater than bacterial biomass in surface sediment (Rublee 1982) and it can account for over 70% of the organic carbon in some size-fractions (Cammen 1982); seasonally, algal carbon (including sedimented phytoplankton) can be abundant even at depths of several thousand meters in connection with bloom events. For surface deposit feeders then, microalgae offer an attractive and abundant source of "available" carbon and in some intertidal and shallow subtidal areas microalgae may be sufficient to satisfy the carbon requirements of the animals (Jensen and Siegismund 1980; Levinton and Bianchi 1981; Christensen and Kanneworff 1983; Bianchi and Levinton 1984). As for sub-surface deposit feeders or for those deposit feeders feeding at depths or locations where bloom inputs do not occur, the question of the actual food resource is an open one.

During this discussion, the organic matter contained in living microbes has been considered separately from that included in the pool of "microbially-derived" material. That pool includes material such as cellular debris from recently dead cells, which may still be quite nutritious, and extra-cellular release products from bacteria and microalgae, which may make up a significant portion of sediment organic matter (Hobbie and Lee 1980). Reports of the nutritional value of these extracellular polymers to deposit feeders are contradictory (Harvey and Luoma 1984; Baird and Thistle 1986), but the differences may simply represent interspecific variation.

In most sediments, however, the predominant fraction of the organic matter is detrital, often of undetermined origin. Since consumption of this pool is so large relative to the microbial pools, even a very low assimilation efficiency could result in a significant uptake of organic carbon; for example, an assimilation efficiency of only 1.8% for the detrital pool would have allowed a population of the polychaete *Nereis succinea* to take up an amount of organic carbon equivalent to that it derived from the microbial pool with an assimilation efficiency of 57% (Cammen 1980a). A variety of studies of deposit feeders or detritivores have found some degree of assimilation of detritus in the absence of microbes (Kofoed 1975; Foulds and Mann 1978; Cammen 1980a; Fong and Mann 1980; Schoenberg et al. 1984; Sinsabaugh et al. 1985; Kemp 1986). However, technical problems have as yet hindered experimental work in this area and we cannot be sure of the importance of non-living organic matter to deposit feeders in nature; new techniques which allow non-specific radiolabeling of sediment organic material (Banks and Wolfinbarger 1981; Lopez and Crenshaw 1982; Wolfinbarger and Crosby 1983) have the potential to provide the answers to this question, but the problem will continue to be a difficult one.

Finally, it must be emphasized that these comments and calculations refer only to carbon or overall energy budgets of deposit feeders. If the nutritional "currency" were to be changed to nitrogen or other essential nutrients, the relative importance of the microbes might be much greater than that calculated above. For example, the assimilation of microbial nitrogen was enough to completely satisfy the requirements for growth of the *Nereis succinea* population mentioned above (Cammen 1980a). Phillips (1984a) has elaborated on this point for a variety of specific, essential nutrients. Thus, it is important to remember that animals have many nutritional needs to satisfy, not just a requirement for a certain rate of overall energy uptake, and that these potentially conflicting demands may make it difficult to describe a complex feeding behavior with simple foraging models; with that caveat in mind, though, it is still useful to make the effort.

Is optimal foraging behavior by marine deposit feeders subject to physiological limitation?

There have been several attempts to explain the variations in ingestion rate by deposit feeders as a function of food quality, where food quality is measured by the concentration of non-living or living organic carbon in the sediment. The basis for most of the discussion has been the optimal foraging model developed by Taghon et al. (1978) to explain particle selection behavior. There is often a wide spectrum of particle sizes in marine sediments and these particles are made up of a complex array of living and non-living organic matter including mineral grains, organic-mineral aggregates, fecal pellets, microalgae, fungi, meiofauna, protozoans and detrital particles (Johnson 1974, 1977; Whitlatch 1974, 1981). Since some of these particles are more nutritious than others, it would be advantageous to deposit feeders to be able to select only the most nutritious particles, if the energetic cost of the selection process were not too great. Taghon et al.'s model examined particle selection behavior in relation to optimal foraging considerations and suggested that deposit feeders should select smaller particles in order to maximize their rate of energy gain. This type of selection is certainly common with deposit feeders, but it is by no means universal since many species feed non-selectively (for example, Gordon 1966; Hughes 1979) and some even select for larger particles (Whitlatch 1974, 1980a; Whitlatch and Weinberg 1982).

The particle selection model begins with the assumption that the nutritional value of a particle is proportional to its surface area, the implication being that smaller particles are more nutritious. This assumption is based on the idea that microbes are the major food source of deposit feeders and that these microbes are concentrated on the surfaces of particles. However, as discussed above, it is now clear that microbes are generally not a major source of carbon or energy for deposit feeders and this means that food quality may not necessarily be a function of particle size at all; a survey of the relationship between nutritional quality and particle size *within* four marine sediments showed that the relationship was generally not predictable (Cammen 1982), thus making it difficult to apply optimal foraging models to explain particle selection. As an alternative to optimal foraging models, more mechanistic views of particle selection have emerged (Self and Jumars 1978; Whitlatch 1980b; Jumars et al. 1981, 1982; Taghon 1982). These studies have identified two critical factors: 1) Probability of contact of the feeding apparatus (such as tentacles) with a given size particle, which can be shown to favor selection of larger particles; and 2) Probability of retention of a particle once it has been contacted, a function of adhesive strength of the mucus on the feeding apparatus, which favors the retention/selection of smaller and less dense particles or particles with an organic coating. Models based on these types of considerations may be better able to explain the particle selection behavior of deposit feeders than those based solely on optimal foraging constraints.

The optimal foraging model has also been extended to cover non-selective deposit feeders (Taghon 1981). For those animals, the model predicts that ingestion rate should increase as food quality increases in order to maximize the net rate of energy gain; the increase in ingestion rate should continue until some maximum ingestion rate is reached and then that maximum rate should be maintained with further increases in food quality.

Several studies of deposit feeders have found results consistent with Taghon's model. For example, ingestion rates were greater for the polychaete *Arenicola marina* as sediment food content was increased (de Wilde and Berghuis 1979) and for the amphipod *Corophium volutator* as the ratio of natural sediment to glass beads increased within the size-fraction of sediment suitable for ingestion (Doyle 1979). Taghon and Jumars (1984) measured ingestion rates for three deposit-feeding polychaetes which were fed glass beads with varying levels of bound protein and, as predicted, ingestion rate increased with increasing protein concentration.

On the other hand, there is also a sizable body of data which appears to contradict this model. Ingestion rates for the polychaetes *Pectinaria gouldii* and *Axiothella rubrocincta* were inversely related to organic matter and pigment concentration in intertidal sediment (Gordon 1966; Kudenov 1982).

A survey of 19 species of deposit feeders and detritivores from three phyla showed that ingestion rate of total dry material varied inversely with the organic content of the food; the result was an ingestion rate of organic matter essentially independent of the concentration in the food source (Cammen 1980b). A similar response has been seen in animals other than deposit feeders: goldfish (Rozin and Mayer 1961); brine shrimp (Reeve 1963); rats (Mercer et al. 1981); insects (Gelperin 1971; Slansky and Feeny 1977); and many non-ruminant domestic animals (McDonald and Edwards 1982). It thus appears that Taghon's model alone may not be sufficient to describe adequately the response of deposit feeders to variable food quality.

An alternative to Taghon's model which may reconcile the apparent discrepancies in the experimental data has been presented by Phillips (1984b). While Taghon's model assumed a maximum ingestion rate, all other physiological processes were assumed to be unbounded. It is highly unlikely, however, that any physiological rate process can increase indefinitely and in order to make the model more realistic, Phillips' model assumes an additional physiological limitation for the organism. This limitation could take the form, for example, of a maximum rate of transport across the gut wall, a maximum rate of metabolism of assimilated material or even a maximum growth rate. With this additional physiological limitation, the optimal response of the animal to variation in food quality changes dramatically since once that limit is reached there no longer is any advantage to increasing ingestion rate; in fact, the energetic cost of additional feeding and the loss of potential food to feces (since most deposit feeders will not immediately reingest their feces) makes it advantageous to feed at the minimum rate which is adequate to reach the limiting factor. The result then is an increase in ingestion rate with increasing food quality until some threshold value is reached at which point ingestion rate should begin to decrease. Calow (1982) has shown that such a homeostatic response is a possible outcome of natural selective pressure. The conflicting results discussed above might then result from various investigators measuring different portions of the feeding curve. Those working with low food qualities (for example, the experimental beads used by Taghon and Jumars (1984) had on the order of 0.01–0.02% organic matter, extremely low for marine sediments) might see an increasing ingestion rate as food quality increased, while those working with more natural levels might see the opposite response. In fact, ingestion rate of the amphipod *Siphonoecetes dellavallei* appeared to follow the response predicted by Phillips with the rate of food gathering being controlled by food concentration below the "incipient limiting concentration" and being controlled by gut capacity above that concentration (Guidi 1986); the result was that the ingestion rate of organic carbon increased with food concentration at low levels of food, but leveled off as food concentrations were increased further. Guidi's study seems to be the first which has been able to show that response in a marine deposit feeder.

There are two hypotheses which might explain regulation of ingestion rates in response to food quality. The first is that the animals have the physiological ability to adjust their ingestion rates in response to short-term variations in food quality either as a result of temporal or spatial changes in their environment. The second would be that the variation in ingestion rates results from long-term adaptation to differing environments by various species populations. These two possibilities have been referred to as two forms of an energy-maximization hypothesis (Doyle 1979); a "special" form which would allow parameters of the feeding model to vary with changing nutritional quality of the food; and a "general" form which would optimize feeding behavior only over a longer time frame, perhaps as long as several generations.

I have investigated this problem with two experimental approaches designed to measure ingestion rates over a range of food quality on natural sediment with a natural population of microbes. In the first set of experiments, food quality was varied by selecting natural sediments with a wide range of concentrations of microalgae and sieving to control the particle size. In the second set of experiments, single grains were separated from particle aggregates within the 40-67 μm particle-size fraction of a natural sediment and various proportions of these two types of particles were recom-

Source of Sediment	Source of *Corophium*	Microalgal C (μg g^{-1})	Egestion rate (μg animal^{-1}h^{-1})
Peck's Cove	Peck's Cove	790	852±169
Peck's Cove	Starr's Point	790	961±137
Starr's Point	Peck's Cove	258	315±106
Starr's Point	Starr's Point	258	398±37

Table 9.3: Egestion rates for two populations of similar-sized *Corophium volutator* feeding on sediment from each location. The sediment was sieved initially to give the $< 67\mu$m fraction, the animals were allowed to feed on that fraction for 24 h, and then the sediment was sieved again through a 102μfm sieve to collect the feces; the incubations were carried out in the dark at 21-23 $^{\circ}$C. The concentration of microalgal C is given for the $< 67\mu$m fraction of the sediment and was determined using a C/Chl a ratio of 40 (Cammen, 1982). Egestion rates are ± 1 standard deviation.

bined to generate sediment fractions of varying food quality, but identical particle size. In both sets of experiments, the resulting sediment fractions were fed to one of two deposit feeders, the amphipod *Corophium volutator* or the snail *Hydrobia ulvae*. I used surface sediment (scraped from the top few millimeters) in all these experiments so that microbial populations (especially microalgae) would be abundant enough to represent a major food source.

In an initial attempt to distinguish between the "special" and "general" forms of the energy-maximization hypothesis, two *Corophium* populations were sampled along with sediment from their respective environments. Similar-sized individuals were then allowed to feed on the $< 67\mu$m fractions of their own sediment and of the sediment from the other location. The intent was to find out whether there was an overriding, genetically fixed control of ingestion rate or whether the response could be a more immediate one; in the former case the ingestion rates should have been constant for each population regardless of the sediment, and in the latter case the ingestion rates should have varied with the sediment. As is obvious from the results (Table 9.3), the ingestion rates were determined by the sediments, not by the differences in the two populations. The second observation from this experiment was that there was a clear increase in ingestion rate with the increase in microalgal biomass in the food. This experiment was not, however, the ideal test of the "general" form of the hypothesis since in the intertidal zone of a temperate region, sediment quality will vary both spatially and temporally; this makes it difficult to determine the "average" food quality experienced by each of the populations.

In order to further examine the variation in ingestion rate with sediment food quality of natural sediments, a series of feeding experiments were carried out using *Corophium* from Maine (USA), Nova Scotia (Canada), and Denmark, and *Hydrobia* sp. from Denmark. These animals were fed the <67 or 38-67 μm fraction of surface sediment. Feeding rates of *Corophium* were scaled to individuals with a length of 5.5 mm using the length-weight relationship from Müller and Rosenberg (1982) and the body weight-ingestion rate relationship from Cammen (1980b); all individuals of *Hydrobia* were similar-sized so no scaling was necessary.

Both deposit feeders were able to adjust their feeding rates to varying concentrations of food (Table 9.3; Fig. 9.1). *Corophium* appears to reach a threshold for ingestion rate within the range of concentrations of microalgae utilized in these experiments (Fig. 9.1). The pattern of the response to varying food quality thus supports the ingestion model of Phillips (1984b) and suggests that *Corophium* may often exist where food is not limiting. The response for *Hydrobia* showed only a decrease in ingestion rate with increasing food quality, but the microalgal concentrations tested did not range as low as those for *Corophium* and thus may have missed the range where the response would have been positive.

The third set of experiments to be reported here was intended to determine the degree of selection by deposit feeders for or against individual sediment grains as opposed to aggregates of smaller particles and to attempt to evaluate the effect of that selection on the nutrition of the animals. Surface sediment was collected from a Danish mudflat and sieved to isolate the 41-67 μm size-fraction. That fraction was then swirled gently in a petri dish to separate the relatively heavy sand grains from the relatively light aggregates; repeating the process several times resulted in two essentially clean fractions, one containing 41- 67 μm sand grains, and one containing 41-67 μm particle aggregates. *Corophium* and *Hydrobia* were allowed to feed on mixtures of these two fractions containing 0, 25, 50, 75, and 100% sand grains and the egestion rates were measured. In separate but similar experiments, the fraction of sand grains was counted prior to and following feeding by the animals so that the degree of selection for or against the individual grains could be determined; these experiments were carried out for the mixtures with 50% and 75% aggregates. In addition, by counting the sediment par-

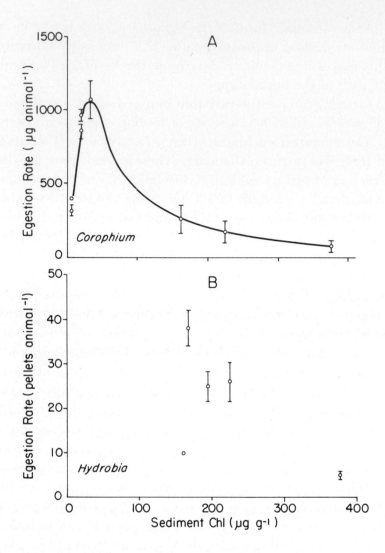

Figure 9.1: Egestion rates for the amphipod *Corophium volutator* (A) and the snail *Hydrobia* sp. (B) feeding on natural sediment fractions (either 38-67 μm or <67 μm in diameter) with varied concentrations of microalgae. Vertical bars represent one standard error.

Type of particle	Mean weight (ng)	C per Particle (ng)		C per weight (ng/ng)	
		Microbial	Total Organic	Microbial	Total Organic
Aggregate	14	0.23	0.85	0.016	0.061
Grain	84	0.27	0.60	0.003	0.007

Table 9.4: Comparison of 41-67 μm sand grain with identical-sized aggregate. Particles were sieved from surface sediment taken from a mudflat at Romo, Denmark. Microbial carbon consists of microalgal C, calculated with a C/Chl a ratio of 40 (Cammen, 1982), and bacterial C, calculated with a conversion factor of 0.22 g C cm^{-3} (Bratbak and Dundas 1984).

ticles in each fraction per unit weight, it was possible to determine various nutritional parameters for the two types of particles; the nutritional benefit of selection for or against the sand grains was then calculated.

As expected, individual sand grains were less nutritious than similar-sized aggregates on a per weight basis, but there was little difference between the two types on a per particle basis (Table 9.4). In terms of the fraction of total organic carbon accounted for by microbes, it could be argued that the organic matter present on a sand grain was potentially of greater value to a deposit feeder than that contained in an aggregate.

Both *Corophium* and *Hydrobia* showed feeding responses consistent with the Phillips model (Fig. 9.2a). Taking into account the degree of selection for particle aggregates within these mixtures of particles, we can calculate the actual amount of microbial carbon ingested by these animals; that amount appeared to reach a maximum when the percentage of aggregates reached 50% and then remained about the same despite an increase in the percentage of aggregates in the mixture. In fact, the actual ingestion rate decreased as the percentage of aggregates increased from 75 to 100%. The response of these two species to changes in food quality could certainly be interpreted as tending toward homeostasis (see Calow 1982).

None of the experiments discussed briefly here are conclusive in themselves, but considered together, they do provide support for the Taghon-Phillips optimal foraging model extended to include compensatory feeding. Although the model is attractive since it explains otherwise contradictory results and initial tests are promising, further experiments with more rigorous

214

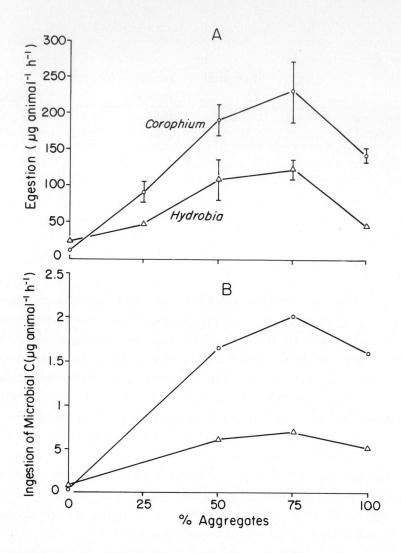

Figure 9.2: Effect of varying fractions of individual grains and particle aggregates on egestion rate of sediment (A) and uptake of microbes (B) by *Corophium volutator* and *Hydrobia* sp. There was no particle selection data for the 25% aggregate mixture, so ingestion of microbes could not be calculated for that fraction. Vertical bars represent one standard error.

controls will be necessary before it can be fully accepted.

Problems in Deposit Feeding Research

The problems discussed in this article are a few of the questions which remain to be addressed in deposit feeding research. For example, questions remain as to the ultimate constraints on feeding behavior: Is control exercised through weight, volume, numbers, quality, or some other attribute of sediment particles or is the feeding rate largely determined by internal physiological constraints? In the first section of this Chapter, we saw that a relatively large fraction of the sediment organic matter must be available to deposit feeders for their nutrition, but our knowledge of the source and composition of that organic matter is lacking. A related problem, addressed elsewhere in this volume, is to determine how variations in ingestion rate interact with those in assimilation efficiency to control the assimilation of organic material by the animals. Ultimately it would be useful to develop these types of models to the point where they could be used in models of ecosystem energetics (e.g. Peters 1978). Describing the transfer of energy through benthic organisms is certainly one of the most intriguing aspects of benthic ecology and the potential significance of that transfer to commercial fisheries makes it even more important to extend our knowledge.

Bigelow Laboratory for Ocean Sciences Contribution No. 87017

Literature Cited

Bader, R.G. 1954. Use of factors for converting carbon or nitrogen to total sedimentary organics. *Science* 120: 709-710.

Baird, B.H. and D. Thistle. 1986. Uptake of bacterial extracellular polymer by a deposit-feeding holothurian (*Isostichopus badionotus*). *Mar. Biol.* 92: 183-187.

Banks, C.W. and L. Wolfinbarger, Jr. 1981. A rapid and convenient method for radiolabeling detritus with [^{14}C]acetic anhydride. *J. Exp. Mar. Biol. Ecol.* 53: 115-123.

Bianchi, T.S. and J.S. Levinton. 1984. The importance of microalgae, bacteria and particulate organic matter in the somatic growth of *Hydrobia totteni. J. Mar. Res.* 42: 431-443.

Bratbak, G. and I. Dundas. 1984. Bacterial dry matter content and biomass estimations. *Appl. Environ. Microbiol.* 48: 755-757.

Bubnova, N.P. 1972. The nutrition of the detritus-feeding mollusks *Macoma balthica* (L.) and *Portlandia arctica* (Gray) and their influence on bottom sediments. *Oceanology* 12: 899-905.

Calow, P. 1982. Homeostasis and fitness. *Am. Nat.* 120: 416-419.

Cammen, L.M. 1980a. The significance of microbial carbon in the nutrition of the deposit feeding polychaete *Nereis succinea*. *Mar. Biol.* 61: 9-20.

Cammen, L.M. 1980b. Ingestion rate: An empirical model for aquatic deposit feeders and detritivores. *Oecologia* 44: 303-310.

Cammen, L.M. 1982. Effect of particle size on organic content and microbial abundance within four marine sediments. *Mar. Ecol. Prog. Ser.* 9: 273-280.

Cammen, L.M. 1987. Polychaetes. pp. 217-260, In: T.J. Pandian and F.J. Vernberg (eds.), *Animal Energetics*. Academic Press, New York.

Christensen, H. and E. Kanneworff. 1985. Sedimenting phytoplankton as major food source for suspension and deposit feeders in the Oresund. *Ophelia* 24: 223-244.

Conover, R.J. 1978. Transformation of organic matter, pp. 221- 299. In: O. Kinne, (ed.), *Marine Ecology*. Vol. IV. Dynamics. John Wiley and Sons, New York.

Doyle, R.W. 1979. Ingestion rate of a selective deposit feeder in a complex mixture of particles: Testing the energy- optimization hypothesis. *Limnol. Oceanogr.* 24: 867-874.

Fenchel, T. 1970. Studies on the decomposition of organic detritus derived from the turtle grass *Thalassia testudinum*. *Limnol. Oceanogr.* 15: 14-20.

Fong, W. and K.H. Mann. 1980. Role of gut flora in the transfer of amino acids through a marine food chain. *Can. J. Fish. Aquat. Sci.* 37: 88-96.

Foulds, J.B. and K.H. Mann. 1978. Cellulose digestion in the mysid shrimp *Mysis stenolepis* and its ecological implications. *Limnol. Oceanogr.* 23: 760-766.

Gelperin, A. 1971. Regulation of feeding. *Ann. Rev. Entomol.* 16: 365-378.

Gerlach, S.A. 1978. Food-chain relationships in subtidal silty sand marine sediments and the role of meiofauna in stimulating bacterial productivity. *Oecologia* 33: 55-69.

Gordon, D.C., Jr. 1966. The effects of the deposit feeding polychaete *Pectinaria gouldii* on the intertidal sediments of Barnstable Harbor. *Limnol. Oceanogr.* 11: 327-332.

Guidi, L.D. 1986. The feeding response of the epibenthic amphipod *Siphonoecetes dellavallei* Stebbing to varying food particle sizes and concentrations. *J. Exp. Mar. Biol. Ecol.* 98: 51-63.

Hargrave, B.T. 1970. The effect of a deposit-feeding amphipod on the metabolism of benthic microflora. *Limnol. Oceanogr.* 15: 21-30.

Hargrave, B.T. 1972. Prediction of egestion by the deposit- feeding amphipod *Hyalella azteca*. *Oikos* 23: 116-124.

Hargrave, B.T. 1976. The central role of invertebrate faeces in sediment decomposition, pp. 301-321. In: J.M. Anderson and A. MacFadyen, (eds.), *The Role of Terrestrial and Aquatic Organisms in Decomposition Processes*. Blackwell Scientific Publications, Oxford.

Harvey, R.W. and S.N. Luoma. 1984. The role of bacterial exopolymer and suspended bacteria in the nutrition of the deposit-feeding clam, *Macoma balthica*. *J. Mar. Res.* 42: 957-968.

Heywood, J. and R.W. Edwards. 1962. Some aspects of the ecology of *Potamopyrgus jenkinsi* Smith. *J. Anim. Ecol.* 31: 239-250.

Hobbie, J. and C. Lee. 1980. Microbial production of extracellular material: Importance in benthic ecology, pp. 341- 346. In: K.R. Tenore and B.C. Coull (eds.), *Marine Benthic Dynamics*. Univ. of S. Carolina Press, Columbia.

Hobson, K.D. 1967. The feeding and ecology of two North Pacific *Abarenicola* species (Arenicolidae, Polychaeta). *Biol. Bull.* 133: 343-354.

Hughes, T.C. 1979. Mode of life and feeding in maldanid polychaetes from St. Margaret's Bay, Nova Scotia. *J. Fish. Res. Board Can.* 36: 1503-1507.

Hylleberg, J. 1975. Selective feeding by *Abarenicola pacifica* with notes on *Abarenicola vagabunda* and a concept of gardening in lugworms. *Ophelia* 14: 113-137.

Jensen, K.T. and H.R. Siegismund. 1980. The importance of diatoms and bacteria in the diet of *Hydrobia* species. *Ophelia* 19(Suppl.): 193-199.

Johnson, R.G. 1974. Particulate matter at the sediment-water interface in coastal environments. *J. Mar. Res.* 32: 313-330.

Johnson, R.G. 1977. Vertical variation in particulate matter in the upper twenty centimeters of marine sediments. *J. Mar. Res.* 35: 273-282.

Jumars, P.A., Nowell, A.R.M., and Self, R.F.L. 1981. A simple model of flow-sediment-organism interaction. *Mar. Geol.* 42: 155-172.

Jumars, P.A., Self, R.F.L., and Nowell, A.R.M. 1982. Mechanics of particle selection by tentaculate deposit-feeders. *J. Exp. Mar. Biol. Ecol.* 64: 47-70.

Kemp, P. 1986. Direct uptake of detrital carbon by the deposit- feeding polychaete *Euzonus mucronata* (Treadwell). *J. Exp. Mar. Biol. Ecol.* 99: 49-61.

Kemp, P.F. 1987. Potential impact on bacteria of grazing by a macrofaunal deposit-feeder, and the fate of bacterial production. *Mar. Ecol. Prog. Ser.* 36: 151-161.

Kennedy, V.S. and J. A. Mihursky. 1972. Effects of temperature on the respiratory metabolism of three Chesapeake Bay bivalves. *Ches. Sci.* 13: 1-22.

Kofoed, L.H. 1975. The feeding biology of *Hydrobia ventrosa* (Montagu). I. The assimilation of different components of the food. *J. Exp. Mar. Biol. Ecol.* 19: 233-241.

Krebs, C.T. 1976. Population dynamics and energetics of the fiddler crab *Uca pugnax* and the effect of contamination with chlorinated hydrocarbons from sewage. Ph.D. thesis, Boston Univ. 141 p.

Kudenov, J.D. 1982. Rates of seasonal sediment reworking in *Axiothella rubrocincta* (Polychaeta:Maldanidae). *Mar. Biol.* 70: 181-186.

Levinton, J.S. 1980. Particle feeding by deposit feeders: Models, data, and a prospectus, pp. 423-429. In: K.R. Tenore and B.C. Coull (eds.), *Marine Benthic Dynamics.* Univ. of S. Carolina Press, Columbia.

Levinton, J.S. and T.S. Bianchi. 1981. Nutrition and food limitation of deposit feeders. I. The role of microbes in the growth of mud snails (Hydrobiidae). *J. Mar. Res.* 39: 531-545.

Lopez, G.R. and Crenshaw, M.A. 1982. Radiolabelling of sedimentary organic matter with ^{14}C-formaldehyde: Preliminary evaluation of a new technique for use in deposit- feeding studies. *Mar. Ecol. Prog. Ser.* 8: 283-289.

Lopez, G.R., J.S. Levinton and L.B. Slobodkin. 1977. The effect of grazing by the detritivore *Orchestia grillus* on *Spartina* litter and its associated microbial community. *Oecologia* 30: 111-127.

McDonald, P. and R.A. Edwards. 1982. *Animal nutrition.* Longman, New York. 475 p.

Mercer, L.P., D.F. Watson and J.S. Ramlet. 1981. Control of food intake in the rat by dietary protein concentration. *J. Nutr.* 111: 1117-1123.

Müller, P. and R. Rosenberg. 1982. Production and abundance of the amphipod *Corophium volutator* on the west coast of Sweden. *Neth. J. Sea Res.* 16: 127-140.

Newell, R.C. 1965. The role of detritus in the nutrition of two marine deposit feeders, the prosobranch *Hydrobia ulvae* and the bivalve *Macoma balthica. Proc. Zool. Soc. London* 144: 25-45.

Peters, R.H. 1978. Empirical physiological models of ecosystem processes. *Verh. Internat. Verein. Limnol.* 20: 110-118.

Phillips, N.W. 1984a. Role of different microbes and substrates as potential suppliers of specific, essential nutrients to marine detritivores. *Bull. Mar. Sci.* 35: 283-298.

Phillips, N.W. 1984b. Compensatory intake can be consistent with an optimal foraging model. *Am. Nat.* 123: 867-872.

Reeve, M.R. 1963. The filter feeding of *Artemia*. II. In suspensions of various particles. J. Exp. Biol. 40: 207-214.

Rozin, P. and J. Mayer. 1961. Regulation of food intake in the goldfish. Am. J. Physiol. 201: 968-974.

Rublee, P.A. 1982. Bacteria and microbial distribution in estuarine sediments, pp. 159-182. In: V.S. Kennedy (ed.), *Estuarine Comparisons*. Academic Press, New York.

Schoenberg, S.A., A.E. Maccubbin and R.E. Hodson. 1984. Cellulose digestion by freshwater microcrustacea. *Limnol. Oceanogr.* 29: 1132-1136.

Self, R.F.L., and Jumars, P.A. 1978. New resource axes for deposit feeders? *J. Mar. Res.* 36: 627-641.

Shanholtzer, S.F. 1973. Energy flow, food habits and population dynamics of *Uca pugnax* in a salt marsh system. Ph.D. thesis, Univ. of Georgia. 91 p.

Sinsabaugh, R.L., A.E. Linkins and E.F. Benfield. 1985. Cellulose digestion and assimilation by three leaf-shredding aquatic insects. *Ecology* 66: 1464-1471.

Slansky, F. and P. Feeny. 1977. Stabilization of the rate of nitrogen accumulation by larvae of the cabbage butterfly on wild and cultivated food plants. Ecol. Monogr. 47: 209-228.

Taghon, G.L. 1981. Beyond selection: Optimal ingestion rate as a function of food value. *Am. Nat.* 118: 202-214.

Taghon, G.L. 1982. Optimal foraging by deposit-feeding invertebrates: Roles of particle size and organic coating. *Oecologia* 52: 295-304.

Taghon, G.L., and Jumars, P.A. 1984. Variable ingestion rate and its role in optimal foraging behavior of marine deposit- feeders. *Ecology* 65: 549-558.

Taghon, G.L., Self, R.F.L., and Jumars, P.A. 1978. Predicting particle selection by deposit feeders: A model and its implications. *Limnol. Oceanogr.* 23: 752-759.

Teal, J.M. 1962. Energy flow in the salt marsh ecosystem of Georgia. *Ecology* 43: 614-624.

Valiela, I., D.F. Babiec, W. Atherton, S. Seitzinger and C. Krebs. 1974. Some consequences of sexual dimorphism: Feeding in male and female fiddler crabs, *Uca pugnax* (Smith). Biol. Bull. 147: 652-660.

Wetzel, R.L. 1977. Carbon resources of a benthic salt marsh invertebrate *Nassarius obsoletus* Say (Mollusca: Nassariidae), pp. 293-308. In: M. Wiley (ed.), *Estuarine Processes*, Vol. 2. Academic Press, New York.

Whitlatch, R.B. 1974. Food-resource partitioning in the deposit feeding polychaete *Pectinaria gouldii*. *Biol. Bull.* 147: 227-235.

Whitlatch, R.B. 1980a. Patterns of resource utilization and coexistence in marine intertidal deposit-feeding communities. *J. Mar. Res.* 38: 743-765.

Whitlatch, R.B. 1980b. Foraging in the deposit-feeding polychaete *Pectinaria gouldii*: Testing the energy- optimization hypothesis. *Am. Zool.* 20: 920.

Whitlatch, R.B. 1981. Animal-sediment relationships in intertidal marine benthic habitats: Some determinants of deposit-feeding species diversity. *J. Exp. Mar. Biol. Ecol.* 53: 31-45.

Whitlatch, R.B., and Weinberg, J.R. 1982. Factors influencing particle selection and feeding rate in the polychaete *Cistenides (Pectinaria) gouldii*. *Mar. Biol.* 71: 33-40.

Wilde, P.A.W.J. de and E.M. Berghuis. 1979. Laboratory experiments on growth of juvenile lugworms, *Arenicola marina*. *Neth. J. Sea Res.* 13: 487-502.

Wolfinbarger, L. and M.P. Crosby. 1983. A convenient procedure for radiolabeling detritus with [^{14}C]dimethylsulfate. *J. Exp. Mar. Biol. Ecol.* 67: 185-198.

Yingst, J.Y. 1976. The utilization of organic matter in shallow marine sediments by an epibenthic deposit-feeding holothurian. *J. Exp. Mar. Biol. Ecol.* 23: 55-69.

Zeuthen, E. 1953. Oxygen uptake as related to body size in organisms. *Quart. Rev. Biol.* 28: 1-12.

Zhukova, A.I. 1963. On the quantitative significance of microorganisms in nutrition of aquatic invertebrates, pp. 699- 710. In: C.H. Oppenheimer (ed.), *Marine Microbiology.* Thomas, Springfield, Ill.

Chapter 10

Modeling Deposit Feeding

Gary L. Taghon
College of Oceanography
Oregon State University
Corvallis, Oregon 97331

Introduction

Models are simplifications of reality. An important goal of modeling is to determine how sensitive the results of the model are to variations in the input terms. Models of the feeding and behavior of deposit feeders are a recent addition to benthic ecology (e.g., Calow, 1975; Jumars et al., 1982; Levinton and Lopez, 1977; Taghon et al., 1978; Taghon, 1981). This chapter discusses models that fall under the general heading of optimal foraging theory.

Optimal foraging theory is used to make predictions about the foraging behavior of animals, subject to several simplifying assumptions (Hughes, 1980; Pyke, 1984; Schoener, 1971). Optimal foraging theory assumes that there are benefits and costs associated with alternative foraging behaviors. Benefits are usually expressed in terms of energy content of the food, but alternative formulations are possible and may be more relevant to some deposit feeders (e.g., essential nutrients such as nitrogen). Costs can also be expressed as the energy needed to search for, capture, ingest, and digest food. Optimal foraging theory also assumes that within the constraints of biologically possible foraging behaviors, one behavior will maximize the difference between benefits and costs. Animals which forage in this "optimal" manner will therefore maximize their fitness, a reasonable assumption in light of evidence that animals in general (Belovsky 1986; White 1978) and deposit feeders in particular (Levinton 1979) are often food-limited.

In this chapter I will discuss recent applications of foraging models to marine deposit feeders and summarize empirical data which can be used to test the predictions of the models. Because the data base specific to marine deposit feeders is still somewhat limited, I will also draw upon a variety of studies of detritivores, herbivores, and predators from freshwater and terrestrial environments. Gaps in our knowledge and possible directions for future research will be discussed. Although the scientific validity of optimal foraging theory has been attacked and defended with some regularity (see Pierce and Ollason (1987) and Stearns and Schmid-Hempel (1987) for the most recent exchange) I will make no such arguments here. The research and spirited debates stimulated by optimal foraging theory are, I believe, justification enough for this modeling approach.

Benefits and Costs of Deposit Feeding

There is no free lunch, yet some types of foods are better bargains than others. The process of obtaining adequate nutrition by deposit feeding can be separated into three components, each with associated benefits and costs: food selection, ingestion rate, and digestion.

Food selection

A major goal of optimal foraging theory is the prediction of an animal's optimal diet. Put simply, out of all the food items available, which should be chosen in order to maximize net gain? For deposit feeders, considerable observational and experimental data on particle selection are available.

I define non-selective feeding as no disproportionate selection of some component of the sediment during feeding. Given the complex composition of natural sediments and consequently the many possibilities that some component will be preferentially included in the diet, a priori one would expect truly non- selective feeding to be rare. However, there are cases where no apparent selection occurs (e.g., George, 1964; Gordon, 1966; Hammond, 1982; Hughes, 1979; Kudenov, 1982; Roberts and Bryce, 1982; Shick et al., 1981).

In by far the majority of cases deposit feeders feed selectively, usually on small particles, on particles of low specific gravity, or on sediment components of higher than average organic content (e.g., Bolton and Phillipson,

1976; Bubnova, 1972; Cadee, 1976; Caine, 1975; Calow, 1975; Ching, 1977; Clements and Stancyk, 1984; Davis, 1974; Fenchel et al., 1975; Ghiold, 1979; Goodbody, 1960; Hart, 1930; Hauksson, 1979; Hickman, 1981; Hughes, 1973, 1975; Hylleberg, 1975; Hylleberg and Gallucci, 1975; Jaccarini, and Schembri, 1977; Jumars et al., 1982; Khripounoff and Sibuet, 1980; Kikuchi and Kurihara 1977; Lane and Lawrence 1982; Marais, 1980; Massin, 1980; Meadows and Bird, 1974; Miller, 1984; Montague, 1980; Moriarty, 1977, 1982; Odum, 1968; Payne, 1976; Petch, 1986; Roberts and Bryce, 1982; Roberts, 1968; Scheibling, 1980; Self and Jumars, 1978; Taghon, 1982; Tevesz et al., 1980; Tietjen and Lee, 1975; Tsuchiya and Kurihara, 1979; Valiela et al., 1974; Warner, 1977; Yingst, 1982).

A third pattern, preferential ingestion of large particles, is less commonly observed (e.g., Connor et al., 1982; Fenchel et al., 1975; Powell, 1977; Roberts and Bryce, 1982; Reading, 1979; Whitlatch, 1974; Whitlatch and Weinberg, 1982).

How do the predictions made by optimal foraging theory compare with these observations? Organic-rich sediment particles are obviously desirable food items and a mathematical analysis is not necessary to provide insights in this case; such particles should be selected. Similarly, selection for particles of low specific gravity is explainable in view of their generally higher organic content (Mayer, this volume). Perhaps not so obvious is the topic of particle size selection. Under the assumption that a deposit feeder's food sources are associated with particle surfaces, optimal foraging theory predicts that small particles should be preferred because of their favorable surface-to-volume ratio. However, if the cost of sorting through particles and rejecting the less desirable larger particles becomes too high, no selection should occur (Taghon et al., 1978). This may explain the results of those studies where no selection on the basis of particle size was found. Unfortunately, there are no data on particle rejection costs but there are indications that such costs may be significant. Dauer (1985) found that a spionid polychaete may reject up to half of the particles that it contacts. Hylleberg and Gallucci (1975) reported that *Macoma nasuta* rejects as pseudofeces up to 97 percent by weight of the material taken in by the inhalant siphon. These data underline the importance of knowing rejection costs and the basis for particle rejection in deposit feeders. If we proceed on the assumptions that rejection costs are low and particle supply is unlimited, optimal foraging theory predicts that only small particles should be selected. Even though some experimental studies have demonstrated that deposit feeders can be highly selective for the "optimal" particles (e.g., Taghon, 1982) selection is never absolute, in the mathematical sense of the model predictions.

Selection of large particles is logical when the particles are benthic diatoms (Connor et al., 1982; Fenchel et al., 1975), but selection for large inorganic sediment particles is in most cases inconsistent with the predictions of current optimal foraging models. Whitlatch (1974) found that a pectinariid polychaete selects large particles, which can be explained by the fact that small natural sediment particles in this case lack the organic encrustations present on large particles. However, this convenient loophole was closed by subsequent experiments with artificial sediments (Whitlatch and Weinberg, 1982) in which large particles were again selected over small, a pattern which was unaffected by the presence or absence of organic coatings (bacteria). Whitlatch and Weinberg's (1982) results contrast with those of Levinton (1987), in which selection for large particles by the gastropod *Hydrobia* was seen only if the particles were protein-coated. The consistent trend for *Pectinaria* to select large particles (Dobbs and Scholly, 1986; Whitlatch, 1974; Whitlatch and Weinberg, 1982) stands in marked contrast to the majority of studies cited above and suggests a distinctly different foraging behavior. This behavior is not predictable from current optimal foraging models.

Data on particle selectivity are usually generated by comparing what is available and what the animal ingests. In some cases, actual particles are not ingested but the attached microflora are scraped off (Lopez and Kofoed, 1980; Nielsen and Kofoed, 1982). Gut or fecal pellet analyses would be inadequate for testing predictions about particle selection in these cases. While it is evident that most deposit feeders are selective to some degree, the actual extent of their selective abilities remains unknown in almost all cases, especially with respect to natural sediments. This is in large part due to inadequate understanding of how deposit feeders perceive and respond to particles in natural sediments (Cammen, Watling, this volume).

The majority of deposit feeders do not move over appreciable distances during feeding. Many are tubicolous and relatively sessile. Those deposit feeders that are motile have the option of moving to or remaining in patches of sediment where the concentration of preferred particles is above average (Forbes and Lopez, 1986; Kitchell, 1979; Lane and Lawrence, 1982; Robertson et al., 1980, 1981). Less motile deposit feeders may forage preferentially in "micropatches" where localized alterations in near-bottom flow result in increased deposition of food particles or enhanced microbial production (Eckman, 1985; Eckman and Nowell, 1984). Models to predict patch selection, movement between patches, and foraging time allocation in different patches have been developed for terrestrial predators (e.g., Charnov, 1976; Cowie and Krebs, 1979; MacArthur and Pianka, 1966; Orians and Pearson, 1979; Speakman, 1986) and may provide insights into patch and micropatch selection by deposit feeders. This would be a fruitful area for further research.

Ingestion rate

Time is an important parameter in optimal foraging theory. Since fitness is assumed to be some function of the net rate of energy gain, the rates at which energy is obtained and expended during foraging are important. Ingestion rate will affect rates of gain and loss. Many deposit feeders feed almost constantly and, depending on their particle-selection behavior, process variable amounts of sediment to extract the organic components. High rates of sediment processing might incur considerable energetic costs, which will be offset to varying degrees depending on the food value of the sediment.

A simple optimal foraging model constructed to examine the trade- offs between benefits and costs of deposit feeding at different rates predicted that ingestion rate should increase asymptotically as food value of sediment increases (Taghon, 1981). Supporting the model are a variety of studies which show a positive relationship between deposit feeding rate or bioturbation rate and some index of sedimentary food value (e.g., Cadee, 1976; Cummins et al., 1973; Ellers and Telford, 1984; Forbes and Lopez, 1986; Frankenberg and Smith, 1967; Guidi, 1986; Hargrave, 1970; Hylleberg, 1975; Jaccarini and Schembri, 1977; Mitchell, 1979; Robertson et al., 1980; Taghon and Jumars, 1984; Tsuchiya and Kurihara, 1979; Whitlatch, this volume; Whitlatch and Weinberg, 1982). Equally various studies showing a negative relation between deposit feeding rate or bioturbation rate and some index of sedimentary food value do not support the model (e.g., Calow, 1975; Cammen, 1980; Falk, 1985; Gordon, 1966; Hobson, 1967; Kudenov, 1982; Mitchell, 1979; Monakov, 1972; Robertson and Newell, 1982; Streit, 1978).

Comparisons among such data sets are complicated by several factors. Probably the most severe problem is inconsistent measures of "sedimentary food value." Clearly, the bulk organic carbon or nitrogen contents of sediments are inappropriate measures of food value (Mayer, this volume) yet their use continues. Another problem is among-species comparisons. As is obvious from Mitchell's (1979) study of isopod and earthworm feeding rates on sewage sludge, different species can respond in opposite manners to the same experimental treatments. Ideally, the model should be tested by determining how individuals of a single species adjust ingestion rate in response to food value.

From a wider perspective, the above studies are a subset of those results which fit either the energy-maximization paradigm (exemplified by the model of Taghon, 1981,), or the homeostasis paradigm (exemplified by the arguments of Calow, 1982). In essence, the former states that animals feed so as to maximize net rate of gain; the latter states that animals forage in a manner which maintains a constant rate of gain. Results from other systems which support the energy-maximization viewpoint are found in the works of of Anderson and Grafius (1975), Grafius and Anderson (1979), and Scriber and Feeny (1979) on various insects. Additional examples of support for the homeostatic viewpoint are found in papers by Barbosa and Greenblatt (1979), Dadd (1960), Gelperin (1971), Iverson (1974), Otto and Svensson 1981; Slansky and Feeny (1977), and Venkatesh and Morrison (1980) on various insects; Hofer (1982) and Hofer et al. (1982) on herbivorous fish; Savory (1980) and Tamm and Gass (1986) on birds; Dalton (1963) on mice; Putnam (1980) on deer.

There are two ready explanations for the opposite results in the data and models. One explanation is that real differences in the energetic strategies of organisms exist; some animals are rate maximizers and for this group optimal foraging theory is valid; other animals maintain a constant rate of gain by compensatory regulation of feeding and for this group the predictions of optimal foraging theory will not be valid. A second explanation, advanced recently by Phillips (1984), is that both strategies are part of a continuum where ingestion rate is maximal at some intermediate food value and decreases for lower and higher food values. Phillips (1984) incorporated a more biologically realistic upper limit on the rate at which food can be absorbed in the earlier model of Taghon (1981). With this modification, both of the ingestion rate-food value relationships seen in the studies cited earlier can be explained as falling on different sides of the "peak" in ingestion rate. Data supporting such a "peaked" ingestion rate at some intermediate food value are found in the studies of Lavelle et al. (1980 cited in Lee, 1985) and Martin (1982) on earthworms, McGinnis and Kasting (1967) on grasshoppers, Dalton (1965) on mice, and Sibbald et al. (1960) on chickens. For deposit feeders, it seems likely that such a relationship also holds (Taghon, unpublished data) and, if so, attention must turn to the ranges of sedimentary food values to which different species respond and their relevance to natural sediments.

Digestion

As is the case for particle selection and ingestion rate, digestion can also be modeled as an optimization process (Jumars and Penry, this volume; Penry and Jumars, 1987; Sibly, 1981). Digestion will depend on, among other factors, the enzymatic capabilities of the animal and the residence time of food in different regions of the digestive tract. Because residence time is related inversely to ingestion rate, the benefit an animal receives in terms of absorbed energy or nutrients will depend on both ingestion rate and digestion efficiency. Far less is known about digestion in deposit feeders than about particle selection and ingestion. In part, slow progress is due to our still inadequate understanding of which sediment components are utilized. Another shortcoming has been the lack of a theoretical framework which would serve to guide experimentation (Box, 1976). Modeling animal guts as chemical reactors (Penry and Jumars, 1987) is a promising approach for generating testable predictions (see chapter by Jumars and Penry, this volume). The costs associated with digestion in deposit feeders are even less well known than the benefits. Animals must invest metabolic energy (partly in the synthesis of enzymes) in the digestion of food and in the transport of the digestive products across membranes.

Because the costs associated with digestion and with the physical transport of sediment during ingestion are poorly known, they were combined in an earlier deposit feeding model and expressed as functions of ingestion rate (Taghon, 1981). While attractive from the viewpoint of simplifying model construction, recent data suggest that it may be inappropriate to combine the costs of ingestion and digestion in this manner. These data are from experiments with *Abarenicola pacifica*, a subsurface deposit-feeding polychaete which processes large amounts of sediment (Hobson, 1967; Hylleberg, 1975). Juvenile *Abarenicola* process up to 400 times their ash-free dry weight of sediment per day (Taghon, unpublished data), an effort which would seem to require a considerable expenditure of energy. In an attempt to separate the mechanical costs of processing sediment from the biochemical costs of digesting sedimentary organic matter, I maintained juveniles in clean foundry sand and measured the ingestion rate and weight loss of individual worms over a 22-day period (*Abarenicola* will feed on clean sediment at variable, but lower, rates than on natural sediment). I expected some form of positive relationship between ingestion rate and rate of weight loss, which would provide an estimate of ingestion costs. Instead, there was no evidence for a significant relationship (Fig. 10.1), which suggests that the mechanical costs

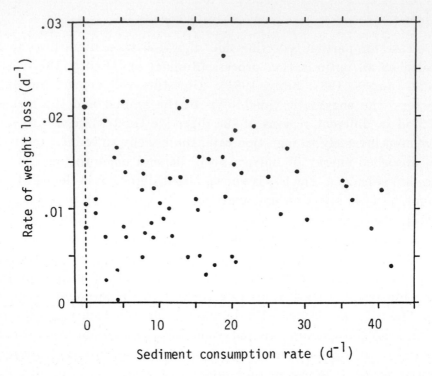

Figure 10.1: Rate of weight loss by juvenile *Abarenicola pacifica* (on ash-free dry weight basis) as a function of sediment consumption rate (normalized to initial ash-free dry weight of worm). Worms fed for 22 days on clean foundry sand (average particle size of 125 μm). The hypothesis of independence cannot be rejected using a nonparametric corner test for association between the two variables.

of feeding are low and that deposit feeders have evolved energetically efficient mechanisms to deal with a food source diluted by large amounts of inorganic and indigestible material.

If mechanical costs are low, then studies of the costs of deposit feeding should focus on the biochemical costs (specific dynamic action) associated with the utilization of sedimentary organic matter (Taghon, in press; see also Forbes, this volume).

Some Future Directions

A better understanding of how deposit feeders perceive or sense the food value of particles is required both for the next generation of deposit feeding models and for appropriate experimental testing of model predictions. Food selection and ingestion are sensitive to chemical cues (Jaccarini and Schembri, 1977; Miller and Jumars, 1986; Valiela et al., 1979, 1984) and the role of these cues as feeding stimulants or deterrents needs much more work. For example, the feces of some deposit feeders appear to contain compounds which act as feeding deterrents (Forbes and Lopez, 1986; Miller and Jumars, 1986; Taghon et al., 1984). Ingestion rate can decrease if pellets accumulate in the foraging area (Miller and Jumars, 1986), a phenomenon which would complicate the interpretation of laboratory experiments for testing feeding model predictions but which would be less important to animals in the field where pellets are dispersed by water flow (Jumars and Self, 1986; Taghon et al., 1984). A further complication is the likelihood that not all species will respond similarly to chemical or physical cues; for example, the spionid polychaete *Streblospio benedicti* does not decrease pellet production rate as pellets accumulate (Fig. 10.2). External cues can elicit elevated feeding rates in mammals (e.g., Weingarten, 1983); increased flow with its associated sediment transport appears to act as a feeding cue for some deposit feeders (Jumars and Self, 1986; Taghon and Jumars, 1984).

Some models of particle selection (Taghon et al., 1978) and ingestion rate (Taghon, 1981) by deposit feeders assume an unlimited supply of particles to the animal. This assumption is an oversimplification. In nature, availability of particles will be affected by sediment transport processes (Miller et al. 1984) and the activities of other animals (Rice et al., 1986). Because optimal foraging theory predictions are sensitive to the abundances of potential food items, more realistic models of deposit feeding should include terms for varying particle availability. Sensitivity analyses of such "dynamic resource" models could then be used to determine which processes had the greatest effect on model results and would be most profitable to measure experimentally or in the field.

The role of temporal variation in foraging behavior of deposit feeders has received little attention. Existing models for particle selection or ingestion rate assume these processes do not change with time or internal state of the animal. Several lines of evidence suggest this too is an oversimplification. Hungry or starved animals are less selective (Hughes, 1979; Kislalioglu and Gibson, 1976), and can modify ingestion rates to make up deficits (Calow, 1975; Hainsworth et al., 1981; Hart and Latta, 1986). Experienced predators are more selective during feeding (Jaeger and Rubin, 1982; McNair, 1981), and experienced copepods are better able to detect phytoplankton and less likely to reject captured cells than inexperienced copepods (Price and Paffen-

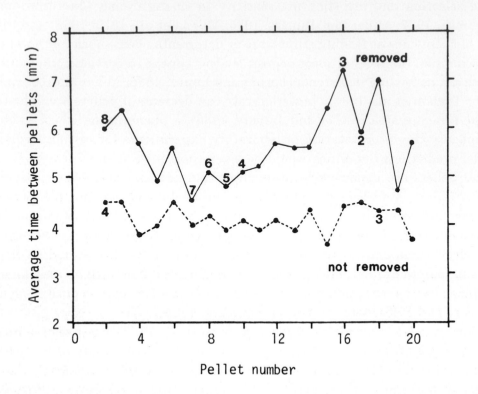

Figure 10.2: The average time between the production of fecal pellets by *Streblospio benedicti* as a function of the number of pellets produced by the animal. Data collected at the Ira C. Darling Center, University of Maine. Data points joined by solid line represent experimental results in which each pellet was removed as soon as it was released by the worm. Dashed line represents data where pellets were left to accumulate in the animal's foraging area. Number above each data point is the number of worms the average time between pellets is based on. In comparison, Miller and Jumars (1986) found that pellet production rate by another spionid polychaete, *Pseudopolydora kempi japonica*, decreased after four pellets accumulated in the foraging area.

hofer, 1984). The only comparable data for deposit feeders I am aware of are those of Miller (1984), who found that *Corophium* becomes more selective for small particles the longer it feeds. Whether deposit feeders can "learn" is an interesting topic with interesting ramifications for modeling deposit feeding. The approach of Doucet and vanStraalen (1980) for determining if a single state variable (e.g., hunger, satiation) is sufficient to describe an animal's feeding may be applicable to some of these questions.

Processes operating over longer time scales may also affect foraging behavior. Optimal diets may change as animals grow and their nutritional needs change. Juveniles may include a greater proportion of protein-rich food (including animal tissue) in their diet while adults include more detrital material (Anderson, 1976; DeSilva and Wijeyaratine, 1977; Moodie and Lindsay, 1972).

Smaller animals have higher size-specific ingestion rates than larger animals, a trend found within (Forbes and Lopez, 1987) and among species (Cammen, 1980). (See Forbes, this volume. Eds.) Assimilation efficiency and assimilation rate are often greater in juveniles than adults (Lee, 1985). These types of ontogenetic shifts in foraging dynamics have been neglected in feeding models. Again, there are important implications for testing model predictions.

Finally, future studies should begin testing the fitness- maximization assumption of optimal foraging theory. Such testing is likely to be a difficult proposition. One of the difficulties involves the relatively long time over which such a test must be conducted. The animal's reproductive lifetime, from birth to cessation of reproduction, is the pertinent time scale for the most rigorous test of foraging theory, since behavior or strategy throughout this period will determine the total contribution to the next generation (Pianka, 1976). For example, animals can compensate for times of food limitation by utilizing energy stores or by "catching up" during more favorable periods, but such compensatory ability is variable (e.g., Cannon, 1929; Williams and Hughes, 1975; Calow, 1977; Townsend and Calow, 1981). The ultimate effects on fitness are likewise variable, with the fecundity of some species fairly resistant (Bongaarts, 1980) or sensitive (Merson and Kirkpatrick, 1983) to fluctuations in food supply. Thus, the observation that the foraging behavior of an animal at one time or under one set of conditions fits the prediction of an appropriate optimal foraging model does not constitute a rigorous test of the underlying fitness- maximization assumption. Sub-optimal foraging might have no practical effect on fitness if compensatory mechanisms are in play. Therefore, rigorous tests of optimal foraging models for deposit feeders, as well as other animals, should occur over time periods sufficient to measure fitness as well as food selection, ingestion rate, and digestion.

Literature Cited

Anderson, N.H. 1976. Carnivory by an aquatic detritivore, *Clistoronia magnifica* (Trichoptera: Limnephilidae). *Ecology* 57: 1081-1085.

Anderson, N.H. and E. Grafius 1975. Utilization and processing of allochthonous material by stream Trichoptera. *Verh. Int. Ver. Limnol.* 19: 3083-3088.

Barbosa, P. and J. Greenblatt 1979. Suitability, digestibility and assimilation of various host plants of the gypsy moth *Lymantria dispar* L. *Oecologia* 43: 111-119.

Belovsky, G.E. 1986. Optimal foraging and community structure: implications for a guild of generalist grassland herbivores. *Oecologia* 70: 35-52.

Bolton, P.J. and J. Phillipson 1976. Burrowing, feeding, egestion and energy budgets of *Allolobophora rosea* (Savigny)(Lumbricidae). *Oecologia* 23: 225-245.

Bongaarts, J. 1980. Does malnutrition affect fecundity? A summary of evidence. *Science* 208: 564-569.

Box, G.E.P. 1976. Science and statistics. *J. Am. Stat. Assoc.* 71: 791-799.

Bubnova, N.P. 1972. The nutrition of the detritus-feeding mollusks *Macoma balthica* (L.) and *Portlandia arctica* (Gray) and their influence on bottom sediments. *Oceanology* 12: 899-905.

Cadee, G.C. 1976. Sediment reworking by *Arenicola marina* on tidal flats in the Dutch Wadden Sea. *Neth. J. Sea Res.* 10: 440-460.

Caine, E.A. 1975. Feeding and masticatory structures of six species of the crayfish genus *Procambarus* (Decapoda, Astacidae). *Forma Functio* 8: 49-66.

Calow, P. 1975. The feeding strategies of two freshwater gastropods, *Ancylus fluviatilis* Mull and *Planorbis contortus* Linn., in terms of ingestion rates and absorption efficiencies. *Oecologia* 20: 33-49.

Calow, P. 1977. Evolution, ecology, and energetics: a study in metabolic adaptation. *Adv. Ecol. Res.* 10: 1-62.

Calow, P. 1982. Homeostasis and fitness. *Am. Nat.* 120: 416-419.

Cammen, L.M. 1980. Ingestion rate: an empirical model for aquatic deposit feeders and detritivores. *Oecologia* 44: 303-310.

Cannon, W.B. 1929. Organization for physiological homeostasis. *Physiol. Rev.* 9: 399-431.

Charnov, E.L. 1976. Optimal foraging: the marginal value theorem. *Theor. Pop. Biol.* 9: 129-136.

Ching, C.V. 1977. Studies on the small grey mullet *Liza malinoptera* (Valenciennes). *J. Fish. Biol.* 11: 293-308.

Clements, L.A.J. and S.E. Stancyk 1984. Particle selection by the burrowing brittlestar *Micropholis gracillima* (Stimpson)(Echinodermata: Ophiuroidea). *J. Exp. Mar. Biol. Ecol.* 84: 1-13.

Connor, M.S., J.M. Teal and I. Valiela 1982. The effect of feeding by mud snails, *Ilyanassa obsoleta* (Say), on the structure and metabolism of a laboratory benthic algal community. *J. Exp. Mar. Biol. Ecol.* 65: 29-45.

Cowie, R.J. and J.R. Krebs 1979. Optimal foraging in patchy environments. In R.M. Anderson, B.D. Turner, and L.R. Taylor (eds), *Population dynamics*. Blackwell, Oxford, pp. 183-205.

Cummins, K.W., R.C. Peterson, F.O. Howard, J.C. Wuycheck and V.I. Holt 1973. The utilization of leaf litter by stream detritivores. *Ecology* 54: 336-345.

Dadd, R.H. 1960. Observations on the palatability and the utilisation of food by locusts, with particular reference to the interpretation of performances in growth trials using synthetic diets. *Entomol. Exp. Appl.* 3: 283-304.

Dalton, D.C. 1963. Effects of dilution of the diet with an indigestible filler on feed intake in the mouse. *Nature* 197: 909-910.

Dalton, D.C. 1965. Dilution of the diet and feed intake in the mouse. *Nature* 205: 807.

Dauer, D.M. 1985. Functional morphology and feeding behavior of *Paraprionospio pinnata* (Polychaeta: Spionidae). *Mar. Biol.* 85: 143-151.

Davis, R.B. 1974. Stratigraphic effects of tubificids in profundal lake sediments. *Limnol. Oceanogr.* 19: 466-488.

DeSilva, S.S. and M.J.S. Wijeyaratine 1977. Studies on the biology of young grey mullet, *Mugil cephalus* L. II. Food and feeding. *Aquaculture* 12: 157-167.

Dobbs, F.C. and T.A. Scholly 1986. Sediment processing and selective feeding by *Pectinaria koreni* (Polychaeta: Pectinariidae). *Mar. Ecol. Prog. Ser.* 29: 165-176.

Doucet, P.G. and N.M. vanStraalen 1980. Analysis of hunger from feeding rate observations. *Anim. Behav.* 28: 913-921.

Eckman, J.E. 1985. Flow disruption by an animal-tube mimic affects sediment bacterial colonization. *J. Mar. Res.* 43: 419-435.

Eckman, J.E. and A.R.M. Nowell 1984. Boundary skin friction and sediment transport about an animal-tube mimic. *Sedimentology* 31: 851-862.

Ellers, O. and M. Telford 1984. Collection of food by oral surface podia in the sand dollar, *Echinarachnius parma* (Lamarck). *Biol. Bull.* 166: 574-582.

Falk, K. 1986. Experimental studies of the feeding ecology of *Scoloplos* spp. (Orbiniidae: Polychaete) from Barnstable Harbor and Boston Harbor. *Biol. Bull.* 117: 479-480.

Fenchel, T., L.H. Kofoed and A. Lappalainen 1975. Particle size-selection of two deposit feeders: the amphipod *Corophium volutator* and the prosobranch *Hydrobia ulvae*. *Mar. Biol.* 30: 119-128.

Forbes, V.E. and G.R. Lopez 1986. Changes in feeding and crawling rates of *Hydrobia truncata* (Prosobranchia: Hydrobiidae) in response to sedimentary chlorophyll-a and recently egested sediment. *Mar. Ecol. Prog. Ser.* 33: 287-294.

Frankenberg, D. and K.L. Smith 1967. Coprophagy in marine animals. *Limnol. Oceanogr.* 12: 443-450.

Gelperin, A. 1971. Regulation of feeding. *Ann. Rev. Entomol.* 16: 365-378.

George, J.D. 1964. Organic matter available to the polychaete *Cirriformia tentaculata* (Montagu) living in an intertidal mudflat. *Limnol. Oceanogr.* 9: 453-455.

Ghiold, J. 1979. Spine morphology and its significance in feeding and burrowing in the sand dollar *Mellita quinquiesperforata* (Echinodermata: Echinoidea). *Bull. Mar. Sci.* 29: 481-490.

Goodbody, I. 1960. The feeding mechanism in the sand dollar *Mellita sexiesperforata* (Leske). *Biol. Bull.* 119: 80-86.

Gordon, D.C. 1966. The effects of the deposit feeding polychaete *Pectinaria gouldii* on the intertidal sediments at Barnstable Harbor. *Limnol. Oceanogr.* 11: 327-332.

Grafius, E. and N.H. Anderson 1979. Population dynamics, bioenergetics, and role of *Lepidostoma quercina* Ross (Trichoptera: Lepidostomatidae) in an Oregon woodland stream. *Ecology* 60: 433-441.

Guidi, L.D. 1986. The feeding response of the epibenthic amphipod *Siphonoecetes dellavallei* Stebbing to varying food particle sizes and concentrations. *J. Exp. Mar. Biol. Ecol.* 98: 51-63.

Hainsworth, F.R., M.F. Tardiff and L.L. Wolf 1981. Proportional control for daily energy regulation in hummingbirds. *Physiol. Zool.* 54: 452-462.

Hammond, L.S. 1982. Analysis of grain-size selection by deposit-feeding holothurians and echinoids (Echinodermata) from a shallow reef lagoon, Discovery Bay, Jamaica. *Mar. Ecol. Prog. Ser.* 8: 25-36.

Hargrave, B.T. 1970. The utilization of benthic microflora by *Hyalella azteca*. *J. Anim. Ecol.* 39: 427-437.

Hart, D.D. and S.C. Latta 1986. Determinants of ingestion rates in filter-feeding larval blackflies (Diptera: Simuliidae). *Freshwat. Biol.* 16: 1-14.

Hart, T.J. 1930. Preliminary notes on the bionomics of the amphipod, *Corophium volutator* Pallas. *J. Mar. Biol. Assoc. U.K.* 16: 761-789.

Hauksson, E. 1979. Feeding biology of *Stichopus tremulus*, a deposit-feeding holothurian. *Sarsia* 64: 155-160.

Hickman, C.S. 1981. Selective deposit feeding by the deep-sea archaeogastropod *Bathybembix aeola*. *Mar. Ecol. Prog. Ser.* 6: 339-342.

Hobson, K.D. 1967. The feeding and ecology of two north Pacific *Abarenicola* species (Arenicolidae, Polychaeta). *Biol. Bull.* 133: 343-354.

Hofer, R. 1982. Protein digestion and proteolytic activity in the digestive tract of an omnivorous cyprinid. *Comp. Biochem. Physiol.* 72A: 55-63.

Hofer, R., H. Forstner and R. Rettenwander 1982. Duration of gut passage and its dependence on temperature and food consumption in roach, *Rutilus*: laboratory and field experiments. *J. Fish. Biol.* 20: 289-299.

Hughes, R.N. 1979. Optimal diets under the energy maximization premise: the effects of recognition time and learning. *Am. Nat.* 113: 209-221.

Hughes, R.N. 1980. Optimal foraging theory in the marine context. *Oceanogr. Mar. Biol. Ann. Rev.* 18: 423-481.

Hughes, T.G. 1973. Deposit feeding in *Abra tenuis* (Bivalvia: Tellinacea). *J. Zool.* 171: 499-512.

Hughes, T.G. 1975. The sorting of food particles by *Abra* sp. (Bivalvia: Tellinacea). *J. Exp. Mar. Biol. Ecol.* 20: 137-156.

Hughes, T.G. 1979. Mode of life and feeding in maldanid polychaetes from St. Margaret's Bay, Nova Scotia. *J. Fish. Res. Board Can.* 36: 1503-1507.

Hylleberg, J. 1975. Selective feeding by *Abarenicola pacifica* with notes on *Abarenicola vagabunda* and a concept of gardening in lugworms. *Ophelia* 14: 113-137.

Hylleberg, J. and V.F. Gallucci 1975. Selectivity in feeding by the deposit-feeding bivalve *Macoma nasuta*. *Mar. Biol.* 32: 167-178.

Iverson, T.M. 1974. Ingestion and growth in *Sericostoma personatum* (Trichoptera) in relation to the nitrogen content of ingested leaves. *Oikos* 25: 278-282.

Jaccarini, V. and P.J. Schembri 1977. Feeding and particle selection in the echiuran worm *Bonellia viridis* Rolands (Echiura: Bonelliidae). J. Exp. Mar. Biol. Ecol. 28: 163-181.

Jaeger, R.G. and A.M. Rubin 1982. Foraging tactics of a terrestrial salamander: judging prey profitability. *J. Anim. Ecol.* 51: 167-176.

Jumars, P.A. and R.F.L. Self 1986. Gut-marker and gut-fullness methods for estimating field and laboratory effects of sediment transport on ingestion rates of deposit feeders. *J. Exp. Mar. Biol. Ecol.* 98: 293-310.

Jumars, P.A., R.F.L. Self and A.R.M. Nowell 1982. Mechanics of particle selection by tentaculate deposit feeders. *J. Exp. Mar. Biol. Ecol.* 64: 47-70.

Khripounoff, A. and M. Sibuet 1980. La nutrition d'echinodermes abyssaux. I. Alimentation des holothuries. *Mar. Biol.* 60: 17-26.

Kikuchi, E. and Y. Kurihara 1977. In vitro studies on the effects of tubificids on the biological, chemical and physical characteristics of submerged ricefield soil and overlying water. *Oikos* 29: 348-356.

Kislalioglu, M. and R.N. Gibson 1976. Prey 'handling time' and its importance in food selection by the 15-spined stickleback, *Spinachia* (L.). *J. Exp. Mar. Biol. Ecol.* 25: 151-158.

Kitchell, J.A. 1979. Deep-sea foraging pathways: an analysis of randomness and resource exploitation. *Paleobiology* 5: 107-125.

Kudenov, J.D. 1982. Rates of seasonal sediment reworking in *Axiothella rubrocincta* (Polychaeta: Maldanidae). *Mar. Biol.* 70: 181-186.

Lane, J.M. and J.M. Lawrence 1982. Food, feeding and absorption efficiencies of the sand dollar, *Mellita quinquiesperforata* (Leske). *Estuar. Coast. Shelf Sci.* 14: 421-431.

Lee, K.E. 1985. *Earthworms - Their Ecology and Relationships With Soil and Land Use*. Academic Press, Sydney, 411 pp.

Levinton, J.S. 1979. Deposit-feeders, their resources, and the study of resource limitation. In R.J. Livingston (ed), *Ecological processes in coastal and marine systems*. Plenum Press, New York, pp. 117-141.

Levinton, J.S. 1987. The body size-prey size hypothesis and *Hydrobia*. *Ecology* 68: 229-231.

Levinton, J.S. and G.R. Lopez 1977. A model of renewable resources and limitations of deposit-feeding benthic populations. *Oecologia* 31: 177-190.

Lopez, G.R. and L.H. Kofoed 1980. Epipsammic browsing and deposit-feeding in mud snails (Hydrobiidae). *J. Mar. Res.* 38: 585-599.

MacArthur, R.H. and E.R. Pianka 1966. On optimal use of a patchy environment. *Am. Nat.* 100: 603-609.

Marais, J.F.K. 1980. Aspects of food intake, food selection, and alimentary canal morphology of *Mugil cephalus* (Linnaeus, 1958 [sic]), *Liza tricuspidens* (Smith, 1935), *L. richardsoni* (Smith, 1846), and *L. dumerili* (Steindachner, 1869). *J. Exp. Mar. Biol. Ecol.* 44: 193-209.

Martin, N.A. 1982. The interaction between organic matter in the soil and the burrowing activity of three species of earthworms (Oligochaeta: Lumbricidae). *Pedobiologia* 24: 1885-190.

Massin, C. 1980. The sediment ingested by *Holothuria tubulosa* Gmel (Holothuroidea: Echinodermata). In M. Jangoux (ed), *Echinoderms: present and past*. A.A. Balkema, Rotterdam, pp. 205-208.

McGinnis, A.J. and R. Kasting 1967. Dietary cellulose: effect on food consumption and growth of a grasshopper. *Can. J. Zool.* 45: 365-367.

McNair, J.N. 1981. A stochastic foraging model with predator training effects. II. Optimal diets. *Theor. Pop. Biol.* 19: 147-162.

Meadows, P.S. and A.H. Bird 1974. Behaviour and local distribution of the freshwater oligochaete *Nais pardalis* Piguet (Family Naididae). *Hydrobiologia* 44: 265-275.

Merson, M.H. and R.L. Kirkpatrick 1983. Role of energy intake in the maintenance of reproduction in female white-footed mice. *Am. Midl. Nat.* 109: 206-208.

Miller, D.C. 1984. Mechanical post-capture particle selection by suspension- and deposit-feeding *Corophium. J. Exp. Mar. Biol. Ecol.* 82: 59-76.

Miller, D.C. and P.A. Jumars 1986. Pellet accumulation, sediment supply, and crowding as determinants of surface deposit- feeding rate in *Pseudopolydora kempi japonica* Imajima and Hartman (Polychaeta: Spionidae). *J. Exp. Mar. Biol. Ecol.* 99: 1-17.

Mitchell, M.J. 1979. Functional relationships of macroinvertebrates in heterotrophic systems with emphasis on sewage sludge decomposition. *Ecology* 60: 1270-1283.

Monakov, A.V. 1972. Review of studies on feeding of aquatic invertebrates conducted at the Institute if Biology of Inland Waters, Academy of Sciences, USSR. *J. Fish. Res. Board Can.* 29: 363-383.

Montague, C.L. 1980. A natural history of temperate Western Atlantic fiddler crabs (genus *Uca*) with reference to their impact on the salt marsh. *Contrib. Mar. Sci.* 23: 25-55.

Moodie, G.E.E. and C.C. Lindsey 1972. Life-history of a unique cyprinid fish, the chiselmouth (*Acrocheilus alutaccus*), in British Columbia. *Syesis* 5: 55-61.

Moriarty, D.J.W. 1977. Quantification of carbon, nitrogen, and bacterial biomass in the food of some penaeid prawns. *Aust. J. Mar. Freshwat. Res.* 28: 113-118.

Moriarty, D.J.W. 1982. Feeding of *Holothuria atra* and *Stichopus chloronotus* on bacteria, organic carbon and organic nitrogen in sediments of the Great Barrier Reef. *Aust. J. Mar. Freshwat. Res.* 33: 255-263.

Nichols, F.H. 1974. Sediment turnover by a deposit-feeding polychaete. *Limnol. Oceanogr.* 19: 945-950.

Nielsen, M.V. and L.H. Kofoed 1982. Selective feeding and epipsammic browsing by the deposit-feeding amphipod *Corophium volutator.* *Mar. Ecol. Prog. Ser.* 10: 81-88.

Odum, W.E. 1968. The ecological significance of fine particle selection by the striped mullet *Mugil cephalus. Limnol. Oceanogr.* 13: 92-98.

Orians, G.H. and N.E. Pearson 1979. On the theory of central place foraging. In D.J. Horn, G.R. Stairs, and R.D. Mitchell (eds), *Analysis of ecological systems.* Ohio State University Press, Columbus, pp. 155-177.

Otto, C. and B.J. Svensson 1981. A comparison between food, feeding and growth of two mayflies, *Ephemera danica* and *Siphlonurus aestivalis* (Ephemeroptera) in a South Swedish stream. *Arch. Hydrobiol.* 91: 341-350.

Payne, A.I. 1976. The relative abundance and feeding habits of the grey mullet species occurring in an estuary in Sierra Leone, West Africa. *Mar. Biol.* 35: 277-286.

Penry, D.L. and P.A. Jumars 1987. Modeling animal guts as chemical reactors. *Am. Nat.* 129: 69-96.

Petch, D.A. 1986. Selective deposit-feeding by *Lumbrineris cf.latreilli* (Polychaeta: Lumbrineridae), with a new method for assessing selectivity by deposit-feeding organisms. *Mar. Biol.* 93: 443-448.

Phillips, N.W. 1984. Compensatory intake can be consistent with an optimal foraging model. *Am. Nat.* 123: 867-872.

Pianka, E.R. 1976. Natural selection of optimal reproductive tactics. *Am. Zool.* 16: 775-784.

Pierce, G.J. and J.G. Ollason 1987. Eight reasons why optimal foraging theory is a complete waste of time. *Oikos* 49: 111-118.

Powell, E.N. 1977. Particle size selection and sediment reworking in a funnel feeder, *Leptosynapta tenuis* (Holothuroidea, Synaptidae). *Int. Revue Ges. Hydrobiol.* 62: 385-408.

Price, H.J. and G.-A. Paffenhöfer 1984. Effects of feeding experience in the copepod *Eucalanus pileatus*: a cinematographic study. *Mar. Biol.* 84: 35-40.

Putnam, R.J. 1980. Consumption, protein and energy intake of fallow deer fawns on diets of differing nutritional quality. *Acta Theriologica* 25: 403-413.

Pyke, G.H. 1984. Optimal foraging theory: a critical review. *Ann. Rev. Ecol. Syst.* 15: 523-575.

Reading, C.J. 1979. Changes in the downshore distribution of *Macoma balthica* (L.) in relation to shell length. *Estuar. Coast. Mar. Sci.* 8: 1-13.

Roberts, D. and C. Bryce 1982. Further observations on tentacular feeding mechanisms in holothurians. *J. Exp. Mar. Biol. Ecol.* 59: 151-163.

Roberts, M.H. 1968. Functional morphology of mouth parts of the hermit crabs, *Pagurus longicarpus* and *Pagurus pollicaris*. *Ches. Sci.* 9: 9-20.

Robertson, J.R., K. Bancroft, G. Vermeer and K. Plaisier 1980. Experimental studies on the foraging behavior of the sand fiddler crab *Uca pugilator* (Bosc, 1802). *J. Exp. Mar. Biol. Ecol.* 44: 67-83.

Robertson, J.R., J.A. Fudge and G.K. Vermeer 1981. Chemical and live feeding stimulants of the sand fiddler crab, *Uca pugilator* (Bosc). *J. Exp. Mar. Biol. Ecol.* 53: 47-64.

Robertson, J.R. and S.Y. Newell 1982. Experimental studies of particle ingestion by the sand fiddler crab *Uca pugilator* (Bosc). *J. Exp. Mar. Biol. Ecol.* 59: 1-21.

Savory, C.J. 1980. Meal occurrence in Japanese quail in relation to particle size and nutrient density. *Anim. Behav.* 28: 160-171.

Scheibling, R.E. 1980. The microphagous feeding behavior of *Oreaster reticulatus* (Echinodermata: Asteroidea). *Mar. Behav. Physiol.* 7: 225-232.

Schoener, T.W. 1971. Theory of feeding strategies. *Ann. Rev. Ecol. Syst.* 2: 369-404.

Scriber, J.M. and P. Feeny 1979. Growth of herbivorous caterpillars in relation to feeding specialization and to the growth form of their food plants. *Ecology* 60: 829-850.

Self, R.F.L. and P.A. Jumars 1978. New resource axes for deposit feeders? *J. Mar. Res.* 36: 627-641.

Shick, J.M., K.C. Edwards and J.H. Dearborn 1981. Physiological ecology of the deposit-feeding sea star *Ctenodiscus crispatus*: ciliated surfaces and animal-sediment interactions. *Mar. Ecol. Prog. Ser.* 5: 165-184.

Sibbald, I.R., S.J. Slinger and G.C. Ashton 1960. The weight gain and feed intake of chicks fed a ration diluted with cellulose or kaolin. *J. Nutrition* 72: 441-446.

Sibly, R.M. 1981. Strategies of digestion and defecation. In C.R. Townsend and P. Calow (eds), *Physiological ecology: an evolutionary approach to resource use.* Sinauer Associates, Sunderland, pp. 109-139.

Slansky, F. and P. Feeny 1977. Stabilization of the rate of nitrogen accumulation by larvae of the cabbage butterfly on wild and cultivated food plants. *Ecol. Monogr.* 47: 209-228.

Speakman, J.R. 1986. The optimum search speed of terrestrial predators when feeding on sedentary prey: a predictive model. *J. Theor. Biol.* 122: 401-407.

Stearns, S.C. and P. Schmid-Hempel 1987. Evolutionary insights should not be wasted. *Oikos* 49: 118-125.

Streit, B. 1978. A note on the nutrition of *Stylaria lacustris* (Oligochaeta: Naididae). *Hydrobiologia* 61: 273-276.

Taghon, G.L. 1981. Beyond selection: optimal ingestion rate as a function of food value. *Am. Nat.* 118: 202-214.

Taghon, G.L. 1982. Optimal foraging by deposit-feeding invertebrates: roles of particle size and organic coating. *Oecologia* 52: 295-304.

Taghon, G.L. and P.A. Jumars 1984. Variable ingestion rate and its role in optimal foraging behavior of marine deposit feeders. *Ecology* 65: 549-558.

Taghon, G.L., A.R.M. Nowell and P.A. Jumars 1984. Transport and breakdown of fecal pellets: biological and sedimentological implications. *Limnol. Oceanogr.* 29: 64-72.

Taghon, G.L., R.F.L. Self and P.A. Jumars 1978. Predicting particle selection by deposit feeders: a model and its implications. *Limnol. Oceanogr.* 23: 752-759.

Tamm, S. and C.L. Gass 1986. Energy intake rates and nectar concentration preferences by hummingbirds. *Oecologia* 70: 20-23.

Tevesz, M.J.S., F.M. Soster and P.L. McCall 1980. The effects of size-selective feeding by oligochaetes on the physical properties of river sediments. *J. Sed. Petrol.* 50: 561-568.

Tietjen, J.H. and J.J. Lee 1975. Axenic culture and uptake of dissolved organic substances by the marine nematode, *Rhabditis marina* Bastian. *Cah. Biol. Mar.* 16: 685-694.

Townsend, C.R. and P. Calow (eds) 1981. Physiological ecology: an evolutionary approach. Sinauer Associates, Sunderland, Mass.

Tsuchiya, T. and Y. Kurihara 1979. The feeding habits and food sources of the deposit-feeding polychaete, *Neanthes japonica* (Izuka). *J. Exp. Mar. Biol. Ecol.* 36: 79-89.

Valiela, I., D.F. Babiec, W. Atherton, S. Seitzinger and C. Krebs 1974. Some consequences of sexual dimorphism: feeding in male and female fiddler crabs, *Uca pugnax* (Smith). *Biol. Bull.* 147: 652-660.

Valiela, I., L. Koumjian, T. Swain, J.M. Teal and J.E. Hobbie 1979. Cinnamic acid inhibition of detritus feeding. *Nature* 280: 55-57.

Valiela, I., J. Wilson, R. Buchsbaum, C. Rietsma, D. Bryant, K. Foreman and J. Teal 1984. Importance of chemical composition of salt marsh litter on decay rates and feeding by detritivores. *Bull. Mar. Sci.* 35: 261-269.

Venkatesh, K. and P.E. Morrison 1980. Crop filling and crop emptying by the stable fly *Stomoxys calcitrans* L. *Can J. Zool.* 58: 57-63.

Warner, G.F. 1977. *The biology of crabs.* Elek, London, 202 pp.

Weingarten, H.P. 1983. Conditioned cues elicit feeding in sated rats: a role for learning in meal inhibition. *Science* 220: 431-433.

White, T.C.R. 1978. The importance of a relative shortage of food in animal ecology. *Oecologia* 33: 71-86.

Whitlatch, R.B. 1974. Food-resource partitioning in the deposit-feeding polychaete *Pectinaria gouldii*. *Biol. Bull.* 147: 227-235.

Whitlatch, R.B. and J.R. Weinberg 1982. Factors influencing particle selection and feeding rate in the polychaete *Cistenides (Pectinaria) gouldii*. *Mar. Biol.* 71: 33-40.

Williams, J.P.G. and P.C.R. Hughes 1975. Catch-up growth in rats undernourished for different periods during the suckling period. *Growth* 39: 179-193.

Yingst, J.Y. 1982. Factors influencing rates of sediment ingestion by *Parastichopus parvimensis* (Clark), an epibenthic deposit-feeding holothurian. *Estuar. Coast. Shelf Sci.* 14: 119-134.

Chapter 11

The Effects of Sediment Transport and Deposition on Infauna: Results Obtained in a Specially Designed Flume

Arthur R.M. Nowell, Peter A. Jumars, Robert F.L. Self
School of Oceanography, WB-10
University of Washington
Seattle, WA 98195
and
John B. Southard
Department of Earth and Planetary Sciences
Massachusetts Institute of Technology
Cambridge, MA 02139.

Introduction

Surprisingly little is known about the effects of steady sediment transport or of natural rates of deposition on the process of deposit feeding. This situation persists despite the theoretical reasons for believing that sediment supply by physical processes in many environments is important or dominant in controlling food supply to individual deposit feeders (Miller et al. 1984), despite newly collected field evidence suggesting that sediment transport rate overwhelms processing rates by deposit feeders in environments of

248

both U.S. coasts (Grant 1983; Miller 1985 and in review), and despite the name "deposit feeders." The reasons are several. One is the technological difficulty of building laboratory devices that realistically can simulate field transport conditions. Another is the difficulty of observing deposit-feeder responses when sediments move. Three other reasons are more subtle. First, it is easy to avoid thinking about sediment movement because it does not occur when one walks out on a sand- or mudflat, and one often avoids it in diving situations as well. Second, very little is known about the mechanics of particle deposition in water, so one cannot extrapolate readily to its biological effects. Third, in the heyday of natural history observations made for their own sake, most observations were done in still water, so the full repertoire of animal behaviors is unknown from classic natural history. Some of these impediments can be overcome simply by being aware of them, while others require more effort. We will focus on the latter.

It is easy to believe that all the important physical processes are well known, and that one simply needs to find someone or some text that deals with them. The state of knowledge of deposition in water, by definition or inspection a process crucial to deposit feeding, shatters that belief. Hjulstrom (1935) published a much-reproduced diagram showing regions of erosion, transport and deposition on a plot of velocity (albeit at an ill- specified height above the bed) versus grain diameter. The original description was careful to state that the plot was largely conjectural. Hjulstrom's diagram fell almost immediately into the hands of sedimentology textbook writers, who quickly dropped his caveats. In actuality there is not a single datum underlying the hypothetical curve of the threshold for deposition, and there are few data (but at least there are better-tested theories) for erosion of fine particles (Nowell et al. 1981). There is no recourse but to go back and generate these data if one wants to use them to begin learning about the importance of deposition to deposit feeders, in terms of either their feeding or their larval recruitment. When one does so for natural quartz particles in the range of 22-250 μm, Hjulstrom's curve for deposition proves to underestimate critical (shear) velocity for deposition by more than two orders of magnitude (Nowell et al., in preparation). Unfortunately, the device used to generate these data is physically too small to accommodate deposit feeders, so it is not the natural tool to make up the deficiency in observations of deposit feeders under sediment transport conditions.

Methodology is at the heart of the problem. Flow devices capable of generating data on thresholds of erosion and interactions of organisms with erosion are comparatively easy to build. Assuming the proper dynamic scaling (Nowell and Jumars 1984), one simply turns up the flow velocity until sediments begin to move, and with the proper measurements a datum is generated. Steady transport and controlled deposition require altogether different devices. Namely, the apparatus must be capable of keeping material entrained indefinitely or until net deposition is to be observed. Transport and deposition problems go hand in hand, because during continuous transport material is continually exchanging place between mobile and immobile layers or fractions; under steady transport both erosion and deposition are going on, but they are balanced. To simulate nature one needs to be able to accommodate not only this exchange, but also organisms of various sizes and also natural bed features.

Ripple migration is arguably the best understood phenomenon of sediment transport (Yalin 1977; Middleton and Southard 1984). Wave- and current-produced ripples can be seen in sands and coarse silts in broad classes of marine and freshwater environments. Compared with suspended load transport of clays and fine silts, the mechanics of grain-by-grain bedload transport in ripple migration produced by steady currents are simple and easily described. Grains hop up the gently inclined stoss (upstream) side of a ripple and avalanche down the steeper lee side, which sits at a maximal angle of repose of non-cohesive and non-adhesive grains (roughly 34 degrees). Such ripples typically have wavelengths of 1000 grain diameters, heights of 100 grain diameters, and migration rates of 0.01 times the boundary shear velocity, u_* (Middleton and Southard 1984). Bulk bedload sediment transport rates per unit width of bed (g/cm/sec) are readily calculated from the velocity at which ripples move (cm/sec) and the average weight of sediment contained per unit area of ripple (g/cm^2).

While ripple migration is occurring, horizontally stationary organisms maintaining contact with the sediment surface must keep pace with 100-grain-diameter vertical excursions of that surface, typically at frequencies exceeding 3/h. Ripples have been implicated in affecting the spatial patterns of larval recruitment (Eckman 1979), the spatial patterns of food supply to meiofauna (Hogue and Miller 1981), modes and rates of food supply to deposit feeders (Miller et al. 1984), and secondary production of populations. There is now field evidence (Jumars and Self 1986) that pulses of sediment transport enhance subsequent rates of deposit feeding and laboratory evidence (Miller and Jumars 1986) that both sediment supply rate and fecal removal rates and frequencies are important in rate control of deposit feeding. There also is an extensive literature on the effects of burial on infauna (Nichols et al. 1978), ranging from applied concerns of dredge-spoil disposal

(Saila and Pratt 1972) to more subtle "sediment-mediated" (Wilson 1981; Thayer 1983) effects of organisms on each other. Given the ubiquity of ripples and the importance of burial in applied and basic research, consideration of the fact that organisms in some environments go through repeated burial and erosion cycles is curiously rare in this literature. There have been no systematic field or laboratory treatments on the effects of ripple migration on infauna where geophysical as well as biological measures have been made. (See Goldring (1962), however, for an interesting discussion in a philological context.)

The apparent reasons for the paucity of information on the biological consequences of ripple migration in particular and sediment transport in general are that the relevant observations are difficult to make in the field, and that continuous, relatively natural sediment transport is difficult to produce in a laboratory system capable of supporting marine organisms. Most laboratory flow tanks or flumes heretofore used (e.g., Rhoads and Yingst 1978; Nowell et al. 1981; Vogel and LaBarbara 1978) have not been designed to allow continuous transport of sediments. Sediments once eroded either went down the drain or deposited in the return section. Flumes that have been designed to allow continuous sediment transport either have had inherent 3-dimensional flow due to their geometries or Froude number and wall effects due to their small sizes (e.g., Taghon et al. 1984; Jumars and Nowell 1984; Miller 1984) that made them unsuitable for production of ripples having natural geometries and dimensions. Conversely, the flumes in use by sediment dynamicists for the study of ripple migration generally either have been remote from sites of ecological expertise and sources of organisms for experimentation or unsuitable for use with corrosive salt water.

There was thus arguable need for a facility capable of maintaining continuous sediment transport in general and ripple migration in particular at a site convenient not only to ecologists and biological oceanographers but also to fluid dynamicists. We have built such a facility at the Friday Harbor Laboratories of the University of Washington, San Juan Island, Washington, U.S.A. We describe here the properties of the flume, together with initial observations of responses of several intertidal organisms to ripple migration. The ubiquity and diversity of responses by these common species underscores the importance of an appreciation of sediment transport phenomena in understanding organisms' interactions with their environments and with each other.

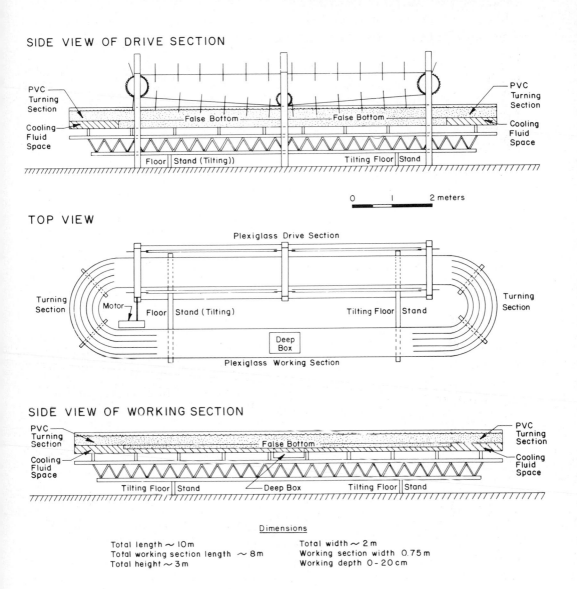

SIDE VIEW OF DRIVE SECTION

PVC Turning Section

Cooling Fluid Space

False Bottom   False Bottom

Floor | Stand (Tilting))   Tilting Floor | Stand

PVC Turning Section

Cooling Fluid Space

0   1   2 meters

TOP VIEW

Plexiglass Drive Section

Turning Section   Motor   Floor | Stand (Tilting)   Tilting Floor | Stand   Turning Section

Deep Box

Plexiglass Working Section

SIDE VIEW OF WORKING SECTION

PVC Turning Section

Cooling Fluid Space

False Bottom

Tilting Floor | Stand   Deep Box   Tilting Floor | Stand

PVC Turning Section

Cooling Fluid Space

Dimensions

Total length ~ 10 m
Total working section length ~ 8 m
Total height ~ 3 m

Total width ~ 2 m
Working section width 0.75 m
Working depth 0 - 20 cm

Figure 11.1: Side and elevation views of the flume and its working section. Because the flow can be driven in either direction, all aspects of the flume are symmetrical. The 2-channel laser-Doppler system can be traversed along the entire working section.

Materials and Methods

Flume design, construction and testing

The goal is to produce a one-dimensional flow and sediment-transport regime resembling that in nature. Ideally, flow velocity and sediment transport would vary only vertically, not in the along-stream or cross-stream direction. General considerations of flume design for bottom boundary-layer and sediment-transport simulation in biologically oriented experiments are discussed elsewhere (Middleton and Southard, 1984; Jumars and Nowell 1984; Nowell and Jumars 1986).

We ruled out impeller-driven pumps (e.g., Miller 1984) and propeller-driven flows for several reasons. They pulse inherently at low rates of the drive mechanisms, producing complex, unsteady 3-dimensional flows. Propellers and impellers also produce strong local shears, affecting the structure and dynamics of particle aggregates and increasing the likelihood that bacteria will be detached from suspended particles. These same shears and the close tolerance of moving parts damage larger organisms that emerge from sediments and circulate with the fluid. In 1979, we designed a circular, paddlewheel drive for a racetrack-shaped channel in an attempt to circumvent these difficulties and started construction in 1981. Boyer and Rhoads (1982) adopted our tentative design and retained the circular paddlewheel drive but allowed the blades to feather, thus reducing undesirable secondary circulation.

Our design effort included estimates of power required for high sediment transport rates. A paddlewheel of reasonable size could be used to impart substantial fluid momentum, but only if it turned rapidly or had a small clearance with respect to the flume bottom and sides. In either case, regions of unnaturally high shear would be produced. For this reason, we elected to distribute the drive mechanism, resembling the tread of a tracked vehicle, over one entire straight stretch of the racetrack (Fig. 11.1); comparatively mild shears are produced by distributing force over an area equivalent to the test section. The drive is built to feather, with 28 paddles of 67.3 by 47.7 cm of clear, 0.64-cm thick acrylic. The paddles reach an adjustable, nearest proximity to the bed at the center point of the return channel. Symmetry of the drive arrangement allows reversibility of paddle direction and thus the flow for simulation of tidal currents. The channel is uniformly 69.8 cm wide (inside diameter) and walled with clear acrylic of 1.91 cm thickness. A false bottom of acrylic, when in place, allows maximal flow depths of 30.5

cm. The working channel (straight section opposite the drive section) accommodates 7 additional cm of sediment throughout when the false bottom is removed, and a central (in the working channel) acrylic box of 76.2 by 50.8 cm accommodates an additional 20.3 cm of sediments for use of natural cores or for work with large or deeply burrowing organisms. The (inside) radius of curvature of the outer edge of each polyvinyl chloride (wall thickness of 0.64 cm) turning section is 122.2 cm. The bottoms of the working section and turning sections are lined with heat exchangers for temperature control. The false bottom of the drive side was designed to accommodate a conveyor belt occupying the full width and length of the return section, for potential use when transporting very delicate clay floccules and particle aggregates. Having the bottom (conveyor belt) and the paddles move in the same direction could reduce the shear across the intervening water column to zero.

For the present experiments all false bottoms indicated in Fig. 11.1 were in place, save that covering the deep box of the working section. Drive blades in the return section were set to be 1.3 cm from the false bottom at their closest approach. Before sediments were emplaced, we checked to see whether the simulated bottom boundary-layer structure was indeed primarily one dimensional. We filled the flume to 14 cm water depth. We then profiled mean velocity vertically and across the channel with a TSI (9100-8) two-axis, laser-Doppler velocimeter.

Approximately 500 liters of sediments were then dug from the uppermost, rippled sediments 1.3 m above MLLW in False Bay, San Juan Island, Washington. The physical and geological environment at this tidal height is described in detail by Miller (1985). Sediments were lain by adding approximately 10 liters at a time to the turning section just upstream of the drive section to fresh water at a paddle velocity capable of maintaining bedload transport (approximately 25 cm/s). The filling took three days of collection (at low tide) and transport of sediments back to our facility. Water and suspended material were siphoned off twice a day during filling and replaced with additional fresh water until dead and injured macrofauna were no longer in evidence and the suspension was dilute enough that the center of the filled working section could be viewed easily (roughly six exchanges of water). This procedure was found in pre-tests to be more efficient than sieving for the removal of undesired macrofauna and very fine silts that would obscure observation. The flume was then thrice drained entirely of water, refilled with seawater, and run under conditions of weak bedload transport to bring it back up to seawater salinity (28.7 to 28.8 ppt during the course of our experiments) and establish a rippled bed. The median grain size of the resultant deposit was 130 μm. Water depth was 14 cm over a 7-cm layer of sediments. Dissolved oxygen was monitored with a polarographic electrode, and never fell below 75% of the saturation value, even when the paddles were still. The flume has a large surface area for gas exchange, and the bulk of labile organic matter was intentionally removed by the rinsing process. Temperature was allowed to rise to that of the room (16° C) before observations began. Temperatures this high are experienced daily at this season by species inhabiting the intertidal zone of False Bay.

Initial observations of bedform geometry as the bed was being lain showed that turning vanes would be necessary for precise quantification of ripple migration. We therefore constructed a makeshift turning "vane" and ran the flume for roughly 4 h at a paddle velocity of 20 cm/s to allow the bed to equilibrate with this new entrance condition.

Experimental organisms and procedures

We chose infaunal surface-deposit and suspension feeders from a range of False Bay environments because their feeding modes oblige them to maintain or repeatedly make connection with the sediment-water interface. The environments and community structure are reviewed thoroughly in Pamatmat (1966) and Brenchley (1981). We chose *Pseudopolydora kempi japonica*, a spionid polychaete (c. 1.5 cm long), and *Macoma nasuta*, a tellinid bivalve (3-5 cm maximal shell length) from the same tidal level at which sediments were gathered. These animals were selected specifically because they are the only conspicuous macro-infauna in the tidal channels that drain False Bay, though our collections were from outside these channels. Ripple migration occurs routinely on outgoing tides in the channels, so we suspected that *M. nasuta* and *P. kempi japonica* would be adapted to the process. Both are surface deposit feeders with functional capability for suspension feeding.

We chose several species from the outer bay because of the high-energy nature of this environment. Ripples apparent there at low tide appear to be produced by surface waves (symmetric oscillatory or cat's back ripples as opposed to asymmetric current ripples). While the surface grain layer on such ripples moves back and forth with the wave period, the ripples may migrate at very slow rates set by the mean or steady component of water motion. Thus it was not clear whether organisms from this environment would have easily characterized responses to the comparatively rapid migration of current-produced ripples. The species chosen were the suspension-feeding bivalves *Transenella tantilla* (c. 5 mm maximal shell length) and *Clinocardium nuttali* (of 5-8 cm maximal shell dimension) and the functionally deposit and suspension-feeding polychaete *Owenia fusiformis* (tube lengths 8-12 cm).

We chose one species specifically because we believed it might be poorly adapted to ripple migration. *Eupolymnia heterobranchiata* is a terebellid polychaete (individuals 7-12 cm long, not including tentacles), which we suspected to be a surface deposit feeder. Terebellids in our previous experiments (Jumars et al. 1982) had shown limited ability to feed under flowing water. *E. heterobranchiata* inhabits about the same tidal level as *Owenia* (near MLLW), but occurs under large patches of nearly complete *Ulva* coverage, which it helps to maintain by cementing pieces of the alga to its tube. This *Ulva* layer effectively armors the bed from fluid forces (Jumars and Nowell 1984) and precludes sediment erosion or ripple migration except in severe storms.

The experimental organisms were introduced to the flume at zero flow velocity, and allowed to burrow and acclimate in the absence of flow for 24 h before experiments with ripple migration. Animals were segregated by species and distributed over the test section from 3 m downstream of the turning section to the end of the straight test section, in the region of strongly two-dimensional ripples. The smallest numbers of individuals observed were for *C. nuttali* (6), *E. heterobranchiata* (7) and *M. nasuta* (15). *M. nasuta* and *C. nuttali* were placed in the deep box to accommodate their potentially deep burrowing and large body sizes, respectively.

We experimented with simulation of tidal periodicity in the strength of sediment transport, starting with no flow, increasing first to weak bedload transport, then to strong, and then slowing the flow again to zero, with the full cycle taking a tidal period. This level of apparent sophistication was discontinued subsequently as premature, given the number of novel qualitative behaviors observed (Results). Each of the resulting behaviors we describe was elicited no matter what the immediately preceding flow and sediment transport history. For purposes of describing behaviors, we examined only two broad stages of sediment transport in addition to observations under still water. Visual observations at the smallest scales were aided by use of a dissecting microscope (Wild) and a long-range microscope (QM-1, Questar Corporation) through the flume wall.

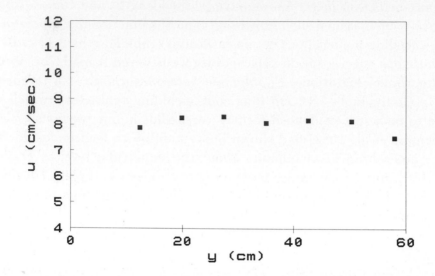

Figure 11.2: Cross section of velocities at a fixed height above the bed in order to demonstrate the nearly one-dimensional nature of the flow field. The Y direction is across the flume.

Results

Flume performance

Laser-Doppler velocimetry validated the presence of mainly one-dimensional flow structure over most of the test section. Some decreases in flow velocity and consequent bed shear stress was measured toward the inner edge of the test section, but this was only of order 10 percent (Fig. 11.2). When sediments were added, they deposited preferentially, as expected, under the comparatively slowly moving fluid at the inner edge of the turning sections (analogous to point bar deposition in meandering channels).

A simple turning device in the upstream turning section ensured that the 3-dimensional structure of ripples exiting the bend disappeared within 3 m, and no depositional bar was present in the turning section. This turning device ensured that the flow around the bend was sufficient to scour the bottom of the turning section clear of sediments. The resulting deceleration of fluid downstream of the flow blockage caused downstream variation (decrease) in ripple wavelength, of about 20%. In this configuration, as a further test of potential performance of a flume of this design, we increased paddle velocity to 35 cm/s (about 20% of maximum achievable). This test was carried out after experiments with animals were finished to demonstrate that the flume can replicate the spectrum of sediment transport observed in the field. Ripples were rapidly "washed out" as abundant material, including sand, went into suspended transport and was maintained in suspended load transport until the paddle velocity was reduced.

Animal responses

The spionid polychaete, *P. kempi japonica*, displayed a highly consistent response to ripple migration over its tube. At slow ripple migration rates it was observed to feed and produce fecal pellets at all phases of the ripple migration. Palps were held in the helical coils characteristic of suspension feeding (Taghon et al. 1980) except between the top and bottom of the lee side of the ripple, when they were appressed to the sediments in the deposit-feeding posture. Deposit feeding resumed immediately upon cessation of flow, no matter what their positions in a ripple. While suspension feeding, the palps were held in the local downstream direction. In the recirculation region in the lee of a ripple crest (Fig. 11.3, discussed in more detail by Nowell and Jumars 1984), the palps thus pointed upstream relative to the primary flow direction of the flume. Downstream orientation of the palps appeared to be effected passively: they oscillated with a period of roughly 1 Hz when the position of the reattachment point of the flow oscillated with that frequency over the animal, the palps seemingly "weathervaning," with the coiled distal portions carried downstream by fluid drag. Feeding was observed at all phases of ripple migration and was substantiated by the appearance of two types of fecal pellets. Flocculent material that traveled in suspension was brownish in color, and some pellets were of the same hue. Others, resulting from material ingested during the deposit-feeding phase, were gray and more granular in appearance.

Active tube building occupied part of the animal's time as the lee side of a ripple marched over it. Material could be seen being transported along the palps to the mouth nearly continuously, with the mouth appearing episodically in tube building, especially immediately after an avalanching episode. Avalanching is not continuous at low rates of ripple migration. As the ripple crest went by, the tube was gradually exposed. At slow ripple migration rates, however, no more than 4 mm of exposed tube was seen, despite greater ripple amplitudes. Closer observation revealed active tube cutting whenever exposed tube length exceeded 2-4 mm. We thought that the stimulus might be the observed strumming by vortex shedding of long, exposed tubes (like

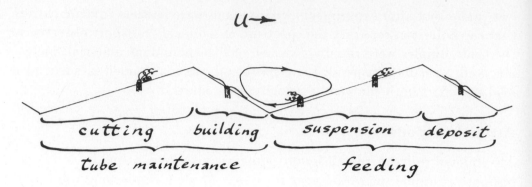

Figure 11.3: Differing palp orientations and positioning of *Pseudopolydora kempi japonica* at selected positions along a sand ripple. Different feeding strategies are identified in the different regions of a ripple.

that heard near telephone lines), but we also observed tube cutting when the flow had been turned off. Cutting apparently is effected by extension of the modified fifth-setiger setae characteristic of the genus. Although details of the process could not be resolved in the natural setting, the animal was extended precisely this far (to the fifth setiger) as the cut section fell, and flashing of reflected light from these large, extended setae could be seen. Drag from the flow on the cut section often aided the final cutting and removal. Even under weak transport, the cut section rolled away and suspension feeding resumed.

Under strong sediment transport conditions, neither feeding nor pellet release was continuous. Individuals were buried soon after the top of the lee side of the ripple passed, though they could be seen building tubes actively until they disappeared from view. Individuals reappeared somewhere along the stoss side by the combination of erosion and tube building and went into suspension-feeding postures, despite strong, turbulent buffeting by the flow. More than 4 mm of tube often was exposed by comparatively rapid rates of erosion on the stoss side at the higher transport rates.

The tellinid bivalve, *M. nasuta*, had the most complex repertoire of behaviors. This species typically maintains its exhalant siphon below the sediment surface, so that the frequency of defecation is not easily monitored. At zero flow velocity, it produced the asterisk-shaped feeding traces characteristic of deposit-feeding tellinids (e.g., Schafer 1972), and individuals moved often. Pseudofecal ejections were frequent. At weak transport levels, movement to new locations was rare, and asterisk-shaped feeing traces were not observed. Movements of siphons that produced asterisk-shaped traces under zero flow conditions occasionally were observed at weak transport, but the resultant depressions were filled by bedload transport. More frequently, inhalant siphons were not extended at all but were used to maintain a small, funnel-shaped depression from which the animal fed. As the lee side of a ripple migrated over, the siphon maintained contact with the surface, the conical depression reappearing at the crest. The animal feeds from the depression, apparently specializing on particles passively collected by deposition into the pit, although we cannot exclude the possibility of suspension feeding as a supplement. Volumetric output per ejection as well as frequency of pseudofecal ejections is reduced from the no-flow case. Under strong transport, most individuals still maintained contact with the sediment surface. They held their inhalant siphons flush with the sediment surface acting like a bedload trap.

The bivalve, *T. tantilla*, which makes abundant surface crawling traces under still water (e.g., Nowell et al. 1981), burrowed in and was rarely observed to move from its position whenever sediment transported. Under zero flow, when not moving, it held both siphons equally and fully extended. Under weak transport, it held the exhalant siphon fully extended, but the inhalant only partially extended. The higher the transport rate, the fewer individuals were evident at the sediment surface. The siphonal tentacles of the bivalve, *C. nuttali*, provided some structural protection of the inhalant stream from coarse grains. As transport rate increased, the inhalant opening was constricted, rotating additional siphonal tentacles into a position where they would intercept transporting grains. When the siphonal tentacle array became sufficiently filled with transporting sand grains that the latter would begin to fall into the inhalant opening, the animal violently "sneezed". This expulsion of fluid from the inhalant opening cleared the tentacle array of sand grains. The frequency of such sneezing increased both as the lee side of a ripple approached upon the inhalant opening and when bedload transport was increased. The cockles used both burrowing and sneezing to keep at the sediment surface.

The polychaete, *O. fusiformis*, under still water formed a moat-like, circular depression about its tube (Eckman et al., 1981, Fig. 11.1). It nodded the protruding section of its tube back and forth at roughly 0.3 Hz, with individuals nodding in different directions. The tentacular crown touched the bed rarely, so that most time it appeared to be suspension feeding. Under weak transport, the nodding stopped, and tubes trailed uniformly downstream. The tubes were arched so that the tentacular crown touched the bed, and came close enough to the bed so that vortex shedding increased the local instantaneous shear. This same posture was maintained under strong transport.

O. fusiformis did not appear to respond to the same recirculation that reversed orientation in *P. kempi japonica*. The top of the arch projected high enough to be affected and oriented by the stronger, primary flow. The most notable behavior, evident at both transport stages but more frequent at the higher, was "unburrowing" as the lee side of a ripple buried the projecting tube. The animal threw the flexible tube into two right angle bends, the first parallel with the sediment surfaces and the second pointing upstream. It would then rotate 90 degrees about its vertical axis, using its "arm" to move sediment. No correspondingly dramatic burying behavior was seen, because the tube is much more easily pulled under by the animal in the direction of imbrication of the grains.

As expected, the terebellid polychaete, *E.heterobranchiata*, showed no apparent active response to ripple migration. Unexpectedly, individuals spent most of their time subsurface either in the presence or absence of sediment movement. The tube was constructed more or less continuously and horizontally about 2 cm below the sediment surface, but a connection to the surface was maintained, facilitating the burrowing mechanism and allowing defecation on the sediment surface. The position of the head could be seen as the animal proceeded forward, characterized by pits indicating subsurface deposit feeding, and new posterior openings appeared when the old ones were far removed from the present position of the head. Head and tail openings sometimes were exchanged. The head could be localized by the emission of a fluid-particle stream. The animal fluidized the bed via antiperistalsis in its tube; fluid could be seen (by virtue of the particles it contained) entering the rear opening of the tube, and a fluid-particle mixture could be seen escaping at the head. Tentacles sometimes emerged on the sediment surface with this excavation stream and engaged temporarily in surface deposit feeding. In the presence of either weak or strong sediment transport, emerging tentacles streamed in the local (including recirculation) downstream direction.

Discussion and Conclusions

Flume performance

Flume design proved entirely sound from the standpoint of power, with complete sediment transport conditions being produced up to and including sands in suspension. The drive mechanism achieved its design objective of producing primarily one-dimensional flow (Fig. 11.4) in the downstream portion of the working section in the absence of sediments. The existence of the logarithmic profile was checked along the test section; fully developed one- dimensional flow (gradients in only the z-direction) was found in the downstream 50% of the test section. The turning vane allowed uniform ripple morphology to develop within 3 flow widths of the turning section.

We had expected some secondary circulation in the racetrack flume. Its extent is in fact predictable from fluid dynamic models (Nelson and Smith, unpublished). The major cause of secondary circulation in a racetrack-shaped flume is the fact that fluid must move faster around the outside of the turn than around the inside in maintaining the average flow velocity of the straight channel. This lowered flow velocity and consequently lower bottom shear stresses allow greater deposition of material at the inside edge, as we observed in the absence of any turning device. The simple turning device, which divided the flume in two in the turning section, reduced problems from cross-stream flow heterogeneity. But to produce steady rates of ripple migration and equilibrium bed configurations, allowing more precise quantification and warranting extensive flow and sediment transport measurements, has required a change from our initial design. Thin turning vanes (5 across the flume's width in the turning section) have now been installed. While fluid flow equilibrium is very rapidly established, long running times will be needed to bring the bed to equilibrium configuration before a given paddle velocity will result in a constant bedload transport rate. Only then can a constant, well-defined set of stimuli be provided for more quantitative (interval or ratio level of measurement) treatment of organism response.

Organismal responses to ripple migration

On a species-by-species basis, the observations of animal response add small increments to an understanding of natural history and raise additional questions. In *P. kempi japonica*, it is apparent that the animal cycles between suspension and deposit feeding at slow ripple migration rates, putting some earlier laboratory observations of switching between feeding modes into an-

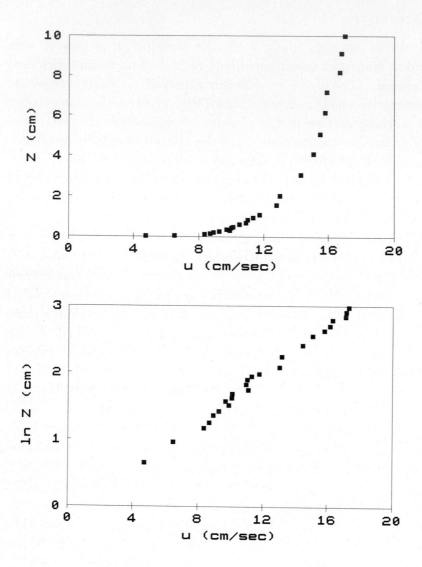

Figure 11.4: Velocity profile over a flat bed of fine sand, plotted in arithmetic and semi-logarithmic form. The former shows the growth of the boundary layer to the free surface, while the semi- log plot shows the existence of the log layer and the viscous sublayer in the region below 0.1 cm.

other environmental context. Tube cutting in polychaetes has been noted before among chaetopterids (MacGinitie and MacGinitie 1968) and terebellids (Aller and Yingst 1978), but only as an activity related to the need for a larger tube as individuals grow. Hence, those previous reports are of an infrequent, lengthwise slitting. The stimulus for *P. kempi japonica*'s tube cutting is less clear, but it may involve the elastic yield of the above-sediment portion of the tube as the animal poles along it with setae. The net results are that the tube opening is kept in a position that allows suspension and deposit feeding and that the bulk of the animal's body remains below "ground" level, presumably safer from both erosion and predation. The energetic costs of building and cutting the tubes must be high; it would appear to be worthwhile because in the field ripple migration rates are quite slow (Middleton and Southard 1984).

In *O. fusiformis*, a longer segment of tube is kept exposed. Its tube is more flexible because only oblate grains are chosen (Fager 1963), and they are glued in imbricated fashion to the flexible tube matrix by only one (the anatomically posterior) edge. Field-collected animals do not appear to add to the tube unless it has been damaged. In the laboratory, and presumably in the field, they carry the tube along as they move. Again the length of tube that is left exposed appears to provide the option for either suspension or deposit feeding. When a shorter tube length is temporarily exposed and the animal occupies it, flexibility appears insufficient for the animal's short tentacular crown to reach the sediment surface for deposit feeding.

E. heterobranchia's mode of movement via continuous or repeated extensions of its tube has been noted before (Fauchald and Jumars 1979), but its proclivity to feed below the surface has not. Our previous observations (Fauchald and Jumars 1979) were made in poorly sorted sediments (including gravel) where the hydraulic tunneling mechanism seen in the present, comparatively well sorted sand presumably would not work well. A common feature of the bivalve behaviors was a lack of horizontal movement during periods of sediment transport, but the apparent reasons for these behaviors are disparate. In *M. nasuta*, the sediment transport prevents both local depletion of deposited resources and accrual of fecal mounds (e.g., Fig. 1 of Jumars and Nowell 1984), two likely stimuli to move horizontally. With its long, extensible siphons, *M. nasuta* appears to have little difficulty maintaining contact with the interface. Adult *C. nuttali*, by virtue of their large sizes and comparatively minor adjustments of siphon length, also appear to require little vertical burrowing in maintaining access to their suspended food, although some upward burrowing was observed as ripples migrated over. Their use of papillae as a "snow fence" to exclude bedload material from the inhalant siphon, with "sneezing" to clear it, appears not to have been noted previously. Because of its small body size and short siphonal lengths, however, *T. tantilla* must burrow frequently to adjust its vertical position when ripples migrate. Also (like the cockle) a suspension feeder on fine particles, it appears to avoid gravitational slumping into the exhalant siphon by holding it above the level of the sediment-water interface and to avoid saltating grains by virtue of the siphon's small size.

The diversity and ubiquity of these animal responses to ripple migration leave little doubt as to the importance of this sediment transport phenomenon in the evolutionary histories of intertidal organisms from False Bay. What remains obscure is the frequency of such events in natural populations and its importance at the individual and population levels from one day to the next. Miller (1985 and in preparation) has suggested that bedload transport of sediments occurs on most days in False Bay. His measurements were carried out at one location, so the degree to which they can be extrapolated to the whole of the bay is unknown. Certainly there are locations, such as in the tidal channels, where ripple migration occurs for a substantial fraction of each day (during outgoing tides). False Bay certainly is not unique among intertidal and shallow subtidal environments in showing frequent ripple migration (e.g., Grant, 1983). The responses we saw thus motivate further study because analogous responses probably occur in many species and locations.

Our previous modeling and measurement effort (Miller et al. 1984; Jumars and Self 1986; Miller and Jumars 1986) has stressed the potential energetic benefits of an enhanced food supply from sediment transport processes, but the present observations also suggest obvious costs of maintaining a connection with the sediment-water interface (Ed. note: The actual costs associated with deposit feeding are not obvious; see chapters by Taghon and Forbes, this volume). At high ripple migration rates, for example, *P. kempi japonica* is unable to maintain contact with the sediment surface while a ripple crest goes by and presumably is unable to feed. "Sneezing" in *C. nuttali* under comparable migration rates is so frequent and convulsive that net energetic gain may well be negative. Resolution of these issues requires two things: feeding and growth rates must be measured under precisely controlled sediment transport conditions that are of much longer periods than we report here, and field ripple migration rates must be better known at sites of ecological interest. The former we hope to accomplish, and the latter is readily achievable by time-course observation or time-lapse photography (e.g., Smith et al. 1986). Similarly, our observations raise questions at the population and community levels about the relative and absolute importance of amensal interactions among trophic (Wilson 1981) or motility (Brenchley 1981) groups. We would not expect, for example, amensalism mediated by defecation to have significant influence on population dynamics in an environment where individuals were routinely buried and exposed by migrating ripples. Potentially sediment-mediated, amensal interactions, whether evaluated in the laboratory or the field, need to be set in the contexts of sedimentary dynamic environments (e.g., Grant 1983). Horizontal mobility has been stressed as an escape from amensal effects (Jumars and Fauchald 1977; Brenchley 1981; Wilson 1981), but the behaviors observed here suggest that vertical mobility deserves substantial attention. We studied only adult specimens here. Before population or community response could be predicted, it would be essential to know whether smaller life stages showed either lesser ability or alternative behaviors. Again, laboratory simulation and precise control of sediment transport conditions and better characterization of field transport regimes are essential. There is a need to progress from empirical correlations between sediment composition and community structure, to a mechanistic understanding of the reasons for them and a consequent need to set biological interactions in the contexts of their physical environments.

Contribution no. 1664 from the School of Oceanography, University of Washington, supported by NSF OCE86-08157.

Literature Cited

Aller, R.C. and J.Y. Yingst. 1978. Biogeochemistry of tube- dwellings: A study of the sedentary polychaete *Amphitrite ornata* (Leidy). *J. Mar. Res.* 36: 201-254.

Boyer, L.F. and D.C. Rhoads. 1982. The effects of marine benthos on physical properties of sediments. In: P.L. McCall and M.J.S. Tevesz (eds.), *Animal-sediment Relations*, pp. 3-52. Plenum Press, N.Y.

Brenchley, G.A. 1978. On the regulation of marine infaunal assemblages at the morphological level: A study of the interactions between sediment stabilizers, destabilizers, and their sedimentary environment. Ph.D. Dissertation, The Johns Hopkins University, Baltimore. 237 pp.

Brenchley, G.A. 1981. Disturbance and community structure: An experimental study of bioturbation in marine soft-bottom environments. *J.*

Mar. Res. 39: 767-790.

Eckman, J.E., A.R.M. Nowell and P.A. Jumars. 1981. Sediment destabilization by animal tubes. J. Mar. Res. 39: 361-374.

Fager, E.W. 1964. Marine sediments: Effects of a tube-building polychaete. Science 143: 356-359.

Fauchald, K. and P.A. Jumars. 1979. The diet of worms: An analysis of polychaete feeding guilds. Oceanogr. Mar. Biol. Annu. Rev. 17: 193-284.

Goldring, R. 1962. The trace fossils of the Baggy Beds (Upper Devonian) of North Devon, England. Palaontologische Zeitschrift 36: 232-251.

Grant, J. 1983. The relative magnitude of biological and physical sediment reworking in an intertidal community. J. Mar. Res. 41: 673-689.

Hogue, E.W. and C.B. Miller. 1981. Effects of sediment microtopography on small-scale spatial distributions of meiobenthic nematodes. J. Exp. Mar. Biol. Ecol. 53: 181-191.

Hjulstrom, F. 1935. Studies of the morphological activity of rivers as illustrated by the River Fyris. Bull. Geol. Inst. Univ. Uppsala 25: 271-528.

Jumars, P.A. and A.R.M. Nowell. 1984. Fluid and sediment dynamic effects on marine benthic community structure. Am. Zool. 24: 45-55.

Jumars, P.A. and R.F.L. Self. 1986. Gut-marker and gut-fullness methods for estimating field and laboratory effects of sediment transport on ingestion rates of deposit feeders. J. Exp. Mar. Biol. Ecol. 98: 293-310.

Jumars, P.A., R.F.L. Self and A.R.M. Nowell. 1982. Mechanics of particle selection by tentaculate deposit feeders. J. Exp. Mar. Biol. Ecol. 64: 47-70.

MacGinitie, G.E. and N. MacGinitie. 1968. Natural History of Marine Animals, 2nd ed. McGraw–Hill, N.Y. 423 pp.

Middleton, S.V. and J.B. Southard. 1984. Mechanics of sediment movement. S.E.P.M. notes for short course no. 3, Providence, Rhode Island, 2nd ed.

Miller, D.C. 1984. Mechanical post-capture selection by suspension- and deposit-feeding *Corophium. J. Exp. Mar. Biol. Ecol.* 82: 59-76.

Miller, D.C. 1985. Interactions of marine sediment transport with deposit feeding and microbial growth. Ph.D. Dissertation, University of Washington, Seattle. 156 pp.

Miller, D.C. and P.A. Jumars. 1986. Pellet accumulation, sediment supply, and crowding as determinants of surface deposit-feeding rates in *Pseudopolydora kempi japonica*, Imajima and Hartman. *J. Exp. Mar. Biol. Ecol.* 99: 1-17.

Miller, D.C., P.A. Jumars and A.R.M. Nowell. 1984. Effects of sediment transport on deposit feeding: Scaling arguments. *Limnol. Oceanogr.* 29: 1202-1217.

Nichols, T.A., G.T. Rowe, C.H. Clifford and R.A. Young. 1978. *In situ* experiments on the burial of marine invertebrates. *J. Sed. Petrol.* 48: 419-425.

Nowell, A.R.M. and P.A. Jumars. 1984. Flow environments of aquatic benthos. *Annu. Rev. Ecol. Syst.* 15: 303-328.

Nowell, A.R.M., P.A. Jumars and J.E. Eckman. 1981. Effects of biological activity on the entrainment of marine sediments. *Mar. Geol.* 42: 133-153.

Pamatmat, M.M. 1966. The ecology and metabolism of a benthic community on an intertidal sandflat (False Bay, San Juan Island, Washington). Ph.D. Dissertation, University of Washington, Seattle. 243 pp.

Rhoads, D.C., J. Yingst and W. Ullman. 1978. Seafloor stability in central Long Island Sound. Part 1. Temporal changes in erodibility of fine-grained sediment. In: M.L. Wiley (ed.), Estuarine interactions, pp. 221-224. Academic Press, N.Y.

Saila, S.B. and S.D. Pratt. 1972. Review of some direct effects of spoil dumping on marine animals. Dredge spoil disposal in Rhode Island Sound, Mar. Tech. Rep. no. 2, University of Rhode Island.

Schafer, W. 1972. *Ecology and palaeoecology of marine environments*. University of Chicago Press. 568 pp.

268

Smith, C.R., P.A. Jumars, and D.J. DeMaster. 1986. *In situ* studies of megafaunal mounds indicate rapid sediment turnover and community response at the deep sea floor. *Nature* 323: 251-253.

Taghon, G.L., A.R.M. Nowell and P.A. Jumars. 1980. Induction of suspension feeding in spionid polychaetes by high particulate fluxes. *Science* 210: 562-564.

Taghon, G.L. 1984. Transport and breakdown of fecal pellets: Biological and sedimentological consequences. *Limnol. Oceanogr.* 29: 64-72.

Thayer, C.W. 1983. Sediment-mediated biological disturbance and the evolution of marine benthos. In: M.J.S. Tevesz and P.L. McCall (eds.), *Biotic Interactions in Recent and Fossil Benthic Communities*, pp. 480-625. Plenum Press, N.Y.

Vogel, S. and M. LaBarbara. 1978. Simple flow tanks for research and teaching. *BioScience* 28: 638-643.

Wilson, W.H. 1981. Sediment-mediated interactions in a densely populated infaunal assemblage: The effects of the polychaete *Abarenicola pacifica*. *J. Mar. Res.* 39: 735-748.

Chapter 12

Small-Scale Features of Marine Sediments and Their Importance to the Study of Deposit Feeding

Les Watling
Darling Center, University of Maine
Walpole, Maine 04573

Introduction

Studies on deposit feeders usually involve parallel samples of both the animal of interest and the sediment in which it is living. To most benthic ecologists, this means that a 'scoopful' of sediment from the sample is removed to the laboratory for analysis of organic carbon and nitrogen, various measures of the mineral fraction, and other bulk properties. To the organism, features of the sediment such as total weight of 'organic carbon' per gram dry weight of inorganic material are probably not perceivable. On the other hand, the quantity (number of mouthfuls?) of sediment needed in order to obtain sufficient amounts of digestible organic material is probably detected via metabolic feedback. If the processes governing the successful maintenance of deposit feeder populations are to be understood, bulk measures of sediment properties must be augmented by methods that will give information relatable to the scale of the organisms under study (see Cammen, this volume). This recommendation was made by Ralph Johnson in 1974, but it has scarcely been heeded. He urged benthic ecologists to devise measures of the food resource and its partitioning that were relevant to the requirements and activities of benthic animals. In order to do this, biological and chemical techniques must be developed that investigate the environment at the correct spatial scale.

Many techniques for the fine-scale study of sediments have been developed by persons interested in the formation and ecology of soils. These methods, such as thin-sectioning, arc not commonly used in the study of marine sediment. Thin sections have been used to study the details of the soil fabric, structural features of soil porosity, microenvironments of soil, the interactions between plant structures and soil particles, as well as features of the mineral components of soil (FitzPatrick 1984). Many of these objectives apply equally well to the study of animal-sediment relationships in the marine realm.

In this paper, small-scale features of marine sediments will be examined, and the thin-sectioning techniques for delimiting these features will be outlined. In addition, the potential importance of some of these features will be discussed in terms of developing an understanding of the relationship between marine deposit feeders, the sediments which they inhabit, and the means by which they ingest the components of these sediments.

Components of Sediment Micromorphology

Here we are concerned with the particles, biogenic structures, and other constituents of sediment and the way in which they are organized or interconnected. Before turning to the individual components, we need to establish an understanding of the terms fabric, structure, and matrix, as these are commonly used to denote the manner and degree of physical relationships between the components.

FitzPatrick (1984) reviewed these terms and offered some solutions to the ambiguity that their use often caused. He recommended, when soil micromorphology is being described, that the following terms be used:

"Coarse material: Individual mineral grains, small rock fragments or fragments of organic matter that are easily resolved with the petrological microscope.

Fabric: The arrangement, size, shape, and frequency of the individual soil constituents.

Fine material: The organic and/or mineral material less than 2 μm that is not easily resolved with the petrological microscope.

Matrix: Material forming a more or less continuous phase and enclosing coarse material, concretions, etc. Generally refers to material less than 2 μm (fine material) but may be much larger. Fine material/matrices are often uniform but may be speckled.

Structure: The spatial distribution and total organization of the soil system as expressed by the degree and type of aggregation and the nature and distribution of pores and pore space" (p. 134-135).

It should be noted that the soil literature is rife with terminology, especially in English. In contrast to the definitions given above, the terms 'structure' and 'fabric' seem combined into the single term 'structure' by French authors: "the term structure refers to the spatial arrangement of mineral particles, and their possible linkage by organic matter and hydroxides of iron or aluminum" (Bonneau and Levy 1982:268). The *Glossaire de Pedologie* (ORSTOM-DGRST 1969) recognizes three major classes of structure: particulate, where the units are not inter-linked; massive, where the units are cemented together to varying degrees; and fragmentary, where the soil is naturally divided into structural units. Bonneau and Levy (1982) noted that a description of the porosity is also important in detailing the structure of a soil. Fedoroff (1982) reviewed many features of the soil fabric that can be observed microscopically, but only hinted at a definition for the term.

I recommend here that marine ecologists follow the usage taken from FitzPatrick (1984) above. As newcomers to this field, I believe we should work first with FitzPatrick's terminology since it seems to be the best defined. As marine sediments are investigated at the micro-morphological level, we will begin to appreciate which aspects of the above terms hold the most meaning for studies of deposit feeders. Further modifications of these terms can then be made as more sediments are examined.

Morphological Features of Marine Sediment

As an introduction into the variety of features that may be seen by using micro-morphological methods, various kinds of sediment structure, matrix, and major biogenic components are outlined below. Where appropriate, features that are of special importance to marine deposit feeders will be discussed.

Structure

Sediment structure is best described as the degree and type of aggregation of the particles in relation to the nature and distribution of pores and pore space. In most soils the individual particles are not distributed randomly, but occur as members of aggregates. The degree of aggregation is often a function of the heterogeneity of particle size. Many types of aggregates have been described in terrestrial soils (see FitzPatrick 1984 for descriptions); however, aggregates in marine sediments have never been examined in thin section, but their occurrence has been inferred from sediments that have been disrupted. Consequently, it is difficult to know what types and sizes of aggregates (if any) might be found. It should be stressed that the term aggregate as used here is quite different from its typical usage in marine benthic studies (e.g., that first proposed by Johnson 1974).

Johnson (1974, 1977) was the first to note the occurrence of what he termed "organic-mineral aggregates" in marine sediments. He used this term to describe mineral grains that were embedded in an amorphous (presumably organic) matrix. Johnson took a small amount of sediment and dispersed it on a slide. As a result, none of the aggregates he saw were necessarily *in situ* structures, but could have been artifacts produced by fragmenting the sediment matrix while dispersing the grains on a microscope slide. He distinguished these structures from encrusted mineral grains, which were composed primarily of mineral material bearing thin organic coats. Using similar techniques, other authors have since recorded the occurrence of organic-mineral aggregates in a variety of marine sediments (e.g., Whitlatch 1974, 1981, Hughes 1979). As noted in the next section, however, these aggregates are almost certainly artifacts of the sediment dispersion process and most probably do not exist *in situ*.

Matrix

The fine material that is not easily resolvable with the light microscope has been termed the matrix. It usually consists of clay particles and amorphous organic matter. The fine material may occur in the form of thin coatings around grains or may encompass several grains and biogenic particles. As seen in thin sections, the matrix forms bridges between grains

Figure 12.1: All figures are of 30 μm thin sections taken from 3 - 4 cm below the surface of the Lowes Cove mudflat. Low magnification view of thin section. Transparent areas are sediment grains while darker particles are plant fragments. Note continuous distribution of mottled material, the matrix, between grains. Scale bar is 0.2 mm.

in marine sands (Frankel and Mead 1973), but completely encompasses all grains in muddy sediments (Fig. 12.1). The matrix has been found to contain polysaccharides in terrestrial soils (Foster 1981) and large amounts of pectic carbohydrates and some proteins in marine sands (Frankel and Mead 1973). Many other organic compounds have been isolated from soils and marine sediments, including the ubiquitous humic substances, proteins, and lipids (Mayer 1985, Mayer et al. 1986), however, the degree to which these compounds occur in the matrix versus in bacteria, protists, faunal and floral elements, or in solution, is unknown. It does seem clear, however, that microorganisms (including both bacteria and diatoms) are one of the major agents producing the organic compounds in the matrix (Webb 1969; Frankel and Mead 1973; DeFlaun and Mayer 1983). Other sources of this material are the mucus products secreted by feeding meiofauna; e.g., mucus nets produced by nematodes (Riemann and Schrage 1978), mucus trails of turbellarians (Klauser 1986) and macrofauna (Lawry 1967) as well as by many organisms for such functions as locomotion (Trueman 1975).

The part of the matrix that has been investigated using histochemical techniques is that which adheres to the larger mineral grains when the grains are dispersed on a microscope slide. This has been referred to as encrusting organic matter. Whitlatch and Johnson (1974) and Whitlatch (1974) were the first to apply standard histological staining techniques to marine sediments. They used the periodic acid-Schiff (PAS) reaction for carbohydrates, mercuric bromphenol blue (MBB) for proteins, and Sudan Black B (SBB) for lipids. Very small amounts of sediment were placed in vials and the stains applied. After staining the grains were dispersed on a microscope slide for evaluation. Whitlatch (1974) noted that only 13.9 % of the material stained positively for PAS, while less than 0.4 % showed MBB reactions and less than 0.1 % SBB reactions. He concluded that less than half of the possible ingestible food items were, in fact, organic in nature.

Gelder (1984) used histochemical techniques and polarizing filters (Gelder 1983) to examine organic coatings on the surface of grains from the Lowes Cove tidal flat in Maine. Acid glycoproteins and compounds containing 1,2 glycol groups were stained with Alcian blue (pH 2.5 or 1.0) and PAS reaction, respectively (AB-PAS). MBB was used for basic proteins while all proteins were stained with Coomassie BB R250 (CR250) following ethanol-acetic acid fixation. Almost half of the material he examined consisted of mineral grains with various types of organic coats. The remaining material was almost entirely organic matter that stained PAS positive and consisted of amorphous flocculent material, micro-organisms, and organic fragments.

Organic films have also been observed on sediment grains by using scanning electron microscopy. Most grains examined from Lowes Cove seemed to have some degree of organic coating, the size and extent of which was qualitatively correlated with changing bacterial activity (DeFlaun and Mayer 1983). Deep-sea sediments and nodules also possess organic coatings. Burnett (1981) described the coatings of the botryoidal surface of manganese nodules as being between 1 and 10 μm thick and bearing several types of microorganisms.

Organic particles

Many different kinds of organic particles may be found in marine sediments. These usually include living diatom and other algal cells, meiofaunal taxa such as Foraminifera, ostracods, copepods, acoel turbellarians, etc., chitinous molts of various crustaceans, shell fragments of molluscs, fragments of terrestrial plants, and setae and jaws of polychaetes (Johnson 1974). In deep-sea sediments a significant proportion of all organic particles consists of nanobiotal elements (Burnett 1981; Snider et al. 1984). The number and type of particles likely to be found will vary with water depth and distance from shore (Hargrave 1975) as well as depth within the sediment column (Johnson 1977). For example, in most nearshore regions where marshes are common, fragments of the marsh grass, *Spartina*, are abundant. In Maine, terrestrial plant fragments seen in the sediment also includes those derived from oak leaves and pine needles, but many of the organic particles may be derived from the large biomass of attached macroalgae living along the shore (Webster et al. 1975; Hughes 1979; Josselyn and Mathieson 1980). In certain deep sea regions, turtle grass (Wiebe et al. 1976; Wolff 1976) has been seen on the seafloor, suggesting that this too may be a source of plant fragments in the sediment. Josselyn et al. (1983) recorded large volumes of seaweed and sea grasses being transported through the Salt River Canyon, St. Croix, U.S. Virgin Islands, most of which must have been deposited to the deep-sea floor as very few organic particles were seen in the canyon floor sediments (Watling and Steneck, in prep.). Large carcass food falls may also provide a source of at least localized particulate organic matter to deep-sea sediments (Stockton and DeLaca 1982).

Microorganisms

While microorganisms are ubiquitous in marine sediments they will not often be seen in thin section preparations; however, they will probably be one of the most important structural agents. The most commonly considered microorganisms in sediments are bacteria and diatoms. In some sediments, the nanobiota (Thiel 1983), or those microorganisms between the size of bacteria and meiofauna, may be more abundant than diatoms (Snider et al. 1984). Much of our perception of the dominance of bacteria and diatoms in marine sediments is derived from studies of sedimentary microbes conducted in very shallow water. Bacteria in these sediments are usually associated with mineral grains or with organic particles (Fenchel 1970) or diatom frustules (personal observations). Many authors have commented that the more angular mineral grains tend to have the greater coverage of bacteria (Nickels et al. 1981, Weise and Rheinheimer 1978), but this has not been demonstrated quantitatively, partly because of the difficulty in quantifying the shape of mineral grains. Bacterial numbers are generally on the order of $10^9 g^{-1}$ dry weight of sediment, but in deep-sea sediments abundances may be at least an order of magnitude lower (personal observation, Aller and Aller 1986). Shallow sediments also harbor diatoms, some being attached to the surface of mineral grains whereas others are mobile and migrate through the upper sediment layers. In deep-sea sediments, Burnett (1979, 1981) has found several nanobiotal species living attached to mineral grains.

Pores and Pore Spaces

Owing to the drainage of water through terrestrial soils, pore space plays a much more important structural role than in marine sediments, with the possible exception of sandy substrata containing very low amounts of silt and clay. Marine clastic sediments have not commonly been examined with thin section techniques (e.g., Frankel and Mead 1973) although many sections are available for sedimentary rocks of clastic origin. Consequently, information about *in situ* pore space volume has been inferred from measures of sediment water content. Harrison and Wass (1965), using a least squares multiple regression analysis, determined that water content was the most useful mass property of marine sediments for predicting the abundances of the three infaunal species they studied. They noted that water content reflected the interrelationships of mean grain size, sorting, grain packing, and mineralogy, which would be expected if it is, in fact, related to pore space. Rhoads (1974) suggested that deposit feeders, by their feeding activities, may exert a strong influence on porosity, water content, cohesion, and compaction of the sediment.

Webb (1969) suggested that the pore space of marine sands could be divisible into two types, based on the degree of water flow. Capillary space is defined as that part of the pore space where water would preferentially flow, with water flow being highly reduced in the remainder, termed cavity space. Through his experiments, Webb determined that organic epipsammic films tended to reduce the capillary space and increase the cavity space, but the overall porosity was increased. This would be a result of the apparent increased size of the grain as the epipsammic film was produced. Water content has been also noted to increase as other factors, such as pelletization (Rhoads and Boyer 1982), increased. However, while there is considerable indirect evidence about the extent of pore spaces in marine sediments, there is little direct information about the existence of these voids, their sizes, or their distributions in the matrix surrounding the mineral grains. From water content data it is known that all of the space between grains in marine muds is not filled completely with matrix. Therefore, one can infer that considerable pore space is present, but that it is cavity space rather than capillary space.

Pellets

Many species of marine invertebrates defecate their ingested material into the environment in the form of pellets. They may take a wide range of shapes and sizes (Kraeuter and Haven 1970). Regions of the sea bottom with high densities of deposit feeders often have a significant proportion of the mineral grains bound into fecal pellets (Rhoads and Young 1971). It has been a popular notion that fecal pellets act as gardens for bacteria (Newell 1965), and that as the pellet ages its food value increases (Johannes and Satomi 1966; Frankenberg and Smith 1967). Recent work on the Lowes Cove tidal flat (as opposed to all the laboratory experiments previously conducted) suggests that there may be an initial, rapid colonization of the pellet surface, probably because it represents available free space (Watling, in prep.). Beyond that, bacterial abundances are seen to fluctuate widely. Hargrave (1976) calculated that only about 1 % of the surface available for bacterial colonization on sediment grains could actually be utilized because of the difficulty in supplying nutrients in an environment governed by diffusive processes. Few pellets are found intact below the surface of the sediment as they are probably disrupted by the movements of organisms living in the surface sediment layers (Levinton 1979).

Burrows, tubes, and other structures

One characteristic of marine infaunal life is the burrow or tube that an organism produces. A burrow may be a temporary excavation made by an organism as it pushes its way through the sediment or settles into the substratum from the water column, or it may be simply lined with mucus to keep the walls from caving in during the short interval it is occupied (Schafer 1972). In both cases, the activity of burrow construction probably has a substantial effect on the structure of the sediment as the cohesive nature of the matrix is disrupted (Jumars and Nowell 1984) and the interstitial waters are 'stirred' (Aller et al. 1983; see also Thayer 1983 for literature review). Tubes are more substantial structures made of agglutinated mineral grains, or other sedimented material such as shell fragments or the refractory remains of plant debris (Schafer 1972). Tubes usually have characteristic features and can be used to identify the taxon level of the organisms that built them. Since tubes extend into the overlying oxygenated waters, and the tube walls are somewhat permeable, many geochemical reactions can be considerably modified by the addition of oxygen into the sediment in the immediate vicinity of an animal's tube (Aller 1982). Tubes also represent a high degree of ordering of sediment grains, usually with a strong organic content in the binding matrix.

Methods of Resin-Embedding Marine Sediment

In order to examine the small-scale features of marine sediment it is necessary to ensure that these features are maintained in their original form during the preparation of thin sections. The techniques used here have, for the most part, been borrowed and modified from those already in the literature on terrestrial soils and from well-known histological procedures.

Sediment samples were taken using small metal forms encompassing a surface of 1 x 3 cm, to a depth of about 3 cm. The protocol follows the same three basic steps of standard histological technique: preservation, dehydration, and embedding. All of the times given below should be adjusted according to the estimated degree of permeability of the sediment block.

Preservation

The sample with its metal form was carefully immersed in 10 % formalin (prepared with seawater) for a period of 3 - 5 days to ensure complete penetration. Two formalin changes follow at 3 day intervals, one made with 50 % seawater and the next with freshwater. The last wash is necessary to remove salt ions which may form crystals in the following steps.

Dehydration

Acetone was used as the dehydration agent. Each step consisted of adding acetone to the solution to achieve a dehydration series of 5 %, 10 %, 25 %, 50 %, 75 %, 85 %, 90 %, 95 %, 100 %, 100 % acetone. Each step lasted about 8 hrs. It was found that the sediment block should not be moved through the solution-air interface as the consequent repeated draining of the sample resulted in the loss of some fine material.

Embedding

After the sample was completely dehydrated, it was moved to an embedding container to which PolyBed 812 resin mix was added until the sample was totally immersed. After curing overnight at 70°C, the sample was removed from its metal form for sectioning. Several sections were cut from each block, glued to glass slides and polished to a thickness of 30 μm.

Micromorphology of a Mudflat Sediment

The only published thin sections for marine sediments which show details of the organic constituents are the few photos in the papers of Frankel and Mead (1973) and Rhoads (1974). In the following account, thin sections of the Lowes Cove, Maine, mudflat sediments will be presented and discussed.

The most striking feature of thin sections of marine muddy sediment is the ubiquitous presence of matrix (Fig. 12.1). In most cases, it is unlikely that grain boundaries ever touch. Grains of all sizes have varying proximity to one another, but they are usually separated by some amount of matrix (Fig. 12.2). Since these sections were cut at 30 μm thickness, there is an apparent differentiation of features. Those larger than 30 μm will stand out from the matrix, whereas those smaller than 30 μm will be completely embedded in the matrix and, therefore, will not be as noticeable. At 100x magnification, the larger grains stand out quite clearly from the matrix (Fig. 12.1), whereas even at 400x the smaller grains cannot easily be discerned and may be missed entirely (Fig. 12.3). Use of crossed polarizers aids in the differentiation of the smaller grains, but is not effective for grains much smaller than 10 μm (Fig. 12.4).

A close examination of the matrix shows that it is not of uniform density. If one examines grain boundaries carefully, certain sites are seen to have higher density of matrix than others (Fig. 12.5. Occasionally, autofluorescence techniques will show these higher density areas to be occupied by living diatoms, but usually it is not possible to determine the nature of the material at these sites.

A large number of autofluorescing chloroplasts were observed in the sections sampled 3-4.5 cm below the sediment surface. Most were associated with large fragments of terrestrially derived organic material, indicating that these plant fragments were either buried quite recently or had resisted microbial attack for some unknown amount of time. Other autofluorescing chloroplasts were seen in diatom cells. Some of these were obviously chain-forming planktonic forms that had become buried, whereas others were clearly associated with large sediment grains. Most of the planktonic forms were enclosed in fecal pellets, suggesting a mode of burial that has not been fully investigated. Two grains that had chloroplasts associated with them were relatively large. In neither case could it be determined from transmitted light that high numbers of diatoms were present although the matrix was of slightly darker color.

Other large particles observed were plant fragments derived from the

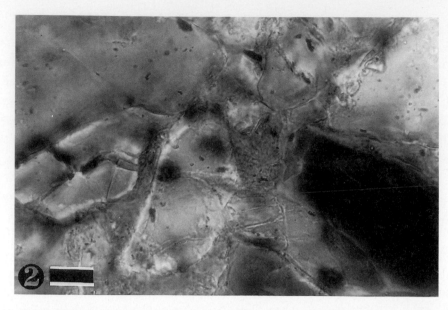

Figure 12.2: While grains exist in very close proximity to one another, there is always at least a thin strand of organic matrix between them. Where the grain surface extends at an angle through the 30 μm of the section the matrix can be seen on the surface of the grain. Scale bar is 0.02 mm.

higher marine fringe. These were from pine, oak, or *Spartina*. In some cases, the plant fragments had pyrite-like nodules within their boundaries (Fig. 12.6). Most plant fragments can be easily identified by using autofluorescence to view the cell walls (Fig. 12.6).

In some areas of the section, intact fecal pellets were observed (Fig. 12.7). It is not known whether these were produced at this depth in the sediment or whether they were produced at the surface and survived burial intact. Pellets contain a higher density matrix and many smaller grains per unit area than is commonly seen throughout most of the thin section (Fig. 12.8).

Quantification of Food Resources for Deposit Feeders

Food resources for deposit feeders have characteristically been studied by taking small amounts of sediment, smearing it on a microscope slide, and then staining the smear to determine the presence of carbohydrates, proteins, or lipids (Whitlatch 1974; Gelder 1983) or by taking larger amounts of sediment and performing bulk chemical analyses for protein, etc. (Mayer

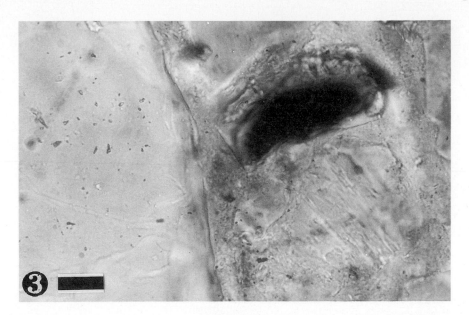

Figure 12.3: Transmitted light view of thin section at high magnification. Very small grains are completely embedded in matrix and are not easily resolvable because they are much smaller than the 30 μm thickness of the thin section. Scale bar is 0.02 mm.

et al. 1986).

The first of these techniques seems to produce major artifacts due to the complete disruption of the sedimentary structure. For example, what has been termed "organic-mineral aggregates" by benthic ecologists do not exist *in situ*. Rather, they are probably fragments of the matrix containing very small embedded mineral particles. That the matrix surrounds all particles, of whatever size, can be seen in the thin sections. There must be some distribution of the adhesive-cohesive forces that results in the formation of "aggregates" as the sediment is disrupted. A second consequence of this disruption is the production of "clean" vs. "encrusted" grains. There is some evidence from the thin sections that encrusted grains exist *in situ*, that is, microbes attach to the surface of a grain and create a layer of material that has stronger adhesive bonds to the grain than to the surrounding matrix. Clean grains are probably those without such microbial attachment and therefore, when the sediment is disrupted, they become separated from the matrix.

Chemical techniques can produce very detailed accounts of the organic components in marine sediments (Klok et al. 1983, 1984), but because of

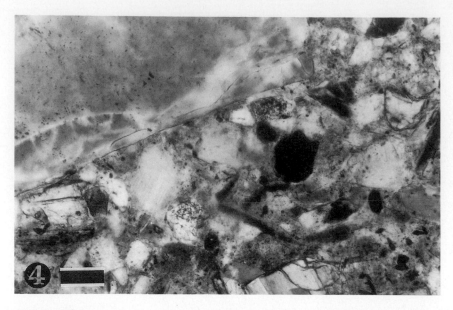

Figure 12.4: Thin section, using partially crossed polarizers. Technique helps to bring out details in the matrix and in some of the smaller grains. The identity of minerals can also be determined using polarized light. Bar is 0.02 mm. (From L. Watling, 1988, *Mar. Ecol. Prog. Ser.* 47:135-144)

the large amounts of material needed and the time and expense to run these analyses, little information can be gained regarding the small-scale spatial distribution of the various compounds. Duchaufour et al. (1984) attempted to overcome some of these problems by using mechanical disaggregation and size fractionation techniques. The various fractions were examined microscopically before being analyzed for organic compounds. In this way it could be determined whether "organic-mineral aggregates", large plant fragments, etc. were being chemically characterized. While it does not seem possible to do detailed chemical analyses on the matrix of thin sections, it may be possible to approximate those results by using histochemical techniques (Gelder 1983). Using autofluorescence or crossed polarizers, it is possible to determine what proportion of the volume of thin section being examined is occupied by large (>40 μm) mineral grains and plant fragments. The remaining volume then is resin (filling the space occupied by water *in situ*), small mineral grains, and the organic material making up the bulk of the matrix. The application of histochemical techniques to the thin sectioned material should allow the direct characterization of the major organic constituents and their spatial arrangements.

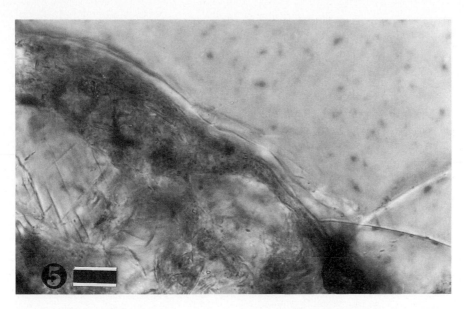

Figure 12.5: In certain places along the grain edge the matrix is thicker than normal. Compare the darkness of the matrix in this photo to that in Fig. 3. In this case autofluorescence techniques showed the presence of diatoms in the matrix. It is likely that the matrix here will strongly adhere to the surface of the grain if the sediment is disturbed. Scale bar is 0.02 mm.

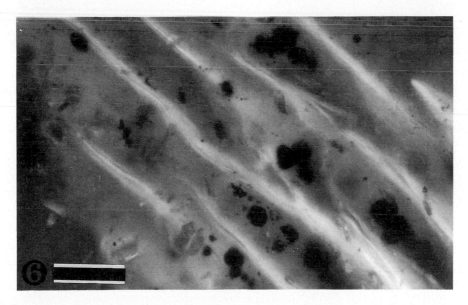

Figure 12.6: Plant fragment (probably piece of pine needle) viewed using epifluorescence light. Inclusions within cells are probably framboids. Scale bar is 0.05 mm.

284

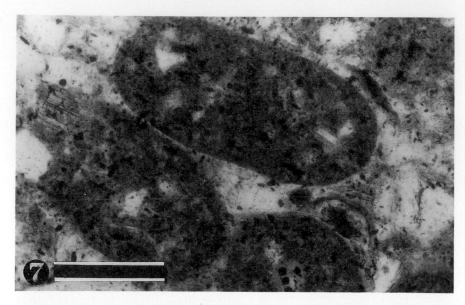

Figure 12.7: Fecal pellets found *in situ*. One is still intact while the other two are beginning to break apart. Scale bar is 0.2 mm. (From L. Watling, 1988, *Mar. Ecol. Prog. Ser.* 47:135-144)

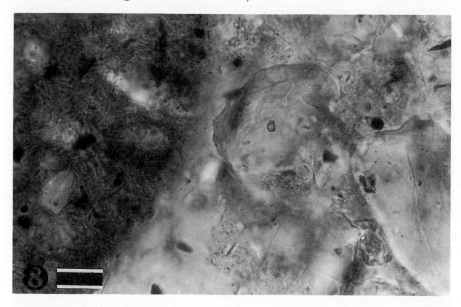

Figure 12.8: Higher magnification of end of fecal pellet and matrix. The pellet matrix is much denser and the enclosed grains are much smaller, suggesting that the organic content of the pellet matrix is greater than that of the matrix or it may have a higher humic content. As the pellets dismember this material enters into the sediment matrix. Scale = 0.02 mm.

The thin sections already examined show a patchiness of large mineral grains that exists on a scale of half a centimeter or so. Where the grains are densely packed, there is little matrix. On the other hand, where fecal pellets, for example, are breaking up in the sediment column, the matrix is very dense. The increased density is probably a direct result of the large number of small grains contained in these pellets. An increase in organic carbon and nitrogen content should be associated with this fine material (Cammen 1982; DeFlaun and Mayer 1983). Thus, a subsurface feeding worm that could 'taste' these differences in organic content may then actively search for such pockets in the sediment. Being able to quantify the micro-distributions of such features may help determine the degree to which a sedimentary environment can support a sub-surface deposit-feeding community.

Acknowledgements

I would like to thank S. Staples, for her help with developing the thin-section technique, and B. McKenzie for producing the photographic prints. This paper benefited from the careful reviews of R. Whitlatch and L. Mayer, and an anonymous reviewer. Many of the ideas contained herein were developed through discussions with the members of the Maine Benthic Oceanography Group, to whom I would like to express my appreciation. This is Darling Marine Center Contribution no. 196. Funds for this research were provided by N.S.F. grant ISP-8011448.

Literature Cited

Aller, J.Y. and R.C. Aller. 1986. Evidence for localized enhancement of biological activity associated with tube and burrow structures in deep-sea sediments at the HEBBLE site, western North Atlantic. *Deep-Sea Res.* 33: 755-790.

Aller, R.C. 1982. The effects of macrobenthos on chemical properties of marine sediment and overlying water. pp. 53-102, in P.L. McCall and M.J.S. Tevesz (eds.), *Animal-Sediment Relations*. Plenum Publishing Corp.

Aller, R.C., J.Y. Yingst and W.J. Ullman. 1983. Comparative biogeochemistry of water in intertidal *Onuphis* (polychaeta) and *Upogebia* (Crustacea) burrows: temporal patterns and causes. *J. Mar. Res.* 41: 571-604.

Bonneau, M. and G. Levy. 1982. Assembly and physical organization of particles. pp. 268-287, in M. Bonneau and B. Souchier (eds.) *Constituents and Properties of Soils.* Academic Press.

Bouma, A.H. 1969. *Methods for the study of sedimentary structures.* John Wiley and sons. New York.

Burnett, B. 1979. Quantitative sampling of the microbiota of the deep-sea benthos. II. Evaluation of technique and introduction to the biota of the San Diego Trough. *Trans. Amer. Micros. Soc.* 98: 233-242.

Burnett, B. 1981. Quantitative sampling of nanobiota (microbiota) of the deep-sea benthos. III. The bathyal San Diego Trough. *Deep-Sea Res.* 28: 649-663.

Burnham, C.P. 1970. The micromorphology of argillaceous sediments: particularly calcareous clays and siltstones. pp. 97-106, in D.A. Osmond and P. Bullock (eds.) *Micromorphological techniques and applications.* Agricultural Research Council of Great Britain, Soil Survey, Tech, Monogr. No. 2.

Cammen, L. 1982. Effect of particle size on organic content and microbial abundance within four marine sediments. *Mar. Ecol. Prog. Ser.* 9: 273-280.

DeFlaun, M.F. and L.M. Mayer. 1983. Relationships between bacteria and grain surfaces in intertidal sediments. *Limnol. Oceanogr.* 28: 873-881.

Duchaufour, H., L.J. Monrozier, and R. Pelet. 1984. Optical and geochemical studies of granulometric fractions from recent marine sediments. *Org. Geochem.* 6: 305-315.

Fedoroff, N. 1982. Soil fabric at the microscopic level. pp. 288-303, in M. Bonneau and B. Souchier (eds.) *Constituents and Properties of Soils.* Academic Press, New York.

Fenchel, T. 1970. Studies on the decomposition of organic detritus derived from the turtle grass *Thalassia testudinum. Limnol. Oceanogr.* 15: 14-20.

FitzPatrick, E.A. 1984. *Micromorphology of Soils.* Chapman and Hall. London.

Foster, R.C. 1981. Polysaccharides in soil fabrics. *Science* 214: 665-667.

Frankel L. and D.J. Mead. 1973. Mucilagenous matrix of some estuarine sands in Connecticut. *J. Sed. Pet.* 43: 1090-1095.

Frankenberg, D. and K.L. Smith. 1967. Coprophagy in marine animals. *Limnol. Oceanogr.* 12: 443-450.

Gelder, S.R. 1983. Enhancement of histochemically demonstrated organic materials on sand-silt grains using polarized light. *Tech. Inf. Bull., Leitz, USA* 1: 11-12.

Gelder, S.R. 1984. Diet and histophysiology of the alimentary canal of *Lumbricillus lineatus* (Oligochaeta, Enchytraeidae). *Hydrobiologia* 115:71-81.

Hargrave, B.T. 1975. The importance of total and mixed-layer depth in the supply of organic material to bottom communities. *Symp. Biol. Hung.* 15: 157-165.

Hargrave, B.T. 1976. The central role of invertebrate faeces in sediment decomposition. pp. 301-321, in J.M. Anderson and A. Macfadyen (eds.) *The role of terrestrial and aquatic organisms in decomposition processes.* Blackwell Scientific Publ., Oxford.

Harrison, W. and M.L. Wass. 1965. Frequencies of infaunal invertebrates related to water content of Chesapeake Bay sediments. *Southeastern Geol.* 6: 177-187.

Hughes, T.G. 1979. Studies on the sediment of St. Margaret's Bay, Nova Scotia. *J. Fish. Res. Bd. Canada* 36: 529-536.

Johannes, R.E. and M. Satomi. 1966. Composition and nutritive value of fecal pellets of a marine crustacean. *Limnol. Oceanogr.* 11: 191-197.

Johnson, R.G. 1974. Particulate matter at the sediment-water interface in coastal environments. *J. mar. Res.* 32: 313-330.

Johnson, R.G. 1977. Vertical variation in particulate matter in the upper twenty centimeters of marine sediments. *J. mar. Res.* 35: 273-282.

Josselyn, M.N. and A.C. Mathieson. 1980. Seasonal influx and decomposition of autochthonous macrophyte litter in a north temperate estuary. *Hydrobiologia* 71: 197-208.

Josselyn, M.N., G.M. Cailliet, T.M. Niesen, R. Cowen, A.C. Hurley, J. Connor and S. Hawes. 1983. Composition, export and faunal utilization of drift vegetation in the Salt River submarine canyon. *Est. Coast. Shelf Sci.* 17: 447-465.

Jumars, P.A. and A.R.M. Nowell. 1984. Effects of benthos sediment transport: difficulties with functional grouping. *Continent. Shelf Res.* 3: 115-130.

Klauser, M.D. 1986. Mucous secretions of the acoel turbellarian *Convoluta* sp. Orsted: an ecological and functional approach. *J. exp. mar. Biol. Ecol.* 97:123-133.

Klok, J., J.M.M. van der Knapp, J.W. DeLeeuw, H.C. Cox, and P.A. Schenck. 1983. Qualitative and quantitative characterization of the total organic matter in a recent marine sediment. pp. 813–818, **In** M. Bjoray et al. (eds.), *Advances in Org. Geochem.*, John Wiley, New York.

Klok, J., M. Baas, H.C. Cox, J.W. DeLeeuw, W.I.C. Rijpstra, and P.A. Schenck. 1984. Qualitative and quantitative characterization of the total organic matter in a recent marine sediment (Part II). *Org. Geochem.* 6: 265-278.

Kraueter, J. and D.S. Haven. 1970. Fecal pellets of common invertebrates of lower York River and lower Chesapeake Bay, Virginia. *Chesapeake Sci.* 11: 159-173.

Lawry, J.V. 1967. Structure and function of the parapodial cirri of the polynoid polychaete *Harmothoe*. *Z. Zellforsch. mikrosc. Anat.* 82: 345-361.

Levinton, J.S. 1979. Deposit-feeders, their resources, and the study of resource limitation. pp. 117-141, in R.J. Livingston (ed.) *Ecological Processes in Coastal and Marine Systems*. Plenum Press, New York.

Mayer, L.M. 1985. Geochemistry of humic substances in estuarine environments. pp. 211-232, in G.R. Aiken, D.M. McKnight, R.L. Wershaw and P. MacCarthy (eds.) *Humic substances in soil, sediment, and water: geochemistry, isolation, and characterization*. John Wiley and Sons, N.Y.

Mayer, L.M., L.L. Schick and F.W. Setchell. 1986. Measurement of protein in nearshore marine sediments. *Mar. Ecol. Prog. Ser.* 30: 159-165.

Newell, R.C. 1965. The role of detritus in the nutrition of two marine deposit feeders, the prosobranch *Hydrobia ulvae* and the bivalve *Macoma balthica. Proc. Zool. Soc. London* 144: 25-45.

Nickels, J.S., R.J. Bobbie, R.F. Martz, G.A. Smith, D.C. White and N.L. Richards. 1981. Effect of silicate grain shape, structure, and location on the biomass and community structure of colonizing marine microbiota. *Appl. Environ. Microbiol.* 41: 1262-1268.

O.R.S.T.O.M. -D.G.R.S.T. 1981. *Glossaire de Pedologie.*

Rhoads, D.C. 1974. Organism-sediment relations on the muddy sea floor. *Oceanogr. Mar. Biol. Ann. Rev.* 12: 263-300.

Rhoads, D.C. and D.K. Young. 1971. Animal-sediment relations in Cape Cod Bay, Massachusetts. II. Reworking by *Molpadia oolitica* (Holothuroidea). *Mar. Biol.* 11: 255-261.

Rhoads, D.C. and L.F. Boyer. 1982. The effects of marine benthos on physical properties of sediments, a successional perspective. pp. 3-52, in P.L. McCall and M.J.S. Tevesz (eds.) *Animal-Sediment Relations.* Plenum Publ. Corp.

Riemann, F. and M. Schrage. 1978. The mucus-trap hypothesis on feeding of aquatic nematodes and implications for biodegradation and sediment texture. *Oecologia* 34: 75-88.

Schafer, W. 1972. *Ecology and paleoecology of marine environments* (I. Oertel and G.Y. Craig, translators). University of Chicago Press.

Snider, L.J., B.R. Burnett and R.R. Hessler. 1984. The composition and distribution of meiofauna and nanobiota in a central North Pacific deep- sea area. *Deep-Sea Res.* 31: 1225-1249.

Stockton, W.L. and T.D. DeLaca. 1982. Food falls in the deep sea: occurrence, quality, and significance. *Deep-Sea Res.* 29: 157-169.

Thayer, C.W. 1983. Morphologic adaptations of benthic invertebrates to soft substrata. *J. Mar. Res.* 33: 177-189.

Thiel, H. 1983. Meiobenthos and nanobenthos of the deep sea, pp. 167-230, in G.T. Rowe (ed.) *Deep-Sea Biology. Vol. 8: The Sea: Ideas and Observations on Progress in the Study of the Seas.* John Wiley and Sons, New York.

Trueman, E.R. 1975. *The locomotion of soft-bodied animals.* Edward Arnold, London.

Webb, J.E. 1969. Biologically significant properties of submerged marine sands. *Proc. Roy. Soc. Lond. B.* 174: 355-402.

Webster, T.J.M., M.A. Paranjape, and K.H. Mann. 1975. Sedimentation of organic matter in St. Margaret's Bay, Nova Scotia. *J. Fish. Res. Board Can.* 32: 1399-1407.

Weise, W. and G. Rheimheimer. 1978. Scanning electron microscopy and epifluorescence investigation of bacterial colonization of marine sand sediments. *Microbial Ecol.* 4: 175-188.

Whitlatch, R.B. 1974. Food-resource partitioning in the deposit feeding polychaete *Pectinaria gouldii. Biol. Bull.* 147: 227-235.

Whitlatch, R.B. 1981. Animal-sediment relationships in intertidal marine benthic habitats: Some determinants of deposit-feeding species diversity. *J. Exp. Mar. Biol. Ecol.* 53: 31-45.

Whitlatch, R.B. and R.G. Johnson. 1974. Methods for staining organic matter in marine sediments. *J. Sed. Pet.* 44: 1310-1312.

Wiebe, P.H., S.H. Boyd and C. Winget. 1976. Particulate matter sinking to the deep-sea floor at 2000 m in the Tongue of the Ocean, Bahamas, with a description of a new sedimentation trap. *J. mar. Res.* 34: 341-354.

Wolff, T. 1976. Utilization of seagrass in the deep sea. *Aquatic Bot.* 2: 161-174.

Chapter 13

On Some Mechanistic Approaches to the Study of Deposit Feeding In Polychaetes

Robert B. Whitlatch
Department of Marine Sciences
The University of Connecticut
Groton, CT 06340

Introduction

Often, foraging models constructed to predict dietary behavior of organisms partition feeding into a series of choices – decisions about where to forage, which types or quantities of food items to ingest, when to move to a new patch of food, etc. (e.g., Krebs 1978, Stephens and Krebs 1986). The rationale underlying this approach relies heavily on the supposition that as a consequence of evolutionary selection pressure(s), organisms tend to use their food resources efficiently. Given this assumption, it is then possible to develop predictions of how an organism should forage in order to maximize its feeding efficiency and evolutionary fitness.

The application of optimal foraging models to deposit-feeding invertebrates has provided insightful and provocative predictions regarding patterns of food item selection (Taghon et al. 1978) and feeding rate (Doyle 1979; Taghon 1981). These models suggest that when given a choice and the ability, deposit feeders should preferentially ingest food particles of highest food value and display consumption rates that are positively related to food availability (see chapters by Cammen and Taghon, this volume). While there is a relative paucity of field and laboratory data which have specifically tested these predictions, often results are consistent with an energy maximization tenet. It is important to note, however, that the notion that deposit feeders behave as optimal foragers appears far from clear. Many species are best described as "imperfect" energy optimizers, and close examination of factors contributing to deposit feeder food-resource selection and consumption rate suggests we are currently facing a rather complex and often opaque issue (e.g., Levinton 1980; Whitlatch and Weinberg 1982).

Aside from difficulties in obtaining appropriate data and designing unambiguous experiments to test the optimality assertion (e.g. Gould and Lewontin 1979), there is a growing concern regarding the utility of optimization theory in general (e.g., Emlen, in press). While it seems reasonable to employ the optimality tenet as a heuristic tool to aid with hypothesis generation, such hypotheses do not necessarily provide a rationale for understanding or explaining foraging behavior. For example, stating a hypothesis that a deposit feeder selects particle sizes which maximize net energy gain is falsifiable and interesting, but it does not provide insight into the organizing principles of deposit feeder foraging behavior.

One approach to understanding the mechanisms of deposit feeder foraging behavior begins by exploring and developing theories regarding principles of food item capture and consumption rate. This approach has a relatively strong theoretical base with other groups of organisms (e.g., insects) and can provide a framework for examining the elements of feeding behavior. This approach need not necessarily be viewed as an alternative to the principles of energy maximization; one is mechanistic, the other strategic.

My purpose here is to examine some possible mechanistic approaches to the study of the foraging behavior of deposit-feeding invertebrates. While I take an admittedly simplified and reductionist view, my purpose is to illustrate two points:

1. Particle selection behavior can be affected by particle encounter rates. Models and experiments designed to examine food item selection, therefore, need to partition "passive" versus "active" selection and assess the degree to which organisms are morphologically and behaviorally

constrained in their particle selection abilities.

2. Consumption rates can be highly variable and depend upon food item availability, particle size, pre- and post-ingestion handling times and particle-specific encounter probabilities. Stochastic (e.g., random or non-optimal) models may generate predictions similar to those derived via energy optimization principles.

Although I will frame my discussion around a particular group of deposit feeders (polychaetous annelids), I believe the approach is general enough to be expanded to other taxonomic groups of deposit-feeding invertebrates (e.g., crustaceans, molluscs), with appropriate modification.

A simplified view of particle selection mechanics

Deposit-feeding polychaetes display a wide array of morphological and behavioral adaptations for collecting particulate food items (see, for example, Fauchald and Jumars, 1979). In order to begin examining the role that morphology can play in food item collection, however, I have divided the polychaetes into two general foraging groups:

1. Gulpers: Organisms which feed by everting a sac-like or weakly or strongly armed proboscides, primarily taking food materials in discrete mouthfuls. Typically these are organisms that burrow through the sediments or forage just below the sediment–water interface (e.g., orbiniids, arenicolids, capitellids).

2. Line-trappers: Species which collect food items with palps (e.g., spionids) or tentacles (e.g., terebellids). Many forms are tubicolous and often feed at, slightly below, or above the sediment-water interface.

Both foraging groups obtain their nutrition by feeding upon a wide variety of organic particulates (e.g., diatoms, detritus, vascular plant fragments, organic-encrusted mineral grains) found in sediments. While these items vary in a variety of quantitative and qualitative ways, for simplicity I will only examine food capture on the basis of particle size (also see Fig. 13.1 for additional assumptions).

Given these assumptions, it is possible to examine particle-specific encounter probabilities using examples of the two contrasting deposit feeder food collection morphologies: a. A "gulper" example (Fig. 13.1a). In this case, the organism moves through the sediment sampling its food resources

"Gulper" model (1a):

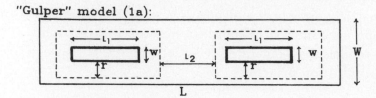

"Line—trapper" model (1b):

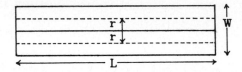

Assumptions:
1. Feeding mechanism has a definable shape.
2. Food particles are two—dimensional discs.
3. Any particle touching a feeding structure is captured.
4. Particles are randomly distributed.

Definitions:

1. $F_{(r)}$ = density of particle distribution

2. $H_{(s|r)}$ = conditional density of being captured, r = size

3. $G_{(s,r)} = F_{(r)} H_{(s|r)}$ = joint density of being captured

4. $K_{(r|s)}$ = conditional density of size r given it is captured

5. $L_{(s)} = \int G_{(s,r)} dr$

6. $K_{(r|s)} = G_{(s,r)} / L_{(s)} = (F_{(r)} H_{(s|r)}) / L_{(s)}$

Figure 13.1: Two simple foraging models (see text for explanation) used to illustrate how deposit feeders' food capture morphologies can influence particle size-specific encounter probabilities.

in discrete mouthfuls. While the food sampling device (e.g., mouth) has a definable area of $(l_1 w)$, according to assumption 3 (Fig. 13.1), the effective area sampled is $(l_1 w)$ plus an envelope around the device of particle radius r (Fig. 13.1a). If the distance between mouthfuls (l_2) is greater than $2r$ (e.g., a food particle of radius r is not potentially sampled twice by the organism with successive mouthfuls), then the conditional probability of a particle of radius r being sampled is:

$$H_{(s/r)} = 2(W + 2r)(l_1 + 2r)/LW \qquad (13.1)$$

$$= (W + 2r)(l_1 + 2r)/(l_1 + l_2)W \qquad (13.2)$$

where L = length of foraging area and W = width of foraging area. If $l_2 < 2r$, then equation 13.2 collapses to:

$$H_{(s/r)} = (w + 2r)/W \qquad (13.3)$$

(Note, however, that equation 13.3 violates assumption 3 (Fig. 13.1) and seems biologically unrealistic for most "gulper"-type deposit-feeding species.)

b. "Line-trapper" model (Fig. 13.1b). In this example the morphological model assumes that the "line-trapper" collects food particles by laying a palp or tentacle on the sediment surface, sampling all of the particulate material that it touches. If we define a similar foraging area sampled by the "gulper" as LW, and a "line-trapper's" sampling device consisting of a "palp" or "tentacle" of length l (where its width, w, is initially small (Fig. 13.1b), then the conditional probability of that structure sampling a food particle of radius r is:

$$H_{(s/r)} = L(2r)/LW = 2r/W. \qquad (13.4)$$

(Note that in all variations of this model, W will not enter into subsequent calculations since W is always greater than r (e.g., boundary conditions are unimportant).

In order to assess how the contrasting feeding structures encounter particles of varying size, Fig. 13.2 illustrates the ratio of conditional probabilities of capturing food particles of varying size. The result is a series of hyperbolic curves varying with different widths of the particle sampling structures. For the gulper model, a greater proportion of small particles are encountered relative to the line-trapper model. As particle size increases, the ratio of the models' conditional probabilities of particle encounter approaches unity. (An example of how the two sampling structures would "sample" a negative exponential distribution of particles sizes is provided in Appendix I.)

While these are only two examples of a wide array of possible morphologies, the point here is simple – morphological structures used to collect particulate food materials have the potential of greatly influencing particle size-specific encounter probabilities and hence apparent particle selection behavior. Even the simplest particle collection morphologies (Fig. 13.1) can potentially sample particulate material in a biased fashion. This finding also points to the necessity of constructing more sophisticated models of particle encounter probabilities and developing approaches which address the interplay of functional morphology and feeding behavior (see, for example, Dauer 1983, 1984). For instance, how morphologically constrained are deposit feeders in coping with variations in food item quantity? The little information available suggests that some species may be rather inflexible (e.g., Whitlatch and Weinberg 1982) to adjustments in food quantity and quality, while other species may possess the capacity for behavioral adjustments (e.g., Jumars et al. 1982). Further, it is important to design studies which partition apparent "decisions of choice" (e.g., active selection) from stochastic (e.g., random) particle-specific encounter probabilities (e.g., passive selection). Lastly, it is imperative to understand the distributional characteristics, form and quality of particulate food items available to deposit feeders and how they are "perceived" by the organisms' food collecting devices. Jumars et al. (1982) have provided important insight on how various physical cues (e.g., particle density, size) affect non-cohesive particle selection in tentaculate deposit-feeding polychaetes. It should be noted, however, that most deposit feeders sample a complex mixture of both non-cohesive and cohesive particulate matter in natural marine sediments. The majority of fine-grained silt and clay sized particles, for instance, is bound in cohesive organic-mineral aggregates (Johnson 1974) and is rarely sampled individually by a deposit feeder. These aggregates can be orders of magnitude greater in size than the inorganic fractions contained within them (Johnson 1974). Since surficial sediments typically contain large quantities of these aggregates (Whitlatch 1981), surface-feeding tentaculate deposit feeders may possess sampling structures to oversample large particulate material in order to maximize organic-mineral aggregate ingestion, as suggested by the "line-trapper" model (Fig. 13.1b).

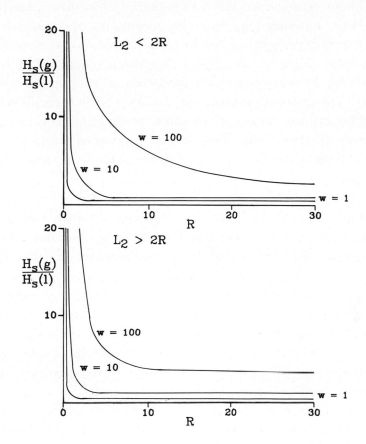

Figure 13.2: Ratios of the conditional probabilities of particle encounter that the "gulper" and "line-trapper" models (see Figs. 13.1a and 13.1b) have in relation to varying particle sizes.

Mechanics of Deposit Feeder Consumption Rate

It is possible to examine the effect that particle-specific encounter rates and handling times have on food ingestion mechanics of deposit feeders. One reasonably well developed approach, termed "functional response" analysis (Soloman 1949; Holling 1959; 1965), provides a quantitative description of the relationship between per capita food consumption as a function of food availability. The approach is quite useful since it focuses on different elements of feeding behavior of an organism and expresses them in terms which can be measured experimentally. This permits a detailed study of the way(s) in which a consumer can alter its foraging behavior in response to variations in food supply.

Since the theoretical development and verification of functional responses has been applied mainly to terrestrial habitats and tightly coupled consumer-prey interactions (see, for example, Hassell 1978), but not deposit feeders, I will present a brief overview of the general features of functional response models.

Intuitively, one would expect that a functional response curve should take the form of an increasing amount of food (e.g., sediment) ingested as food concentration (e.g., protein, nitrogen, diatoms) in the sediment increases; at least to some limiting value representing maximum ingestion rate within a given time-frame. While a variety of theoretically possible functional response curves exist (Abrams 1982), they tend to fall into three general categories (Holling 1959; Hassell 1978). Figure 13.3 depicts these groupings and shows that while each curve reflects different patterns of monotonic rise, common to all is an upper bound on the ingestion rate of a consumer. Type I (food-concentration independent) responses increase linearly to a plateau, while Type II responses are hyperbolic (inversely food-concentration independent) and Type III responses are sigmoid (food-concentration dependent).

Various conceptual models are available to characterize both the form of a functional response and estimate biologically meaningful parameters (e.g., prey encounter rate, handling times, etc.). These can be further categorized as continuous-time (e.g., Holling 1959; Hassell 1970) and discrete-time (Royama 1971; Rogers 1972; Hassell et al. 1977) models. Discrete-time models relate the amount of food eaten (N_t) to food availability (N_a), whereas continuous-time models compare the number of food encounters (N_e) to a function of food availability (N_a). The functions of food availability involve several parameters (Table 13.1) and Figure 13.4 illustrates how ingestion

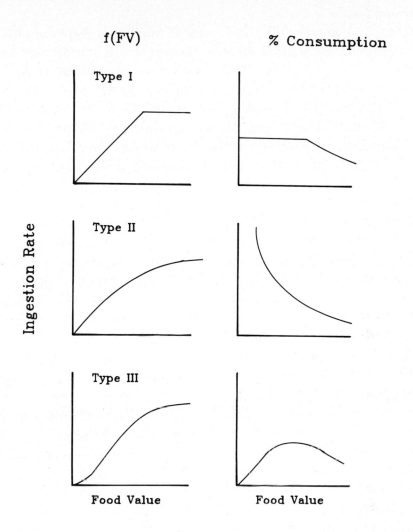

Figure 13.3: Three common classes of functional response curves.

rate, encounter rate and handling time components can contribute to each functional response curve.

Also, there are a variety of empirical functional response models (typically adapted from enzyme kinetics theory) which can be used to describe functional response curves. These are commonly applied to fish and zooplankton predators (see overviews provided by Durban 1979 and Valiela 1984). Although these models estimate feeding rate constants, they fail to provide much insight into the mechanism(s) which produce(s) the various consumer-prey feeding curves. In contrast, the conceptual functional response models (Table I) separate feeding into a variety of behavioral components.

While there is presently no explicit application of the functional response approach to deposit feeders, Taghon and Jumars (1984) examined the ingestion rates of several species of deposit feeding polychaetes in situations where food value of artificial sediments varied. These deposit feeders appear to fit a Type I or Type II functional response (Fig. 13.5), though it is not possible to discern which model fits best, let alone infer the mechanism(s) of feeding by a fit to a specific curve. Interestingly, several species show no indication of an asymptote in feeding rate (Fig. 13.5). Whether the range of food values was insufficient to adequately detect a plateau, or whether the relatively short-term nature of the feeding experiments failed to provide an entire picture of the functional response is unknown. For example, Mayer et al. (1986) recently noted that surficial marine sediments can contain as much as 1-2 mg of protein per gram dry weight. Perhaps these species are operating at the lower, linear end of their functional response curves, below the food levels where satiation would show an effect.

I have collected limited data on functional responses of two species of deposit-feeding polychaetes from the Dutch Wadden Sea. Figure 13.6 shows the effect of particle size on feeding rate, when food value (protein concentration) was systematically varied. Generally, as particle size increases, not only does feeding rate change but so does the form of the organisms' response to food availability (Type I to Type II functional response curve). While it is premature to speculate on the generality of these results, an important finding is that deposit feeder functional responses are flexible and can vary in relation to the available particle size spectrum. The specific mechanism(s) mediating differences in observed responses probably involves differences in pre- and post-ingestion particle handling times. One can postulate that these species are acting as "bulk" sediment processors when food sizes are small relative to gut volumes and/or food capturing structures. In this case,

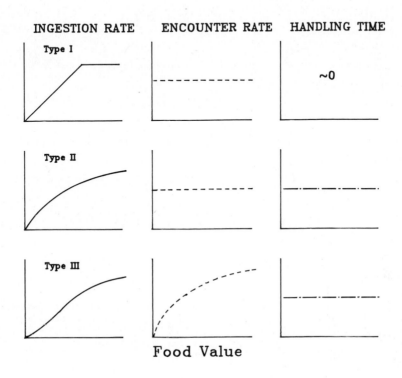

Figure 13.4: A description of how the various components of the functional response curves can contribute to the overall consumer-prey response.

Equation type	Model Type	Equation	Ref.
Continuous	I	$N_e = a'TN_t$	(1)
	II	$N_e = \dfrac{a'TN_t}{1+a'T_hN_t}$	(2)
	II	$N_e = \dfrac{bTN_t}{1+(cN_t)+(bT_hN_t^2}$	(1)
Discrete	I	$N_A = N_t(1 - e^{-a'T})$	(1)
	II	$N_A = N_t(1 - e^{-a(T-T_hN_a)})$	(1)
	III	$N_A = N_t(1 - e^{\frac{-bN_t}{1+cN_t}(T-T_hN_a)})$	(3)

Definitions:

Type	Symbol	Definitions
Variable	N_e	Number or amount of food items encountered
	N_t	Number or amount of food items ingested
	N_a	Amount of available food
Constant	T	Total available foraging time
Parameters	T_h	Food handling time[1]
	a'	Instantaneous search time[2]
	b, c	Variable search time[2]

[1] While typically denoted as the time from initial food capture, through feeding and initiation of search for a subsequent food item (Hassell, 1978), for deposit feeders it is more simply defined as time from first food item contact to egestion.

[2] In most cases this term is vanishingly small for deposit feeding invertebrates.

Table 13.1: Various linear and non-linear functional response curves (modified from Lipcius and Hines 1986). References are: (1) Hassell 1978; (2) Holling 1959; (3) Hassell et al. 1979

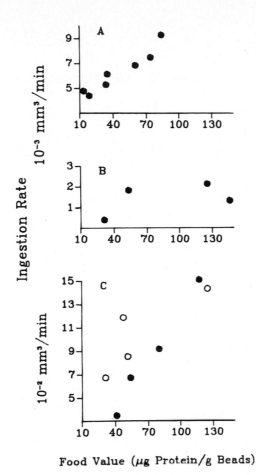

Figure 13.5: The relationship of food value to ingestion for three species of deposit-feeding polychaetes (from Taghon and Jumars, 1984; Tables 1-5). A = *Pseudopolydora kempi japonica*; B = *Hobsonia florida*; C = *Amphicteis scaphobranchiata* - closed circles indicate ingestion rates on glass beads 13-44 μm in diameter while open circles refer to consumption rates on glass beads 44-62 μm in diameter. Food value is expressed as the amount of bovine serum albumin (e.g., protein) attached to glass beads (see Taghon and Jumars, 1984 for details).

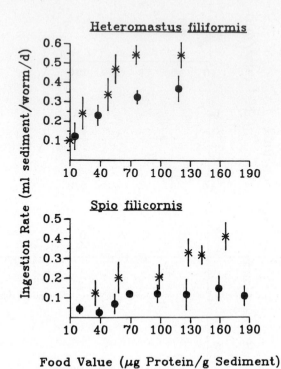

Figure 13.6: Functional response curves for two species of deposit-feeding polychaetes. A = *Heteromastus filiformis*; B = *Spio filicornis*. Open circles indicate ingestion rate on quartz grains 20-45 μm in diameter while closed circles indicate ingestion rates on grains 100-150 μm in diameter. Each point = mean +/- 1 s.d. (N = 5 to 7). Food value is expressed as the amount of bovine serum albumin bonded to the natural sediments (see Taghon, 1982 for details).

particle handling time is at or near zero. As particle size increases, handling times also increase, resulting in both decreased feeding rates and alterations in the form of the functional response curve (as depicted in Fig. 13.4). This finding is somewhat analogous to the queing theory ingestion model developed by Sjoberg (1980) which relates the form of a zooplankter's ingestion curve to a size ratio of the consumer and its particulate food resource.

Though further, more detailed studies are needed to dissect how the various components of the functional response equations contribute to deposit feeder foraging behavior, mechanistic approaches to foraging seem to provide interesting insights into questions related to both particle selection and feeding rate activities. Such an approach appears useful in enhancing our understanding of how deposit-feeding invertebrates adjust their feeding behavior in response to variations in food quality and/or quantity.

Acknowledgements

I am grateful to R. Lipcius, R. Zajac, T. DeWitt, L. Gypson and an anonymous reviewer for comments and the National Science Foundation for support. This is contribution number 190 of the Marine Sciences Institute, The University of Connecticut.

Literature Cited

Abrams, P. 1982. Functional responses of optimal foragers. *Am. Nat.* 120: 382-390.

Dauer, D.M. 1983. Functional morphology and feeding behavior of *Scolelepis squamata* (Polychaeta: Spionidae). *Mar. Biol.* 77: 279-285.

Dauer, D.M. 1984. Functional morphology and feeding behaviour of *Streblospio benedicti* (Polychaeta; Spionidae). Pages 418-429 In: P.A. Hutchings (ed.), Proceedings of the First International Polychaete Conference. Linnean Soc. New South Wales, Australia.

Doyle, R.W. 1979. Ingestion rate of a selective deposit feeder in a complex mixture of particles: testing the energy optimization hypothesis. *Limnol. Oceanogr.* 24: 867-874.

Durban, A.G. 1979. Food selection by plankton feeding fishes. Pages 203-218. In: H. Clepper (ed.), *Predator-Prey Systems in Fisheries Management*. Sport Fishing Institute, Washington.

Emlen, J.M. in press. Evolutionary ecology and the optimality assertion.

Fauchald, K. and P.A. Jumars. 1979. The diet of worms: a study of polychaete feeding guilds. *Oceanogr. Mar. Biol. Ann. Rev.* 17: 193-284.

Gould, S.J. and R.C. Lewontin. 1979. The spandrels of San Marco and the Panglossian paradigm: A critique of the adaptationist programme. *Proc. R. Soc. Lond.* B 205: 581-598.

Hassell, M.P. 1978. *The Dynamics of Arthropod Predator-prey Systems*. Princeton Univ. Press.

Hassell, M.P., J.H. Lawton and J.R. Beddington. 1977. Sigmoid functional responses by invertebrate predators and parasitoids. *J. Anim. Ecol.* 46: 249-262.

Holling, C.S. 1959. Some characteristics of simple types of predation and parasitism. *Can. Entomol.* 91: 385-398.

Holling, C.S. 1965. The functional response of predators to prey density and its role in mimicry and population regulation. *Mem. Entomol. Soc. Can.* 45: 3-60.

Johnson, R.G. 1974. Particulate matter at the sediment-water interface in coastal environments. *J. Mar. Res.* 32: 313-330.

Jumars, P.A., R.F.L. Self and A.R.M. Nowell. 1982. Mechanics of particle selection by tentaculate deposit-feeders. *J. Exp. Mar. Biol. Ecol.* 64: 47-70.

Krebs, J.R. 1978. Optimal foraging: decision rules for predators. Pages 23-63. In: J.R. Krebs and N.B. Davies (eds.), *Behavioural Ecology*. Blackwell Sci. Publ., London.

Levinton, J.S. 1980. Particle feeding by deposit feeders: models, data and a prospectus. Pages 423-439. In: K.R. Tenore and B.C. Coull (eds.), *Marine Benthic Dynamics*. Univ. South Carolina Press, Columbia.

Lipcius, R.N and A.H. Hines. 1986. Variable functional responses of a marine predator in dissimilar homogeneous microhabitats. *Ecology* 67: 1361-1371.

Mayer, L.M., L.L. Schick and F.W. Setchell. 1986. Measurement of protein in nearshore marine sediments. *Mar. Ecol., Progr. Ser.* 30: 159-165.

Rogers, D. 1972. Random search and insect population models. *J. Anim. Ecol.* 41: 369-383.

Royama, T. 1971. A comparative study of models for predation and parasitism. *Res. Popul. Ecol., Suppl.* 1: 1-91.

Solomon, M.E. 1949. The natural control of animal populations. *J. Anim. Ecol.* 18: 1-35.

Sjoberg, S. 1980. Zooplankton feeding and queing theory. *Ecol. Modell.* 10: 215-225.

Stephens, D.W. and J.R. Krebs. 1986. *Foraging Theory.* Princeton University Press, Princeton.

Taghon, G.L. 1981. Beyond selection: optimal ingestion rate as a function of food value. *Am. Nat.* 118: 202-214.

Taghon, G.L. 1982. Optimal foraging by deposit-feeding invertebrates: roles of particle size and organic coating. *Oecologia* 52: 295-304.

Taghon, G.L., R.F.L. Self and P.A. Jumars. 1978. Predicting particle selection by deposit-feeders: a model and its implications. *Limnol. Oceanogr.* 23: 752-759.

Taghon, G.L. and P.A. Jumars. 1984. Variable ingestion rate and its role in optimal foraging behavior of marine deposit-feeders. *Ecology* 65: 549-558.

Valiela, I. 1984. *Marine Ecological Processes.* Springer-Verlag, New York.

Whitlatch, R.B. 1981. Animal-sediment relationships in intertidal marine benthic habitats: some determinants of deposit-feeder species diversity. *J. Exp. Mar. Biol. Ecol.* 53: 31-45.

Whitlatch, R.B. and J.R. Weinberg. 1982. Factors influencing particle selection and feeding rate in the polychaete *Cistenides (Pectinaria) gouldii. Mar. Biol.* 71: 33-40.

Appendix 1. How the two feeding models (Fig. 1) sample a negative exponential distribution ($F_{(r)}$) of particles.

Assume that:

$$F_{(r)} = \frac{1}{\theta}e^{-r/\theta}, r > 0$$

For the "line-trapper":

$$G_{(s,r)} = K\frac{2r}{\theta}e^{-r/\theta}$$

$$\int G_{(s,r)}dr = K2\theta\int\frac{r}{\theta}e^{-r/\theta}\frac{dr}{\theta} = K2\theta$$

$$K_{(r|s)} = \frac{r}{\theta^2}e^{-r/\theta}$$

For the "gulper":

If $L_2 > 2r$, then

$$G_{s,r} = [1/(L_1 + L_2)](L_1 + 2r)(w + 2r)\frac{1}{\theta}e^{-r/\theta}$$

$$K_{(r|s)} = [1/(L_1 + L_2)\theta H_\theta](L_1 + 2r)(w + 2r)e^{-r/\theta}$$

If $L_2 < 2r$, then

$$G_{(s,r)} = (w + 2r)\frac{1}{\theta}e^{-r/\theta}$$

$$K_{(r|s)} = \frac{1}{H_\theta}(w + 2r)e^{-r/\theta},$$

where θ is the parameter of the negative binomial distribution.

Chapter 14

Some Ecological Perspectives in the Study of the Nutrition of Deposit Feeders

Kenneth R. Tenore
Chesapeake Biological Laboratory
Center for Environmental and Estuarine Studies
Solomons, Maryland 20688-0038 USA

Introduction

Even after several decades of research on the ecology of marine deposit feeders we are still unsure about what are the food resources that are exploited and still debate what one regulatory mechanism controls distribution and abundance. Two observations, neither new nor startling, might help us to understand why we need knowledge of the nutritional needs of, and resources available to deposit feeders:

1. We have usually searched for a single limiting factor that controls all species' distribution, abundance, and production rather than delineate the "interactive hierarchy" of several regulatory mechanisms.

2. We have often correlated and modeled point-in-time-specific, "snapshot" data of biotic units (individuals, populations, communities) with concomitant environmental physical/chemical controls; we have only played lip service to the varying time sequencing over which regulatory

mechanisms exert influence, i.e., the density at which a population of a deposit feeder exists at a given point in time has been caused by conditions of different environmental factors at varying previous points in time. Although I believe that these observations are generic problems in ecological research, they are particularly relevant to questions about nutritional sources available to, and exploited by, deposit feeders. In this Chapter, I would like to explore the hierarchy of the regulatory mechanisms that, interactively, result in observed distributions, abundances, and production of a population of a deposit feeder. Specifically, where are, and are not, feedback regulatory mechanisms between levels of hierarchical controls and how should this affect our designing of experiments studying the ecology of deposit feeders.

The "interactive hierarchy" of regulatory mechanisms

A variety of controls can, to a greater or lesser degree, affect species' distribution, abundance, and food chain parameters (e.g., egestion and assimilation rates and production, and calculated efficiencies.) Even when Liebig formulated his law of the limiting factor, he emphasized how various environmental factors could interact. He initially stated: "at any time and under a given set of environmental conditions, one factor limits the physiological growth of an organism." He then developed the interactive nature of controls by pointing out, for example, that high light levels could be concomitant with higher temperature levels and that light levels would affect photosynthetic rate, but also higher temperatures would affect a variety of enzymatic rates associated with plant growth. Furthermore, as initially formulated the concept of limiting factor dealt *specifically* with the regulatory effect of physical/chemical environmental parameters on physiological responses. Only more recently has this concept come also to view interspecific processes such as competition and predation as possible limiting factors.

As a way of illustrating the "interactive hierarchy" of potential regulatory mechanisms, it may be instructive to discuss different regulatory levels that control the final expression of production and trophic transfer in a simple detrital food chain (Figure 14.1).

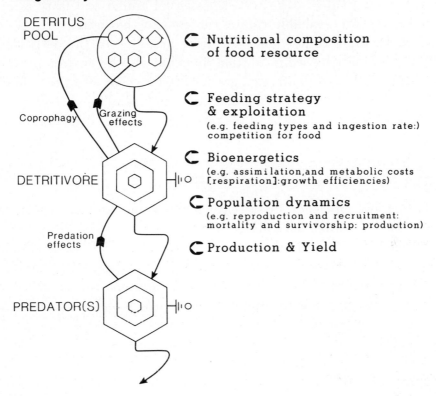

Regulatory Mechanisms of Detritus Food Chains

DETRITUS POOL

⊂ Nutritional composition
of food resource

⊂ Feeding strategy
& exploitation
(e.g. feeding types and ingestion rate:)
competition for food

⊂ Bioenergetics
(e.g. assimilation,and metabolic costs
[respiration]:growth efficiencies)

⊂ Population dynamics
(e.g. reproduction and recruitment:
mortality and survivorship: production)

⊂ Production & Yield

Coprophagy Grazing effects

DETRITIVORE

Predation effects

PREDATOR(S)

Figure 14.1: Hierarchy of regulatory mechanisms controlling detritus food chains.

Nutritional composition of food resources

Detritus is a heterogeneous pool derived from plant materials of varying nutritional quality (seagrasses, seaweeds), fecal pellets, and also a suite of trophic levels of populations of microalgae, bacteria, fungi, and protozoa. These varying sources of food can have quite different nutrient values of typically limiting substrates (protein, essential amino and fatty acids) and assimilable energy (available caloric content) to the detritivore. Also, the rate at which these components are made available to the detritivore can be affected not only by sedimentation rates but also by environmental (e.g., temperature) and food chain (e.g., grazing) factors that affect the physiology, growth, and production of the populations of potential food items associated with the dead organic matter and the rate of decay of the dead organic matter itself.

Feeding Strategies and Exploitation

The feeding and efficiency rates (e.g., assimilation rate) of deposit feeders are initially, i.e. proximally, determined by physiological constraints. An obvious example of the fundamental "proximal" control of environmental factors is that of temperature and salinity. In a hypothetical habitat with a water temperature of 50^0C, the polychaete *Capitella capitata* will not live because it is not physiologically adapted to such a high temperature. One feels confident in saying that food, or interactive controls like predation, is not controlling *C. capitata* in this environment, but the very proximal control of biophysics on the physiology of living organisms. There is a temperature range, say 5–25^0C, within which *C. capitata* can live (survive), and another narrower temperature range within which *C. capitata* successfully reproduces and populations exist. At some point in this temperature range, individual growth is optimal; at the extremes it will be suboptimal and stress will result in lower growth rate. Within the temperature range where *C. capitata* grows, we would expect to see varying food supply and competition and predation affecting (and possibly limiting?) population growth. However, even within this range, optimal vs. suboptimal temperature levels will result in varying physiological rates upon which more distal potential limiting factors must interface. Simply put, if a population of *C. capitata* is at stressful temperature levels such that population increase is not optimal, then the effect of increasing predation rates on population decline is exacerbated; the environmental factor (in this case temperature) is a more proximal control upon which the more distal control of predation intensity is super-imposed.

Detritivores exhibit a variety of feeding strategies (subsurface vs. surface feeders; selective vs. non-selective feeding) that will affect what components of the total detrital pool the organism can potentially exploit. Also, the morphology of the food particles (size and shape) can determine the availability (e.g., ability to ingest) an otherwise nutritious food. Furthermore, the feeding rate of an organism, after physiological constraints discussed above, can be affected by food quality and quantity. The ingestion rate of some animals will vary with food quality; other animals, like *C. capitata*, at least over a wide range of food quality, do not change ingestion rate. There may be a wide variety of potential food resources in the habitat but the physiological, morphological and behavioral characteristics of the deposit feeder can determine what and how much of these food resources can even be potentially utilized.

The abundance of a potential food item in the habitat does not assure that "it is important" in the nutrition of a particular deposit feeder unless it supplies essential nutrients and energy needed by the deposit feeder. The initial studies of the ecology of deposit feeders centered around the "enriching" role microbes played on otherwise refractive fecal pellets or vascular plant detritus (an excellent review of resource studies in deposit feeders is Lopez and Levinton 1987.) This idea dominated our thinking for several decades, without any actual growth data showing the growth potential of such "enrichment." It was only in the 1980's when some simple mass budgets (Cammen 1980) and actual growth data (Tenore 1977 started to emphasize the real complexity of so-called "simple" detritus-microbe-detritivore food chains (see Tenore et. al. 1982 for a review.) Phillips (1984) categorized the potential of different detritus substrates and associated microbes as to their potential as suppliers of specific essential nutrients to marine detritivores. Basically, deposit-feeders, like most marine invertebrates, need energy source and essential nutrients that they cannot themselves synthesize. Two important categories of such macronutrients are essential amino acids (from the protein content) and essential fatty acids (long-chain polyunsaturated, PUFA's, from lipid content). Bacteria may be able to supply the "carbon" source for a deposit feeder[1]; they cannot be the food source for deposit feeders because it cannot supply all the essential A.A. and F.A. because bacteria are deficient in methionine and PUFA's. The recent interest

---

[1] In reality we should be discussing not carbon but caloric source as it is the assimilable energy content that we are trying to characterize and not carbon content, e.g., equal carbon values of sawdust and sugar will have quite different assimilable energy contents for deposit feeders!

in benthic microalgae as a food resource for deposit feeders (Bianchi and Levinton 1984) does have sound theoretical support in that algae, especially diatoms, contain not only high assimilable energy (lipids) but an abundance of the essential fatty acids (PUFA's) low in many of the other potential food resources (Tenore 1987).

Bioenergetics

The efficiency at which a detritivore assimilates and incorporates ingested food and the metabolic costs of the organism results in individual growth. These efficiencies can be influenced by: (1) physical environmental factors such as temperature; (2) physiological changes in organisms with age; (3) quality and quantity of ingested food.

Population Dynamics

The bioenergetics is ultimately expressed in the population dynamics of the detritivore. Besides somatic growth, reproductive growth of an organism leads to reproduction and recruitment into the parent population. Coupled with mortality and survivorship rates, these parameters lead to changes in standing biomass (carrying capacity), and population production. At this level, a whole suite of inter- and intra-specific relations can affect the resultant production: intra- and inter-specific competition, interference, and predation. An example of the value of understanding nutritional resource levels and population carrying capacity is the work by Chesney (e.g., Chesney and Tenore 1985) in which he showed that the crash of spring bursts of opportunist deposit feeders like *C. capitata* could be the result, most proximally, of overshooting carrying capacity. The effect of further regulatory mechanisms, such as predation, are superimposed on the major pattern defined by the food resource control.

A major point that stands out after this exercise is that production and potential trophic transfers are in reality controlled by physical-chemical, physiological, organismal, and ecological factors. There is considerable interaction and feedback among these regulating mechanisms but, generally as you move up the scale from physical to community factors, the final expression of growth builds, and is directly affected, by succeeding regulatory mechanisms. For example, temperature affects rates of metabolic processes and too high a temperature will denature protein and kill the organism. This will occur regardless of changes in predation intensity. In contrast, when temperatures inhibit growth, an increase in predation might more quickly decimate a population than when temperature levels favor maximum growth and population increase. Similarly, the attainable maximum growth efficiency of an individual organism (production/food ingested) will be little influenced by changes in predation levels. Population production, however, will be affected by changes in standing biomass and size class structure because of mortality due to predation. When food supplies are abundant and a detritivore population is undergoing maximum growth, high predation levels (density independent?) have less of an effect than when a population is declining because of low food supply. The point to be made is that, if we attempt to study at the level of community or ecosystem, we have to take into account the potential levels allowed by physical, physiological and biosynthetic regulatory mechanisms. Whitlatch and Zajac (1985) has the best delineation and discussion of this interactive hierarchy of regulatory mechanisms.

The varying sequence over which regulatory mechanisms exert influence

Ecosystems, at a given point in time, are not necessarily (and probably not usually) in equilibrium. Specifically, this non-equilibrium means that the population characteristics (e.g., density, size class structure) of species are the expression of a suite of regulatory mechanisms whose controlling influence occurs over various periods of time prior to what we are seeing at a given point in time. For example, the spring bloom of benthos, which characterizes temperate-mesohaline benthic regimes, results from a series of past conditions and events: population recruitment events resulting in population growth (e.g., food potential, potential growth rates, competition, interference, facilitation, predation); food sedimenting to the bottom allowing reproductive growth of adult spawning members; water temperature affecting potential reproductive growth; interspecific interactions affecting adult spawning stock; previous years bloom resulting in population stocks from which present broods develop; that hurricane three years ago that drastically changed sedimentary characteristics and community structure. As we can see, besides differing in magnitude of control, such mechanisms differ in their time sequence and duration previous to that expression we are seeing in today's "snapshot." This is hardly a new insight but it is one that we subconsciously ignore when relating (e.g., correlating) the population structure of biota to present food or predation levels.

In studies of benthic detritus food-chains we, again subconsciously, of-

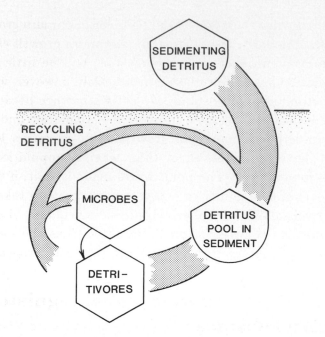

Figure 14.2: Schematic showing extrinsic vs. recycling components of sedimenting detritus pool available to detritivores.

ten treat the sediment detritus pool as a closed, never-ending cycle that is modified (pelletized, depelletized, decomposed, transformed, etc.) without any change in mass (this is somewhat against the laws of thermodynamics). What in reality we have (Figure 14.2) is a detritus pool in sediment that has two main sources: (1) sedimenting detritus and (2) recycled detritus. The microbe/detritivore feeding results in a mass reduction of the recycling detritus component of the detritus pool. The contribution of the external-source, sedimenting detritus can vary depending on water column even. If, however, this external source of detritus were cut off from the benthic regime, the mass of the recycling non-detritus component (at least the nutritionally available component) would reduce to nothing. This does not include microbes, such as benthic diatoms, that in fact can be the major supplier of energy and essential nutrients, i.e., essential fatty acids and amino acids. In the present discussion of regulatory mechanisms occurring previous to the "snapshot" situation, it is obvious that the concentrations and even rates of supply of different food resources do not necessarily reflect levels resulting in the current densities of detritivores. For example, at a "snapshot" sampling event, there may be a low influx rate of sedimenting detritus and a high standing amount of recycled detritus in the sediment. The current standing biomass of the detritivore(s) are not caused by the amounts of those current food resources; a high sedimentation rate occurring some time before (e.g., three weeks) the current situation could have resulted in recruitment and growth of the fast growing opportunists, or emigrating adult forms into food-enriched areas. In the process of population growth the potential food resources, specifically the more labile assimilable components of detritus, have been readily utilized. What remains may be the unutilizable components.

Literature Cited

Bianchi, T. and J. Levinton. 1984. The importance of microalgae, bacteria and particulate organic matter in the somatic growth of *Hydrobia totteni*. *J. Mar. Res.* 42:431-443.

Cammen, L. 1980. The significance of microbial carbon in the nutrition of the deposit feeding polychaete *Nereis succinea*. *Mar. Biol.*, 61:9-20.

Chesney, E. and K. Tenore. 1985. Oscillations of laboratory populations of the polychaete, *Capitella capitata* (type 1): their cause and implications for natural populations. Mar. Ecol. Prog. Ser. 20:289-296.

Lopez, G. and J. Levinton. 1987. Ecology of deposit feeding animals in marine sediments. *Quart. Rev. Biol.*, 62:235-260.

Phillips, N. 1984. The potential of different microbes and substrates as suppliers of specific essential nutrients to marine detritivores. *Bull. Mar. Sci.*, 35:283-298.

Tenore, K.R. 1987. Nitrogen in benthic food chains, pp 191-205. In: T.H. Blackburn and J. Sorensen (eds.), *Nitrogen Cycling in Coastal Marine Environments*. John Wiley and Sons, Ltd.

Tenore, K., L. Cammen, S. Findlay and N. Phillips. 1982. Perspectives in factors controlling detritus mineralization depending on detritus source. *J. Mar. Res.*, 40:473-490.

Whitlatch, R. and R. Zajac. 1985. A hierarchical approach to modelling soft-bottom successional dynamics. P.E. Gibbs (ed.), Proc. 19th EMBS, Plymouth, U.K., Cambridge University Press.

Index